Scharinger

Industrial AI: from Pilot to Profit

Boris Scharinger

Industrial AI: from Pilot to Profit

Key Concepts, Success Factors, Use Cases and Market Mechanics

HANSER

Print-ISBN: 978-1-56990-610-1
E-Book-ISBN: 978-1-56990-974-4
EPUB-ISBN: 978-1-56990-978-2

Bibliographic information of the German National Library:
The German National Library lists this publication in the German National Bibliography; detailed bibliographic data are available on the Internet at http://dnb.d-nb.de.

Vilshofener Straße 10 | 81679 Munich | info@hanser.de
www.hanserpublications.com
www.hanser-fachbuch.de
Editor: Sylvia Hasselbach, Kristin Rothe
Production Management: Grazyna Lada
Copy editing: Ian Travis, Neuharlingersiel
Cover concept: Marc Müller-Bremer, www.rebranding.de, Munich
Cover design: Max Kostopoulos
Typesetting: Eberl & Koesel Studio, Kempten

Contents

Part I: Introduction and Key Concepts

1 Introduction

1.1 About the Author

Boris Scharinger serves Siemens Digital Industries, the Industry 4.0 and PLM software division of Siemens, in numerous initiatives centered on industrial-grade AI.

With a professional career spanning more than three decades, Boris possesses a uniquely broad background that bridges the gap between complex IT infrastructure and strategic business innovation.

His diverse roles have included Enterprise IT Architecture Management for digital services, leading a large-scale IT carve-out program, leading innovation campaigns in IT outsourcing, directing IT audits in North America with a focus on data analytics and cybersecurity, moderating cross-company data collaboration initiatives, and defining global technology roadmaps.

He plays a vital role in identifying and mentoring pioneering startups through initiatives such as the Siemens Industrial AI Awards and co-hosting the annual AI with Purpose Summit, which foster collaboration between established industrial players and innovative newcomers to make AI *industrial-grade*.

Contact the author via his website *www.industrial-ai-book.com*!

1.2 Foreword by Prof. Wil v. d. Aalst

It is a great pleasure to write this foreword for *Industrial AI: From Pilot to Profit* by Boris Scharinger. We are living in a moment when the public imagination has been captivated by AI, triggered by the "ChatGPT moment" of November 2022. From generating poetry and PowerPoint slides to drafting business plans and writing Python code, the promises of AI can appear limitless.

Yet, as this book rightly observes, the industrial world is now entering a necessary and sobering phase. As Boris notes, roughly 95% of enterprise GenAI initiatives fail to deliver measurable return on investment and are abandoned before reaching production. The gap between impressive demos and sustained industrial impact remains wide.

After providing an excellent historical overview and a clear survey of emerging AI-based technologies, Boris explains why AI applications in industrial settings are fundamentally more challenging. He identifies three core reasons:

1. High-stakes consequences;
2. Physical constraints and long-lived assets; and
3. Brownfield complexity and legacy integration.

In industry, AI errors can have severe real-world consequences – financial losses, safety incidents, environmental damage, or even loss of life. Unlike consumer-facing AI, where mistakes are usually benign, industrial AI must meet far higher standards of reliability, validation, and accountability, and this inevitably slows down adoption and deployment. Moreover, industrial systems are governed by the laws of physics and embedded in expensive physical assets with lifecycles that often span decades. AI models must respect physical limits, engineering constraints, and safety margins, while integrating with machinery and processes that cannot be frequently redesigned or replaced. Most industrial environments are brownfield systems: heterogeneous, highly customized, and developed over many years using legacy equipment, proprietary protocols, and siloed data sources. This fragmentation makes data integration, model deployment, and continuous updating far more difficult than in greenfield, cloud-native digital environments.

This analysis is both accurate and insightful. I would add that many successful AI applications focus on optimizing a single task or isolated step. However, true complexity emerges when we consider end-to-end processes. This is precisely why my own work has increasingly focused on *Object-Centric Process Mining* (OCPM). OCPM moves beyond simplified, case-centric representations and models processes as they actually occur in industrial reality. Real-world industrial processes involve interactions among multiple object types – machines, orders, materials, products, sensors, and assets – that evolve over long lifecycles, operate under physical constraints, and interact in dynamic environments. OCPM is particularly well-suited to brownfield settings, as it integrates fragmented event data originating from heterogeneous legacy systems.

However, seeing the problem is not enough. Moving the needle on productivity requires sustained commitment to motivation, implementation, and change management. We have seen this before with Industry 4.0, where substantial upfront investments often failed to deliver the promised returns because organizations struggled to scale beyond siloed pilots. The digital gap is as much a cultural and organizational challenge as it is a technical one. For this reason, the book wisely addresses not only technology but also economic, legal, and organizational dimensions. In particular, it emphasizes the importance of governance of AI systems, data infrastructures, and decision rights – as a prerequisite for lasting success.

This book serves as a vital map for navigating the transition from experimentation to value creation. It performs the essential task of translating the world of business to technologists and the world of technology to business leaders. Along the way, it demystifies technical concepts such as retrieval-augmented generation and surrogate models, grounding them firmly in the operational realities of enterprise environments.

Importantly, the book also looks beyond today's hurdles to offer an inspiring outlook on the next frontier of industrial intelligence. We are entering a phase where the intersection of agentic AI and process mining will enable entirely new paradigms. In such environments, process mining provides a transparent "mirror" for autonomous agents, ensuring that as AI systems begin to plan and execute multi-step actions independently, they do so within the boundaries defined by process models, compliance requirements, and quality standards.

At *Celonis*, we summarize this philosophy under the "no AI without PI" banner, where AI refers to *artificial intelligence* in organizations and industries, and PI stands for *process intelligence* powered by OCPM. AI needs context to make sound decisions, and process models combined with event data provide exactly that context. Most data stored in industrial systems already describes events and objects – machines, people, suppliers, products, tools, and assets. From bills of material and SCADA data to supply chain and CRM systems, a large share of industrial data is structured, operational, and readily available. It is, therefore, naïve to assume that general-purpose large language models trained primarily on text and images can, on their own, manage and improve complex industrial systems.

For those ready to move from ambition to action, this book offers the guidance needed to ensure that industrial AI does not remain a collection of costly experiments. Instead, it becomes a true engine of the next revolution in intelligence.

Enjoy reading!

Prof. Dr. Wil van der Aalst

Full professor at RWTH Aachen University & Chief Scientist at Celonis

1.3 Navigating the Industrial Revolution of Intelligence

Industry doesn't need another hype cycle; it requires tools that work. While consumer AI tolerates hallucination, industrial AI demands precision. This book is a compendium that provides guidance for transitioning from experimental pilots to mission-critical operations. It explains the buzzwords while still focusing on the engineering and shop-floor realities: reliability, safety, and Return on Investment. Insights into the mechanics of market and business cases help us understand why industrial AI takes longer.

And last but not least: This book inspires by crawling through all the primary functions of an industrial enterprise: Each function is explained and its potential AI support laid out while commercial solution briefs for each function provide a valid entry point into market screenings for any reader with the ambition to tackle AI's potential in these functions.

1.4 Target Audience

Of course, every person on this planet (and beyond) must read this book! However, the way it is shaped aims to be *particularly useful* to the following roles:

- *Corporate Decision Makers* (e.g., CEOs, CIOs, Supervisory board members) who require a broad overview of the potential of AI for their enterprise and guidelines to understand risks, both on the technical and business side of life.
- *MBA students* of AI, IT, Engineering, and Business Administration – requiring a generalist's insight into the most critical enterprise functions and the way AI can provide a competitive difference.
- *Consultants* on a mission to monetize their technical and managerial capabilities within corporate environments.
- *Startups* where great technology seeks practical application. And where insights into market and business case mechanics are vital to success.
- Finally: *Anyone wanting to join the mission to make AI industrial-grade.*

1.5 How to Read this Book

This book is designed to guide readers through a structured journey, from foundational knowledge to practical application.

Part I: Introduction and Concepts begins by establishing a solid foundation. It traces the history of AI from its origins to the current era of generative models, providing the essential context for understanding today's landscape. It then clarifies key modern concepts, including generative AI, agentic AI, the Digital Twin, and the Industrial Metaverse, thereby establishing a precise vocabulary for the subsequent discussions. Part I also examines various AI technologies, at least to some degree, to understand their differences and their relevance to industry AI approaches.

Part II: Adoption Hurdles confronts the practical challenges head-on. It examines the paradox of slower industrial adoption than in other sectors and delves into the specifics of making AI "industrial-grade". This section provides an honest look at the unique data challenges, the mechanics of the business case, and the critical need for new engineering disciplines to bridge the gap between algorithm and application.

Part III: from Ambition to Action offers a strategic framework for getting started, outlining the necessary organizational capabilities, the crucial role of partnerships, and a methodology for assessing and prioritizing use cases.

Part IV: Enterprise Functions and AI Use Cases makes the potential of Industrial AI tangible. It presents a comprehensive functional breakdown of a modern industrial enterprise. It showcases examples of how AI is creating value at every stage – from innovation management and product design to production engineering, operations, and service.

Part V: Conclusion and Annexes summarizes and adds a comprehensive references list, table, and figure indexes, abbreviations, keywords, and a company register.

1.6 A Big Thank You

This book is inspired by *Prof. Peter Mertens*. Prof. Mertens is a key pioneer in the field of *Business Information Systems*, and both his lectures and his books have shaped my passion and skills for my professional career, bridging technology and business. The structure of his book, Integrated Information Systems [1], served as the blueprint for Part IV of this book.

This book would not have been possible without input and advice from many industrial AI experts out there, namely

- *Robert Weber and Peter Seeberg*, running the Industrial AI Podcast (*aipod.de*) and orchestrating a lively community of industrial AI practitioners and startup entrepreneurs;
- *Roberto d'Ippolito, Volkmar Sterzing*, and *Peter Mas* from Siemens, as well as *Moritz Frenzel* from Altair, who helped me understand the impact of AI in engineering, particularly in simulation and design space exploration;
- *Erik Scepanski* and *Armin Hadzalic* from Siemens on what it takes to mature industrial copilot technology, and *Filippos Petridis* (Siemens) and *Tom Cadera* (Cadera Design) for their input on (and passion for) AI user experience;
- *Vlad Larichev* from Accenture for our great discussions on Agentic AI and the Digital (Reasoning) Thread concepts;
- *Torsten Kroeger* and the Intrinsic team for helping me capture where AI-based industrial robotics is heading;
- *Tom Hurd* from ZEKI Data for both data points and insights on AI talent movement trends;
- *Prof. Marco Huber* from Fraunhofer IPA and the University of Stuttgart for reviewing this book diligently and for providing excellent use case examples; and
- *Prof. Wil van der Aalst* from the RWTH Aachen University and Chief Scientist at Celonis for this review of the process mining-related sections and his highly appreciated foreword!

A tremendous amount of inspiration and input came from the industrial AI startup community, including Assemblio, Blockbrain, Celus, Compute Maritime, Cybord, Drimco, Easy2Parts, Ethon.ai, Katulu, Lambda Function AI, Node Robotics, PAILOT, Plus10, Riiico, NXAI, Werk24, WeSort, Xplain Data, and many more.

Thank you all for driving AI to become industrial-grade – keep on rockin'!

Last but not least: Thank you from the very bottom of my heart to my wife, *Martina*, and my kids, *Emma* and *Nicklas*, for your support and tolerance of my dedication to getting this book project finished in a pretty short time frame!

2
Key Concepts

2.1 From the Beginning to Today

2.1.1 Foundations (before the 1950s)

In the 1930s, *Alan Turing* envisioned a theoretical device – now known as the *Turing Machine* – capable of performing any computation through predefined rules. Turing also formulated the Imitation Game (later called the *Turing Test*), a conceptual framework for assessing whether a machine can demonstrate behavior indistinguishable from that of a human. He posited that if a machine could convincingly simulate human responses, it might reasonably be considered intelligent. Combined with the invention of electronic computers in the 1940s, this intellectual development marked the transition of artificial intelligence from myth and speculation to tangible scientific possibility.

2.1.2 The Birth of Artificial Intelligence (1950s–1970s)

The formal inception of AI as an academic discipline dates back to the summer of 1956, when a group of prominent researchers convened at Dartmouth College in the United States for a foundational workshop. They theorized that "every aspect of learning or any other feature of intelligence can in principle be so precisely described that a machine can be made to simulate it", and the term *Artificial Intelligence* was introduced during this event.

The initial architects of AI were notably optimistic, hypothesizing that machines would be capable of performing any intellectual task undertaken by humans within one or two decades. Their methodology primarily relied on *symbolic AI*, which entailed programming systems with explicit sets of rules and knowledge – similar to providing comprehensive instructions for each task.

Illustrative early AI programs include the *Logic Theorist*, which could prove mathematical theorems, and ELIZA, which simulated a psychotherapist by identifying keywords and responding with pre-defined phrases. These applications demonstrated the potential for computers to engage in complex logical reasoning.

Despite these early achievements, such systems soon encountered significant limitations. Although effective at solving specific, well-structured problems, they were inadequate for addressing the ambiguous and unpredictable challenges of real-world situations. These systems lacked common-sense reasoning, had limited capacity for experiential learning, and required considerable manual effort to encode all necessary rules. This approach proved unsustainable because it required an exhaustive, rule-based description of the world, which is inherently impractical.

2.1.3 The AI Winters (1970s–1980s)

The initial optimism of the 1950s and 60s began to fade. The grand promises of brilliant machines weren't materializing:

- Early forms of *artificial neural networks*, known as *Perceptrons*, had profound limitations, spotted by thoughtleaders such as Minsky and Papert in the 1970s [2].
- The momentum of *Expert Systems* dried out in the 1980s as researchers realized that intelligence was far more complex than just following a set of rules. It involved intuition, learning from experience, adapting to new situations, and understanding the nuances of human language and the world. The early AI systems simply weren't equipped for this.

Funding for AI research dried up, and public interest waned. These periods are often referred to as the *AI Winters* – a time of reduced enthusiasm and investment.

Despite the winters, important foundational work continued quietly. Researchers explored new ideas that would prove crucial for AI's resurgence.

2.1.4 Learning from Data (1990s–Early 2010s)

As the 1990s dawned, a confluence of factors began to thaw the AI winter. First, computers became exponentially more powerful and cheaper, thanks to *Moore's Law*[1]. This meant machines could process far more information. Second, the Internet began

---

[1] The observation respectively pace setting, that the number of transistors on a microchip doubles roughly every two years.

to take off, generating vast amounts of data – text, images, sounds – that could be used to train AI systems.

This era saw a significant shift from symbolic AI to *Machine Learning* (ML). Instead of explicitly programming every rule, machine learning algorithms *learn* patterns and make predictions from data. Think of it as teaching a child by showing them many examples, rather than giving them a rulebook.

Suddenly, AI started to become genuinely valuable for everyday applications:

- *Spam filters* learned to identify junk email by analyzing patterns in messages.
- *Recommendation engines* on websites like Amazon or Netflix learned what we might like based on our past choices and what similar users enjoyed.
- *Search engines* became incredibly good at finding relevant information.

LeNet-5, developed by Yann LeCun in 1998, is a pioneering example of deep learning: Designed for handwritten digit recognition, it introduced key architectures such as convolutional layers, pooling, and fully connected layers. Its success in processing bank checks demonstrated the commercial viability of neural networks, laying the foundation for modern computer vision and subsequent advances in deep learning.

In 2011, IBM's *Watson* AI gained attention by defeating human contestants on *Jeopardy!*, showcasing its ability to process natural language and deliver real-time answers. IBM aimed to expand Watson's use to business and healthcare, especially medicine, where it was expected to analyze research, assess patient data, and support clinical decisions. However, Watson struggled with messy medical records, sometimes making irrelevant or unsafe recommendations. Data entry requirements also increased clinicians' workloads. Watson's modular design worked well for narrow tasks but was incapable of adapting to complex hospital environments. High deployment costs and limited benefits led to client dissatisfaction, and IBM eventually sold Watson Health assets in 2022.

Watson's failures were both technical and strategic; it relied on advanced search and rule-based processing rather than actual intelligence. This experience underscored the need for realistic expectations and adaptable solutions capable of handling real-world data in industrial AI applications [3].

This period was a quiet revolution. AI wasn't making headlines with promises of human-level intelligence, but it was steadily becoming an indispensable tool, learning from the growing sea of data.

2.1.5 The Deep Learning Revolution (2010s–2020)

The 2010s witnessed an explosion in AI capabilities, driven primarily by a technique known as *Deep Learning*. This is a specific type of machine learning that uses extensive neural networks – complex, multi-layered mathematical structures loosely inspired by the way neurons connect in the human brain.

What made deep learning so powerful?

- *Even more data:* The Internet and social media generated unprecedented amounts of data for training.
- *Even more computing power:* Graphics Processing Units (GPUs), originally designed for video games, turned out to be perfect for the massive parallel computations needed for deep learning.
- *Improved algorithms:* Researchers developed smarter ways to train these deep networks.

The results were astonishing:

- *Image Recognition:* Deep learning systems became incredibly accurate at identifying objects, faces, and scenes in images, often surpassing human performance in specific tasks.
- *Natural Language Processing:* Machines started to genuinely understand and generate human language, leading to better translation tools, chatbots, and voice assistants like *Siri* and *Alexa*.
- *Speech Recognition:* Converting spoken words into text became remarkably reliable.

In autumn 2012, a significant advancement occurred at a relatively unknown computer vision competition. The *ImageNet Large Scale Visual Recognition Challenge* consistently posed substantial challenges for researchers, who competed to train machines to identify everyday objects such as cats, cars, and chairs across millions of images. Although accuracy had gradually improved, progress was incremental until an unexpected breakthrough emerged. A team led by Geoffrey Hinton and his students, Alex Krizhevsky and Ilya Sutskever, introduced a deep neural network – later known as AlexNet – that dramatically outperformed its competitors by halving the error rate.

For the first time, an automated system achieved image recognition capabilities approaching human reliability. This innovation was highly regarded within academic circles and garnered strong interest from industry stakeholders due to its commercial potential. The application of deep learning quickly expanded: factories transitioned from rigid, rule-based vision systems – which often failed under varying conditions – to models that learned directly from extensive product datasets, thereby improving defect detection efficiency and accuracy.

The adoption of these technologies extended to logistics, where organizations trained AI systems to scan packages, track inventory, and minimize errors in warehouse operations. The medical sector followed suit, with radiologists leveraging *Convolutional Neural Network*-based tools to detect early indicators of disease in imaging studies. Agricultural professionals also benefited, using drones and camera-equipped AI platforms to identify plant health issues and promptly mitigate crop losses.

John Deere's Autonomous Farm Vision

John Deere's journey toward precision agriculture began with the launch of its *MyJohnDeere platform* in 2012, which enabled farmers to collect and manage data from their connected equipment. This laid the foundation for the *autonomous farm vision* unveiled around 2013. A significant acceleration came in 2017 with the acquisition of a Silicon Valley startup specializing in computer vision and machine learning. This expertise enabled the development of advanced solutions, such as the *See & Spray* system, which uses smart cameras and AI to distinguish between crops and weeds, enabling targeted spraying and a significant reduction in herbicide use.

Another iconic moment arrived in 2016 when Google's *AlphaGo*, a deep learning system, defeated the world's top Go player, Lee Sedol. Go is an ancient board game far more complex than chess, requiring intuition and strategic depth. AlphaGo's victory showed that AI could master tasks that seemed uniquely human.

The *Industrial Internet of Things* (IIoT) emerged from the broader IoT concept, applying network connectivity and data exchange to industrial processes and equipment [4]. The early 2010s saw a surge of interest as major industrial companies, aiming to build digital ecosystems for factories and supply chains, developed their own platforms to monetize on the industrial "Big Data" hype. General Electric, a pioneer in this area, introduced its *Predix* platform, positioning it as an open-source operating system for the Industrial Internet [5]. Meanwhile, German industrial giant Siemens launched *MindSphere*, a cloud-based IIoT platform for its own machinery and third-party assets. European companies, including German machine builders like DMG MORI and Dürr, partnered with Software AG to form *Adamos*, a collaborative platform designed specifically for the mechanical and plant engineering sector. Around the same time, American software company PTC made significant acquisitions, including ThingWorx, to build its own IIoT platform focused on rapid application development and connectivity.

Despite the initial hype and significant investment from these major players, the IIoT failed to meet its projected growth, and adoption was far slower than anticipated. This was primarily due to a confluence of technological, cultural, and economic challenges.

From a technological standpoint, integrating new IIoT solutions with legacy operational technology proved to be difficult and costly. Older machines were never designed to be "smart", leading to compatibility issues and a lack of standardized protocols for data communication. Ultimately, this led to data format initiatives such as OPC UA (see Section 9.2.1).

Furthermore, data protection was a significant concern. Connecting sensitive industrial systems to the Internet increased the risk of cyberattacks and the loss of intellectual property and trade secrets.

Beyond technology, other factors contributed to the slow adoption: The high upfront investment costs for hardware, software, and implementation were a significant barrier for many companies, who were also skeptical about the return on investment. The perceived benefits of IIoT – such as predictive maintenance and increased efficiency – were often difficult to quantify in advance (see also Section 5.4).

In this context of applying AI to real-world, high-stakes problems, the term *Industrial AI* began to gain prominence. The concept was notably championed and defined by Professor Jay Lee, who distinguished it from general AI by its focus on industrial systems. He emphasized that Industrial AI required not only predictive accuracy but also extreme reliability, safety, and deep integration with domain-specific physics and engineering knowledge [6].

2.1.6 The Era of Transformer Models (2020+)

More recently, we've entered the era of *Generative AI* (GenAI). Based on an algorithmic class called *Transformers*, systems like ChatGPT can generate coherent, creative text, write code, and even compose poetry. Tools like DALL·E and Midjourney can create stunning, original images from simple text descriptions. These systems don't just analyze data: They create entirely new content, in many cases undistinguishable from content created by human authors.

Launched in late 2022, *ChatGPT* by OpenAI achieved a historic milestone, reaching one million users in just five days, far outpacing the growth rates of previous tech giants such as Instagram and Netflix. This momentum continued, reaching 100 million monthly active users within two months and making ChatGPT the fastest-growing consumer application at the time. Its rapid adoption highlighted a global fascination with generative AI, as the platform quickly transitioned from a viral experiment to an essential tool for millions.

In January 2025, the "DeepSeek moment" sent ripples through the global AI landscape, as a team of leading Chinese algorithmic experts demonstrated that sophisticated model architecture and innovative training approaches could rival or surpass models built primarily on brute-force computational power.

This achievement challenged the prevailing narrative that success in AI development was predominantly determined by access to vast GPU clusters and massive training budgets. The DeepSeek team's accomplishment highlighted the importance of algorithmic efficiency, clever parameter optimization and architectural innovation over raw computational might, achieving comparable or superior performance to leading US models while utilizing significantly fewer computational resources.

Recent research on DeepSeek's development indicates that public claims about its minimal resource footprint have been overstated and significantly understate the GPU resources and costs required to train the model [7]. DeepSeek also faces substantial challenges for industrial deployment in European contexts: the model lacks essential features such as explainable decision-making, comprehensive audit trails, and verified data governance mechanisms. These limitations effectively limit DeepSeek's European industrial applications to experimental and non-critical use cases, despite its impressive technical achievements.

2.1.7 AI as an Innovation Catalyst

AI has delivered disruptive breakthroughs by solving complex, seemingly intractable problems in science and engineering. In biochemistry, DeepMind's *AlphaFold* effectively solved the decades-old challenge of protein folding, accurately predicting proteins' 3D structures from their amino acid sequences. This has revolutionized drug discovery and materials science to the extent that John Jumper and Demis Hassabis at DeepMind received the Nobel Prize for Chemistry in 2024 for AlphaFold [8].

Similarly, in energy, AI accelerates the path to viable *fusion reactor design*. Using deep reinforcement learning, AI systems can stabilize and control the super-hot plasma in a Tokamak in real time, preventing destructive instabilities. By processing massive sensor data and optimizing confinement, AI is significantly reducing the time and cost required to achieve clean, limitless fusion power [9].

While *autonomous driving* is undergoing a sobering recalibration of expectations, the prospect of freeing human capacity from the steering wheel of a car or truck has fueled its own perception and processing innovation cycle in AI and has, in turn, been fueled by AI.

2.1.8 The Accelerating Velocity of AI Innovation

The AI field is advancing at a breakneck pace, turning once-theoretical ideas into practical tools within weeks or months. This rapid progress signals a significant shift in how AI is developed and deployed across industries.

Key drivers include enhanced computational resources, such as powerful GPUs and cloud platforms, greater data availability, and significant algorithmic breakthroughs. Open-source frameworks (e.g., TensorFlow, PyTorch, Hugging Face) have made AI tools widely accessible, reducing entry barriers and fostering global collaboration. Tech companies often open-source their tools to attract talent and spur innovation, thereby building strong developer communities and accelerating innovation. The pool of AI professionals is expanding rapidly, thanks to universities and online education, while research is spreading rapidly through preprint servers like arXiv (*arxiv.org*), further accelerating innovation cycles. Recent milestones highlight this acceleration: generative AI models, text-to-image systems (DALL·E, Midjourney, Stable Diffusion), and scientific breakthroughs such as AlphaFold are transforming industries and research.

Finally, *Venture Capital* (VC) investment in AI startups continues to rise, even in times of economic uncertainty, empowering firms to scale research, hire top talent, and accelerate product launches (see Figure 2.1).

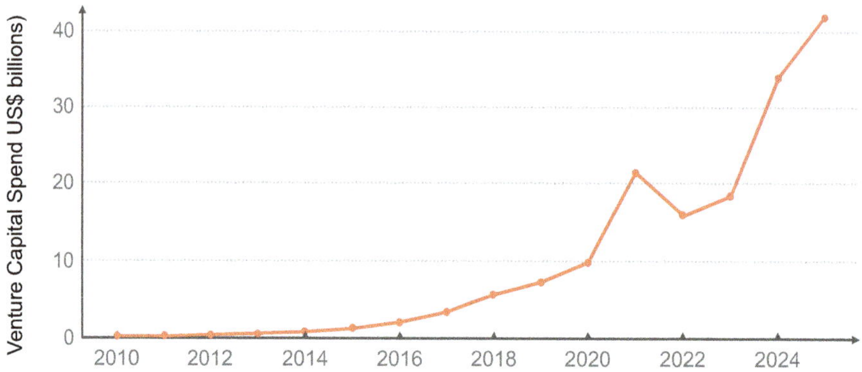

Figure 2.1 Estimated annual VC spend on industrial AI startups

2.2 From Today to Tomorrow

2.2.1 Next Stop: Trough of Disillusionment?

The explosive arrival of generative AI has propelled artificial intelligence to the peak of Gartner's *Hype Cycle*. Public fascination and media coverage have created a peak of inflated expectations, with many viewing technologies such as ChatGPT as a panacea for every business problem. However, history shows that what follows this peak is an inevitable slide into the *Trough of Disillusionment*.

This phase begins when the initial excitement fades and the harsh realities of implementation set in. Companies find that transitioning from a clever demonstration to a reliable, scalable, and profitable industrial application is extraordinarily difficult.

For the industrial sector, this disillusionment may be particularly acute: Unlike the digital world, where the cost of failure is often low, a mistake in an industrial AI system can have catastrophic consequences for physical assets, the environment, and human safety. The hype promises intelligent factories and autonomous supply chains, but for many, the reality will be a frustrating series of costly pilot projects that fail to scale. Navigating this valley will be the first significant test for organizations serious about deploying Industrial AI, separating those with a durable, realistic strategy from those just chasing the trend.

Simultaneously, the euphoria surrounding the AI infrastructure build-out is waning, as evidenced by reports that major companies, including Microsoft, are canceling or postponing large-scale AI data center leases. This retreat suggests a re-evaluation of aggressive capacity forecasts, as many companies struggle to identify a viable path to production that justifies the substantial infrastructure investment [10].

2.2.2 AI in Mathematics

In July 2025, OpenAI, DeepMind, and Harmonic achieved gold-medal performance at the prestigious high school competition, the *International Mathematical Olympiad* (IMO), competing against human participants.

The convergence of AI and mathematics is rapidly forming a distinct research domain. While AI demonstrating proficiency in solving problems such as those in the IMO is a significant milestone, future goals are far more ambitious, potentially including solving open mathematical problems or formalizing a substantial portion of existing mathematics. Initiatives such as DeepMind's work on the Lean Proof Assistant and OpenAI's advances in automated reasoning will accelerate this field [11].

This intensification is expected to lead to more sophisticated AI models, such as *neural theorem provers* that integrate symbolic reasoning, and the co-development of *entirely new mathematics* with AI assistance [12].

2.2.3 AI in Biology

The current momentum in the use of generative AI for biological applications is strong, signaling a fundamental transformation of the life sciences and drug discovery. The industry views biological data (DNA, RNA, proteins) as the "language of life", making it an ideal domain for the same transformer-based models (like LLMs) that power general-purpose applications.

The trend toward developing Biological Foundation Models is accelerating. *Evo 2* by the *Arc Institute* has been trained on massive datasets of nucleotides and whole genomes (up to 9 trillion nucleotides) across species. These models can generalize and predict the function of DNA, RNA, and protein sequences.

Instead of screening millions of existing molecules, Gen AI models can generate entirely novel sequences and small molecules with desired properties that have never existed in nature (*De Novo Drug and Protein Design*):

- The world's first completely AI-discovered drug, *rentosertib*, has advanced to clinical trials.
- New platforms are emerging to create bespoke molecules, such as those pioneering generative covalent chemistry to design small molecule medicines for *previously undruggable* protein targets.
- Models such as *BoltzGen* from MIT have demonstrated the ability to design protein binders with high affinity for multiple targets, showing strong generalization and controllability.

2.2.4 Continual Learning

Continual Learning is an advanced ML paradigm that enables an AI system to acquire, update, and retain knowledge from a continuous stream of non-stationary data throughout its operational lifetime. It aims to mimic the natural, adaptive learning process of the human brain, which continually integrates new experiences without forgetting core skills.

The primary obstacle in achieving true continual learning is *catastrophic forgetting*:

- *The problem:* Traditional neural networks are typically trained on a static, fixed dataset. When these models are subsequently trained on a new, distinct task, the gradient-based optimization process for the new task often overwrites the weights that encoded knowledge from the previous tasks. This causes a drastic and sudden drop in performance on the old tasks.
- *The dilemma:* Continual learning must solve the stability-plasticity tradeoff: it must be plastic enough to digest new information effectively, yet stable enough to consolidate and retain existing knowledge.

Continual learning is a precondition for achieving *Artificial General Intelligence* (see Section 2.2.7).

2.2.5 Humanoid Robots

The compelling promise of universality fuels the current drive toward *Humanoid Robots* in industrial settings: The core appeal is that of creating a single, general-purpose machine that can leverage the human-centric infrastructure already present in factories, warehouses, and assembly lines – using tools, opening doors, and navigating stairs designed for humans [13]. This contrasts sharply with current specialized industrial robots, which require costly, bespoke environmental restructuring.

A heated conceptual debate centers on movement, specifically *legged* versus *wheeled* designs. While wheeled or tracked robots are highly efficient and stable on flat factory floors, they fail immediately at negotiating stairs, uneven terrain, or obstacles. Legged designs (like the bipedal humanoids from Tesla's Optimus and Agility's Digit) offer superior adaptability and mobility in complex environments. Still, they currently face higher costs, greater complexity, and significantly lower energy efficiency and durability than wheeled platforms. Despite the hype, several major challenges must be solved before humanoids can make a tangible difference in industry. Mechanically, they lag far behind biological capability; robotic hands lack the dexterity and degrees of freedom needed for nuanced manipulation, and actuators lack the necessary force density. Computationally, they struggle with sensorimotor skills and learning efficiency, often requiring billions of simulated interactions to master simple tasks with poor generalization (see also Section 2.7.4.3 "Embodied AI" and Section 2.7.4.4 "World Models").

Furthermore, the total cost of ownership (including ongoing maintenance and significant capital expenditures) makes them economically unviable compared with lower-cost, highly specialized automation systems or even low-wage human labor. Truly practical industrial humanoids require breakthroughs in whole-body control, tactile sensing, and significant cost reduction.

2.2.6 Machine Economy

The *Machine Economy* refers to a future system in which intelligent, autonomous machines – enabled by IoT, AI, and blockchains or similar trust mechanisms – perform economic transactions, make decisions, and even act as agents with economic identity, all with little or no human intervention. For example, machines could autonomously reorder supplies when inventory runs low, pay for charging or maintenance, or enter into self-executing contracts (*smart contracts*) with other machines [14].

Indications that the Machine Economy is already coming include: The growing number of IoT devices connected and generating real-time data; early implementations of machines automatically performing purchases (e. g., smart appliances, autonomous vehicles) without manual input; development of decentralized infrastructure where physical devices share and trade resources and business models shift from ownership toward pay-per-use or outcome-based services in which machines become service providers themselves [15].

These trends suggest a transition where machines increasingly contribute directly to economic value creation, and financial systems adapt to include them as active participants.

2.2.7 Artificial General Intelligence

Artificial General Intelligence (AGI) refers to systems that can understand, learn, and apply their intelligence to solve any problem a human can, across a wide variety of tasks. Unlike the *Narrow AI* prevalent today (such as current LLMs), AGI exhibits generalizable reasoning, common sense, and the ability to apply knowledge from one domain to a completely different one.

The promise of AGI is immense, potentially leading to unprecedented economic growth (some forecasts predict sustained 5%+ GDP growth) and breakthroughs in science, healthcare, and medicine (e. g., curing diseases and addressing climate change). AGI could effectively act as a superhuman researcher.

However, the primary challenge is achieving agency and common sense (quoting Moravec's Paradox: what is hard for humans is easy for AI, and vice-versa). Other challenges include safety and alignment (ensuring the AGI's goals align with human values), data scarcity for training, and managing the inevitable mass job displacement it would cause.

Timelines for AGI are highly contentious, even among experts. *Epoch.ai* researchers present a range of forecasts [16]:

- *Optimistic/short timelines:* Some researchers predict a high probability of transformative AI (often equated with AGI capabilities) emerging within five to 15 years (around 2030 to 2040), driven by the exponential scaling of compute power. Epoch's modeling of *superhuman coder capabilities* sometimes points to a median around 2028 to 2030.
- *Conservative/long timelines:* Others, like some at Epoch, maintain a more cautious median timeline of 30+ years (2055 to 2060), emphasizing that solving real-world agency and common sense remains a persistent, unsolved problem that scaling alone may not fix.
- *Consensus forecasts* from AI expert surveys generally place a 50% probability of AGI emerging between 2040 and 2061.

2.3 Infrastructure for AI

While AI may seem like a purely digital phenomenon, it is anchored in a massive and rapidly growing physical infrastructure. The AI revolution is built on three physical pillars: data centers, specialized chips, and vast amounts of electricity.

2.3.1 Data Centers

The adoption momentum of GenAI has triggered a Capital Expenditure (CapEx) technology history that the world has never seen before, transforming the data center from a passive utility into a high-value strategic asset. Unlike traditional cloud facilities designed for general storage, these new *AI factories* are purpose-built to house massive GPU clusters, requiring entirely new architectural standards for density and cooling. Industry forecasts now project global data center investment to exceed US$ 2.5 trillion by the end of the decade, with hyperscalers nearly doubling their capital expenditures in 2025 alone to secure their dominance [17].

In the *United States*, the scale of construction has shifted from individual buildings to city-sized campuses. A defining example is the reported *Stargate* project, a collaboration involving OpenAI and Oracle. This initiative aims to deploy infrastructure across multiple US states with a potential total investment value rumored to approach US$ 100 billion over time. Similarly, Blackstone has committed US$ 25 billion to develop a series of AI-ready data center campuses, effectively reshaping the local economy around digital infrastructure. AWS has broken ground on a US$ 11 billion campus, further cementing the Midwest as a new corridor for silicon and steel.

The growth of AI investments is primarily driven by hyperscalers: AWS, Microsoft, Google, and Meta account for most new projects. By the end of the decade, hyperscalers are projected to account for over 60% of all data centers [17].

2.3.2 AI Semiconductor Technology

2.3.2.1 General Purpose Chip Architectures

The engine of the AI data center is a specialized semiconductor architecture: the *Graphics Processing Unit* (GPU), originally designed for video games, which is ideally suited to the parallel computation of neural networks.

AI workloads are shifting, challenging traditional hardware roles. Training large, complex models is still GPU-intensive due to their massive parallelism, making these models the superior choice for deep learning development. However, inference (deployment/use) increasingly relies on *Central Processing Units* (CPUs), especially for lightweight models or edge devices. Modern CPUs with specialized vector instructions (such as the Intel VNNI) handle high-volume, low-latency inference tasks in an efficiently and cost-effective way, complementing the GPU's dominance in training.

NVIDIA's *Compute Unified Device Architecture* (CUDA) is a parallel computing platform and programming model that enables developers to harness GPU processing power for general-purpose computing. Instead of relying solely on CPUs, CUDA enables massive parallelism by allowing thousands of GPU cores to execute computations simultaneously. This architecture is particularly well-suited for large-scale data processing tasks, including deep learning, scientific simulations, and high-performance computing. In the AI hardware market, CUDA plays a central role by providing the foundation for most of NVIDIA's AI acceleration technologies.

Apple has launched *MLX* to mimic CUDA in Apple MacBook environments, while AMD seeks to counter CUDA's market dominance with *ROCm*. However, due to its maturity and ecosystem adoption, CUDA has become the industry standard for GPU-based AI development, giving NVIDIA a dominant position in the AI hardware ecosystem and driving innovation in machine learning and data-intensive applications.

NVIDIA holds a significant market position that drives ecosystem alignment around its release cycles. The company's annual chip release schedule and its impact on a key segment of the AI compute stack create supply chain dependencies. Consequently, the strategies, cooling technology decisions, and energy management approaches adopted by hyperscalers are increasingly shaped by NVIDIA's product roadmap. This roadmap largely determines the timing of hyperscaler capacity expansions, facility design considerations, and cooling solution selection [17].

Field-Programmable Gate Arrays (FPGAs) provide a flexible, reconfigurable hardware platform that bridges the gap between general-purpose processors and custom ASICs. They enable developers to tailor hardware architectures to specific AI workloads, such as neural network inference or data preprocessing, delivering higher performance and energy efficiency than CPUs or GPUs for those tasks. FPGAs excel in low-latency, real-time applications – like autonomous systems and edge AI – due to their parallel processing and customizable data paths. Their reprogrammability also enables rapid prototyping and adaptation, allowing AI models to evolve without requiring new hardware fabrication.

Chiplets are small, specialized integrated circuits designed to work together as a single, cohesive processing unit within a larger package. Instead of manufacturing an entire complex system as a single monolithic die, the functions (such as CPU cores, memory controllers, and I/O) are separated into individual chiplets. This modular approach leverages advanced packaging technology to connect them, allowing manufacturers to mix and match best-of-breed components, use smaller dies, and combine different node sizes (e. g., a CPU core with 5 nm while an I/O module uses 10 nm technology). This improves manufacturing yields for complex designs and enables greater scalability, offering a cost-effective path to building powerful processors.

2.3.2.2 AI-specific Chip Architectures

Google's *Tensor Processing Units* (TPUs) are *Application-Specific Integrated Circuits* (ASICs) designed for tensor processing. Tensor processing is a form of high-speed parallel computing that focuses on performing large-scale matrix operations, such as multidimensional additions and multiplications, to efficiently handle the heavy data workloads required by neural networks. Unlike more general-purpose GPUs, TPUs use matrix processing units to accelerate the linear algebra at the heart of deep learning.

Wafer-sized AI chips, such as those built by Cerebras (*cerebras.ai*), represent a radical shift in accelerator design. Instead of tiling many smaller chips, Cerebras constructs a single processor spanning nearly an entire silicon wafer. Their WSE-3 model, for example, contains about 900,000 AI-optimized cores and delivers ~125 petaflops of compute power. Having all cores and memory on a single large chip reduces communication latency, eliminates many off-chip bottlenecks (such as slower external memory), and increases bandwidth dramatically. This means that models with trillions of parameters can be trained more efficiently.

Other AI chip architectures emulate biological and physical principles: Photonic chips use light rather than electrons to perform computations, enabling ultra-fast data transmission and low power consumption. By exploiting optical interference and parallelism, they can process vast amounts of information simultaneously, making them ideal for large-scale neural network inference. *Memristor-based chips* mimic the behavior of biological synapses by combining memory and processing in a single unit, reducing data movement and energy use. Their resistance varies with historical electrical activity, enabling them to learn and exhibit adaptive behaviors natively in hardware. *Analog AI chips* process information using continuous voltage levels rather than binary signals, enabling inherently parallel, energy-efficient computation well suited to matrix operations in neural networks. However, they face challenges in precision and noise control. *Spiking neural network chips*, as a subclass of *Neuromorphic Chips*, model the event-driven communication of biological neurons, transmitting information only when neurons spike. This sparse temporal coding dramatically reduces power consumption and improves efficiency for real-time sensory and edge applications (e. g., *spinncloud.com*). Together, these architectures represent a shift toward brain-inspired and physics-driven computing paradigms that aim to overcome the limitations of conventional digital AI hardware. They have clearly not yet gained commercial traction.

There is some enthusiasm for *Quantum Computing* (QC) and QC-enabled machine learning. While the commercial relevance of QC itself is still disputed, no research currently available indicates that QC will make a difference to AI's computational challenges.

2.3.2.3 Performance Gain Predictions

AI chip performance is likely to see several interlocking improvements rooted in advances in manufacturing, architectures, and energy efficiency:

- First, process node shrinkage toward 2 nm and eventually 1 nm-class transistors (with techniques like Gate-All-Around, backside power delivery, and nanosheet/nanowire approaches) will yield higher transistor density, lower power consumption, and faster clock speeds [18].
- Second, hybrid packaging, chiplets, and 3D stacking will reduce data path distances and interconnect bottlenecks, boosting effective throughput and performance per watt [19].
- Third, memory subsystem improvements – especially more widespread use of high-bandwidth memory, and tighter integration between memory and logic – will remove one of the current limiting factors in large AI model workloads [20].
- Fourth, architectural optimizations, such as specialized accelerators, more efficient AI inference hardware, quantization, sparsity, and specialized precision formats, will continue to drive gains in both throughput and energy efficiency.
- Finally, manufacturing scale and yield improvements will augment raw performance gains – better tooling, EUV lithography, and more robust fabs will become more capable and cheaper per unit performance.

Taken together, we can expect AI chips that deliver multiple-fold increases in performance per watt, far larger on-chip memory and bandwidth, and significant improvements in inference and training latency (see Figure 2.2).

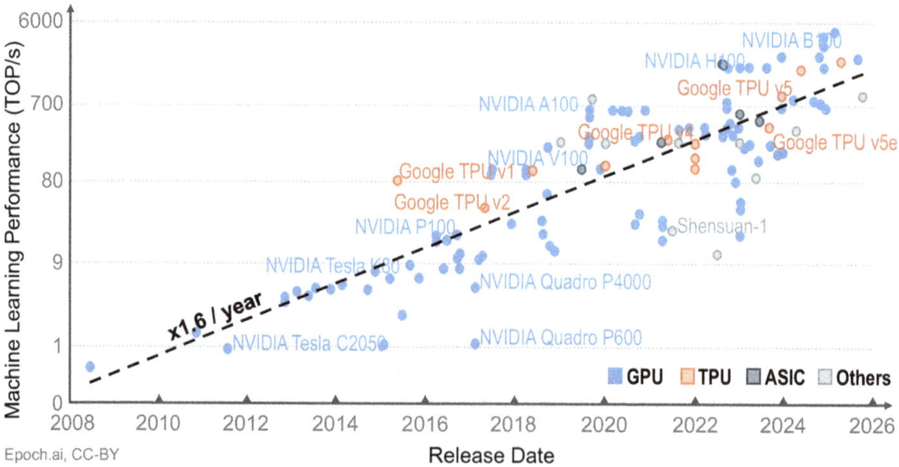

Figure 2.2 Increases in ML chip performance 2008–2026 [21]

2.3.2.4 Edge Applications

The resource requirements for training are exponentially higher than those for inference. Training is fundamentally memory-bound, requiring sufficient high-speed memory to hold not only model weights but also massive volumes of activation maps, gradients, and optimizer states. To handle iterative optimization, training models typically require twice to four times the memory footprint of the model weights themselves [22].

In sharp contrast, inference is designed to be efficient once the model parameters are fixed. Inference demands are primarily limited to the memory required to store the quantized model weights. Hence, inference-only platforms can operate effectively with highly constrained on-chip memory pools, thereby minimizing power requirements for applications where power (and heat) is a concern and on-edge training capabilities are not needed.

Cloud data storage and higher data transfer costs are often underestimated, negatively impacting ROI for industrial use cases. This issue is exacerbated by the high volume of production data, while data points on anomalies (e. g., quality defects) are scarce. Edge AI applications can process large volumes of data locally, reducing cloud storage and data transfer costs.

Examples of AI edge applications include:

- *Engineering workstations* such as HP Z8 Fury Workstation, NVIDIA's DGX Spark, or AMD's Strix Halo. These appliances cover local training and execution of AI workloads, for example, for local simulation and design space exploration (see Section 23.2.2 "Design Space Exploration"), and for the application of LLMs in classified local environments. Power consumption varies between 240 W (DGX Spark) and ~1500 W (HP's Z8 Fury, depending on configuration). Active cooling is a necessity.
- *Inference-only AI chips and appliances* to embed AI in autonomous vehicles, drones, machine-vision cameras for navigation, robotics, and quality inspection. Examples include XILINX's Versal AI core offerings, focused on ultra-low latency (e. g., an autonomous robot performing a safety stop or a controller for a CNC machine), and Sima.ai's MLSoc family (*sima.ai/mlsoc-family*). Power-consumption-optimized – and therefore heat-optimized – edge architectures are an important enabler for fan-less edge designs, which are useful in dusty industrial environments or settings with high hygiene standards (e. g., implying water-based cleaning procedures).

2.3.3 Energy Consumption

The energy consumption of this infrastructure is staggering and growing extraordinarily. Training a single large AI model can consume as much electricity as hundreds of households do in a year. As AI becomes more integrated into everyday products, the energy required for *inference* will also soar. This immense appetite for power poses a major challenge to sustainability goals and may become a fundamental constraint on AI's future growth.

Of course, the portion of a data center's operational costs attributable to electricity varies significantly by location, age, and efficiency. Electricity typically accounts for 30% to 60% of a data center's total annual operating expenses. For older or less efficient enterprise data centers, this can increase to 60% to 70%, while modern, highly efficient hyperscaler facilities with optimized cooling and electrical infrastructure (achieving a low Power Usage Effectiveness, or PUE) may operate at the lower end of the range, around 30% to 40%.

DeepL's Data Center in Iceland

DeepL is leveraging its data center strategy in Iceland's unique geographic advantages to significantly reduce the energy costs associated with training and running its demanding translation AI. The core cost advantage stems from two geographical factors: Firstly, Iceland provides a low-cost, stable supply of *100% renewable energy*, sourced entirely from reliable geothermal and hydroelectric power. Secondly, the island's cold climate enables *free-air cooling year-round*, eliminating the need for energy-intensive mechanical refrigeration. This highly efficient operational model dramatically reduces the facility's PUE, enabling DeepL to reduce its largest expense while meeting demand for scalable compute resources.

It's also noteworthy how electricity is used within the facility [23]:

- *Servers and IT equipment* (compute) consume ~40% to 60% of the total power entering the facility.
- *Cooling systems* need anything from 7% to over 30% of the total electricity, depending on the facility's design and PUE score. Cooling is the fastest-growing facility segment, with annual growth rates of 24% and 20% through 2030, respectively. The rise in dense, GPU-intensive workloads is accelerating the adoption and replacement cycles of liquid cooling, positioning it as a significant beneficiary of AI infrastructure changes [17].
- The remaining power goes to power distribution units, uninterruptible power supply, lighting, security, and the like.

The current AI boom is increasing energy consumption, as AI servers with GPUs can consume 3 to 6 times the power of traditional servers, necessitating higher density and greater cooling requirements, as shown in Figure 2.3.

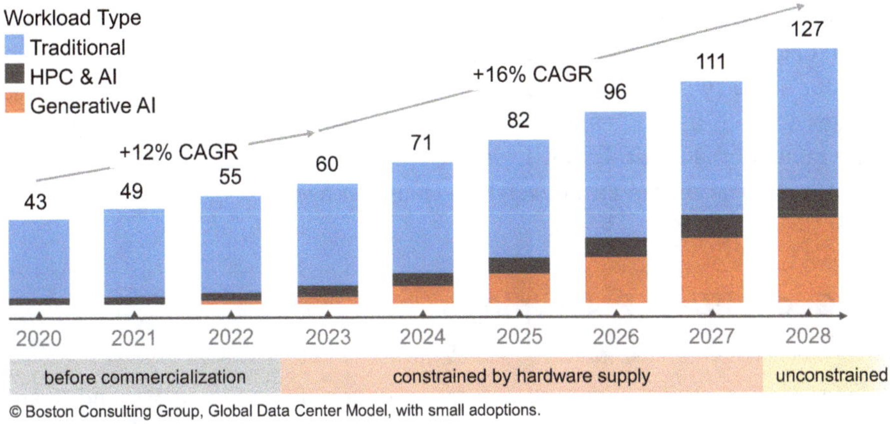

Figure 2.3 Global data center power required for projected compute in Gigawatts [24]

2.3.4 Sustainability Impact

The explosive growth of AI, particularly GenAI, has created a profound sustainability paradox: The intensive training and continuous inference (usage) of these models demand immense computational power, making AI one of the fastest-growing consumers of global electricity.

Training a single state-of-the-art LLM can consume hundreds of megawatt-hours, releasing substantial carbon emissions, especially when powered by fossil fuels. Beyond power, this algorithmic footprint involves significant water use in both semiconductor production and the cooling of high-density servers. It contributes to e-waste from the rapid turnover of specialized hardware. If left unchecked, this escalating energy hunger threatens to derail net-zero commitments and strain local power grids.

The AI industry is developing aggressive countermeasures focused on hardware, software, and operational efficiency. On the software side, techniques such as model pruning and quantization are used to compress models by removing redundant parameters, dramatically reducing inference energy requirements with minimal accuracy loss. Furthermore, researchers are focusing on model efficiency, shifting from building exponentially larger foundational models to developing smaller, task-specific, and less resource-intensive models.

Operationally, companies are deploying strategies to ensure AI is carbon-aware. This involves shifting compute workloads to data centers in regions with abundant renewable energy (e. g., hydropower in Nordic countries) and using software to schedule non-critical jobs during periods of peak renewable generation. Advances in cooling, such as liquid-immersion cooling, further reduce the facility's PUE, while reducing the non-IT power load and demonstrating that the drive for efficiency can align sustainability with economic advantage.

The negative environmental footprint of AI will not be offset by consumers writing poems on ChatGPT or kids doing their homework with AI assistance. However, leveraging AI for industry in the context of Zero-Waste-Zero-Defect strategies, discovering new materials with a significantly lower environmental footprint, and using AI to optimize humanity's logistical challenges will lead to a situation in which the advantages of AI optimization can far outweigh its energy hunger.

2.4 A Geopolitical Powerplay

AI is no longer just a technology – it is a primary vector of national power and a central theater for geopolitical competition. The rivalry between the United States and China has crystallized into an AI race, in which leadership in AI is regarded as synonymous with future economic dominance and national security.

This power play is most visible in the battle for the physical components of AI: semiconductors. What are known as the *chip wars* have seen the United States implement stringent export controls to prevent advanced AI chips, particularly those designed by companies such as NVIDIA, from reaching China. The goal is to slow China's progress in developing the large-scale models that underpin modern AI. In response, China is pouring massive state resources into developing its own domestic semiconductor industry to achieve self-sufficiency.

In September 2025, China's Internet regulator has barred the country's largest tech companies from purchasing Nvidia's artificial intelligence chips, as Beijing intensified efforts to strengthen its domestic sector and rival the US. The Cyberspace Administration of China instructed firms such as ByteDance and Alibaba to halt testing and orders of the RTX Pro 6000D – Nvidia's customized product for China [25].

This competition extends beyond hardware to talent, data, and international standards. Nations are vying to attract the world's top AI researchers, build massive national data repositories, and influence global regulations to favor their own technological and ethical frameworks.

Even at the model usage level, fierce competition is evident: Recent research by CrowdStrike concludes that the Chinese AI model DeepSeek intentionally produces fewer or more coding errors by design when tasked by different regions or political groups [26].

China's *AI+ initiative*, launched in late 2024, represents a strategic shift from developing general-purpose models to the large-scale integration of AI across manufacturing, healthcare, and energy: By aiming for 70% penetration of AI-powered end devices by 2027, Beijing seeks to dominate *embodied AI* (see Section 2.7.4.3) and industrial automation – sectors where Europe has traditionally excelled. This "grand steering" approach, supported by state funding and open-source breakthroughs like DeepSeek, has created a formidable sovereign AI stack [27].

For any global industrial company, this means the landscape is no longer flat. The choice of where to develop AI, where to source components, and on which markets to deploy solutions is now fraught with geopolitical risk and regulatory complexity.

A machine tool builder integrates AI technologies into their machines, which are sold globally. US export controls limit their ability to integrate US LLM technology into machines sold in China, forcing them to develop product variants that use local models for machines targeting the Chinese market.

2.4.1 AI and Critical Infrastructure

The integration of AI into critical infrastructure – such as power grids, water treatment facilities, transportation networks, and manufacturing plants – presents a profound duality of promise and peril.

On one hand, AI offers transformative potential for optimization and resilience. It can predict equipment failures in power plants, optimize traffic flow in smart cities, manage complex energy loads to prevent blackouts, and detect anomalies in water supply systems. These applications can enhance our infrastructure's efficiency, sustainability, and robustness.

On the other hand, this integration creates a new and highly sensitive attack surface. An AI system controlling a power grid could be compromised by malicious actors, potentially leading to widespread outages. Autonomous vehicle networks could be hacked, and smart factories could be shut down remotely. The very complexity and autonomy of AI systems can make them difficult to secure and audit, potentially hiding vulnerabilities that can be exploited at scale. As we embed AI more deeply into the systems that underpin our society, ensuring AI's security and safety is not merely a technical challenge but a matter of national security.

The conflict between *Ukraine* and *Russia* has seen the Ukrainian power grid become a significant target for cyber warfare. This isn't a new development; state-sponsored Russian hackers have been testing their capabilities against Ukraine's energy infrastructure for years, notably with the 2015 and 2016 attacks that caused widespread blackouts [28].

2.4.2 Digital Sovereignty

Digital Sovereignty in the age of AI refers to the capacity of a nation or organization to maintain independent control over its digital assets – specifically data, algorithms, and computing infrastructure – without reliance on external actors that could compromise its security or autonomy [29]. As AI systems become critical national infrastructure, sovereignty is no longer merely about where data resides (residency) but about who ultimately holds the power to access and manipulate the intelligence derived from it.

The industry distinguishes between several approaches to achieving this:

- *Sovereignty by Contract* (or Legal Sovereignty) relies on legal frameworks and agreements to protect digital assets. Organizations use foreign technology (e. g., from American hyperscalers) but sign strict, binding contracts or Service Level Agreements to ensure compliance with local laws, such as GDPR. While flexible, this model is often criticized as fragile because extraterritorial laws (such as the U. S. CLOUD Act) can, in theory, override private contracts, thereby compelling providers to disclose data despite contractual commitments.

AI Infrastructure Build-up in Europe and the Gulf States

Europe is seeing a surge in sovereign AI infrastructure to reduce latency and regulatory risk. Microsoft recently announced a landmark US$ 10 billion investment to build an AI hub in Portugal, while Google is deepening its footprint in Germany and Belgium with EUR 5.5 billion commitments in both countries, designed to support local enterprise AI adoption. National IT champions such as Deutsche Telekom, IONOS, and the German Schwarz Group, with their IT branch StackIT, are investing in building AI Giga Factories, partially subsidized by the German Government.

The *Gulf monarchies* are aggressively positioning themselves as the world's 'neutral' AI superpowers, effectively pivoting their economic base from exporting hydrocarbons to exporting services. Leveraging vast sovereign wealth, nations like the *UAE* and *Saudi Arabia* are building state-of-the-art infrastructure to capture global compute demand. This strategy relies on a "sovereignty by purchase" model: By funding the world's most expensive infrastructure, these nations aim to become indispensable nodes in the global AI supply chain, ensuring that even if the software is American, the "engine room" of the future economy resides in the Gulf.

- *Sovereignty by Origin* (or Technological Sovereignty) offers a tighter form of control rooted in the provenance of the technology. It requires that the software, hardware, and AI models are developed, owned, and operated by local entities within the sovereign jurisdiction [30]. By eliminating foreign supply chain dependencies, this approach ensures that no hidden backdoors or foreign judicial levers exist, offering the highest assurance of independence at the cost of reduced vendor choice.

Pursuing strict sovereignty by origin effectively isolates an ecosystem from the massive economies of scale and Research and Development (R&D) budgets of US hyperscalers, who currently drive the frontier of AI capability. This decoupling can create a dangerous innovation gap, where sovereign entities are forced to rely on domestic technology that is often generations behind global state-of-the-art systems in terms of capability and efficiency. Ultimately, this approach risks prioritizing jurisdictional control over functional utility, leaving nations with secure but obsolete infrastructure that cannot compete in a global economy defined by rapid technological velocity.

- *Data Embassies* have emerged as a further approach: Physical data centers located in allied nations that are granted diplomatic immunity. Just as a physical embassy in a foreign capital is legally considered the soil of the guest nation, a data embassy is a server room on foreign soil where the host country has no legal jurisdiction, right to search, or ability to seize content. Data embassies decouple a nation's survival from its territory, ensuring that even if the capital falls or the land sinks, the digital state continues to operate from a secure, inviolable enclave abroad.

Digital Backups of Whole Nations

As a small Baltic state wary of Russian aggression, *Estonia* established the world's first data embassy in *Luxembourg* in 2017. This Tier-4 data center hosts critical government clouds (e-Land Registry, e-Tax) under a bilateral treaty ensuring that Luxembourg police or courts have no authority over the servers. It serves as a digital backup of the entire country.

Following the 2022 invasion, *Ukraine* passed emergency legislation to allow state data to leave the country. Working with *AWS*, they effectively migrated the government applications to the cloud (using AWS Snowball devices to move petabytes of data physically). While not a formal embassy treaty in the same legal sense, this effectively utilized the cloud as sanctuary, allowing the government to issue pensions and document war crimes even as missiles targeted physical servers in Kyiv.

2.4.3 AI Regulation

Understanding the diverse regulatory landscapes has become essential for manufacturers implementing AI systems. The approach to AI regulation varies dramatically across regions, with each framework reflecting distinct priorities, governance philosophies, and risk tolerance.

2.4.3.1 European Union

The *European Union*'s approach to AI regulation faces substantial criticism:

- EU regulation imposed on corporations has increased to such an extent that regulatory duties become an unbearable burden – the EU AI Act is yet another one.
- AI specific: The EU AI Act was coined with societal concerns in mind and does not allow lean approaches to AI governance for industry.

The *EU AI Act* categorizes AI systems into four risk tiers: unacceptable, high, limited, and minimal (see Figure 2.4). For industrial applications, this means stringent requirements for high-risk systems used in critical infrastructure, manufacturing safety systems, and industrial robotics. Manufacturers must conduct conformity assessments, implement robust data governance, ensure human oversight, maintain technical documentation, and perform ongoing monitoring.

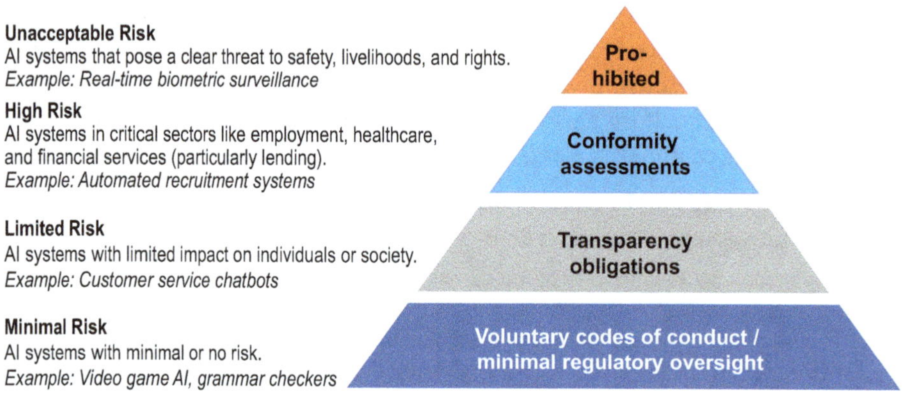

Figure 2.4 Risk pyramid according to the EU AI Act

While the EU AI Act provides a binding legislative framework, its technical implementation requirements – sensibly – are subject to vertical industry standards, such as the *Machinery Directive*, which are continuously developed. The overall situation implies several challenges:

- A *timing issue*: The EU AI Act is about to become legally binding prior to technical standards being available (and with sufficient time to implement them).
- A *content issue*: Several aspects of technical feasibility in industry contradict the current legislation, which would suggest an iterative approach to EU AI Act refinement.

> The logging requirements for AI in critical systems under the EU AI Act can hardly be implemented in industry, where the AI model is an embedded component within an overall system that prescribes the system's logging infrastructure.

- A *systemic business model challenge*: The work on technical standards for EU AI Act implementation is dominated by consultants, assessment, and certification experts whose business models are geared to earning money with assessments and certifications; this naturally prevents a lean approach to technical standards.

2.4.3.2 United States

The *US* employs a fragmented regulatory landscape without a comprehensive federal AI law:

- Industrial AI faces oversight from various agencies depending on the application: OSHA for workplace safety, FDA for medical device manufacturing, EPA for environmental monitoring systems, and NHTSA for autonomous industrial vehicles.
- Societal concerns are addressed by a plethora of state-by-state regulations and laws, such as the recent California Senate Bill 53 [31] or New York's RAISE Act and AI Companion Law.

This decentralized approach has created a complex patchwork of requirements for multi-state industrial operations, while the current administration emphasizes the need for creating a streamlined national approach to AI regulation.

2.4.3.3 China

China implements a state-directed approach that aligns AI deployment with national strategic priorities. Industrial AI systems must register with authorities, undergo security reviews, and make sure data and models come from legitimate sources. China's framework focuses on eight critical scenarios, including manufacturing applications that could affect national security. The centralized model enables rapid implementation but requires close alignment with government priorities. Penalties for non-compliance are severe, including substantial fines, service suspension, or criminal charges for serious violations.

2.4.3.4 Japan

Japan has adopted a light-touch regulatory model based on voluntary guidelines rather than binding legislation. The *AI Governance Guidelines for Business* emphasize practical risk management while encouraging innovation. This approach gives industrial AI developers significant flexibility while still establishing clear expectations for ethical AI development. Japan's focus on human-centric AI principles promotes dignity, fairness, and inclusivity in industrial applications.

2.4.3.5 South Korea

South Korea has passed a comprehensive *AI Basic Act*, set to take effect in 2026, focusing on high-impact systems in critical sectors. Industrial AI systems must enable meaningful human monitoring, provide transparency about AI-generated decisions, and undergo risk assessments. Foreign AI companies must appoint local representatives, creating additional compliance requirements for international industrial AI providers.

2.4.3.6 Gulf Nations

The regulatory landscape for AI in the Gulf region is emerging as a nuanced patchwork, driven primarily by countries such as the *United Arab Emirates* (UAE) and *Saudi Arabia*. These countries, with ambitious national AI strategies, generally favor a business-friendly, innovation-first approach, often using "soft law" ethical guidelines and regulatory sandboxes rather than strict, dedicated AI legislation. Oversight often falls under comprehensive Personal Data Protection Laws, which indirectly govern AI by focusing on data handling, consent, and transparency.

A major challenge remains in establishing unified governance frameworks and developing culturally relevant Arabic-language models to ensure the responsible and equitable adoption of AI across the broader region [32].

2.4.3.7 Implications for Industrial AI

In most cases, AI regulation aims to mitigate societal issues caused by AI, such as the use of large-scale AI systems to influence public opinion or for surveillance. Only very few industrial use cases match these risk profiles. However, for industrial AI deployments, these regulatory differences necessitate the establishment of a systematic methodology:

- *Risk Assessment Framework*: Evaluates each industrial AI application's risk profile across jurisdictions where it will operate.
- *Regulatory Stack Approach*: Designs core capabilities to meet the strictest applicable requirements (typically the EU's) with modular compliance components for different regions.
- *Documentation Systems*: Implement robust documentation practices capturing development decisions, data sources, testing methodologies, and performance metrics from the earliest design stages.
- *Continuous Monitoring*: Establishes processes to track evolving requirements across regions, as AI governance frameworks continue to develop rapidly.
- *Transparency Mechanisms*: Invest in explainability capabilities for industrial AI systems, particularly for high-risk manufacturing applications.

2.4.3.8 Industry-driven Trustworthy AI

Industry-driven initiatives often take the form of consortia and internal governance frameworks, aiming to embed principles such as fairness, transparency, robustness, and accountability throughout the AI lifecycle, from design through deployment.

The initiative *Partnership on AI* (*partnershiponai.org*) brings together major tech companies, civil society, and academics to share best practices and develop common standards. Individual giants, such as IBM and Google, publish their own detailed AI principles and establish responsible technology boards to govern internal development, with a focus on human-centric AI that augments, but does not replace, human judgment.

The *AI Trust Alliance* (*trustalliance.ai*), in collaboration with the French *Confiance.ai* consortium and the VDE technology organization, have established a combined German-French label for trustworthy and responsible AI. The resulting *Trustworthy AI Label* is a voluntary standard for characterizing the trustworthiness of AI-based systems, using a VCIO (Values, Criteria, Indicators, Observables) model to describe how well a system adheres to core socio-technical values.

Switzerland launched the *Swiss AI Initiative for trustworthy AI*, including digital sovereignty [33]. The focus of this initiative is joint research supported by a substantial contribution of AI resources from the Swiss National Supercomputing Centre.

Applied AI (*appliedai.de*), an AI dissemination accelerator in the ecosystem of Munich's top-notch university TUM, provides an AI risk and hazard assessment methodology helping users navigate through compliance requirements of the EU AI Act [34].

2.5 AI and the Labor Markets

The global race for AI dominance begins and ends with talent:

- At the highest level, fierce *international competition* is underway, as leading nations strategically invest in research hubs and immigration to attract the world's elite researchers (see Section 2.5.1).
- This geopolitical rivalry is mirrored by intense *national and industry-level competition*, where sectors such as Big Tech, finance, and healthcare engage in aggressive talent wars for specialists who can drive innovation (see Section 2.5.2).
- Finally, at the *enterprise level*, companies compete through escalating compensation and by offering purpose-driven projects and a culture of continuous development to secure the scarce expertise needed for AI maturity (see Section 2.5.3).
- Section 2.5.4 provides the first data points on *AI's job replacement effects* in software engineering and process outsourcing services. Chapter 10 provides guidance on addressing AI talent challenges in our corporate environment.

2.5.1 AI Talent at the International Level

AI professionals are now more mobile and discerning, seeking roles where they can pioneer new technologies and ensure their work is socially meaningful and trustworthy. Often referred to as "walking intellectual property", these experts are highly sought after beyond just Silicon Valley. The influx of foreign talent has played a key role in establishing and sustaining the *United States*' leadership in AI, as Figure 2.5 shows.

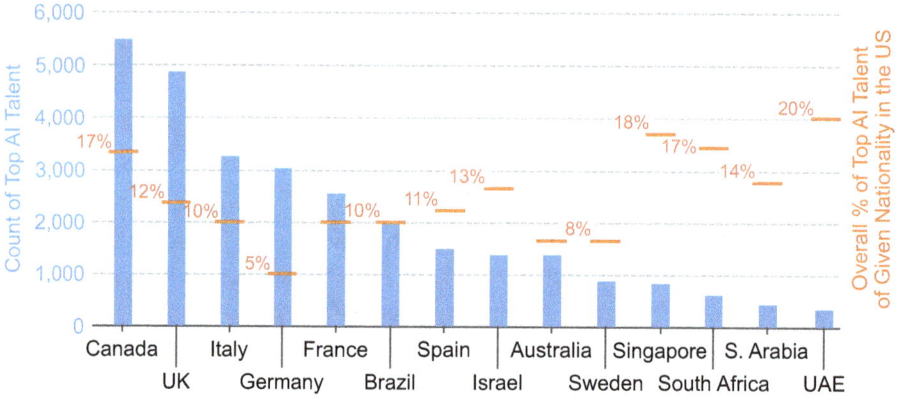

Underlying data for this insight is from Zeki Data's tool Talent IQ.

Figure 2.5 US Top AI talent count by nationality

However, this pipeline is shrinking quickly, as fewer leading AI experts are willing to relocate to the US – in part due to concerns about the political environment and shifts in visa policies and processing times by immigration authorities (see Figure 2.6 and [35]).

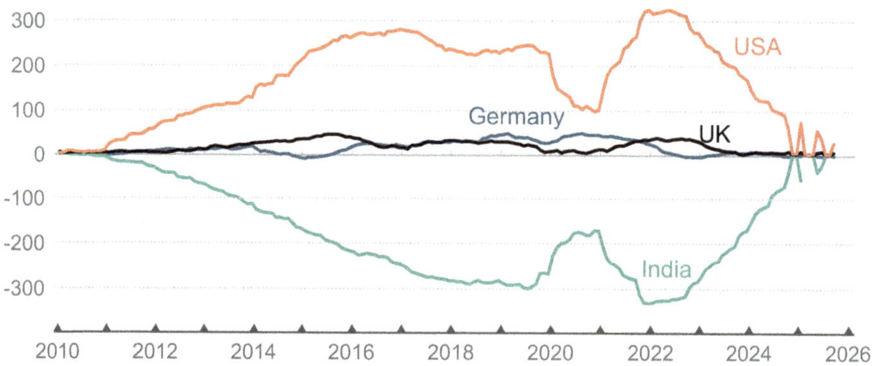

Underlying data for this insight is from Zeki Data's tool Talent IQ.

Figure 2.6 Net flow of top AI talent of selected nations (12 months rolling average)

Several *European nations* – such as the UK, Germany, the Netherlands, and Nordic countries – are beginning to achieve net AI talent inflows, supported by national champions and diverse startup ecosystems. In January 2025, the *UK* government announced plans to develop an internal headhunting team modelled after top recruitment companies to recruit elite AI scientists and engineers to the UK. Additionally, the government proposed a dedicated global AI talent visa to help reduce barriers for top researchers and engineers.

In February 2024, the *Singaporean* government unveiled a US$1 billion, five-year plan to support AI computing, talent development, and industry growth. In April 2024, the Canadian government announced a US$ 2.4 billion package to secure *Canada*'s AI advantage. And last but not least, it appears that emerging AI talent in *India* are choosing to pursue their careers or complete advanced degrees there. This is supported by numerous well-funded initiatives that have established strong ecosystems that bridge academia, Indian deep-tech champions, and emerging startups.

2.5.2 AI Talent at National Level and Industry Level

Highly skilled individuals tend to be concentrated within a select group of major technology firms and hyperscalers, making it challenging for industrial organizations to secure and retain the expertise necessary to develop competitive solutions.

Additionally, a secondary self-reinforcing cycle is emerging. Leading technology companies originally developed core business models focused on primary markets – Google in search and advertising, Amazon and their Chinese counterparts in e-commerce, and Meta in social media. To support these operations, they built extensive data centers, AI frameworks, and cloud infrastructure. These resources subsequently evolved into independent hyperscaler and AI businesses. Currently, a substantial portion of hyperscaler efforts is directed towards building applications that fully utilize their own capacity, including further expansion into the industrial sector (see Table 2.1).

Not all of these initiatives have been commercially successful, and some have been scaled back (e. g., Apple's attempt to build cars, AWS's attempt to enter industrial monitoring with "Monitron"). The effect on AI talent recruitment remains: industry competes with Big Tech players not just for algorithmic AI talent but also for "applied AI" talent, where domain expertise intersects with AI expertise.

Table 2.1 Big Tech initiatives entering the industrial space

Big Tech	Industrial Market Segment	Value Driver
Alphabet	▪ Autonomous Driving (Waymo) ▪ Lifescience/precision medicine (Verily) ▪ Industrial Robotics (intrinsic)	▪ AI capabilities (e. g., proprietary chips) ▪ Cloud resources
Amazon	▪ Intralogistics (AGVs, Robotics) and Distribution Logistics ▪ Industrial machine monitoring (e. g., Monitron)	▪ Leadership in logistic processes ▪ Cloud resources
NVIDIA	▪ Robotics simulation ▪ Computational Fluid Dynamics ▪ Autonomous driving ▪ Industrial Metaverse	▪ AI capabilities (e. g., proprietary chips)
Apple	▪ Autonomous Driving ▪ Personalized Healthcare (e. g., hearing aids)	▪ Consumer Access ▪ App store ecosystem

2.5.3 AI Talent at Corporate Level

The hiring and headhunting of elite AI talent have surged into an unprecedented bidding war, with compensation packages now regularly reaching millions of dollars and, in some extreme cases, even hundreds of millions of dollars over several years. Major tech giants such as Meta, Google, and OpenAI are aggressively competing for a limited pool of top researchers and engineers, particularly experts for

- physical AI and world models (see Section 2.7.4.4 "World Models");
- energy efficiency tuning in hardware and software; and
- product engineering for technical and commercial scale.

This hyperinflation in salaries, equity, and bonuses is driven by the perceived massive economic leverage that a single AI breakthrough could generate. Companies view this spending as a rational investment, after all, the cost of securing a world-class AI expert is relatively small compared to the billions spent on training LLMs and the potential revenue from establishing long-term competitive advantages in the AI race. This trend has not only reshaped the entire tech labor market but also intensified the industry's growing wealth disparity.

2.5.4 AI Effects on the Labor Markets

Prof. Holger Schmidt, a prominent digital economist and professor at TU Darmstadt, has collaborated extensively with the job portal *Indeed* to track the *AI-Job-Index*. His work focuses on how GenAI is reshaping labor demand, skill requirements, and productivity. According to the AI-Job-Index analysis [36], the specific breakdown of job exposure to GenAI is as follows:

- *High exposure:* Roughly *one-fifth* of all job postings on Indeed are considered "highly exposed" to GenAI. In these roles, AI can handle *80% or more* of the typical tasks. This category primarily includes knowledge-intensive fields such as software development, marketing, and legal services.
- *Medium exposure:* Nearly *half* of the jobs show a moderate level of exposure, where AI can assist with *50% to 80% of tasks*. These roles are likely to undergo significant augmentation, with the human worker remaining essential but their workflow fundamentally transformed.
- *Low exposure:* About *one-third* of jobs have low exposure, where AI can perform *less than 50%* of tasks. These are typically "hands-on" or blue-collar roles that require physical presence and manual dexterity, such as nursing, construction, or specialized craft trades.

Schmidt emphasizes that high exposure does not equal job loss. Instead, his data suggests that these highly exposed roles are seeing a surge in demand for workers with AI skills, as companies prioritize hiring people who can leverage these tools to drive 10x productivity. In other words, Indeed's data suggest that the German and global markets are in a "learning phase" rather than a "replacement phase".

This is, in a sense, countered by Stanford's *Digital Economy Lab*, which analyzed payroll data from millions of US workers from late 2022 through mid-2025. They find a *~16% decline* in employment among 22- to 25-year-olds in AI-exposed industries, such as software development and customer service. Employers are reportedly using AI tools to automate many tasks that junior developers once performed (e.g., basic coding and debugging), thereby reducing demand for entry-level hires [37]. This obviously raises the question of how software development staff can grow senior when young talent is cut off from entry-level positions.

A similar effect is observed by *ZEKI Data*, as shown in Figure 2.7: Among US companies with the highest level of AI maturity, hiring of junior software developers declined significantly [35].

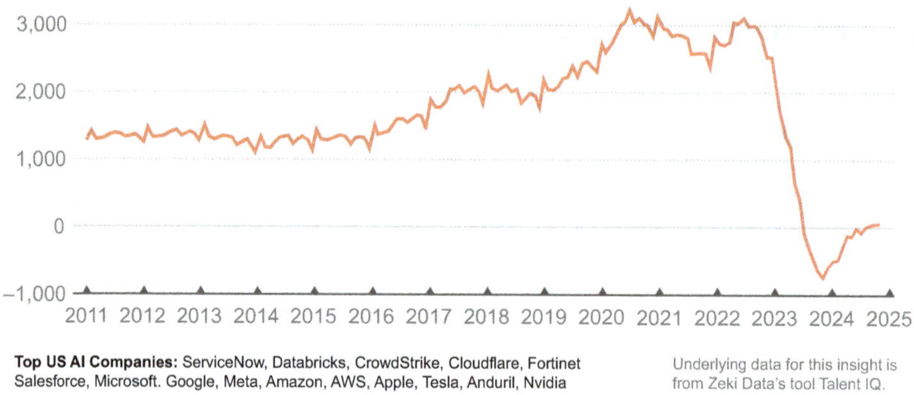

Figure 2.7 Software engineering monthly hires of top US AI companies

Kraków, Poland, has become a center for business process outsourcing, particularly in Shared Services (see Chapter 32), with around 100,000 people employed in this domain. Recent employment statistics reveal a surge in mass layoffs, recording nearly 1,900 job cuts in Q1/2025, as the region's business services sector undergoes structural transformation driven by AI and automation. Major global firms are shedding white-collar roles in finance and tech, signaling the erosion of the traditional low-cost outsourcing model. Companies are increasingly automating repetitive tasks or consolidating operations in lower-cost markets such as India. This trend extends across Central and Eastern Europe, with similar shifts observed in Romania and Hungary [38].

One possible interpretation of these statistics, restoring compatibility with Professor Schmidt's AI-Job-Index-based findings, is that in both scenarios, software engineering in top US AI companies and business process outsourcing services in Eastern Europe, AI design competency and actual process execution are separate functions. A small group of experts handles process redesign and AI-driven automation, while productivity gains in process execution have negative labor-market effects.

2.6 Industrial Context

2.6.1 Digital Twins

2.6.1.1 Value Proposition

Digital Twins are virtual replicas of physical assets, processes, or systems that continuously update via a real-time data exchange. Unlike static simulations, these dynamic virtual models evolve alongside their physical counterparts, reflecting current conditions and predicting future states through AI (and non-AI) algorithms [39, 40]. Their virtual nature enables users to conduct virtual experiments, simulate scenarios, and test modifications without disrupting actual production. They also democratize expertise by digitizing institutional knowledge, enabling less-experienced operators to benefit from AI-enhanced guidance. As manufacturing faces increasing pressure to be sustainable, Digital Twins optimize resource use and energy consumption, reducing waste and environmental impact while maintaining productivity.

2.6.1.2 Digital Twin Interoperability

Analyzing a system as a whole, rather than focusing on its individual components in isolation, reveals deeper synergies and hidden bottlenecks, allowing for the discovery and realization of significantly greater optimization potential. Projected into the world of Digital Twins, this immediately brings us to the topic of Digital Twin interoperability. Its challenges are indeed manyfold:

- A *lack of standardization* across the rapidly evolving ecosystem impedes seamless integration and communication between different Digital Twin models and platforms. Specific obstacles include the *semantic gap*, where different vendors or domains use heterogeneous data models, terminology, and definitions for the same physical assets, making it difficult for one twin to interpret information from another correctly.
- Furthermore, twins must integrate with a vast array of *legacy systems* that were not designed for a modern, real-time data exchange, requiring complex middleware and proprietary connectors.
- The *absence of a distinct boundary between the authoring tools* used to create a Digital Twin *and the execution environments* that run it locks users into proprietary ecosystems.
- Finally, achieving real-time synchronization and ensuring security and trust when exchanging sensitive, high-velocity data between federated, multi-vendor twins adds complexity, preventing the formation of truly cohesive and scalable "systems of Digital Twins".

The *Asset Administration Shell* (AAS) significantly advances Digital Twin interoperability by serving as a standardized digital wrapper for any industrial asset. It decouples asset information from its underlying proprietary IT/OT systems, providing a unified, technology-agnostic interface. The AAS achieves this through sub-models, which are standardized, machine-readable data structures (such as "Nameplate" or "Technical Data") that consistently describe an asset's features, capabilities, and functions, regardless of the manufacturer or data source. This common structure and the defined API enable software applications from companies across the entire value chain (e. g., PLM, MES, ERP) to understand, communicate with, and exchange data about the asset seamlessly [41].

2.6.1.3 AI for Digital Twins

While the Digital Twin provides the structure and data (the *what* and *where*), AI can provide the reasoning and foresight (the *why* and *when*). Predictive Maintenance is undoubtedly the most common use case: The Digital Twin mirrors the current state of a machine (e. g., a turbine or vPLC). AI algorithms analyze historical and real-time data streams from the twin to detect subtle patterns indicating wear or impending failure:

- *Without AI*: The Digital Twin shows us that the temperature is rising.
- *With AI*: The Digital Twin alerts us that the temperature rise mimics a failure pattern from three years ago and predicts a breakdown in 48 hours.

AI runs thousands of virtual scenarios on the Digital Twin without risking the physical equipment. *Reinforcement Learning* agents can interact with the Digital Twin to learn optimal control strategies in a "What-If" Simulation.

An AI can test 10,000 different cooling configurations on a factory's Digital Twin to find the one that minimizes energy consumption by 15%, then apply that logic to the real facility.

Complex systems contain too many variables for a human to monitor. AI establishes a baseline of normal behavior for the Digital Twin and instantly flags anomalies that logic-based rules might miss. If an AI model suggests a parameter set for a complex machine calibration, a Digital Twin can be used to verify the AI-generated parameter set before deployment.

2.6.2 Software-Defined Automation

Historically, industrial automation has been tied to the physical world, anchored in proprietary PLC hardware. While the robustness of such architectures is acknowledged, this hardware-centric orientation has led to hardwired automation infrastructure that severely restricts operational flexibility. *Software-Defined Automation* (SDA) "liberates" control algorithms from their underlying hardware constraints. Central to this transformation is the deployment of *virtual PLC* (vPLC) technology. Contemporary vPLCs are containerized, real-time applications that run on standard commercial-off-the-shelf servers or industrial edge devices. Through the utilization of hypervisors and specifically the recent extension of IT hypervisors to work with OT network protocols (and determinism), these virtualized controllers afford deterministic performance comparable to traditional PLC hardware, while offering the kind of scalability inherent to enterprise software. Ideally, a manufacturing facility might host multiple vPLC instances on a single, robust server, thereby centralizing administration and reducing the required hardware footprint on the factory floor.

Audi Virtualizes PLCs

Audi and *Siemens* virtualized part of Audi's PLC infrastructure for its factory in Neckarsulm, Germany. vPLC technology is located in a central data center, reasonably close to the factory. I/Os are connected via dark fiber, and a central VMware-based orchestration stack manages the vPLCs and virtual servers for IT workloads within a single environment.

The promises of SDA extend well beyond mere hardware consolidation: the paradigm enables the adoption of DevOps in the OT domain (see Figure 2.8).

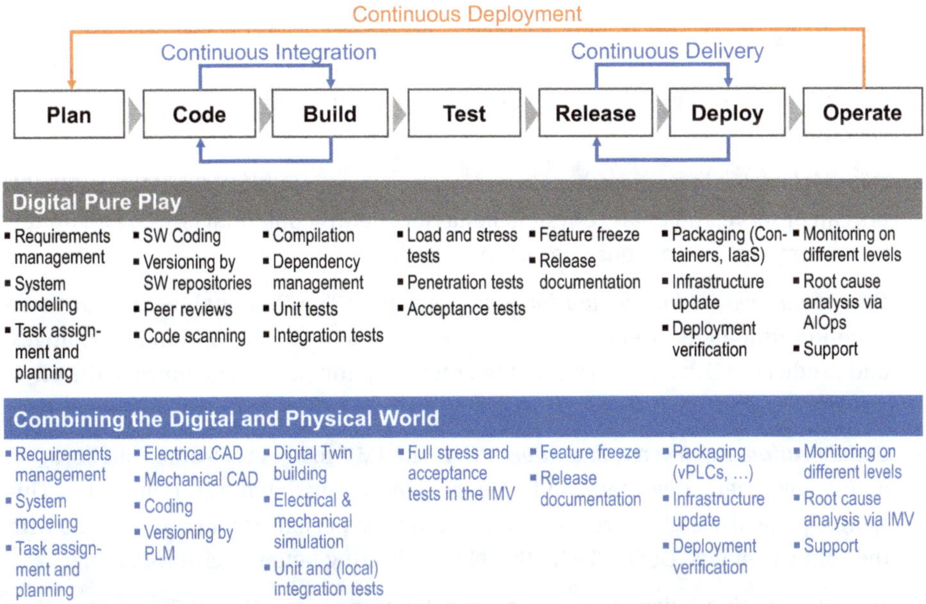

Figure 2.8 Projection of IT's DevOps concept onto the OT world

However, production technology still moves physical objects with all their potential for disaster. This is why the ability to simulate physics with Digital Twins is a precondition for successfully exploiting SDA: control logic is developed, validated, and verified in a purely virtual environment before deployment on physical machinery. The deployment itself leverages virtual PLCs, so modifications to machine logic can be propagated globally across facilities, eliminating the need for manual, on-site intervention by technical personnel.

2.6.3 Industrial Metaverse

The *Industrial Metaverse* (IMV) is a virtual environment designed to mirror and enhance real-world industrial operations. It's more than just a Digital Twin; it is a comprehensive, immersive, and collaborative platform that visualizes, simulates, and optimizes an entire industrial ecosystem.

2.6.3.1 Value Proposition

At its core, the IMV is a platform for simulating complex systems at a granular level. Imagine a factory, a power plant, or an entire supply chain replicated in a rich, interactive digital space. This digital realm allows for:

- *Visualizing the Digital Twin in context:* It provides a realistic environment to see and interact with comprehensive Digital Twins of assets, processes, and even entire facilities. This goes beyond static models, offering dynamic, real-time representations.
- *Gaining insights in a realistic environment:* By operating within the IMV, stakeholders can observe and analyze system behavior, identify potential issues, and understand complex interactions in a risk-free setting.
- *Continuous evaluation, simulation, and prediction:* The IMV enables constant testing and refinement. Users can interactively evaluate scenarios, simulate changes, and predict the Digital Twin's behavior, thereby anticipating outcomes in the physical world.
- *Collaboration, experience, and interaction:* The IMV fosters real-time collaboration among engineers, operators, and managers, breaking down traditional silos. This “single pane of glass” approach enables shared experiences and interactions with the comprehensive Digital Twin, thereby facilitating better decision-making.
- *System-level simulation:* The IMV aggregates component Digital Twins to reflect and optimize complex system behavior, allowing for a holistic view and optimization of industrial operations.

2.6.3.2 Supplementing Technologies

- *Augmented reality* enhances real-world operations by overlaying digital information – such as schematics, maintenance instructions, or sensor data – directly onto physical equipment, improving accuracy, safety, and productivity.
- *Virtual reality* technology enables fully immersive simulations where engineers, designers, and operators can collaborate in virtual factories or training environments without physical constraints or risks.

- *Universal Scene Description* (USD) is an open-source 3D scene description technology (*openusd.org*) developed by *Pixar Animation Studios*. It was invented to address the complex challenges of collaborative 3D content creation in large-scale animation and visual effects pipelines, allowing multiple artists and departments to work on the same scene simultaneously and non-destructively. In 2016, Pixar open-sourced USD and, in 2023, formed the *Alliance for OpenUSD* (*aousd.org*) with other industry leaders.

  For the IMV, USD provides a robust, extensible, and interoperable framework for representing and aggregating vast amounts of 3D data, including geometry, materials, physics, and simple kinematic behaviors, from various sources and software tools.

  USD's initial design is biased toward "dumb geometry" yet lacks native, comprehensive schemas for specialized metadata found in industrial systems such as *Building Information Modeling* (BIM) and *Product Lifecycle Management* (PLM). This data would include things like electrical information, sensor types, maintenance history, and engineering properties. Furthermore, industrial Digital Twins are "live" and require real-time streaming of IoT sensor data from the physical asset to the virtual model (bidirectional flow for a true Digital Twin). USD does not natively support the connections or protocols for this vast, continuous data flow, though efforts are underway to integrate USD with IoT data-streaming protocols. The *Metaverse Standards Forum* (*metaverse-standards.org*) addresses these shortcomings through its various working groups.

- The *Industrial Internet of Things* (IIoT) complements the IMV by connecting machines, sensors, and systems to collect and share real-time operational data. By providing accurate, continuous data streams, IIoT bridges the gap between physical assets and their digital counterparts, enhancing visibility, decision-making, and automation.

  Examples: IIoT sensor data from the real world calibrates a Digital Twin's prediction model, improving predictions. In another scenario, real-world sensor and PLC data are used to "replay" machine behavior in the virtual world to identify the root cause of a production issue.

2.6.3.3 AI for the Industrial Metaverse

The interaction between Industrial AI and the IMV can be understood through several key contributions:

- *Content generation:* AI plays a catalytic role in the initial creation and ongoing population of the IMV. This includes generating realistic 3D models, textures, and environmental details, often from existing CAD data or real-world scans, to build an immersive virtual environment.

Solution Brief 2-1: AI-based Extraction of CAD models from 3D Scans (Riiico)

Challenge
- Redesigning and retrofitting existing factories is slow and costly.
- Converting 3D scan data (LiDAR) into usable CAD models takes too long.
- Difficult to plan and collaborate on new factory layouts and processes.
- Inefficient and error-prone robot programming in complex facilities.

Solution
- AI automatically generates precise 3D Digital Twins from LiDAR scans.
- Platform segments and pre-classifies all factory equipment and objects.
- Provides CAD-ready models for simulation and collaboration tools.
- Enables drag-and-drop design for virtual factory planning.

Benefits
- Reduces 3D modeling time by up to 80% with AI automation.
- Speeds up redesign processes, making factories more agile and resilient.
- 30% faster robot programming and up to 15% reduced project costs.
- Allows global teams to collaborate using one virtual ground truth.

Customers: Porsche, Schaeffler, Schmitz Cargobull, Siemens, Volkswagen, Volvo Cars

Provider: Riiico, Düsseldorf, Germany; *riiico.com*

- *Integrating real-time data streams:* Industrial operations generate vast amounts of data from sensors, machines, and control systems. AI algorithms are essential for ingesting, processing, and integrating these real-time data streams into the IMV, ensuring that the Digital Twin remains synchronized with its physical counterpart.
- *Analysis for optimization:* Once data is integrated, AI analyzes it to identify patterns, anomalies, and opportunities for optimization. This can involve predictive maintenance, process optimization, quality control, and energy efficiency improvements within the virtual environment.
- *Training autonomous systems through simulation:* One of the most powerful interactions is using the IMV as a training ground for autonomous systems: AI models, particularly those controlling robotic arms or automated guided vehicles (AGVs, see also Section 24.7.1), can be trained extensively within the simulation environment of the IMV, for example using Reinforcement Learning (see Section 2.7.1.7), alternatively the use of synthetic training data (see Section 9.3). This includes the following propositions:
  - Training AI in the virtual space allows it to learn complex tasks, adapt to various conditions, and refine its control strategies accordingly.
  - There is no risk of damage or disruption in the physical world, such as a humanoid robot in training damaging the lab environment.

  - It is the basis for parallelization of AI training and only limited by available compute power.
  - It is catalytic for generating statistically relevant scenarios, as opposed to chasing or waiting for rare events to happen in reality.
- *Accelerating simulation:* AI significantly accelerates simulation processes. By leveraging advanced algorithms, AI can speed up complex calculations and model predictions, enabling more systems and dimensions to be simulated within a given timeframe. This results in shorter iteration cycles for design, optimization, and validation.
- *Conversational AI for user interaction:* To make the IMV accessible and intuitive, conversational AI helps users interact with the IMV. This could involve natural language interfaces that enable engineers to query the system, request simulations, or receive insights without specialized programming knowledge.

2.6.4 Digital Threads

The *Digital Thread* redefines how manufacturing enterprises connect, contextualize, and leverage data across the entire product lifecycle. Unlike traditional siloed approaches, where information remains trapped within departmental boundaries, a Digital Thread creates a seamless, bidirectional flow of digital information that links every stage from initial concept and design through manufacturing, quality control, field deployment, to end-of-life.

At its core, the Digital Thread represents the evolution from *document-centric* to *data-centric* manufacturing, where authoritative product and process information maintains its context and relationships as it traverses organizational boundaries, systems, and lifecycle phases [42].

The Digital Thread serves as the essential foundation upon which advanced industrial AI applications are built, providing the contextual intelligence necessary for meaningful analytics and automation: When manufacturing systems can access a complete historical and real-time record of a product's digital life – from engineering requirements and design intent to production parameters, quality measurements, and field performance – AI algorithms can gain the comprehensive perspective needed to deliver truly transformative insights.

When product engineers modify a design specification, the Digital Thread ensures this change propagates automatically to manufacturing execution systems, quality control protocols, and supply chain partners, while simultaneously preserving the decision context and approval history. This bidirectional information flow enables closed-loop validation, in which field performance data informs future design iterations, creating a continuous improvement cycle previously impossible at scale.

Similarly, the Digital Thread powers adaptive manufacturing systems that can automatically adjust production parameters based on real-time feedback and historical performance data. In complex, highly regulated industries such as aerospace, automotive, and medical devices, the Digital Thread provides end-to-end traceability for regulatory compliance while accelerating innovation cycles through rapid, data-driven experimentation. As manufacturing faces increasing pressure to be sustainable, the Digital Thread also enables precise tracking of materials, energy use, and environmental impact throughout the product lifecycle, allowing AI systems to optimize for both economic and ecological outcomes [43, 44].

Northrop Grumman's Digital Pathfinder

Northrop Grumman's Digital Pathfinder initiative successfully integrated a continuous digital thread across the "Model 437 Vanguard" aircraft lifecycle. By integrating design, supply chain, and manufacturing into a single source of truth, they reduced engineering rework from the industry average of 15–20% to less than 1%, while achieving 30% cost and schedule savings [45].

2.7 AI Technology

2.7.1 Traditional AI

2.7.1.1 Rule-Based Reasoning

Rule-Based Reasoning (RBR) is an AI approach that uses explicit "if-then" rules to process information and draw conclusions. The system's intelligence stems from a detailed knowledge base created by human experts. RBR is highly transparent and easy to explain, making it suitable for fields that require clear audit trails.

Early, successful examples included the first *expert systems*, such as *MYCIN* (1970s), which diagnosed infectious diseases, and *DENDRAL* (late 1960s), which used rules to identify chemical structures from mass spectrometry data. While newer AI systems excel at pattern recognition, RBR remains valuable when logic and clarity are paramount.

2.7.1.2 Artificial Neural Networks and Machine Learning

Artificial Neural Networks (ANNs) are computational models inspired by the structure and function of the human brain, designed to recognize patterns, process data, and make predictions. They consist of interconnected layers of nodes (*neurons*) that work together to transform input data into meaningful outputs. An ANN typically includes an input layer, one or more hidden layers, and an output layer. Each neuron receives inputs, multiplies them by associated weights, adds a bias term, and applies an activation function to introduce nonlinearity, allowing the network to capture complex relationships in the data.

The learning process in neural networks occurs through *forward and back propagation*. In the forward propagation phase, data moves from the input layer through the hidden layers to the output, where predictions are generated. The network's output is then compared to the actual target values, and an error (or loss) is calculated. During backpropagation, this error is backpropagated through the network to adjust the weights and biases. Using algorithms such as gradient descent, the network minimizes the loss by adjusting its parameters slightly at each iteration, gradually improving its accuracy.

Through many cycles of forward and backward propagation, the network learns how to generalize patterns and make accurate predictions for previously unseen data. This is *Machine Learning* (ML). ML is broadly categorized into supervised and unsupervised learning based on the nature of the training data:

- *Supervised learning* relies on labeled data, where each input example is paired with the correct output or label (e. g., an image of a cat labeled "cat"). The crucial process of adding these labels is known as *annotation* or *labeling*. Significant human effort and domain expertise is required to provide the ground truth to allow the model to learn the input-output mapping for tasks like classification or regression.
- Conversely, *unsupervised learning* works with unlabeled data, aiming to discover hidden patterns, clusters, or structures within the data on its own and is suitable for tasks like customer segmentation or anomaly detection.

In both paradigms, *feature engineering* is vital, transforming raw data into meaningful, predictive features (input variables) that capture essential characteristics, enabling the algorithm to learn more effectively. Feature engineering used to be an elite task where data scientists met with domain experts. Today, increasing numbers of ML approaches leverage data analytics to handle feature engineering, such as *AutoML* (see Section 2.7.1.5).

Solution Brief 2-2: High Quality Annotation Services (Responsible Annotation)

Challenge

- The quality of data annotation directly affects model performance and reliability.
- Achieving high accuracy and consistency across large, complex datasets is difficult.
- Inaccurate labeling can lead to significant errors, biases, and rework.

Solution

- Applies a multi-stage quality control process, including the consultative creation of detailed annotation handbooks, reviews, and client acceptance.
- Utilizes proprietary software and rigorous workflows for high-quality results.
- Employs a team of neuro-diverse annotators for precise and consistent labeling.

Benefits

- Ensures a high-quality, precise ground truth dataset for model training.
- Employs neuro-diverse team members for the benefit of society and output quality.

Customers: Frequentis, Keba, Universidade Federal do Espírito Santo

Provider: Responsible Annotation Services, Vienna, Austria; *annotation.at*

2.7.1.3 Natural Language Processing

Before the advent of LLMs, *Natural Language Processing* (NLP) was characterized by a blend of rule-based and statistical methodologies: Early efforts relied heavily on hand-crafted linguistic rules, dictionaries, and ontologies to parse and understand human language. Resulting models were adept at tasks such as part-of-speech tagging, named entity recognition, and sentiment analysis, often requiring extensive feature engineering. While groundbreaking for their time, these traditional NLP systems faced significant challenges: They were frequently brittle, struggling with ambiguity, context-dependent meanings, and the sheer variability of human expression. Generalization was complex, and text generation was typically formulaic and constrained, far from the fluid, creative outputs we see today with LLMs.

2.7.1.4 Deep Learning

Traditional Machine Learning typically uses “shallow” structures: Their neural network structures are often fairly transparent (we can see exactly why a decision was made), but they hit a performance ceiling once the data becomes too complex.

Deep Learning (DL) uses ANNs with many “hidden” layers (hence the term “deep”). This enables the model to handle nonlinear relationships and high-dimensional data such as images, audio, and raw text.

Let's imagine a neural network as a series of filters: When we feed it an image of a cat, the first layer might detect edges, the next might identify shapes like ears or whiskers, and a deeper layer might recognize the combination of these features as a "cat". The "deep" in deep learning refers to these many layers of processing.

2.7.1.5 Automated Machine Learning

Automated Machine Learning (AutoML) is an AI subfield that automates the end-to-end process of applying ML to real-world problems. Traditionally, building effective ML models requires human expertise in data preprocessing, feature engineering, model selection, and hyperparameter tuning. AutoML reduces this complexity by providing tools and frameworks that automate these tasks, making ML more accessible to non-experts while saving experienced practitioners time.

At its core, AutoML frameworks search through combinations of algorithms, features, and parameters to find the optimal model for a given dataset. For example, AutoML can automatically select from decision trees, neural networks, and ensemble methods, tune hyperparameters, and even engineer new features to improve model performance.

Solution Brief 2-3: Industrial AutoML (Weidmüller)

Challenge

- Automation engineers lack the data science skills to build ML models.
- Difficult to gain valuable insights from existing machine data.
- Implementing ML models is traditionally slow and expensive.

Solution

- AI/AutoML software automatically builds ML models from existing data.
- Requires no prior knowledge of data science for use.
- Models are deployable on-premises or in the cloud for real-time analytics.
- ModelBuilder creates, and ModelRuntime operates and optimizes the solution.

Benefits

- Accelerate innovation and optimize industrial operational processes: Creaing a functional ML model in just about one hour.
- Achieving greater productivity with predictive maintenance and anomaly detection.
- Developing new data-driven business models and increasing customer satisfaction.

Customers: Boge Compressors, GEA, MIELE

Provider: Weidmüller, Detmold, Germany; *weidmuller.com/en/solutions/solutions/industrial_analytics/automated_machine_learning.jsp*

Beyond unlocking analytics for non-experts, AutoML can serve as evidence to regulatory bodies that the AI model has achieved optimal performance on a given dataset. Performance statistics on different AI model architectures, feature significance, hyperparameter settings, and comparisons between them are by-products of AutoML and, therefore, a natural way to document the diligence in those design choices.

2.7.1.6 Physics-Informed Neural Networks

Physics-Informed Neural Networks (PINNs) combine the strengths of ML with the fundamental laws of physics. To understand why this is important, we need to consider how most AI models work. Traditional neural networks learn patterns by training on large datasets. For example, if we wanted a network to predict how heat moves through a piece of metal, we would need thousands of temperature measurements across different situations. But in many industries, collecting that volume of data is expensive, time-consuming, or even impossible. This is where PINNs stand out: Instead of learning from raw data only, they are designed to also "know" the physical equations that govern how the real world behaves. These are the same equations that engineers and scientists have used for centuries to describe phenomena such as fluid flow, material deformation under stress, and energy conservation. By incorporating these equations directly into the training process, a PINN produces predictions that remain consistent with the laws of nature.

2.7.1.7 Reinforcement Learning

Reinforcement Learning (RL) is a type of ML in which an agent learns to behave in an environment by performing actions and receiving rewards or penalties (negative rewards). Unlike supervised learning, which uses labeled data, or unsupervised learning, which finds patterns, RL focuses on goal-directed sequential decision-making. The agent's objective is to learn a strategy (named *policy*) that maps states of the environment to the best possible actions – to maximize the cumulative reward over time. The process is a continuous loop (see Figure 2.9): The *Agent* executes *Action A*, which transitions the environment to the *Current state* (S). The *Observer* assesses the current state and provides a *Reward* (R) to the Agent which then selects the next action, and so on.

The best way for non-experts to understand RL is to imagine a computer game such as *Super Mario* and the challenge of teaching an AI to play it: the AI model uses a virtual joystick to move the character across the screen. The high-score and finishing a level are reward functions, while the character's death (falling into traps and such) is a penalty function. When we allow the AI to learn by playing the game 100,000 times, it will eventually become a pretty good Super Mario player and even succeed in previously unseen game levels.

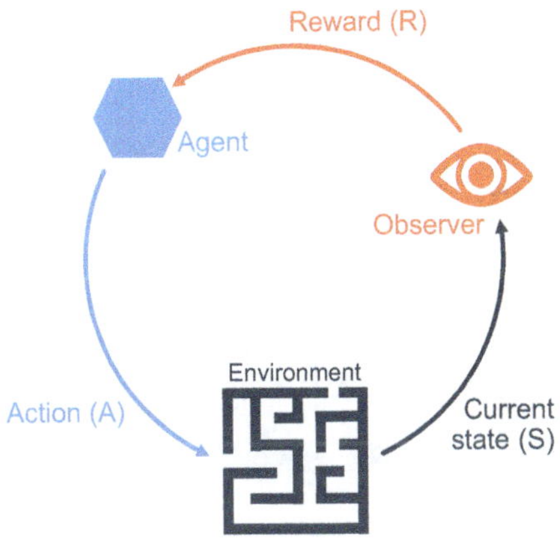

Figure 2.9
Reinforcement Learning Principle

RL has proven highly effective in complex domains such as robotic control, game-playing (e. g., AlphaGo), and resource management.

Machine Throughput +30% in Packaging

Sollas, a machine tool builder for packaging machines, significantly improved their machines' performance through an RL collaboration with *Siemens*: a Digital Twin simulation of the packaging machines' motion components fed an RL approach with rewards for increased throughput and penalties for increased wear and tear. The resulting neural network was compiled to run on a PLC. While the machine output improved by more than 30%, the lifetime of the motion components increased by 20% [46].

2.7.1.8 Federated Learning

Federated Learning (FL) is a paradigm that directly addresses data privacy and confidentiality concerns, as outlined in Section 4.6.1. Instead of moving massive amounts of sensitive data to a central server for model training, the model goes to the data. In a typical setup, a global AI model is sent to local nodes (e. g., individual factories or machines). The model is trained locally on the nodes' private data. Afterwards, only the updated model parameters – the mathematical learnings, not the raw data – are sent back to the central server for aggregation into an improved global model. These updates are then aggregated securely on a central server to improve the global model while preserving the protection of local trade secrets. The updated global model is redeployed to the local nodes, and the cycle restarts (see Figure 2.10).

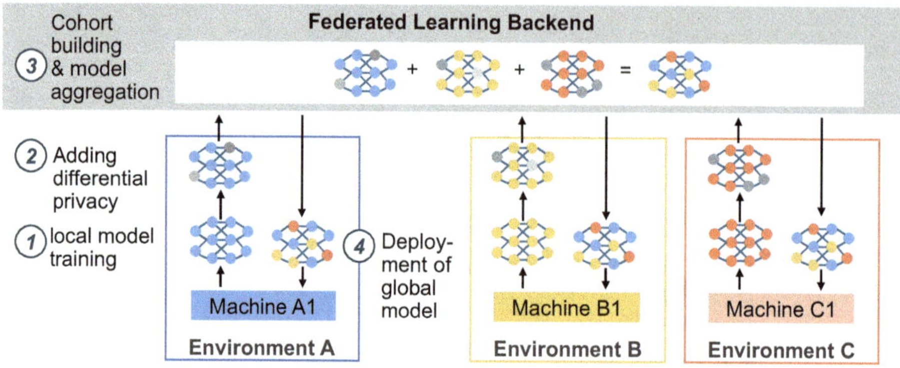

Figure 2.10 Federated Learning Principle

How the Smartphone Industry Leverages FL

Google was one of the first to deploy FL at scale, using it to improve predictive typing and autocorrect in Android's "Gboard" keyboard, the modern successor to T9 text prediction. Similarly, *Apple* applies FL to enhance features such as QuickType and Siri suggestions, enabling devices to learn from user behavior without exposing private messages or interactions.

By processing data locally and sharing only anonymized models, FL achieves a balance between personalization and privacy.

FL can solve multiple data protection issues. Examples are:

- Several automotive factories within one car brand regularly compete for production orders of new product lines. Although they share the same use cases, each factory is reluctant to share data that could reveal productivity key performance indicators to a competing factory.
- An electronic manufacturer runs factories in Europe and China. Chinese legislation imposes barriers to cross-border data transfers, but all factories want to deploy the same high-quality inspection AI models.
- A CPG producer uses organic raw materials such as cotton. Varying properties, such as humidity or density, require different machine parameter settings for optimal production. The supplier encodes raw material properties per batch into an ML model, enabling the customer to calibrate.

Pharmaceutical Competitors Join Forces

The MELLODDY project (2019–2022, *https://www.melloddy.eu/about-1*) was a EUR 18.4 million collaboration among ten major European pharmaceutical companies, academic groups, and tech partners to accelerate drug discovery using FL. By applying the open-source *Substra* framework – supported by blockchain for secure, decentralized data management – partners jointly trained models on over 10 million compounds and 1 billion test results without sharing sensitive data. The project demonstrated that FL can produce strong, privacy-preserving models across organizations, improving the efficiency of identifying new drug candidates while maintaining complete data confidentiality and control.

Due to the complexity of FL as a mixture of distributed systems management and ML, industry adoption lags behind its potential. Complexity drivers include intelligent model grouping ("which local models should be clustered to become a global model?") and mastering the creation of noise for differential privacy, which, in a nutshell, prevents local data from being re-identified by comparing multiple local model versions.

2.7.1.9 Knowledge Graphs

Knowledge Graphs (KGs) are a powerful paradigm for organizing and understanding complex information by structuring data as a network of interconnected entities and their relationships. In this model, nodes represent real-world entities (e. g., people, products, or concepts), and edges represent semantic relationships between them (e. g., "Siemens *manufactures* a PLC" or "Germany *is located in* Europe").

KGs break with the tabular constraints of traditional "relational" databases: Relational databases rely on predefined, rigid schemas with tables, rows, and columns, where relationships are established through foreign keys. Adding new relationship types or entities requires schema alterations, which are complex and affect existing data. In contrast, KGs can accommodate new entities and relationships without requiring a complete structural overhaul, making them

- highly adaptable to evolving data landscapes; and
- a fit for scenarios where entities and their relations are not known ex-ante but discovered by a crawling through engineering documents.

Furthermore, KGs are a great way to add determinism to AI models, as they can hold "rule bases" for concluding and reasoning in a graph representation easily (see Section 2.7.2.7 "Retrieval Augmented Generation").

2.7.1.10 Process Mining

Process Mining (PM) is a data-driven technique that bridges the gap between traditional process analysis and modern data analytics. It involves extracting process traces from event logs and transaction tables to visualize, analyze, and improve real business processes (see Figure 2.11).

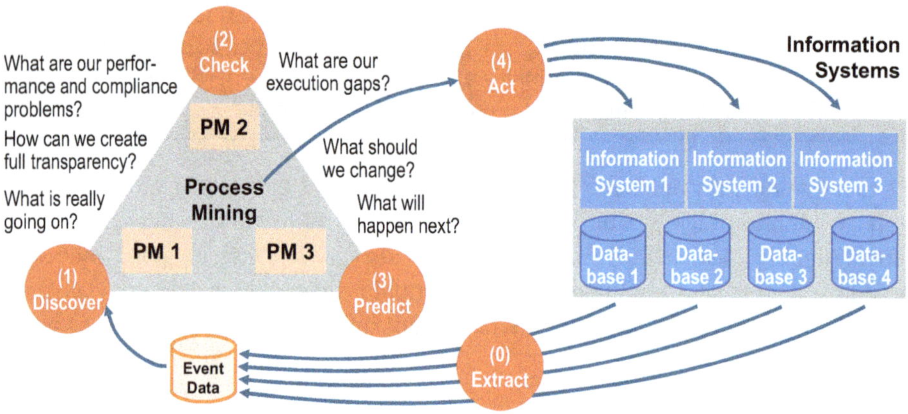

Figure 2.11 Process Mining Principle

Unlike conventional process modeling, which relies on assumptions or interviews, PM uses actual recorded data to uncover how processes truly operate in practice. The technique identifies process flows, bottlenecks, deviations, and inefficiencies by mapping the actual sequence of activities and comparing it against the intended process model.

Object-centric PM enriches the core concept by grouping event data around specific information entities such as a “purchase order” or an “invoice”.

There are three main application types of process mining:

- *Discovery*, which automatically generates a process model from event data (see Figure 2.12 as an example);
- *Conformance checking*, which compares actual behavior with expected workflows; and
- *Enhancement*, which refines or optimizes processes based on insights gained.

A leading global bank successfully applied PM to its loan origination workflow. By analyzing event logs, they identified significant bottlenecks and unnecessary handoffs, streamlining approvals. This resulted in a 25% reduction in cycle time for small-business loans, greatly improving the customer experience and operational efficiency.

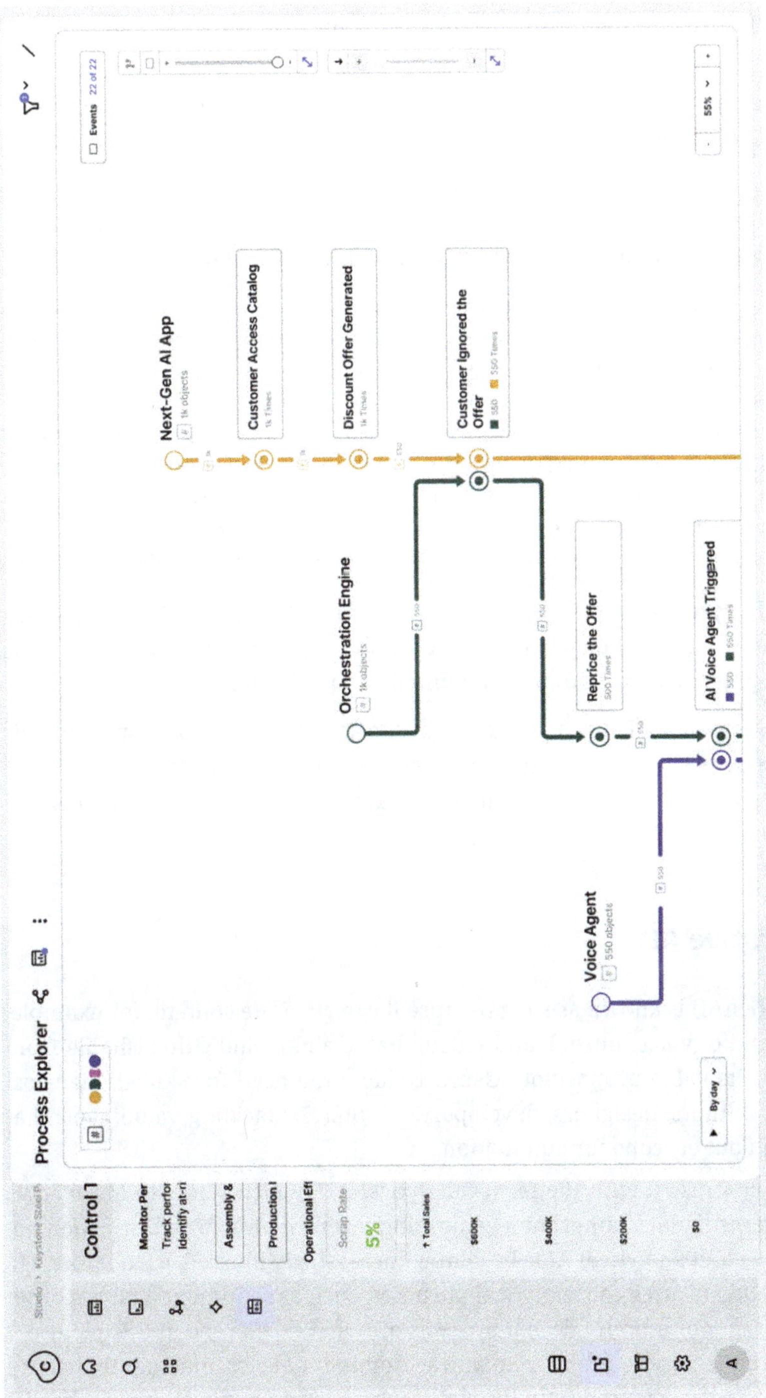

Figure 2.12 Process Mining analysis example (Celonis)

The relationship between GenAI (see Section 2.7.2), with its power to interpret natural language, and PM is highly synergic and noteworthy:

- GenAI can support the cumbersome task of relating log and event file entries to business transactions, reducing the preparation time for PM projects.
- LLMs and NLP can leverage entity extraction in unstructured texts (consider take emails and chat messages as an example) to expand PM from transaction environments (such as workflow management tools) to "human communication".

A company implemented a stringent approach to approver determination in its SAP procurement workflows. Almost every approval request resulted in a three- to four-week email exchange, primarily because the system-determined approver lacked the business context for the related procurement activity and therefore felt uncomfortable approving without substantial briefing. Leveraging entity extraction helped anonymize email threads and integrate them into a process mining workflow to improve approver-determination algorithms in the ERP system.

- GenAI can analyze the process-related documentation that typically exists in every organization as a means to depict the "to-be" state of processes. First experiments to generate process models from documentation have been promising [47].
- Research indicates that PM can play a role in supervising the complex and dynamic interactions between agents in an agentic environment and therefore contribute towards solving the quality management challenge of agentic environments [48] (see Section 4.10.3).

2.7.2 Generative AI

Generative AI (GenAI) is known as such because it can generate content, for example, texts, images, audio (voice, music), and video, that is almost indistinguishable from human content. Its value proposition: GenAI reduces the need for skilled, high-cost labor (lawyers, authors, designers, developers, ...), thereby tackling value pools that have so far been out of scope for automation.

GenAI is often contrasted with the term "analytical AI", which refers to ML models that *detect patterns* in data rather than generating text or images. The distinction between generative and analytical AI is becoming increasingly blurred, as today's large models can already be used for analytical purposes, such as sentiment analysis of social media messages or a pretty decent analysis of "what do you see in this picture?" Transformer architectures – which remain the dominant algorithmic family behind large models – are already used in industrial machine-vision applications, so the distinction between generative and analytical AI will remain a short-term phenomenon.

2.7.2.1 Foundation Models

The term Foundation Model is a business model statement: one party invests significant effort to train a foundational model that can then be used by hundreds or thousands of application providers with only incremental effort. In other words, AI scales as a product, not as a project for the many AI application providers. This change in business case mechanics has driven the shift toward foundation models. California's Senate Bill 53 [31], on regulating AI, defines foundation models as AI models with the following attributes:

1. Trained on a broad dataset.
2. Designed for generality of output.
3. Adaptable to a wide range of distinctive tasks.

Thomson Reuters' CoCounsel AI

AI applications for lawyers excel at legal research, document analysis, and drafting, resulting in significant efficiency gains. The key benefit is that they free up lawyers for high-value strategic work that requires human judgment and client interaction. For instance, *CoCounsel* (by Thomson Reuters) can summarize a million-page discovery document in minutes, and platforms such as *Spellbook* can draft and redline contracts by flagging risky clauses and comparing them to market standards. CoCounsel is a legal AI application implemented on top of OpenAI's o1-mini LLM.

2.7.2.2 General Purpose Language Models

Large Language Models (LLMs) are advanced DL models, typically based on the *transformer* architecture, trained on massive amounts of text data. Their primary function is to understand, generate, and process human language. LLMs predict the next word in a sequence, enabling them to perform diverse tasks such as translation, summarization, creative writing, and answering questions. Their "largeness" refers to their large number of parameters and the scale of their training data, which together enable complex linguistic comprehension.

LLMs fundamentally change how humans interact with machines and software systems: Many decades of user interface design, all needed to accommodate the fact that software systems require structured, validated input via screens, can now be replaced with natural language input via text or voice.

A *token* is the elemental particle of language for GenAI (almost like a syllable). As a standard digital chunk, it enables models to decompose, comprehend, and generate coherent text. *Tokenization* is how an LLM converts raw text or other media into a simplified, understandable digital representation.

Modalities are the types of data or sensory inputs that a model can process, understand, and generate. Initially, LLMs were unimodal, processing only text. *Multimodal LLMs* have expanded this capability to include other modalities, such as images (visual data), audio (speech and sound), and, in some cases, video or structured data. For example, a multimodal model can take an image and a text prompt as input, and generate a text description or a new image as output. This allows them to perform complex tasks, such as answering questions about an image or describing a scene from a video.

Small Language Models (SLMs) are compact versions of LLMs, characterized by significantly fewer parameters (typically a few million to around 10–30 billion) and requiring substantially less computational power for training and inference. Unlike general-purpose LLMs, SLMs are often trained or fine-tuned on smaller, more focused, domain-specific datasets to excel at specific tasks, balancing performance with efficiency. This reduced size yields several practical advantages: faster inference (response time), lower operational costs, and deployment on resource-constrained environments such as edge devices and mobile phones, enabling on-device AI for enhanced privacy and offline functionality.

SiMa's Embedded Language Models

SiMa.ai is a software-centric company providing a Machine Learning System-on-Chip platform for the embedded edge market. Its technology is purpose-built to accelerate diverse AI workloads, including SLMs, thereby enabling previously unseen natural language interaction between humans and machines, specifically with cars [49].

2.7.2.3 Domain-Specific Language Models

Domain-Specific Language Models (DSLMs) move beyond the broad, general-purpose capabilities of LLMs. DSLMs are GenAI models that have been meticulously trained or fine-tuned on specialized datasets specific to a particular industry, business function, or regulatory process. Unlike generic models that often lack contextual precision, DSLMs understand the unique jargon, nuances, and intent of a given domain – whether this be finance, healthcare, legal compliance, or manufacturing.

By 2027, *Gartner* predicts that more than half of the GenAI models used by enterprises will be domain-specific (up from 1% in 2024) [50]. This dramatic acceleration reflects a move from AI experimentation to operationalization, as customers seek specificity for their (industrial) applications. Furthermore, DSLMs are viewed as essential differentiators for AI agents, enabling them to interpret highly specific industry context and make sound, explainable decisions.

Solution Brief 2-4: Large Mechanical Model-based Engineering (Leo AI)

Challenge

- Engineers are burdened by tedious work searching for technical data.
- Relying on generalist AI leads to inaccurate, non-validated answers for complex mechanics.
- High error rates in early-stage documentation and initial conceptual designs.

Solution "Leo Large Mechanical Model"

- Uses a proprietary model trained on millions of engineering-grade sources.
- Connects with CAD tools to interpret 3D geometry and design constraints.
- Generates verified technical reports, bill of materials, and specifications based on engineering standards.

Benefits

- Saves engineers approximately 5 hours per week by automating repetitive tasks.
- Reduces design and documentation errors by 30% through automated validation.
- Accelerates reviews and time-to-market by shortening initial development stages.

Customers: Bosch, HP, Philips, Scania, Toyota

Provider: Leo AI, Cambridge, Massachusetts, USA; *getleo.ai*

2.7.2.4 Vision Language Action Models

Vision-Language-Action Models (VLAMs) are a major leap toward embodied AI (see Section 2.7.4.3), unifying visual perception, natural language understanding, and physical action generation within a single integrated computational framework. They are essentially DSLMs for robotics, in which the output is not just text but a sequence of executable motor commands. VLAMs take an image (or video) of a robot's surroundings and natural language instructions as input, reason about the scene, and directly generate low-level robot actions to accomplish the task. Google (including its internal division), NVIDIA, Figure AI, and other commercial players are developing VLAMs, while the first open-source initiatives are emerging, such as OpenVLA (*openvla.github.io*).

2.7.2.5 Prompt Engineering

Prompt engineering is the rapidly evolving discipline of designing and optimizing the inputs – or prompts – that guide LLMs to produce accurate, relevant, and context-aware outputs. Since LLMs do not inherently "understand" tasks but instead generate responses based on patterns in data, the way a problem or instruction is phrased plays a critical role in shaping model behavior. Prompt engineering involves structuring queries, constraints, and examples to elicit the desired reasoning and response style from the model. Within this framework, there are two key types of prompts:

- The *system prompt* defines the overarching behavior, tone, and constraints of the AI assistant – it acts as a persistent instruction that guides all interactions, such as maintaining factuality, politeness, or domain expertise.

- The *user prompt*, by contrast, represents a specific request or query from the user and operates within the boundaries set by the system-level directives.

Beyond textual prompting, LLMs extend their capabilities through *function calling*, a mechanism that allows the model to integrate external data sources or execute predefined operations. For example, when a user requests real-time weather information, the model can call an external API to retrieve current data rather than relying on its static training data (i. e., historical data). Function calling, as a primary mechanism of integration, is increasingly being replaced by the *Model Context Protocol*, which enables prebuilt providers of data from external sources (see Section 2.7.3.2).

2.7.2.6 Context Engineering

Context engineering refers to designing and managing the information environment in which an LLM operates, ensuring that it has access to appropriate data, background knowledge, and constraints to generate accurate and meaningful responses. While prompt engineering focuses on crafting specific instructions or questions to guide the model's immediate behavior, context engineering shapes the surrounding knowledge that informs how the model interprets and reasons about a task.

This includes curating relevant documents, memory states, conversation history, or structured data that provide situational awareness. For example, in an enterprise assistant, context engineering might involve dynamically retrieving a user's past interactions or company policies before forming a response. In essence, prompt engineering specifies what the model should do. In contrast, context engineering ensures *it knows what it needs to do* effectively, together enabling more coherent, reliable, and domain-specific AI interactions.

2.7.2.7 Retrieval Augmented Generation

Retrieval-Augmented Generation (RAG) enhances LLMs by integrating external knowledge retrieval with generative reasoning. Instead of relying solely on information embedded during model training, RAG systems dynamically access up-to-date, domain-specific data from external sources to produce accurate, explainable, and context-aware responses.

The process involves two main components: retrieval and generation. In the retrieval phase, a query or prompt is converted into a numerical representation – called an embedding – and compared against a *vector database*, which stores embeddings of documents, passages, or structured data. These databases use similarity searching to efficiently identify the most relevant information based on semantic meaning rather than exact keyword matches. The retrieved content is then injected into the model's context, guiding the generative phase to produce fluent, factually grounded answers.

One of RAG's key evolution lies in its intersection with *knowledge graphs* (see Section 2.7.1.9). By combining the unstructured semantic retrieval of vector databases with the structured reasoning capabilities of KGs, RAG systems can achieve a deeper understanding of context and relationships. For example, vector retrieval might discover relevant research papers on a medical topic, whereas a knowledge graph can trace causal links between drugs, symptoms, and diseases. This hybrid approach not only improves retrieval precision but also supports *explainability* by linking generated statements back to structured sources.

RAG leveraging KGs represents a decisive step toward industrial-grade AI, merging the creative flexibility of generative models with the factual reliability of external knowledge systems – enabling applications such as intelligent assistants, research copilots, and enterprise analytics tools that can reason over both text and data in a coherent, verifiable manner.

2.7.3 Agentic AI

Agentic AI defines a new paradigm in which an AI system can autonomously pursue complex goals by forming its own action plan, executing it, monitoring its progress, and adapting dynamically to environmental feedback. Essentially, it does not simply respond to a single prompt; it maintains a state, memory, and an internal context in order to complete multi-step tasks.

An agentic system uses a loop that generates sub-goals, calls external tools or models (e.g., search or code execution), and iteratively refines its approach until the main objective is met.

This makes the system less of a reactive tool and more of a proactive, goal-oriented worker capable of independent reasoning and problem-solving (see Figure 2.13).

	Traditional AI	Generative AI	Agentic AI
Primary Function	Executes predefined rules and models to **analyze data** with fixed parameters	**Generates human-like content**, predictions or insights based on learned patterns	**Autonomously decides, adapts and acts** with minimal human input
Decision-making process	**Deterministic** (rules) and **pattern-based** (ML)	**Pattern-based**	**Goal-oriented** (plans, reasons and makes autonomous decisions)
Adaptability	◔ Requires painstaking updates	◑ Learns patterns but lacks independent action	● Adapts to changing supply chain conditions
Memory & Learning	○ Static – relies on historical data updates	◕ Context-aware 'by session' but lacks long-term memory	● Retains, learns and improves from past actions
Multisystem Integration	○ Static – relies on predefined data connections	◕ Context-aware but lacks long-term system-interoperability	● Integrates and orchestrates systems in real-time
Human Involvement	● Rules set by humans	◑ Relies on user prompts, assists with prompting	◔ Acts independently, adjusting strategies dynamically

Figure 2.13 Differences between traditional, generative, and agentic AI [51]

2.7.3.1 Agents

In our context, *agents* are autonomous entities designed to perceive their environment, process information, and act on it to achieve defined objectives. They can exist as software systems, physical robots, or Digital Twins that interact with sensors, machines, and humans within industrial processes.

- *AI agents* are intelligent systems that utilize AI techniques – such as ML, reasoning, and natural language understanding – to analyze data, learn from experience, and make dynamic decisions. They are capable of adapting to new conditions, predicting equipment failures, optimizing resource use, and improving production efficiency. Examples include predictive maintenance systems, intelligent scheduling agents, and self-learning process controllers.
- In contrast, *Non-AI agents* follow fixed, rule-based logic or deterministic algorithms. They operate on the basis of predefined instructions and lack learning capabilities. Examples include programmable logic controllers (PLCs), rule-based monitoring systems, and workflow automation scripts. Although less flexible, non-AI agents are highly reliable, predictable, and well-suited for safety-critical tasks.

A hybrid approach that combines AI and non-AI agents is compelling for industrial-grade AI applications as it provides consistency, validation, and verification of AI-driven outcomes. This synergy ensures both innovation and reliability – AI agents drive performance improvements, while Non-AI agents safeguard operational integrity, compliance, and safety, resulting in robust, trustworthy, and efficient industrial solutions.

2.7.3.2 Model Context Protocol

The *Model Context Protocol* (MCP), published in late 2024 by Anthropic, is an emerging standard designed to streamline communication between LLMs and external systems. At its core, MCP defines a consistent way for models to access tools, data sources, and applications, thereby reducing integration friction. Rather than relying on custom-built adapters or APIs for each use case, MCP provides a unified protocol. This ensures that LLMs can interact with external environments in a predictable, secure, and extensible manner – whether they are retrieving structured data, triggering workflows, or accessing proprietary databases.

Before MCP, LLM integration was largely ad hoc. Developers often had to create bespoke solutions that involved crafting API wrappers, exposing data through middleware, or embedding contextual information directly into prompts. These methods worked, but they were fragmented and inefficient. Prompt engineering served as a workaround for missing context, whereas system-specific plug-ins required ongoing maintenance. As a result, organizations faced scalability issues: Every new tool or dataset required fresh integration work, and interoperability between LLMs and enterprise systems remained limited.

MCP shifts this paradigm by offering a standard protocol, reducing the burden of integration, and enhancing reliability. LLMs can now leverage external capabilities without developers having to reinvent the wheel for each new connection.

2.7.3.3 Agent-to-Agent Protocols

In agentic systems, the agents' ability to interact with one another has become vital. This is where *Agent-to-Agent* (A2A) protocols enter the scene – standards that govern how autonomous agents exchange messages, share state, and coordinate action. Much like Internet protocols enable computers to communicate across networks, A2A protocols aim to provide intelligent agents with a common language for reasoning and collaboration.

Several initiatives are emerging in this space. The *Agent Communication Protocol* provides structured message-passing rules that define how agents can request, inform, or negotiate with one another. The *NANDA protocol* (Negotiation and Agreement for Networked Distributed Agents) emphasizes consensus-building and contract formation among agents, which are essential features of multi-agent cooperation in business and research settings. More broadly, A2A standards encapsulate messaging patterns and ontologies to ensure that agents interpret each other's goals and context consistently.

While MCP establishes a reliable bridge between a single model and its environment, agent-to-agent protocols extend that bridge to entire networks of models. Together, they create a layered ecosystem: MCP ensures that each agent can access the appropriate context, while A2A frameworks enable those agents to coordinate, delegate, and negotiate intelligently.

For the development of agentic AI, this dual structure is essential. A single agent may perform well in isolation, but real-world applications – from supply chain optimization to automated research assistants – require collaboration across specialized agents. A2A protocols thus lay the groundwork for multi-agent societies, in which intelligence is not merely individual but emerges from structured communication.

2.7.3.4 Agentic Economy

The *agentic economy* builds directly on the concept of Agentic AI, but expands it to a multi-agent, *multi-party* ecosystem. While Agentic AI focuses on a single autonomous agent performing complex tasks, the Agentic Economy describes a future in which numerous specialized agents, provided by and representing different companies and even individual consumers, interact and transact with one another [52].

One key feature of this new economy is *dynamic monetization* of these interactions. A supply chain agent, for example, could automatically pay an inventory management agent for real-time data or a logistics agent for securing transport – all without human intervention.

The tourism industry is a "hot" candidate for the agentic economy: Instead of simply displaying flights and hotels like traditional booking engines, agentic platforms act as personalized agents. They take a user's broad goals (e.g., "a seven-day relaxing beach vacation in Greece for two in July with a budget of US$ 4,000") and autonomously reason, plan, and execute a complex itinerary. This includes dynamically booking interconnected components such as flights, specific resort rooms, and local transportation, and even suggesting and securing reservations for activities and dining, all of this while continuously monitoring prices and availability to maximize the user's value and experience without requiring constant manual oversight. This level of autonomous, goal-directed planning and action in a multi-party environment is the core characteristic of the agentic economy [51].

Agent payment protocols are open technical standards that enable AI agents to securely, auditably, and autonomously transact on behalf of users. They address issues of authorization, authenticity, and accountability in machine-to-machine commerce. These protocols use cryptographically signed digital contracts, known as "mandates" (e.g., intent mandates and cart mandates), to verify a user's permissions and set boundaries for the agent's actions. Examples are:

- *Agent Payments Protocol*: Developed by Google and partners, it uses mandates to secure transactions.
- *Agentic Commerce Protocol*: Developed by OpenAI and Stripe, it makes online checkouts in Internet shops "agent-ready".

An *agent store* is a digital marketplace or platform where users can discover, deploy, and manage autonomous software agents designed to perform specific tasks using AI. These agents can handle functions such as data analysis, automation, customer support, or industrial process optimization. The store typically offers both pre-built AI agents and customizable options for enterprise integration. Examples include OpenAI's *GPT Store*, where users can access specialized GPT-based agents; Microsoft's *Copilot Studio*, which hosts workflow automation agents; and *Hugging Face Spaces*, where developers share and deploy intelligent models and interactive AI applications across industries.

2.7.3.5 Software Architecture and Business Model Impact

Agentic AI is likely to fundamentally change how we access software, and this will be disruptive both on the customer side of life as well as on the software provider side (see Figure 2.14):

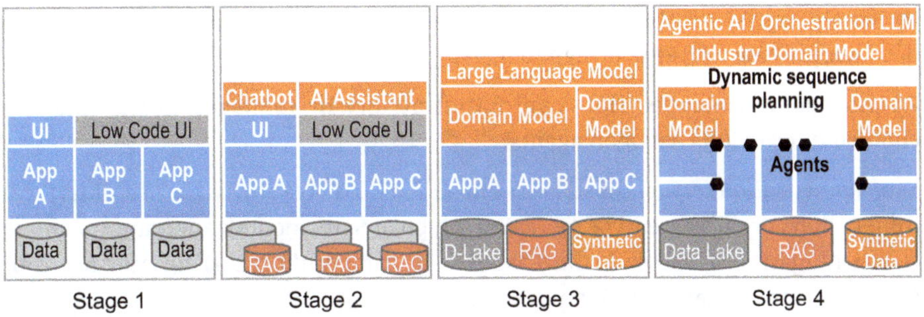

Figure 2.14 Stages of software architecture evolution

- *Current state (Stage 1)*: Applications are tied to their data pools. Each application owns its user interface (UI), and semantics are application-specific. Occasionally, application integration is performed using low-code or robotic process automation paradigms.
- *AI-Infused applications (Stage 2)*: Applications are enhanced with chatbots and AI Assistants. A RAG layer is added to each application's technology stack, as AI language models require a vector database to access content effectively (see Section 2.7.2.7).

  Example: Teamcenter X, Siemens' PLM platform, provides users with an AI Assistant to interact with Bills of Materials and other PLM data objects.
- *LLM-interfaced applications (Stage 3)*: A generic or domain-specific language model becomes the primary user interface. To leverage enterprise data as fully as possible, cross-application data lakes are built, and an enterprise RAG layer is established that is no longer limited to the semantics of a single application. Synthetic data is used to enhance model performance where required.
- *Agentic AI (Stage 4)*: The orchestrating LLM understands business processes and context sufficiently well to define and continuously evolve task sequences dynamically (this can span from simple workflows to full Digital Threads). Applications are organized into functional modules, which are accessed via agents (AI and non-AI). Agents leverage both domain-specific AI models and application functionality to execute their tasks as needed.

The development towards stage 4 imposes a couple of essential questions:

- *Reproducibility concerns:* An overarching LLM that dynamically defines workflows across several agents imposes the challenge of reproducibility. Let's assume an AI-generated production line design has just undergone a machine safety assessment. The safety approval has been granted, subject to the condition that one or two flaws be corrected through a design change. The automation engineers must process these design changes using the same design toolchain used to create the line design. However, the agentic LLM's dynamic task-sequencing behavior does not provide a "freeze design tool chain mode".

- *Output quality concerns:* How can output quality be managed in dynamically chained interactions between agents?
- *SaaS monetization impact:* In stages 3 and 4, the LLM layer *owns the user interface.* Applications are accessed via API calls. A typical SaaS monetization approach assumes human user access is time-based (e.g., a monthly recurring user license). Currently, users interact with an overarching layer.

Autodesk Revisits Its License Models

Autodesk launched its Neural 3D offering, an AI model that converts a natural language prompt into a 3D design, in the summer of 2025. During their Q3/2025 earnings call, Autodesk's CEO announced the need to revisit their current license models. As engineers spend time prompting CAD models, the actual use of Autodesk's CAD environment shrinks to minutes per month. An outcome-based licensing model is intended to address the situation described in [53].

- *Value flow ownership:* Stage 4 represents a scenario where many parties provide agents representing business functionality, whether they be internal feature providers or external ones. In cases where there are competing offerings, which is a natural situation in agent stores and hyperscaler marketplaces, who decides which agent performs a task? Will we be entering a scenario where software modules are pre-licensed by a customer, and the agentic layer selects from a registry of pre-licensed agents? Or will the orchestration LLM chase the best bargain agents? Will there be multi-sided markets in which application providers pay the provider of the orchestration LLM to prioritize their software?

2.7.4 Technology Outlook

2.7.4.1 Physics AI

Physics-Informed Neural Networks (PINNs) are a powerful new class of ML models that embed physical laws (expressed as differential equations) directly into the neural network's loss function. Unlike traditional numerical solvers, PINNs can learn solutions from sparse, noisy data while enforcing fundamental constraints, such as conservation laws.

This approach significantly impacts simulation by enabling engineers to bypass complex meshing and intensive computation, thereby accelerating the development of Digital Twins and predictive models. PINNs enable faster, more robust simulations across fields such as fluid dynamics and materials science, democratizing high-fidelity modeling.

Weather forecasting shifts its focus from complex numerical weather prediction models to data-driven ML systems (see Figure 2.15). These AI models are trained on large volumes of atmospheric data to identify patterns and rapidly generate forecasts for variables such as precipitation and temperature. The primary benefit is speed: AI can produce highly accurate forecasts, especially for nowcasting (predictions hours out), far faster than traditional methods.

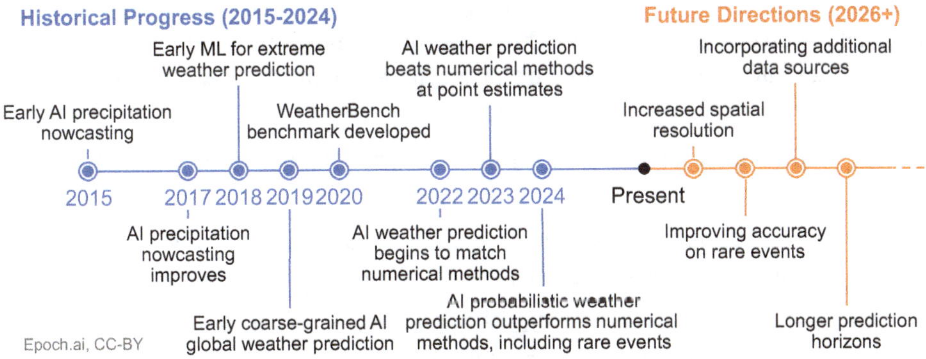

Figure 2.15 Evolution of AI in weather forecasting [21]

2.7.4.2 Physical AI

Physical AI is an emerging discipline that extends AI beyond perception and decision-making into the realm of physically interacting with and manipulating the real world. Unlike traditional AI systems confined to digital environments, physical AI integrates ML with an understanding of physics, enabling intelligent agents to reason about forces, motion, and material properties. In robotics, physical AI powers *robot manipulation*, allowing machines to handle objects with precision and adaptability. By learning the dynamics of contact, friction, and balance, robots can perform complex assembly tasks or safely collaborate with humans in industrial and domestic settings. Beyond solid mechanics, physical AI also encompasses *Computational Fluid Dynamics* (CFD), where AI models simulate and optimize fluid behavior. For example, in the process industry, AI-driven CFD can predict and control the mixing of two chemicals, ensuring uniformity, safety, and efficiency without extensive physical experimentation. Through these capabilities, physical AI bridges the gap between computation and the physical world, enabling systems that not only think and perceive but also *act* and *interact* effectively within the constraints of physical laws. Physical AI is a key component of various simulations in the *Industrial Metaverse*.

2.7.4.3 Embodied AI

Embodied AI is an AI approach that integrates into physical bodies, typically robots. Embodied AI agents perceive, interact with, and learn from the real world through their sensors and actuators. This physical presence is crucial, enabling them to develop a richer understanding of causality, spatial relationships, and the nuances of human interaction – skills often difficult to acquire through simulation alone. By experiencing the world directly, these systems can refine motor skills, adapt to unforeseen circumstances, and even develop forms of common sense through physical engagement. This field is pivotal to advancing robotics beyond pre-programmed movements, enabling truly autonomous and intelligent machines capable of performing complex tasks in unstructured environments. Key characteristics of Embodied AI include:

- *Perception and reasoning:* Using sensors, cameras, and algorithms to interpret the environment.
- *Learning and adaptation:* Employing techniques such as reinforcement learning and imitation learning to improve performance over time.
- *Multimodal interaction:* Integrating vision, language, and action for tasks like object recognition, navigation, and human-robot interaction.

2.7.4.4 World Models

AI *world models* are learned internal representations of environments that enable an agent to predict, simulate, and plan future states, rather than simply reacting to inputs. These models combine perception (e. g., vision sensors), state encoding, dynamic prediction, and, often, a decoder to map back to observations. Using world models, AI can imagine what-if scenarios: "What happens if I move forward, if I push that object, or if certain external conditions change, ...?" This allows far more sample-efficient learning, especially in RL and robotics, since many trials can be handles virtually rather than purely in the real world [54]. Recent research emphasizes integrating physics, causality, neurosymbolic representations, and continual learning to make world models more robust and interpretable (Ser, Lobo, Müller, & Holzinger, 2025). Naturally, they are key ingredients for Embodied AI.

World models are a highly sought-after venture capital target, as they offer the same level of universality for autonomous devices that LLMs do for language-based applications. The investment required to develop them is an entry barrier in itself. Prominent players include World Labs (*worldlabs.ai*), Google DeepMind (*deepmind.google*), and General Intuition (*generalintuition.com*).

World models carry the promise of greatest universality, and we are likely to see a platform-and-model "wrestling match" (Universality vs. Specificity) at the boundaries between world models and domain-specific large models, such as a model that helps control dozens of welding variants (see Table 2.2).

Table 2.2 Domain-Specific Large Models versus World Models

	Domain-Specific Large Model (Applied AI)	AI World Model (Theoretical/Embodied AI)
Core Goal	To master the language, context, and data of a single specialized field.	To simulate the environment and its dynamics, enabling planning and prediction of future states.
Scope of Data	Highly curated, narrow dataset (legal documents, medical research, financial reports, etc.)	Multimodal data (video, images, audio, continuous sensory input, text) is designed to capture physical causality.
Function	Excels at tasks requiring niche expertise: diagnosing diseases, citing specific case law, or analyzing financial reports.	Enables an AI agent to build a "mental model" of the external world (like physics or robot movement) to rehearse actions internally.
Output Type	Precise, accurate, context-aware textual output (summaries, reports, code, answers) within its domain.	Predicted future states, simulated environments, or optimal action sequences (often used in robotics/Reinforcement Learning).
Examples	Models such as BloombergGPT (finance) or the Siemens Industrial Foundation Model.	Architectures such as DeepMind's systems for game environments and models for autonomous vehicles.

Part II: Adoption Hurdles

3 Why Industry is Harder

Following the rapid adoption of GenAI technology in 2024, there is limited evidence of its impact on business. A recent study by MIT's Nanda initiative reports that 95% of organizations are not realizing returns from their GenAI investments. One reason is the well-documented stalling of use cases during the Proof of Concept (PoC) phase, due to a lack of capabilities and suitable landing zones for production deployment. Another, perhaps less explored, reason is the challenge of deciding between custom AI development and the purchase of third-party products. Nanda's report indicates that externally sourced systems have a 67% higher success rate compared to internally developed tools [56].

What about analytical AI applications in industry? Research indicates that 70% of predictive maintenance programs fail to achieve their objectives, primarily because they cannot integrate the solution into daily workflows [57]. And of course, the specifics of data: While manufacturers collect vast amounts of sensor data, they use only 44% of it effectively. The majority remains trapped in historians or siloed machines, inaccessible for real-time analysis, according to a Rockwell Automation study [58].

3.1 Industry Among Industries

The industrial world is fundamentally different from the data-native environments of social media or e-commerce. These differences create noteworthy barriers to rapid AI deployment:

High-Stakes Environment: The cost of failure is the primary differentiator. If a consumer AI recommends the wrong song, the consequences are trivial. If an Industrial AI miscalculates a parameter in a chemical reactor or fails to detect a flaw in an aircraft engine, the consequences can be catastrophic, involving financial ruin, environmental damage, and loss of life.

Physics and Physical Assets: Industrial systems are governed by the laws of physics, not just by data correlations. AI models must respect these physical constraints to be credible and safe. Furthermore, these systems involve massive, expensive physical assets with lifespans measured in decades, rather than the months or years of a software application.

Brownfield vs. Greenfield: Most industrial environments are brownfield, a complex patchwork of legacy equipment, proprietary control systems, and outdated data protocols from dozens of vendors over many years. This contrasts sharply with the greenfield digital world, where systems are designed from the ground up with modern, standardized data infrastructure.

Beyond shop-floor environments, this also affects PLM, CRM, ERP, and MES environments: wherever stringent Software-as-a-Service strategies are leveraged, rapid AI innovation spreads more quickly than in environments where highly customized systems impede rapid update cycles.

A leading producer of airplane turbines misses out on AI productivity gains as their highly customized PLM system cannot be smoothly updated, hence preventing new AI features from being deployed as they are published by the PLM software vendor.

3.2 Specifics of Sub-Industries

Both the discrete manufacturing and process industries have several sub-industries with varying AI adoption rates. Table 3.1 lists the number and points to the AI adoption drivers:

Table 3.1 AI adoption speed in different sub-industries

Industry	Adoption Speed	Adoption Drivers
Pharma	High	▪ High R&D investment ▪ Large biological and chemical datasets ▪ High-value drug discovery use cases
Automotive	High	▪ High digital maturity in R&D and design ▪ Investment in autonomous vehicles ▪ High costs of recalls
Aerospace & Defense	High	▪ Critical need for reliability and simulation ▪ Complex engineering challenges ▪ High government R&D funding

Industry	Adoption Speed	Adoption Drivers
Consumer Packaged Goods	Medium	▪ High volume of sales/transactional data ▪ Demand forecasting ▪ Personalized marketing and retail analytics
Food & Beverage	Medium	▪ Supply chain optimization ▪ Production scheduling ▪ Quality control and safety monitoring, high costs of recalls
Chemicals	Medium	▪ Process optimization and safety ▪ Asset performance management ▪ High energy costs ▪ Complex simulation needs.
Machine Tool Building	Low-Medium	▪ Smart factory initiatives ▪ Predictive maintenance ▪ Automation of complex production lines.

3.3 Potential by Function

According to a McKinsey study, GenAI has substantial economic potential across enterprise functions, with an estimated annual value creation of US$ 2.6–4.4 trillion globally across 63 analyzed use cases. Approximately 75% of GenAI's value creation is said to be concentrated within four key areas [59] (see Figure 3.1).

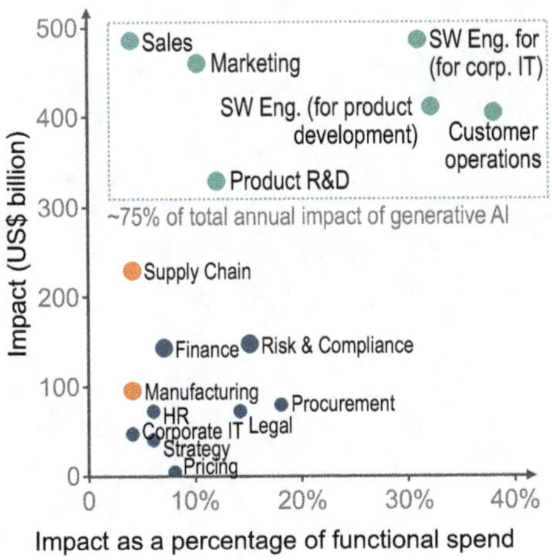

Figure 3.1
Economic potential by enterprise function [59]

- In *Customer Operations*, GenAI enhances agent productivity and the customer experience, with the potential to automate up to 50% of human-serviced contacts and increase productivity by 30–45% of current functional costs.
- *Marketing and Sales* benefit immensely from personalized content creation and enhanced data utilization, with estimated productivity increases of 5–15% of marketing spending and 3–5% of global sales expenditures.
- In *Software Engineering*, GenAI accelerates coding by acting as a virtual collaborator and generating draft code, with the potential to increase productivity by 20–45% relative to current annual spending.
- Finally, in *Product R&D*, the technology streamlines processes such as generative design and early research analysis, potentially unlocking a value equivalent to 10–15% of overall R&D costs.

4 Making AI Industrial-grade

Building AI solutions for industrial environments requires a far higher bar for robustness, reliability, and longevity than typical consumer or enterprise applications. Industrial-grade AI must be designed to withstand not only technical challenges but also the operational, organizational, and regulatory realities of design, engineering, and production environments.

4.1 Model Level

At the core there are the models themselves. Industrial AI models must be robust– able to cope with shifts in input data distributions without breaking down.

In the context of generative AI, robustness is defined by minimizing hallucinations, as inaccurate outputs can lead to significant or even hazardous outcomes. Hallucinations also tend to impact on acceptance among user groups. Based on our observations, AI models achieving 80% accuracy often generate initial enthusiasm at the management level and are sufficient to proceed to lab testing. However, for genuine user adoption in industrial environments – particularly within engineering cultures – a model typically needs to achieve 95% accuracy.

> An engineering team using a third-party LLM to generate PLC code noticed that code produced for identical prompts varied across days, confusing the automation engineers who used the solution. Implementing more than 1,500 test cases that run nightly helps them identify differences and adjust the system prompt to ensure consistent output for users.

Ideally, models are highly capable of generalization and can be transferred across similar machines, processes, or sites without extensive retraining.

An AI model for vibration analysis detects anomalies in pump operation, such as a pump cavity. However, the vibration anomalies would appear in different frequency bands depending on the pump base material (concrete, wood, or steel). In its early versions, the AI model did not generalize well enough to scale as a product. It was only when the model was enriched with a preprocessing function that used noise-filtering algorithms from hearing aid technology that the anomaly detection model became independent of pump location.

Overfitting is a widely recognized issue in AI model training, especially in deep learning. It happens when a model fits the training data – and even its noise – too closely, creating an overly intricate hypothesis that matches the training set exactly but does not work well with unfamiliar data. This results in high variance and weak performance on validation or test sets. The model ultimately "memorizes" examples rather than learning core patterns. Overfitting often stems from using a model that is too complex for the available data or from training it for too many iterations. Increasing the dataset size and employing regularization methods that discourage complex models can help address this problem. A focus on high-quality data is important, as is urging data scientists to move beyond the "easy wins" of overfitting and to adopt a data-centric mindset [60].

AI model performance, when continuously evaluated in an industrial environment, can become a financial liability when AI-driven services are sold based on outcomes or when customers request model performance guarantees. One important mechanism for managing financial liabilities (e.g., those of an AI startup) and associated risks is AI model performance insurance.

Solution Brief 4-1: Insurance against AI Model Liabilities (Munich Re)

Challenge

- Customers lack trust in "black box" AI algorithms and their consistency.
- Uncertainty regarding Return on Investment creates hesitation to invest.
- Companies fear liabilities from AI errors such as hallucinations or IP infringement.
- Risk of financial losses or business interruption due to model underperformance.

Solution aiSure™

- Munich Re evaluates the quality and performance of the specific AI model.
- Provides a performance guarantee backed by insurance to the AI vendor or user.
- Indemnifies clients for financial losses or legal liabilities if the AI errs.
- Covers prediction errors, data drift, and unexpected deviations in behavior

Benefits

- De-risks the purchase decision, allowing for faster AI adoption.
- Protects the balance sheet by transferring financial risk to Munich Re.
- Builds trust with stakeholders and clients through validated model performance.
- Enables companies to scale AI usage without fear of uncapped downside.

Solution Brief 4-1: Insurance against AI Model Liabilities (Munich Re)

Customers: FUGU, TWAICE

Provider: Munich Re, Munich, Germany; *munichre.com/insure-ai*

4.2 Execution Environment Level

Beyond the model, execution must be hardened for industrial conditions. This includes tight integration with cybersecurity frameworks, with every IT/OT service minimized to reduce attack surfaces.

The vast majority of AI workloads are IT workloads, in the sense that they introduce attack vectors that stability-focused OT environments try to avoid at all costs. Particularly when working with industrial AI startups, this can lead to a situation in which ten innovation partners put forward ten different IT stacks and ten different levels of maturity in terms of how stringent these stacks are (security), how they are monitored, patched, and backed up.

A chemical manufacturer learned the importance of execution hardening the hard way. A predictive quality AI system was connected directly to the plant network without proper patching. When malware hit the broader IT environment, the unprotected AI system went offline, halting production for several hours. The incident led to a company-wide overhaul of cybersecurity integration.

Solution Brief 4-2: Industrial Edge Platform (Siemens)

Challenge

- Critical machine data remains trapped on the shop floor without easy cloud access.
- Real-time processing is impossible when relying solely on slow, distant cloud connections.
- Managing software and security updates across thousands of decentralized industrial devices is difficult.

Solution "Industrial Edge"

- Processes high-frequency data locally at the machine level with support for OT network protocols, MQTT, and PLC connectivity.
- Provides a global hub to deploy, update, and monitor apps across all devices.
- Supports diverse industrial applications and Docker-based software for flexible, customized functionality, based on a hardened Linux stack ('Industrial OS').

Solution Brief 4-2: Industrial Edge Platform (Siemens) *(continued)*

Benefits

- Protects industrial assets with automated security patches and secure, isolated data processing.
- Bridges need for innovation (e. g., startup solutions) and stability in corporate large-scale up to global OT environments.

Customers: BMW, Festo, Volkswagen

Provider: Siemens, Berlin/Munich, Germany; *siemens.com/industrial-edge*

When the execution environment is cloud-based, common hardening methods include API monitoring (network traffic to and from the AI solution), network traffic monitoring between cloud components, and robust identity and access management, including session-based usage tokens.

4.3 Hardware Considerations

Industrial AI hardware presents its own set of challenges, some related to technical performance, but many more to supply chain resilience and other factors. It is fair to say that Proof of Concept projects hardly embrace the hardware dimension in their feasibility focus, which is one of several reasons for expensive "Lab to Reality" gaps:

- *AI chip power consumption:* The sheer amount of power required by some AI chips imposes challenges, specifically when the AI system is embedded into battery-driven, mobile systems such as AGVs or AMRs.
- *AI chip heat dissipation:* As a function of power consumption, AI chip heat must be safely dissipated. Does this require a fan, or can the edge device operate with a fanless design, which offers many advantages in dusty or hygienic shop-floor environments?
- *AI chip floating point calculations:* Different AI chips show small differences in their calculation routines, which means their floating point numbers differ in terms of the last decimal digits. This causes the AI model's outputs to differ depending on the hardware on which it is executed.
- *AI chip export control restrictions:* The rising geopolitical tensions and AI technology in the middle of an international powerplay have already led to restrictions on AI chip exports. Developing globally available products (e. g., AGVs) already requires regional product variants with different AI chips.

- *System resilience against electro-magnetic impulses:* Consumer-grade hardware is not designed to withstand the reality of a shop floor, such as legacy electrical drive systems causing electro-magnetic impulses that can ruin a GPU card.

> An electronics assembly factory in Europe implemented a proof of concept solution on a gaming GPU card, as procurement time was of the essence. The GPU card died a "sudden death" after just a few weeks on the shop floor due to electromagnetic interference from the electrical drives. The electrostatic shielding of a consumer-grade GPU card wasn't enough.

- *Spare part warranties:* Consumer-grade hardware schemes provide spare part availability and software driver updates for around three years. Specific long-term product schemes provide warranties for the availability of support and replacement parts for approximately five years. Given the fact that production line investment horizons in industry start at seven years or more, there is still a significant support gap between AI chip providers and their industrial end customers.
- *Spare part availability:* Geographic availability also matters: can critical components be shipped to facilities worldwide within reasonable timeframes?

> An electronics assembly plant in Southeast Asia invested heavily in GPU-based inspection systems. When a cooling issue forced multiple GPU replacements, they discovered that spare parts had to be shipped from Europe, resulting in multi-week downtime. The lesson: Hardware availability and logistics can matter as much as processing power.

4.4 User Experience and Adoption

Even the most technically advanced AI system will fail if users reject it. A system designed by data scientists for data scientists often struggles on the shop floor, where intuitive interfaces and traceable decisions are essential. Effective visualization, alignment with company-specific terminology, and active user involvement in rollout projects increase acceptance. In industrial contexts, explainability is not just a property of algorithms but also of interface design.

Let's look at a couple of dimensions:

- *Multimodality:* The popularity of chatbots has led to an overemphasis on textual interaction with copilot technology, which may work for engineers. However, shop-floor realities (think globally!) differ: illiteracy, or even an immigration-heavy workforce, makes emphasizing text input and output suboptimal. Visualization enables users to grasp status (and localization) information much more quickly (see Figure 4.1). Voice output reaches machine operators wherever they are, not just when they are standing in front of a machine.

A major CPG provider with ambitious industrial AI plans stated that their shop-floor personnel supervise several machines in parallel while also managing material inflow. They do not have time to read the text output from a copilot for machine operations *on-screen*. Instead, the only acceptable means of communication would be machine status and diagnostic information provided via voice output to earbuds, as this reaches workers wherever they are on the shop floor.

- *Explainability* transforms opaque “black-box” models into transparent partners, allowing domain experts to validate AI recommendations against their own technical knowledge. By providing a clear rationale for decisions, *explainable AI* (XAI) mitigates algorithm aversion and builds the high-stakes trust necessary for operators to confidently leverage AI in their daily work.

An aerospace company developed a defect-detection AI system for composites. Early prototypes required operators to interpret raw confidence scores, which created confusion and mistrust. After redesigning the interface to visually highlight detected defects using the operators’ terminology, adoption increased substantially, and false-rejection rates declined.

- *Personifying AI* – by giving it a name, a conversational voice, or a “co-pilot” persona – increases adoption by tapping into human social instincts, making the technology feel like a supportive teammate rather than a cold, intimidating tool. This human-centric framing helps bridge the “trust gap” in industrial settings, as operators are more likely to engage with and rely on a system that communicates in a familiar, relational manner during high-pressure workflows.

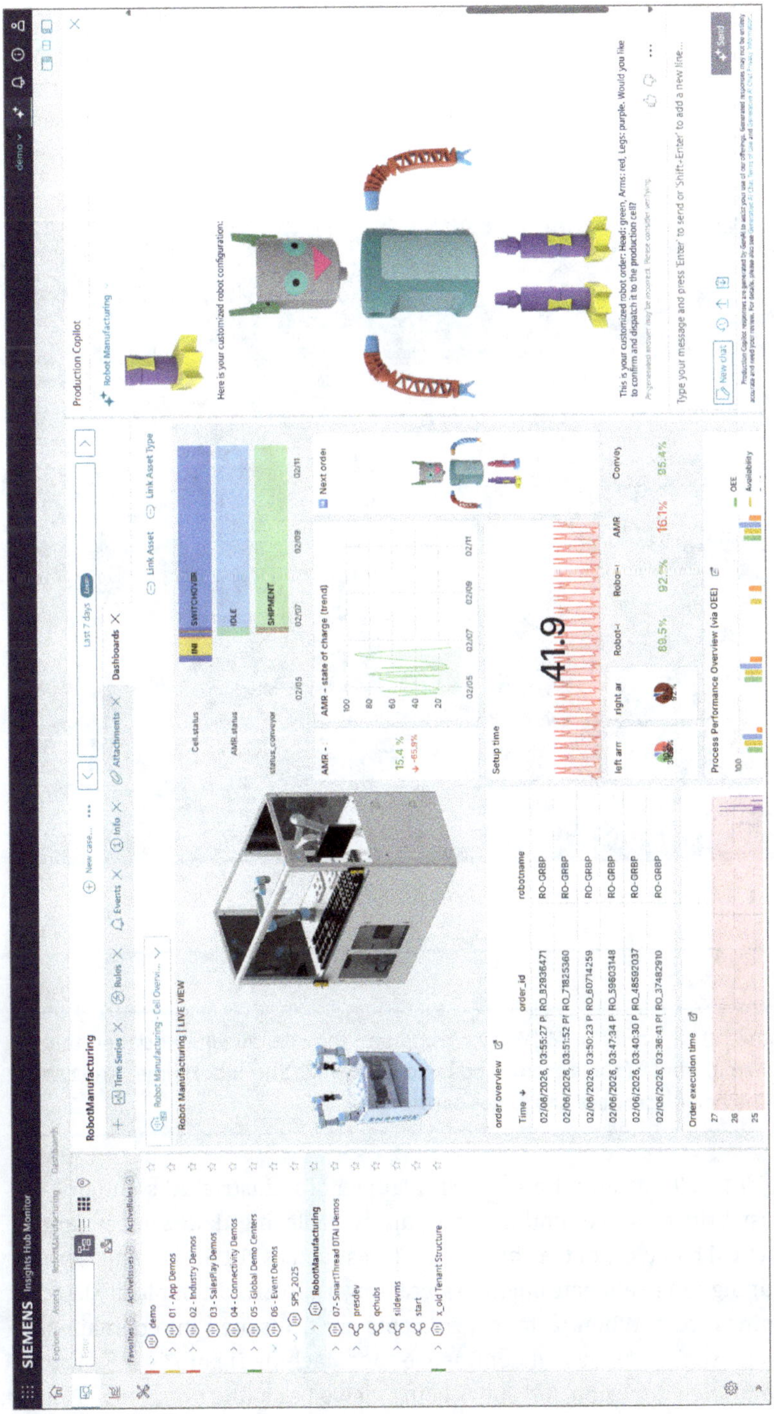

Figure 4.1 Siemens Copilot user interface design

Shibaura Machine collaborated with *Spur Insights* in Switzerland to develop the LEO AI Assistant to support operators of its injection molding machines. LEO has been personified as a helpful blue-collar colleague with a very positive impact on user acceptance (see Figure 4.2).

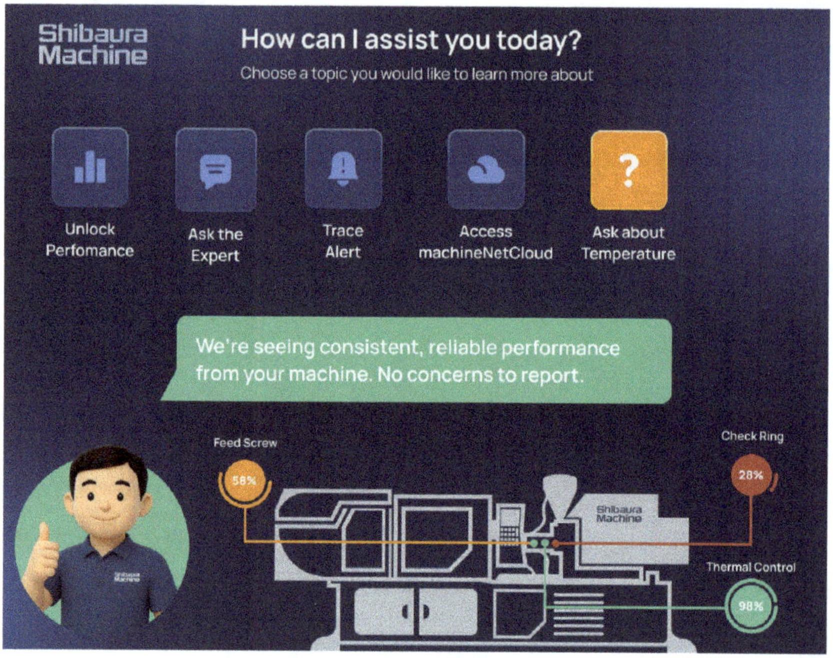

Figure 4.2 Shibaura Machine's LEO AI Assistent

IBM named their powerful AI "Watson", creating the subliminal association that the human in front of the system is equal to the genius Sherlock Holmes and can rely on the helpful services of a junior partner.

- *Avoiding AI jargon:* To ensure the successful launch of industrial AI solutions, developers must bridge the communication gap by replacing data science jargon with the practical language of the shop floor. Terms such as "F1 Score" and "hyperparameter tuning" often alienate operators, creating a perceived complexity barrier that undermines trust. When technical concepts are translated into domain-specific outcomes – such as "Decision Confidence" or "Machine Health" – the AI stops feeling like a foreign intrusion and starts being viewed as a functional tool. Prioritizing clear, outcome-based communication reduces "tech-shame" and empowers workers to embrace innovation without needing a degree in mathematics.

4.5 AI and ML Operations

AI solutions are not static; they must be managed across their entire lifecycle. Data distributions evolve, requiring ongoing retraining and recalibration. This challenge is amplified in the age of LLMs, where providers can update model weights overnight without notice. Without robust quality assurance, such changes can cause identical prompts to yield different results from one day to the next – undermining user trust in mission-critical environments.

Technologically, the challenge lies in building robust, automated, and reproducible pipelines that handle massive volumes of industrial IoT data, ensuring model versioning, data lineage, and continuous monitoring for performance decay or *data respectively model drift*.

Culturally, organizations must transition from experimental Proofs of Concept to treating AI models as production-grade software assets that require continuous integration, delivery, and monitoring. This is equally challenging as establishing a DevOps culture: Programmers and data scientists tend to favor change (change culture), while IT administrators, as well as any role operating a complex system, such as a production line, favor robustness (stability culture). The power of successful DevOps and AI/ML pipelines lies in these different cultures finding common ground through appreciation.

The financial institution *Hauck Aufhäuser Lampe* partnered with startup *embraceable.ai* to build the HALLEY AI platform, which serves as a foundation for highly regulated core banking processes. HALLEY's specific application architecture ensures that all artifacts (e.g., AI knowledge bases, AI models, etc.) are thoroughly version-controlled, all changes and updates immutably logged, and all components (application components, models, and datasets) governed by strict configuration management. [61].

4.6 Data Access and Acquisition

More Data Beats Better Algorithms

In 2006, *Netflix* announced a million-dollar competition that would reshape how the tech world thought about AI: The company released a massive dataset of user ratings – 100 million judgments on 18,000 movies – and challenged researchers to improve its recommendation engine, Cinematch, by at least 10%. Teams from around the world poured in with algorithms rooted in collaborative filtering, matrix factorization, and ensemble methods. For years, the leaderboard shifted as tiny improvements in accuracy were eked out.

The contest revealed a striking truth: the more data a team could leverage, the more accurate its predictions became, often outpacing teams with cleverer mathematical tricks but less effective use of the dataset. This insight fueled the now-famous mantra: *More data beats better algorithms.*

In practice, it meant that feeding ML systems larger, richer datasets often delivered greater gains than inventing entirely new approaches. The Netflix prize also foreshadowed debates about diminishing returns. After the winning team finally surpassed the 10% threshold in 2009, Netflix opted not to implement the algorithm, citing engineering complexity and privacy concerns as the company shifted toward streaming. Yet, it crystallized a cultural shift in AI: data, not just algorithms, was the decisive factor in achieving performance breakthroughs.

Andrew Ng, founder of *Landing.ai*, advocates a *data-centric AI* paradigm (as opposed to model-centricity) that systematically engineers the data needed to build successful AI systems. High-quality data is crucial for AI systems, as it significantly impacts the performance, accuracy, and reliability of AI models. His philosophy encourages a shift away from obsessing over model size toward optimizing data quality and domain adaptation, ensuring that AI systems are built on robust, consistent data [65].

Easier said than done in industrial environments! Let's look at the specific challenges of industrial data access:

- *Intellectual property and trade secrets* concerns prevent many companies from unlocking access to their industrial data for their AI co-creation partners. Although data-related industrial collaborations are increasing, they remain rare at the outset.
- *Intellectual property rights on training data* themselves are an issue that is, in many cases, fuzzy and unresolved – specifically when industrial AI models are built on top of commercial LLM offerings.
- *Data valuation and taxation:* As industrial data becomes a precious ingredient for the creation of AI models with commercial impact, data valuation and tax-compliant transfer pricing become a challenge whenever data crosses legal entities and country borders.

- *Semantics:* Inconsistent naming conventions, varying data unit interpretations, and a lack of standardized context across different machinery and systems require much effort as a precondition to AI projects.
- *Data scarcity:* Obtain enough failure and "edge case" data is difficult, as industrial processes are designed to fail rarely.
- *Data quality:* Sensor noise, missing values, and inconsistent labeling reduce model training effectiveness.
- *Data bias:* Training data often reflects historical sub-optimal processes, inadvertently encoding existing inefficiencies or unfairness.
- *Data drift:* System performance degrades as real-world operational conditions and equipment subtly change over time.

4.6.1 Intellectual Property and Trade Secrets in Data

Industrial data is the crown jewels of a company. Process parameters, production recipes, and material compositions are all key *Intellectual Property* (IP). The fear of this IP being exposed through industrial espionage or a data breach is a primary inhibitor of AI adoption, particularly for solutions that rely on public cloud infrastructure.

In addition to IP, there are other areas of confidential *trade secrets*, such as pricing or production throughput.

When *Tesla* launched the Model 3, closely monitored by the financial markets, every piece of news about Tesla's production throughput moved the stock markets dramatically. One of Tesla's most innovative production systems was the Giga Press: a giant press shop that produced the car underbody as a single piece, whereas competitors would assemble hundreds of individual parts. Access to the log files of that Giga Press, including timestamp information, would constitute a regulated stock-market trade secret and must not be disclosed to anyone outside Tesla.

Companies are highly reluctant to allow sensitive operational data to leave their own secure networks, creating a significant barrier for centralized AI training and analysis. Federated Learning (see Section 2.7.1.8) is a framework that enables training AI models without moving training data out of local environments.

4.6.2 Intellectual Property Rights on Data

For organizations that leverage third-party foundation models, compliance with legal and ethical data-sourcing standards is critical. Many widely-used LLMs fail this test, making them unsuitable for commercial-industrial deployment that adheres to sourcing compliance rules.

> A German machinery company paused an AI rollout after a legal review revealed that the foundation model provider could not guarantee compliance with EU data regulations. While the delay was costly, it prevented the risk of future legal penalties and forced the company to build a compliant, in-house dataset - an investment that paid off in later projects.

4.6.3 Valuation and Taxation of Data

When internal data is shared across national borders or between separate legal entities within a multinational group, its valuation and the establishment of a transfer pricing scheme are required for tax compliance. Data, as an intangible asset – especially valuable, unique datasets – must be priced in accordance with the *arm's length principle*. This principle, mandated by tax authorities worldwide (following OECD rules for international taxation), requires that the price of an internal transaction be the same as if it occurred between two independent, uncontrolled parties. Failure to accurately value the data's contribution to profit and apply an appropriate transfer price can lead to accusations of profit shifting, triggering significant tax audits, penalties, and double taxation across jurisdictions [66].

4.6.4 Shop-floor Semantics

Data without context is just numbers. A critical challenge on the shop floor is the lack of a shared semantic model. A temperature reading of "85.2" is meaningless without knowing the unit (Celsius or Fahrenheit?), the asset it belongs to (which motor?), and its position (bearing or casing?).

Without this semantic context, it is impossible to reliably aggregate and analyze data across different assets, let alone across multiple factories. This lack of a common language is a fundamental barrier to developing scalable AI solutions.

In industry, PLCs pose a specific challenge: their I/O interfaces (I/Os) are typically labeled generically. You need to understand the PLC code to know that "I/O 3" provides an analog signal that corresponds to temperature. In all cases where source code access is prohibited, for example when the PLC is part of an acquired machine by a machine tool builder ("black box"), the only further options are documentation in manuals, or the machine tool builder could provide a semantic interface (e.g., an OPC UA server) as a part of their machine.

4.6.5 Data Scarcity

It may seem paradoxical that a factory generating terabytes of sensor data could suffer from data scarcity. Still, the issue is highly relevant: For many critical applications, such as predictive maintenance and predictive quality, the most important data points are those associated with failures or rare events. A machine may run flawlessly for years, generating vast amounts of data on normal operations, but provide only a handful of examples of the specific fault condition we want the AI to predict. This class imbalance makes it incredibly difficult to train a robust model.

In many cases, the related analysis used to identify these scarce records (e.g., anomaly detection) is performed in the cloud. This can lead to substantial costs for cloud storage and data transfer.

4.6.6 Data Quality

Raw industrial data is rarely clean or ready for analysis. It is often plagued by a host of quality issues that require significant and costly data engineering efforts to fix:

- *Noise:* Sensor readings can be imprecise or subject to drift (e.g., due to electromagnetic interference, changes in temperature, and lighting conditions).
- *Missing data:* Obvious potential reasons for gaps in data streams are network outages, sensor failures, or systems being taken offline for maintenance. However, a significant challenge lies in the software engineering paradigms of the IT and OT worlds: the timing differences between PLC polling cycles (typically 5 ms) and the system layer above (SCADA or MES), which typically polls data from the PLC layer every second. As a consequence, critical signals appearing on a PLC are lost before data is pulled from the layer above. Hence, critical analytical functions, such as predictive maintenance's anomaly detection, are doomed to fail if the PLC programmer does not log high-frequency signals in a dedicated, persistent queue or log file [67].
- *Time (stamp) alignment:* Synchronizing data from multiple systems with different clocks is a non-trivial problem, making it difficult to establish accurate causal relationships (time/clock synchronization challenge). Furthermore, sensors and their node systems provide data at different sampling rates; for example, one sensor

delivers data every 10 ms, while another provides data only twice per second (non-equidistant timestamps).

- *Inconsistent formats:* Different machines and control systems often use proprietary, incompatible data formats, requiring custom integrations.
- *Labeling quality:* The quality of data annotation is challenging due to the complexity of domain-specific features, high cost, and the need for subject matter expert consistency (see Solution Brief 2–2 "Responsible Annotation Services" in Section 2.7.1.2)

4.7 Ecosystem Partnerships

The scarcity of AI experts makes it difficult for companies to build and retain in-house expertise. As a result, many organizations turn to ecosystem partnerships early in their AI journey. Partner selection, however, has a direct impact on long-term industrial viability:

- Is the partner financially stable? Wherever investments touch the shop floor, seven-year and longer investment cycles are standard; hence, this must be the shortest time horizon an innovation partner's stability must offer.
- Do they have a culture of ongoing support, or will the burden of operations ultimately fall back on the customer?
- Can our AI partner support international scaling of their AI solution, for example, when rollouts into a global factory network are on the roadmap for scale-up?

Choosing the right ecosystem partner can be just as critical as the AI solution's technical design.

A mid-sized manufacturer partnered with a startup to deploy an AI scheduling system. When the startup was acquired, support quickly evaporated, leaving the manufacturer responsible for maintaining an unfamiliar system. In contrast, another division partnered with an established industrial software vendor to ensure long-term support and integration with existing systems.

4.8 Requirements Engineering for AI

Classical *Requirements Engineering* (RE) practices, which were originally developed for deterministic software systems, often fall short when applied to AI because they do not adequately account for the probabilistic, data-dependent, and evolving nature of ML-driven solutions.

AI systems are not merely programmed but also trained, rendering their behavior contingent on the quality, representativeness, and governance of the data. Yet, requirements for data – its adequacy, fairness, and compliance with ethical standards – remain under-specified or absent in many projects.

Similarly, non-functional requirements such as explainability, robustness, and accountability, which are critical for fostering trust and meeting regulatory obligations, are frequently treated as secondary considerations rather than central design imperatives.

The lack of systematic traceability further compounds this problem, as requirements are rarely linked across datasets, model architectures, evaluation metrics, and business objectives, thereby undermining transparency and accountability [62].

> A data scientist at a large automation company was tasked with building an ML model for anomaly detection. They selected an algorithm they felt comfortable with based on their university project work. A proper review of formally documented requirements revealed that a different algorithm class would have been a significantly better fit for the use case.

Moreover, requirements must be conceptualized as dynamic and evolving artifacts, continuously refined through iterative validation and monitoring as models adapt to changing operational environments. However, in practice, organizations often fail to institutionalize such living requirements processes, resulting in AI systems that degrade over time or deviate from stakeholder expectations. The absence of inclusive, multidisciplinary stakeholder engagement in requirements definition exacerbates these challenges, as critical perspectives from ethicists, domain experts, and end users are often marginalized in favor of purely technical considerations.

4.9 The Role of an AI Bill of Materials

An *AI Bill of Materials* (AIBOM) is an important extension of the traditional software bill of materials, specifically designed to address the unique complexities and risks inherent to AI. Its primary significance lies in providing a comprehensive, structured inventory of all components that constitute an AI system, including not only software libraries and dependencies but also foundational training datasets, model architectures, and hardware configurations. By documenting data provenance and the specific versions of algorithms used, an AIBOM transforms the black box nature of AI into a transparent asset.

In industrial and enterprise settings, adopting an AIBOM is essential for managing supply chain risks and meeting increasingly stringent regulatory requirements, such as the EU AI Act and NIST frameworks. It enables security teams to identify vulnerabilities in third-party libraries, detect potential data poisoning, and monitor model drift over time. Ultimately, establishing a clear record of an AI system's ingredients not only secures the AI lifecycle but also ensures that the technology remains a reliable and accountable tool for long-term operational success [63].

Complementing the technical inventory of an AIBOM, *Model Cards* and *Dataset Cards* serve as essential "nutrition labels" that advance AI transparency:

- *Model Cards* offer standardized summaries outlining an algorithm's strengths and limitations, with particular emphasis on biases and environmental factors that may affect functionality.
- Similarly, *Dataset Cards* specify the provenance and structure of training data, addressing privacy issues and identifying any potential sampling gaps.

4.10 Managing Quality in Agentic Environments

Managing the output quality of Agentic AI in industrial settings poses unique challenges. AI agents often rely on *non-deterministic LLMs* to reason through engineering problems, which can lead to "agentic drift" or subtle hallucinations that are difficult to detect in real-time. On the shop floor, a minor reasoning error by a maintenance agent could lead to an incorrect tool selection or a safety violation, thereby converting a productivity gain into a physical risk.

Distributed Software Architectures

Distributed software architectures gained significant traction in the late 1980s and early 1990s. Despite their theoretical advantages in modularity and scalability, they were avoided in mainstream commercial applications due to the extreme complexity of managing data consistency and network latency across multiple nodes. Furthermore, the lack of standardized, developer-friendly tooling made the simpler monolithic architecture a far more reliable choice for businesses at the time.

The primary difficulty lies in the multi-step nature of agentic workflows. Because a task sequence chains several tool calls (known as a *propagation chain*) – such as querying a technical manual, calculating a load limit, and then sending a command to a PLC – errors can compound across the sequence. Traditional quality gates struggle here because the "correct" answer isn't always binary; it requires deep domain-specific context that general-purpose AI often lacks. Furthermore, managing output quality is complicated by the "replication gap", where a system that performs perfectly in a Digital Twin simulation may fail when confronted with the noisy, unstructured data of a brownfield factory environment.

4.10.1 Supervisor Agents

To bridge this gap, engineers must implement *layered governance*, using secondary supervisor agents to verify the primary agent's logic. Particularly, non-AI agents, often serving as a façade to traditional software applications, are well-suited:

- *Design Rule Checks:* A supervisor agent uses a deterministic rule base to check the AI agent (or human) output against engineering constraints. These rule bases can be fed and maintained by in-house domain experts, and they can also incorporate industry codes and regulations when expressed in a software-readable format.

Airbus, Boeing, and Renault leveraged Dessia's AI design and validation platform. A design verification app holds design rules related to geometry, expressed formally via Dessia's geometry processing SDK, which integrates with leading CAD software suites (see Figure 4.3).

- *Traditional simulation:* AI agent output can be fed into traditional simulation applications via a supervisor agent as an interface and challenge the output with simulation results.

When supervisor agents differ in their assessment from the "creator" agent, a human-in-the-loop mechanism checks in between results or asks for the authorization of high-consequence actions. Ensuring reliability requires moving beyond simple accuracy metrics to "prevention metrics", such as the frequency of guardrail triggers or the consistency of reasoning chains over time.

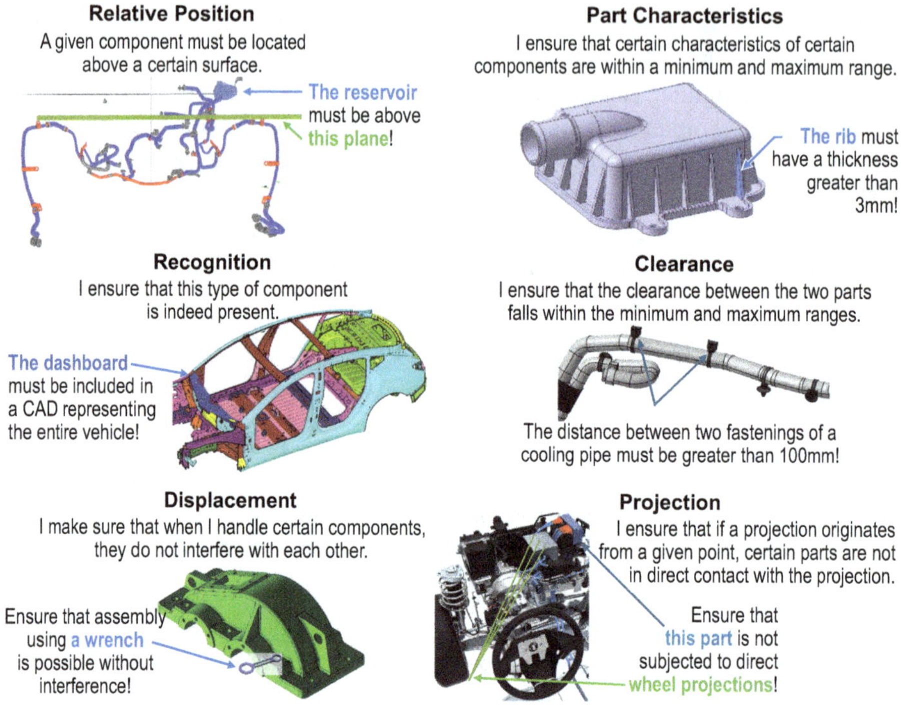

Figure 4.3 Design rule formulation (Dessia)

Solution Brief 4-3: Design Rule Checking (Dessia)

Challenge

- Repetitive manual verification tasks slow down innovation and delay time-to-market.
- Complex engineering designs are prone to human error and inconsistency during manual checks.
- Siloed data and manual rules make enforcing compliance and design standards difficult.

Solution "AI-Verification App"

- AI automatically enforces design rules and compliance standards across models.
- Smart integration through AI-powered 3D clash verification and geometric recognition.
- Custom AI apps connect to PLM systems to automate engineering workflows.
- A specific Python SDK uses routines to understand the geometry of engineered objects and helps express design rules formally.

Benefits

- Reduces development time by up to 80% by automated validation and exploration.
- Improves design quality by eliminating errors early in the cycle.

Customers: Airbus, Boeing, Renault

Provider: Dessia, Antony, France; *dessia.io*

4.10.2 Digital Reasoning Thread

Accenture proposes a *Digital Reasoning Thread* (DRT) architecture (*digital-reasoning-thread.com*), that provides an active, federated intelligence layer that connects disparate components – from PLCs and SCADAs to HMI and Resource Planning. It addresses the challenge of siloed data by creating a unified environment where autonomous agents can execute complex sequence planning, predictive maintenance, and quality assurance. By emphasizing the knowledge graph-driven capture of domain expertise and a set of technical and human feedback loops, the framework facilitates adaptive, yet quality-managed, agentic AI workflows (see Figure 4.4).

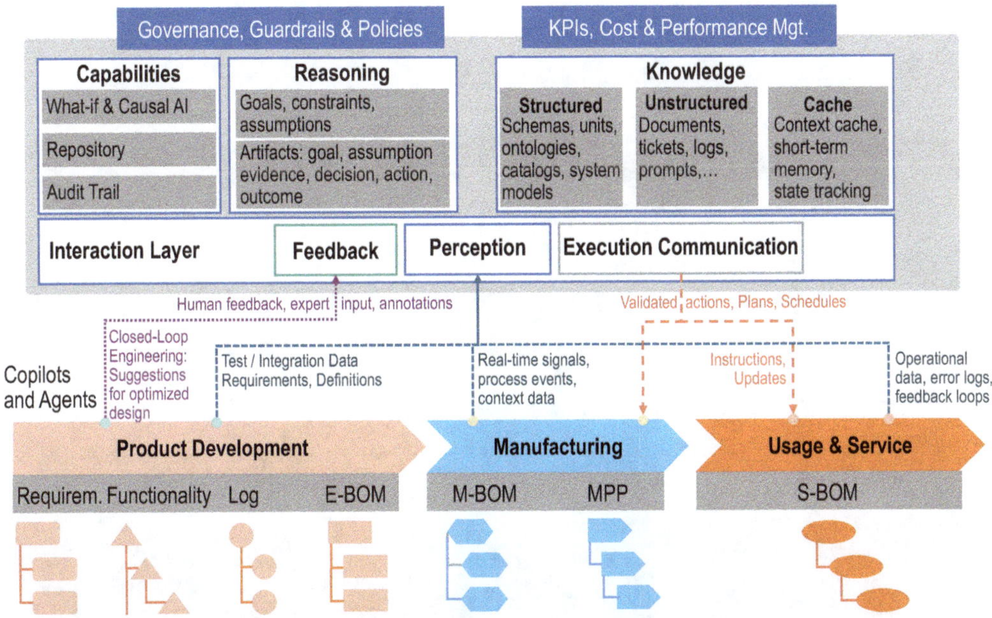

Figure 4.4 Conceptual architecture "Digital Reasoning Thread"

4.10.3 Process Mining for Agent and Process Compliance

Where autonomous agents dynamically orchestrate complex workflows, *Process Mining* is emerging as a potential tool for quality management. The inherent challenges of ensuring reliability and predictability in distributed software architectures are not new; they have been well documented since the 1990s. As systems became more decentralized, the difficulty of monitoring "emergent behavior" grew. This historical precedent led researchers as early as 2009 to examine process mining specifically as a quality management mechanism within multi-agent systems. By extracting knowledge from event logs, process mining provides a transparent "mirror" of how agents actually interact, rather than how they were theoretically designed to perform [48].

This academic foundation is becoming relevant as we speak: Process mining enables real-time sequence compliance checks, identifying when an AI agent deviates from a "golden path" or enters an inefficient loop. By comparing live-agent behavior with formal process models, organizations can ensure that autonomy does not compromise quality, thereby providing the governance framework needed for trusted, large-scale agentic deployments. An example of related recent research is [64].

5 Business Case Mechanics

5.1 The Macroeconomic Perspective

AI is projected to deliver a massive positive "supply shock" to the global economy, potentially adding US$7–13 trillion to global GDP by 2030, according to estimates by Goldman Sachs and McKinsey [68]. JP Morgan projects a cumulative U. S. productivity gain of ~17.5% over the next 20 years, translating to *US$ 7 trillion* in added economic potential beyond current projections [69].

However, this growth will likely follow a *productivity J-curve*: Initial gains may be muted or even negative as corporations incur the high costs of retooling infrastructure and retraining workforces, before a sharp acceleration in output occurs.

The core macroeconomic tension lies in the ratio of augmentation to displacement. While AI promises to reverse the global productivity slowdown by automating routine cognitive tasks (augmenting labor), the International Monetary Fund warns that *40% of global employment* is at risk of AI disruption. If displacement outpaces the creation of new high-value roles, the economy could experience a "jobless recovery" where capital owners capture the vast majority of efficiency gains. This risks a structural divergence: Advanced economies with robust digital infrastructure could see exponential growth. At the same time, developing nations – lacking the capital to sovereignize their AI stacks – may fall further behind, exacerbating global inequality even as aggregate global wealth soars [70].

On the other hand, the AI industry would need to generate US$ 650 billion in annual revenue to deliver a modest 10% return on the massive investments expected through 2030, which nourishes concerns about an investment bubble [71].

5.2 The Productivity Promises of Industry 4.0

Despite all the excitement about AI's economic potential across all industries: Discrete manufacturing and the process industries are still going through a phase of sobering up from the fact that *Industry 4.0* (I4.0) has not delivered the promised productivity gains and its results significantly diverge from previous technological eras: the period of *Lean Manufacturing/ERP* (1991–2002) and *Automation/Robotics* (2002–2010) each delivered over 30% productivity growth, whereas the *Industry 4.0 era* (since 2010) has only produced an approximately 5% increase in productivity per employee (see Figure 5.1).

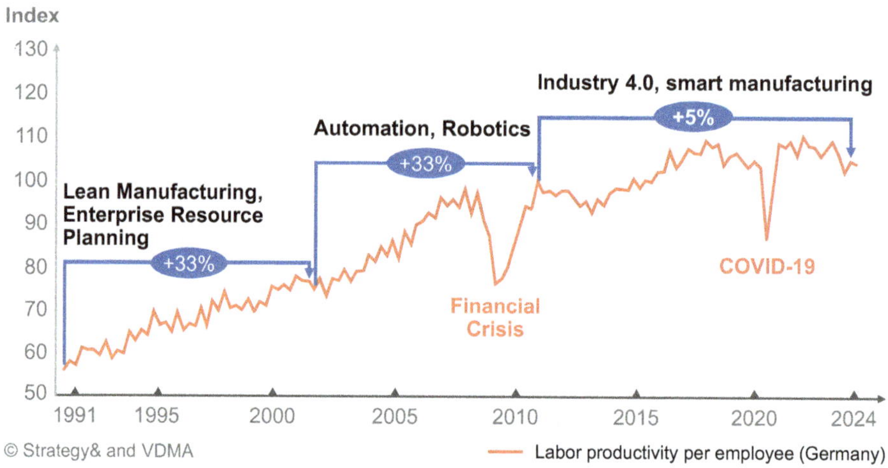

Figure 5.1 Labor productivity in the German machine tool industry [72]

Primary reasons for this shortfall are:

- The *productivity-cost imbalance:* The most tangible evidence of I4.0's failure to deliver is the financial reversal faced by manufacturers:
  - *Stagnant productivity vs. rising costs:* Since 2010, the meager gains in labor productivity have been outstripped by rising factor costs. Labor costs, in particular, increased by 22%, while productivity rose by only 11% during that period, rapidly diminishing profitability.
  - *Lack of capitalization:* Companies have struggled to find the optimal balance between investments and measurable benefits from I4.0 technologies. This points to a failure to capitalize on technological advancements, resulting in high upfront investment costs that have not yet yielded quantifiable long-term returns. Furthermore, digital transformation initiatives suffer from common investment cycles in industry: Machines and production lines are (commer-

cially) designed to run for seven years+; replacing a legacy machine generation (maybe with data access limitations) does not fall in line with the timing needs of a transformation initiative.

- *Implementation and integration barriers:* The fundamental challenge of I4.0 lies in connecting siloed systems, which has proven difficult in practice:
  - *Fragmented implementation:* Many organizations launch I4.0 as small-scale pilot projects but struggle to scale the technology enterprise-wide. These individual initiatives remain siloed (e.g., a sensor on a single machine) and fail to integrate the entire value chain, preventing the realization of holistic benefits.
  - *Legacy system interoperability:* Manufacturing environments often rely on decades-old machinery and established IT systems. Integrating these legacy assets with modern, connected I4.0 technologies is complex, costly, and difficult to standardize.
  - *Lack of standards:* The market is flooded with proprietary solutions from different vendors, leading to a lack of standardized protocols. This creates compatibility issues and vendor lock-in, which limits flexibility and scalability.
- *Data, skills, and strategic mindset*: I4.0 requires a new way of thinking, which many organizations have been slow to adopt:
  - *Data overload without insight:* The core of I4.0 turns big data into actionable insights. However, companies often generate massive amounts of data from IoT devices while lacking the sophisticated analytics tools and expertise to derive meaningful intelligence from it. Without high-quality data and data integrity, the systems underperform.
  - *Defensive investment mindset:* Executives tend to focus digital transformation initiatives on operational improvements (doing the same thing better and faster). This defensive mindset aims to protect existing margins rather than leverage I4.0 for radical innovation, new business models, or R&D-driven revenue growth, limiting the ultimate profit impact.
  - The *digital gap:* This refers to the organizational and cultural difficulty in transitioning from traditional operations to a digitally-driven reality, leading to a paradoxical situation where the profitability criteria for digital investments remain unclear. This digital gap multiplies across a fragmented industrial supply chain of production operators, machine tool builders, and system integrators: different commercial interests, different levels of digital maturity, and the painstaking process of digital alignment through consensus rather than top-down decision-making are wear-and-tear factors on the momentum of innovation.

5.3 Business-to-Consumer vs. Business-to-Business Scaling

Since the momentum of Deep Learning AI technology development has been fueled by social media companies, such as e-commerce (Amazon, Alibaba) and ad placements via search and social media (Google, Meta, Baidu, Tencent), it has become a multi-trillion-dollar business. In the discrete manufacturing and process industries, AI adoption has been comparatively low due to the significantly more complex business case mechanics (see Table 5.1).

Table 5.1 Comparison of AI value creation in social media vs. industry

	Business to Consumer (B2C)/ Social Media	Discrete Manufacturing/Process Industries
Value per Use Case instance	**Low** Example: US$ 0.05 for a successful ad placement	**Medium to high** Example: US$ 200 saved if a faulty PLC is identified before being sent to a customer.
Potential Customers	**Extreme** Example: Meta with 1billion users on Facebook.	**Very low** Rationale: Every production line is different. Differences in production setups are linked to competitive differentiation.
Effort to acquire data	**Very low** Rationale: Related platforms have been built as data collectors in the first place.	**Very high** Rationale: All challenges as listed in Section 4.6.
Return on Investment	**Very high**	**Low-medium**
Other factors	Innovation investment cycles based on software and IT (<3–5 years).	Innovation Investment cycles based on machine parks and factories (>7–10 years).

Table 5.1's comparison of the structural business case mechanics in B2B versus B2C grounds the somewhat irrational discussion about rapid AI adoption in the US versus slower AI adoption in Europe: Europe has no noteworthy social media industry. There are no indications that the adoption rate of Industrial AI differs between the two geographies.

5.4 Foundational Capability vs. Use Case ROI

The pervasive investment in AI and its supporting capabilities has created an organizational challenge: accurately quantifying the Return on Investment (ROI) across disparate investment horizons. Organizations are currently investing heavily in AI, yet they report that returns often materialize slowly and are difficult to measure. This challenge is exacerbated by the fact that inadequate infrastructure and poor data quality are cited by one in four executives as a principal barrier to realizing AI ROI, confirming that the foundation itself is a critical strategic necessity [73].

This financial ambiguity suggests a multi-tiered methodology (see Figure 5.2) that formally separates expenditure and attributes value generation *across the AI stack*:

- *Tier 1 – foundational capability creation:* This tier encompasses the investments in the unified data platform, industrial data sources, data governance structures, infrastructure modernization, and the development of core, reusable AI engines. These investments are analogous to the historic transition to factory electrification – they demand massive organizational change, workflow redesign, and reskilling before their full economic benefits manifest [73]. Because the value accrues slowly and broadly, this category requires a longer measurement timeframe. It relies heavily on capability benchmarks, such as self-service adoption rates or improvements in time-to-insight, rather than immediate financial profits.
- *Tier 2 – individual AI use cases:* This tier includes the direct costs and benefits associated with specific AI models, such as a predictive maintenance system or an AI agent in customer service. These applications leverage Tier 1's foundational capabilities, such as data access. Measurement here is typically short-cycle and focused on direct financial outcomes, such as productivity lift, immediate cost savings, and revenue contribution.

Relying on vast amounts of data without the capability to analyze and act on it effectively constitutes an investment with no return. Therefore, the foundational Tier 1 investment must be justified by its role as a prerequisite for risk mitigation and value creation, rather than solely on direct profit generation. Strong data governance, for instance, is associated with a 20-fold increase in the likelihood of regulatory compliance [74]. If poor data quality actively constrains AI ROI [73], then Tier 1 investment functions as an essential, quantifiable strategy for avoiding regulatory exposure and operational failure.

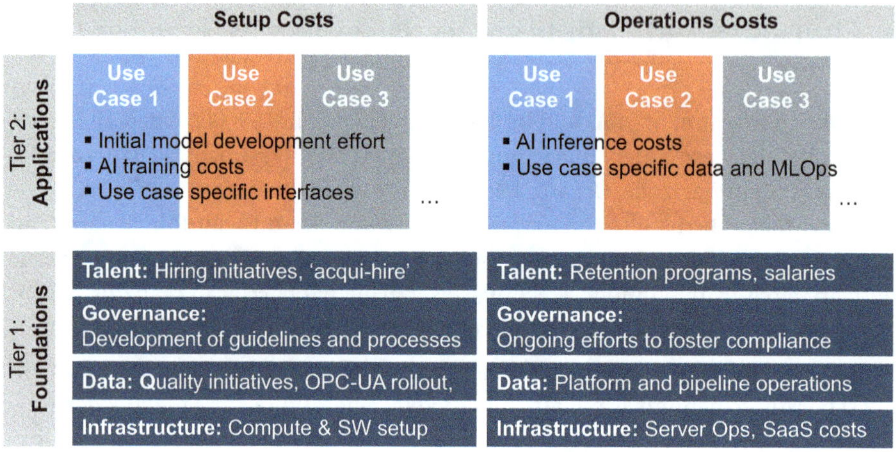

Figure 5.2 Tiered approach to foundational capabilities and AI use cases

5.4.1 Foundational Capability Value

The returns generated by core data capabilities are often indirect, system-wide, and precede the direct financial benefits of specific AI applications. This is why Tier 1 ROI measurement must focus on operational de-risking, efficiency benchmarks, and strategic option value.

Tier 1 investment justification relies heavily on establishing the internal monetary value derived from the optimized data management processes that are prerequisites to successful Tier 2 deployment.

- *Operational efficiency and cost savings:* Robust data governance frameworks directly translate into tangible cost savings by reducing redundancies and inefficiencies [75]. Mature governance has been shown to increase operational efficiency by 33% and reduce overall data management costs by 15% [74]. These benefits are monetized by quantifying the time and resources saved by teams through manual data cleansing, validation, and preparation. This streamlining of operations reduces friction, enabling the organization to allocate resources toward innovation rather than infrastructure maintenance [75].
- *Data quality assurance:* High-quality data is an immediate and measurable financial asset [76]. Investment in governance structures enables the tracking of key metrics, including d*ata accuracy rates, data completeness scores,* and *error detection and resolution times* [76]. These metrics quantify the improvement in internal quality control.
- *Quantifying negative impact avoidance:* One critical component of Tier 1 ROI is the financial quantification of risk mitigation. Poor data quality creates "negative

value" through costly operational errors. Organizations must monetize the costs of potential failures, such as exposure to real regulatory risk, penalties, duplicate invoices, and financial write-offs resulting from incorrect use of master data. Quantifying this negative impact shifts data governance from a compliance-only task to a core financial de-risking strategy. For instance, leaders who have deployed data access governance solutions stand to achieve *an average ROI of 175% over three years*. This return is achieved by minimizing business friction and legal exposure, proving that the baseline justification for data governance rests on minimizing operational losses and regulatory penalties, irrespective of the success of any specific new AI application [74].

The value of the foundational investment can be demonstrated by comparing it to the barriers cited by non-leaders: inadequate infrastructure and data. By eliminating these barriers, the organization purchases a competitive option. The platform is justified not only by the use cases it enables but also by the great cost and risk avoidance it offers as a ready-state capability.

5.4.2 AI Use Case Value

Tier 2 investments deliver direct financial returns and are measured using traditional financial metrics applied to the product increment. However, these returns must be formally attributed to acknowledge their intrinsic reliance on the Tier 1 platform.

Specific AI applications create value that can be categorized into three distinct layers, ensuring that both direct and indirect benefits are captured [77]:

- *Productivity lift:* Direct gains in efficiency, measured by time savings and optimization. This is often the first measurable return from generative AI solutions, which focus on augmenting employees so they can spend more time on strategic and creative tasks [73].
- *Cost avoidance:* The reduction of operational expenses and the mitigation of specific, quantifiable risks. A classic example is predictive maintenance, which avoids thousands of dollars in unplanned downtime costs by transforming siloed data into actionable insights.
- *Revenue contribution:* Creation of new business opportunities, enhanced customer value, and business model reimagination. This category reflects actual transformative value and is often associated with AI ROI Leaders, who define their most critical wins in these strategic terms [73].

5.5 Pilot Purgatory

Sobering reports indicate that up to 95% of enterprise GenAI projects fail to deliver measurable ROI and are scrapped before reaching production, a failure rate far exceeding that of standard IT initiatives [56]. While the shocking percentage stems from a cross-industry study, industrial AI projects face a distinct set of Go-Live challenges, as outlined earlier, many of which also relate to traditional AI use (see Table 5.2).

Table 5.2 Cost-driver differences between AI PoC and production setups

	Proof of Concept Focus	Production Focus
Model Level	▪ Primary PoC focus	▪ Model just one component in a larger system.
Execution Environment	▪ Ignored or minimal ("sandbox")	▪ Comprehensive security, compliance, and governance (e. g., audit logging, explainability, data protection), which requires extensive legal and technical review.
Hardware Compute & Scalability	▪ Low-cost, on-demand cloud resources (e. g., dedicated Lab server)	▪ Fault-tolerant, high-availability infrastructure (often using expensive GPUs) that can handle peak load, low latency requirements, and 24/7 uptime.
User Experience & Adoption	▪ Ignored or minimal	▪ Requires training and potentially process changes.
Data Access & Acquisition	▪ Small, clean, static dataset ▪ Minimal or no integration with core systems	▪ Real-time, large-volume data pipelines that clean, validate, and feed data continuously from dozens of varied sources. ▪ Deep, resilient integration with existing legacy ERP, CRM, and OT systems.
MLOps & Engineering	▪ Model trained on a laptop ▪ Lab environment	▪ Building a robust MLOps platform for automated retraining, continuous integration/deployment (CI/CD), version control, and model monitoring.
Partner Ecosystem	▪ Agile startups	▪ Reliable and stable partners. ▪ Ability to operate.

This does not mean that proof of concept projects are easy: Many PoCs start with an overly ambitious timeline and face delays, primarily for the following reasons:

- Access to quality datasets runs into typical challenges (see Section 4.6), resulting in delays.
- Missing Performance Baselining: Data scientists keep on tuning the AI model 'forever' (which often results in an overfitting problem, see Section 4.1); it is unclear when the AI model delivers sufficient value, as the performance baseline of the existing process is exceeded.

An industrial PoC team spent several months seeking additional datasets to improve the quality inspection model's performance from 92% to 95%, while human performance via visual inspection only reached 85%.

Industrial AI startups suffer in particular from the problematic dynamics of pilot purgatory: A startup's well-articulated value proposition leads to a high number of proof of concept engagements, which are often capacity-consuming to run. The number of pilot projects signals market demand to venture capitalists and naturally stirs investment appetite. However, financial returns are contingent on successful deployments at scale; disappointment is inevitable given the industry's current high "drop-out" rates.

5.6 Use Case Scalability Assessment

Siemens and Inpro developed a scalability assessment approach for industrial AI use cases, which follows the CRISP-DM methodology for data analytics projects [78]. In each project phase (*Business Understanding, Data Understanding, Data Preparation, Model Development, Evaluation, and Deployment*), several assessment questions are used to generate a scalability score. The scalability score is particularly useful when a *relative* assessment is needed: "We have 18 different ideas. Which five of them should we pursue?"

One of the principal challenges in AI use case assessments is that not all relevant questions can be answered in advance, at least not with a high degree of certainty.

The complexity of AI model deployment can depend on findings from the "data understanding" project phase; that is, once the team determines which brownfield connectivity wall they have encountered.

Consequently, this scalability assessment is an approach to accompanying an AI project and stopping it at the earliest possible point if fundamental scalability hurdles are identified. Given this, the recommendation is to make assessment updates a required activity within a project's quality-gate approach.

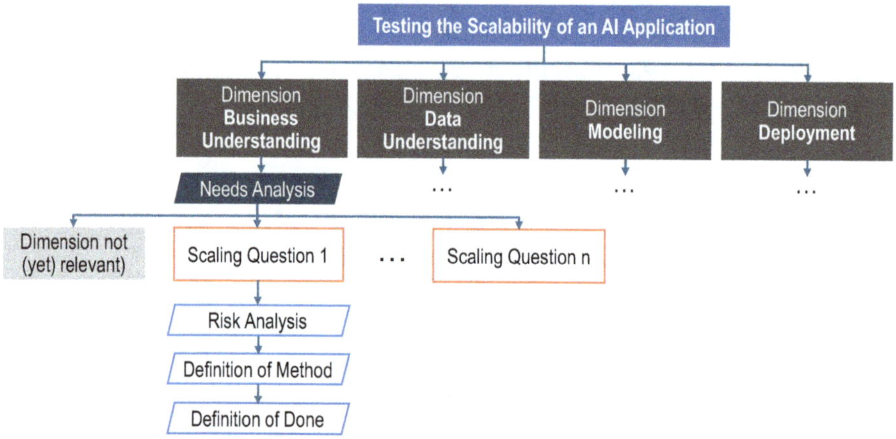

Figure 5.3 Structure of Inpro's AI use case scalability checklist [78]

Typical questions in the *Business Understanding* dimension are:

1. *"Can the rollout potential be quantified, have all the relevant basic numbers for calculations been determined?"*, such as the number of identical production units in the group brand/ scaling over production units (e. g., for a robot application), units in the whole group, in the market, etc.
2. *"Can the costs of development be split between the use case in focus and all possible use cases/solutions (estimation)?"* (see Section 5.4).
3. *"Can the costs of the development be determined, and can the benefits of the use case be quantified?"*
   - *In Production:* The main benefits are difficult to quantify (e. g., unplanned downtime). The customer often has no reliable figures or figures traceable to a specific cause. Local cycle-time improvements do not typically translate into improvements across the entire production chain or cannot be substantiated with figures.
   - *In Planning:* Often, external contracts (e. g., for drawing tests with steel, combinations of sheet thicknesses, ...)/services are awarded, and the replaceable project volumes can be quantified more easily.
4. *"Is the Domain Expert team role staffed?"*, especially given that experts are rarely available customer-side. This is an important basis for estimating the costs of data understanding (splitting the expenses between the customer and the supplier)

5. *"Has software architecture development for the use case been coordinated with the customer's overall architecture roadmap (midterm/long-term)?"*; this influences the technical scaling factor as it avoids reimplementation overhead at later stages.
6. *"Are all involved suppliers known, including their responsibilities and their (data) IP?"* For example, robotics vendors will charge an additional license fee for data access to their robots.
7. *"Are brownfield restrictions known?"* For example, outdated machine interfaces that lead to proprietary formats.

5.7 AI-driven Business Models

AI can enable manufacturers to shift their focus from selling products (say, a one-time CapEx sale of a machine) to offering a continuously optimized service paid for by the *measurable outcome* it delivers. This is powered by embedding IoT sensors and AI-driven predictive maintenance platforms into the equipment. These systems continuously analyze vibration, temperature, and performance data to accurately predict failures.

Instead of buying a new industrial 3D printer, a customer could pay a fee for *guaranteed part yield* or *X components produced per month*. The manufacturer uses AI to dynamically manage the printer's operational parameters (e. g., print speed and material flow) to minimize material waste and maintain a consistently high quality, thereby mitigating the risk of poor performance.

Reality shows that switching from CapEx to OpEx is rarely a sufficient motivation for customers.

Trumpf's Pay per Part Model

Metal laser cutting machine provider *Trumpf* combined a technologically advanced machine operations strategy with financing and leasing capabilities to market its machines in an outcome-based way. However, the primary concern of their customers was not *output quality* but *machine utilization*, i. e., a financial risk that Trumpf could not address with the given approach. From a customer perspective, the OpEx model, with its financial overhead costs, just increased the price point; hence, the offering proved unsuccessful.

Outcome-based models are most successful when the provider can onboard customer risk and manage it more effectively using AI and IoT than the customer can. "Significantly better" can be anchored in specific domain expertise in a niche area (making it costly for customers to maintain that niche expertise themselves) or in access to data points across a broader customer base, enabling fleet learning and, in turn, better AI models to drive operational equipment efficiency.

Rhein-Ruhr-Express: Guaranteed Moved Passenger Volume

Siemens Mobility closed a first-of-a-kind deal with a group of mass-transport providers in the north of Germany: The "*Rhein-Ruhr-Express*" train was sold as a "guaranteed moved passenger volume" package. IoT sensor data from Siemens Mobility's installed base of trains helps optimize both train design and predictive maintenance procedures to support guaranteed passenger movements with as few train cars as possible [79].

6 Cultural Adoption Hurdles

6.1 Engineering Culture

> *"A good scientist is a person with original ideas. A good engineer is a person who makes a design that works with as few original ideas as possible." [80]*

This quote points to a notable adoption hurdle for AI, specifically in the art form of engineering: Engineers strive to master complexity, typically by reducing it. Changing LLM weights overnight, hallucinations, black box AI architectures or a lack of explainability, the idea that a plethora of AI agents produces a multi-disciplinary solution design and the perspective that debugging this solution design by tuning the agents' work is hindered by a lack of *reproducibility* – this is nightmare material for engineers as it substantially increases the complexity of their work and potentially even the complexity of solutions.

6.2 The Competence Penalty

A recent study identifies a *competence penalty* as a hidden cultural barrier to AI adoption in the workplace [81]. Research reveals that employees who utilize AI tools are often judged by peers as less competent and lazier, even if the technology helps them produce superior work. Unlike complex traditional software that signals expertise, user-friendly AI is frequently viewed as a "shortcut", leading colleagues to undervalue the user's actual skills. This social stigma creates a paradox in which the method of work is scrutinized more than the outcome. Consequently, workers may avoid adopting AI or conceal its usage to protect their professional reputations.

To overcome this, the study suggests that organizations must reframe AI not as a walking aid but as a specialized tool that requires skill to master. By shifting the focus from effort to outcomes, companies can help dismantle this bias and encourage effective AI integration.

7 Legal Hurdles

The use of AI in product design, product engineering, and production engineering is currently encumbered by jurisprudential uncertainty, specifically regarding *Intellectual Property* (IP) rights and liability frameworks.

7.1 IP Protection of AI-generated Outcomes

One primary impediment is the prevailing legal requirement that human authorship or inventorship be established to secure patents and copyrights (see Table 7.1). Consequently, AI-generated assets – ranging from optimized structural schematics to autonomous source code – risk failing to qualify for protection, potentially relegating proprietary innovations to the public domain. Furthermore, the opacity of "black box" algorithms complicates avoiding inadvertent infringement of third-party IP embedded in training datasets.

Table 7.1 National differences in IP protection of AI outcomes

	United States	European Union	United Kingdom
Copyrightability of AI Output	**Strictly Human-Centric.** The US Copyright Office (USCO) refuses registration for works created without significant human creative input. AI-generated content is generally in the public domain.	**Human-Centric** The "originality" standard requires a work to be the "author's own intellectual creation". Wholly AI-generated works generally lack the necessary human personality to qualify.	**Unique "Computer-Generated" Category** The UK is an outlier: the CDPA 1988 protects "computer-generated works" in which no human author exists. Authorship is assigned to the person who "undertook the arrangements" (e. g., the prompter/developer).
Patent Inventorship	**Humans Only** The Federal Circuit ruled that an "inventor" under the Patent Act must be a natural person. AI cannot be listed as an inventor.	**Humans Only** The European Patent Office (EPO) ruled that an inventor must have legal personality (i. e., be a human). Naming an AI as an inventor renders the application invalid.	**Humans Only** The UK Supreme Court unanimously ruled that an AI cannot be an inventor. The inventor must be a natural person.
Patent Eligibility of AI Inventions	**Subject Matter Eligibility** AI inventions face hurdles under the Alice/Mayo test: They must not be "abstract ideas" and must show a specific practical application or technical improvement.	**Technical Character** AI inventions are patentable if they solve a specific technical problem (e. g., image processing) rather than being purely abstract algorithms or business methods.	**Technical Contribution** As in the EU, software/AI is patentable if it provides a "technical contribution" beyond the computer itself or operates the computer in a new technical way.

Enterprises can deal with this along the following lines:

- Have humans modify the output sufficiently to flip it back so that it becomes 'a human invention'. This must be driven by awareness training and can potentially be monitored by technical means (e. g., source code scanning)
- Protect the production system as opposed to the output. This means that the system of data, AI pipelines, and prompts is protected rather than just the output.

Cogniwerk's Creative Record

The *Cogniwerk.ai* AI-assisted image creation platform (*cogniwerk.ai*) is built such that a human controls the creation pipeline, which is scripted or visually modelled as a sequence of image creation and modification steps (e. g., upload image, remove background, modify content, apply filters, etc.). The human designer remains the originator of the output, as they define and parameterize the pipeline. The essential output of the system is not just the final image but includes a 'creative record' that documents the workflow and any external AI components in an auditable and, to a certain extent, protectible way [82].

7.2 IP Rights on Training Data

IP rights regarding AI training data are a critical legal and strategic minefield. Unlike traditional software code, which is clearly copyrightable, the status of the insights derived from training data remains legally complex. In an industrial context, the core tension lies between the data creator (the machine operator) and the model creator (the solution provider).

If an AI model is trained on proprietary operational data from a factory, does the factory owner have a claim on the resulting algorithm? Without explicit contractual frameworks defining usage rights – specifically the right to use customer data to improve a global model – companies risk building "poisoned" assets that cannot be legally deployed to other clients, stifling commercial growth.

A "Fleet Learning" Business Model at Stake

An OEM develops a smart predictive maintenance service intended to be a scalable SaaS offering. The value proposition relies on "Fleet Learning" – using failure data from Customer A to prevent failures for Customer B. Customer A, a large chemical manufacturer, refuses to grant the OEM rights to use their operational data for any purpose other than servicing their specific machines. They regard their machine parameters as trade secrets and fear that improving the OEM's global model could indirectly help a competitor (Customer B) achieve higher uptime. Because the OEM cannot aggregate data to build a robust, generalizable model, it is forced to train bespoke, isolated models for each customer. The product fails to scale as a low-touch SaaS platform and instead becomes a high-cost consulting service, severely limiting revenue potential and market penetration.

7.3 IP Protection of AI Models

When AI solutions begin to scale as products, the question of how to protect them from use beyond the contractually agreed scope becomes unavoidable. A multi-layered approach combines technical measures with a contractual/legal framework. The technical measures comprise:

- *API-based access:* Instead of delivering the model file (weights and architecture) to the client, host it on a secure server and provide access via an API. This prevents the client or third parties from copying the underlying code. However, it can be a hard sell to industrial clients who require on-premises deployments for performance and/or confidentiality reasons.
- *Model watermarking*: This involves embedding a hidden, unique signal or "backdoor" into the model's behavior during training. If we suspect that someone has stolen our model, we can feed it a specific, secret input (a trigger) to determine whether it produces a predetermined output, thereby proving ownership [83].
- *Model extraction attack detection:* AI models could be copied using random sampling attacks. A copycat basically feeds random input data to the AI model, measures the output, and then uses both datasets to train a new AI model. This approach is limited to smaller models, such as an AI model for controlling a chemical process based on time-series data, and it circumvents the aforementioned *model watermarking* strategy. One countermeasure is to monitor input data so that random input does not trigger an alert that would inform a supervisor.
- *Confidential (AI) computing:* Confidential AI computing is an emerging security framework that applies confidential computing technologies to the AI lifecycle, ensuring cryptographically verifiable protection for data and models while they are in use. It leverages hardware-based *trusted execution environments* on specific CPUs and GPUs, enabling organizations to run AI against sensitive information without exposing either the AI or the data to cloud providers or other partners. However, confidential AI is not yet mainstream: key infrastructure, such as confidential VMs and GPUs, is still in the early-adopter phase rather than a widely deployed standard [84].

Noised Model Research

The *KI-Fogger* research project (6/2025–5/2028) develops innovative security techniques to protect AI models against unauthorized access and data extraction. By repurposing adversarial methods such as data poisoning and backdooring, researchers create "noised" models that produce meaningless results without proper authorization. Using multi-level encryption keys, the system keeps intellectual property securely in industrial environments and delivers precise outputs only to verified users.

Further information: *forschung-it-sicherheit-kommunikationssysteme.de/projekte/ki-fogger*.

Legal and other measures include:

- *Trade secrets:* Since algorithms are often complicated to patent, many companies treat their model weights and hyperparameters as trade secrets, which are legally protected in most jurisdictions [85]. However, this requires strict non-disclosure agreements and internal security protocols to clearly document the trade secret character of the information.
- *Terms of service:* Explicitly prohibit model extraction attacks (querying the API repeatedly to reconstruct the model) or reverse engineering in commercial contracts.
- *Patents:* While abstract algorithms are complicated to patent, specific applications of AI in an industrial process (e. g., "A method for controlling a gas turbine using a neural network to optimize fuel flow") can sometimes be patented [86].
- *Defensive publication:* Publishing some aspects of the research to establish 'prior art', preventing competitors from patenting the same techniques, while keeping the specific implementation details proprietary [87].

7.4 Liabilities

The primary legal challenge regarding generative AI is determining liability for copyright infringement at two levels [88]:

- *Input stage:* using protected works for model training; and
- *Output stage:* generating content that is substantially similar to existing works.

Since AI lacks legal personhood, courts are currently deciding whether the developer, the user, or both bear responsibility when an infringement occurs. Many platforms argue that AI training constitutes "fair use" or "transformative work", while creators maintain that unauthorized scraping violates their exclusive rights to reproduction and derivative works.

For enterprises, these risks are significant, as an enterprise may face litigation for using AI-generated logos, code, or marketing copy that inadvertently infringes a third party's intellectual property. However, it is essential to note that liability for copyright infringement can be avoided if specific contractual terms are in place to exclude it. For instance, many GenAI providers now offer IP indemnification clauses for their enterprise tiers, legally shifting the financial burden of potential infringement claims from the user to the developer.

Parallel to IP challenges there is the unsettled doctrine of *safety liability*: Unlike traditional deterministic engineering tools, AI models are probabilistic. In high-stakes industrial environments where software errors can lead to physical hazards, establishing a chain of causation for AI-induced failures remains legally ambiguous. Current product liability statutes struggle to apportion accountability among model developers, data curators, and deploying engineers when autonomous systems exhibit unforeseeable, emergent behaviors.

Until legislative bodies clarify the duty of care regarding probabilistic outputs and modernize IP statutes to accommodate non-human generation, industrial enterprises face uncapped exposure to litigation.

This legal vacuum acts as a substantial deterrent, forcing organizations to weigh the efficiency gains of automation against the existential risks of undefined accountability and unprotected assets.

Part III: from Ambition to Action

The journey from recognizing the potential of industrial AI to realizing tangible, scaled-up value is fraught with organizational, technical, and strategic challenges. Many companies falter not because of a lack of ambition, but because they lack a cohesive, practical starting point. Part III is designed as a helpful roadmap, moving beyond the "why" and diving deep into the "how":

- We begin by addressing the critical issues of *motivation and timing*, helping to ground our AI initiative soundly and to understand the time needed to mature.
- We then immediately tackle the most significant hurdle: establishing *access to industrial data*, ensuring that our models are fed with high-quality, relevant information.
- Success depends equally on human capital, so we detail strategies for securing *access to AI talent*, whether through hiring or upskilling.

The subsequent sections guide us through the technical and operational backbone:

- *Mastering AI Technology* and establishing rigorous *AI governance* to ensure models are trustworthy, compliant, and scalable.
- We explore the modern integration of workflows through *DevOps, DataOps,* and *MLOps*, the machine that keeps our models running effectively.

8 Motivation and Timing

Firstly, let's look at this top-down: Industry serves to fulfill humanity's consumption needs. While doing this, the industry's environmental footprint is substantial: the industrial sector is responsible for approximately 21% of global greenhouse gas emissions, primarily from heavy industries such as steel, cement, and chemical production. These industries require substantial energy, often derived from fossil fuels, thereby contributing to substantial CO_2 emissions [89].

In addition to the term Industry 4.0, Germans have coined the term 'enkel-fähiges Unternehmertum', which translates to "grandchild-compatible entrepreneurship". In other words, entrepreneurship that values saving our planet's resources so that our grandchildren have a world worth living in.

AI is a powerful tool for significantly reducing the industry's resource footprint: According to PWC, AI could cut 0.9 to 2.4 gigatons of CO_2 emissions by 2030 – which is equal to the combined yearly emissions of Australia, Canada, and Japan [90]. This is why we must start leveraging AI *now*.

Decarbonization across Complex Supply Chains

The "De:karb" research project by *Trumpf*, *Thyssen Materials*, and *Fraunhofer IPA* leverages AI-driven automation to transform how product carbon footprints are calculated across complex supply chains. By utilizing AI to harmonize disparate data and identify emissions hotspots, the system provides precise, real-time insights into a product's environmental impact. Combined with a secure blockchain-based "Carbon Ledger", these capabilities allow manufacturers to optimize decarbonization strategies and automate regulatory compliance. This intelligent approach ensures that companies can transparently manage CO_2 data while maintaining the highest levels of industrial competitiveness.

Many corporations view sustainability not just from a regulatory requirements perspective but also actively seek *Zero Defect Zero Waste* (ZDZW) strategies [191] and *zero defect manufacturing* [192] as differentiating factors. Achieving excellence in these domains requires waste and defect reduction considerations in the earliest design phases of products and production setups – again, an area where simulation and specifically *design space exploration* (see Section 20.2.2) unfold their impact.

Of course, this includes learning curves to master AI as a tool. Starting these learning curves, first experimenting, and finding, hiring, and training the right people are not matters for an individual use case-based ROI assessment. ROI assessments can help prioritize use cases later on, once AI core capabilities have been established. Table 8.1 provides an overview of AI initiative stages and their approximate durations.

Table 8.1 Learning curve phases and typical durations [91]

Stage	Focus/Activity	Duration	Key Challenge
Awareness & Experimentation (1)	Identifying key use cases (e. g., predictive maintenance pilot), building internal interest, and running initial proof of concepts.	6–12 months	Securing executive buy-in and a dedicated budget.
Active Adoption & Capability Building (2)	Formalizing successful PoCs in pilot projects, developing an initial AI strategy, and building a dedicated internal team (AI center of excellence).	1–2 years	Transitioning from isolated pilots to governed, repeatable, and scalable solutions.
Operationalization & Scaling (3)	Integrating AI models into core manufacturing processes (e. g., embedding AI agents into production workflows), establishing clear ROI metrics, and standardizing data governance.	1–2 years	Overcoming system integration complexity and maintaining high-quality model performance in a live industrial environment.
Transformation (4)	AI becomes a fundamental part of the business DNA, driving new products, redesigning entire business models, and achieving continuous, measurable strategic advantage.	Ongoing (3+ years)	Fostering a sustained AI-first culture and continuously adapting the workforce's skills.

Secondly, agility has become a mandatory capability for entrepreneurial survival. Whether due to the COVID-19 pandemic, geopolitical tensions that led to import tariffs, rare-earth supply challenges, or logistical nightmares caused by disruptions to maritime routes, our supply chains have become fragile. Saturated markets require fast responses to competitor moves.

Tesla's Agile Response to Supply Chain Disruption

While legacy automakers such as Ford and Volkswagen were forced to shut down factories because they couldn't source specific chips during the COVID supply chain crisis, Tesla's engineers took a radical approach: Within a matter of weeks, Tesla's software team validated 19 new controller variants. They took alternative, available semiconductors - some not initially intended for automotive use - and wrote entirely new code to make them compatible with their vehicles. Hence, Tesla gained market share.

Whether using supply chain analytics to understand microcontroller availability (see Section 20.3.3) or leveraging GenAI for software development (see Section 31.4), AI can become a powerful tool for addressing these challenges.

A McKinsey study [92] modeling the economic impact of AI predicts that *AI front-runners* could boost economic value by 122% by 2030, equating to roughly 6% annual growth in cash generation. These front-runners tend to dominate profits, potentially creating "superstar" companies and increasing market concentration.

Followers, accounting for 20–30% of firms by 2030, are more cautious adopters of AI and likely to experience moderate changes in cash flow. They benefit from spill-overs from the front-runners but also face competition from them, and eventually from other followers.

Laggards or nonadopters (60–70% of firms) risk losing approximately 23% of cash flow relative to current levels. Their delayed or non-existant investment in AI limits their revenues, often forcing them to cut costs and reduce investment.

According to McKinsey, late adopters and nonadopters are more likely than their peers to reduce employment and spending, reflecting how firms adapt to the threat of market exit in changing economic environments.

9 Access to Industrial Data

Access to data as a foundational capability ensures a steady, high-quality stream of information from across the operational value chain. This necessitates implementing scalable data ingestion pipelines, centralized data lakes, and a comprehensive data management strategy that addresses data quality, security, and accessibility. Without a robust, well-organized data foundation, even the most sophisticated algorithms become ineffective.

9.1 Soft Sensors

Soft sensors, also known as virtual sensors, are computational models that estimate hard-to-measure process variables using readily available data from existing instruments. Instead of installing costly or impractical physical sensors, soft sensors use statistical, machine-learning, or physics-based models to infer critical values such as temperature, viscosity, or emissions. In industry, they help to address the persistent challenge of poor data quality by filling measurement gaps, filtering noise, and validating inconsistent readings. By providing reliable, continuous estimates, soft sensors improve process monitoring, enable predictive maintenance, and support real-time optimization, ensuring that decisions are based on accurate, consistent operational data.

9.2 Data Standards

9.2.1 Open Platform Communication Unified Architecture

The *Open Platform Communication Unified* Architecture (OPC UA) is a machine-to-machine communication protocol for a secure and reliable data exchange in industrial automation [93]. It provides a standardized framework for machines from different vendors in order to communicate and add semantic context to data.

Harmonized Semantics for Injection Molding

The injection molding industry has achieved technical and semantic standardization, primarily through the efforts of EUROMAP (European Association for Plastics and Rubber Machinery Manufacturers). The key technical driver is the adoption of OPC UA. It is semantically realized through the EUROMAP Companion Specifications, specifically EUROMAP 77 (Injection Molding Machine to MES) and EUROMAP 82 series (Machine to Peripheral devices) [94].

9.2.2 Asset Administration Shell

The *Asset Administration Shell* (AAS) is a cornerstone technology that enables a seamless data exchange and interoperability in the evolving Industry 4.0 landscape. At its core, an AAS is the standardized digital representation, or Digital Twin (see Section 2.6.1), of an industrial asset – be it a physical component, a machine, a production line, or even a software service. An AAS is a universal, open interface that encapsulates all relevant information about an asset throughout its lifecycle, from design and manufacturing to operation and maintenance, and decommissioning.

The industrial sector has long grappled with heterogeneous systems, proprietary data formats, and a lack of standardized communication protocols. This fragmentation has historically hindered efficient data exchange, resulting in significant engineering overhead, costly integration projects, and limited agility to adapt to new market demands. The AAS addresses these critical issues by providing a standardized, semantic framework for describing and accessing asset information. It breaks down data silos by defining a common data language and structure, and enabling different systems, regardless of origin or technology, to understand and interact with one another's data.

Through its modular structure, composed of submodels, the AAS organizes specific aspects of an asset's data – such as technical specifications, maintenance history, energy consumption, and operational parameters – into easily accessible, understandable units. These submodels are defined by standardized templates, ensuring consistency across various manufacturers and industries. This standardization enables true plug-and-play, allowing new machines or components to be integrated into existing production environments with minimal configuration overhead.

9.2.3 The Digital Product Passport

The *Digital Product Passport* (DPP, also known as the *Digital Product Plate*) aims to encase extensive product data – such as manufacturing processes, maintenance records, component origin, and recyclability – in an accessible digital file [95]. A data carrier with a unique identifier link a physical item to its DPP – much like a license plate links a car to a registration database.

Regulations require that the data carrier be attached to the product (or to packaging/documentation if direct attachment is impractical), endure the product's normal use over time (typically ≥10 years), and provide easy access to meet diverse stakeholder needs. Candidate technologies include QR codes, barcodes, and RFID. QR codes and barcodes are low-cost and smartphone-readable but are vulnerable to wear and require a line of sight; RFID tags enable hidden, long-term, bulk, non-line-of-sight reading.

The *Battery Passport*, required from February 2027 under the EU Battery Regulation, is the first pilot of the DPP concept. It leverages the same digital infrastructure but with highly specific content, including mandatory data points on carbon footprint, material origin, and recyclability for all electric vehicles and industrial batteries.

9.2.4 NAMUR Open Architecture

In the process automation industry (e.g., chemicals and pharmaceuticals), NAMUR has developed standards, such as the *NAMUR Open Architecture* (NOA). NOA is designed to securely extract data for monitoring and optimization from traditional, closed process control systems without interfering with the core, safety-critical control loop (via a defined "second channel"). NOA leverages both OPC UA and the AAS.

9.2.5 Hermes and Gerber

HERMES is an open, modern, machine-to-machine communication standard for the electronics manufacturing industry. It is designed to replace outdated standards for *surface mount technology* (SMT) assembly lines, enabling seamless data exchange between machines from different vendors to improve efficiency and traceability. GERBER is the standard file format for PCB manufacturing and SMT assembly, defining copper layers, solder masks, silkscreens, and drill data to ensure precise communication between design software and fabrication equipment.

9.3 Synthetic Data

Synthetic Data is artificially generated data that mimics the statistical properties of real-world data. By using simulation or generative AI, engineers can generate vast amounts of realistic data to train AI models. Gartner predicts that synthetic data generation will surpass training AI models on real data by 2030 [96].

Synthetic data for industrial machine vision applications is an innovative field with significant momentum, as evidenced by numerous specialized startups, including Artificial Pixels, Green Matter AI, CVEDIA, bifrost.ai, and Idealworks. Table 9.1 lists key differences between real and synthetic data.

Table 9.1 Comparison of real and synthetic data usage

	Real Data	Synthetic Data
Definition	Actual data collected from real-world sources.	Data generated to simulate real-world data patterns.
Source	Collected directly from user interactions, transactions, or events.	Created through algorithms, simulations, or pattern generation.
Data Utility	Essential for production and insights requiring actual trends.	Effective for testing, model training, and simulations.
Data Protection	Can contain sensitive information, revealing trade secrets.	Can work with statistical methods (differential privacy) to camouflage trade secrets.
Accuracy	High, as it represents real events and interactions.	May approximate real data patterns but lacks true authenticity.
Acquisition Costs	Higher, often requiring data collection efforts and compliance. Data labeling for supervised learning is an additional overhead.	Generally lower, as it can be generated programmatically, including data labels for supervised learning.
Scalability	Limited by the availability and accessibility of real data.	Easily scalable, as it can be generated in large quantities.

Table 9.1 Comparison of real and synthetic data usage *(continued)*

	Real Data	Synthetic Data
Timing	Can only be harvested when a physical environment with sensors has been configured and is operational.	Digital Twins can generate data before the physical environment exists.
Bias and Representativeness	May contain biases reflective of actual populations and collection methods.	Potentially less biased if designed well.

Beyond generating numerous examples of rare failure events, synthetic data generation enables AI training to begin long before a physical product or factory exists, using data from a Digital Twin.

AI Model Ready for Production Line Start

When introducing new car models, a leading German car manufacturer struggled with lengthy pilot-production ramp-up times. A core issue was their machine vision quality control, which required time-consuming image capture and labeling to train the AI model on new parts. *Inpro* countered this with a custom *CAD-to-CAQ pipeline*. They used CAD files of the latest parts and sensors to render them realistically. An AI algorithm then digitally captured known fault patterns from parts of older car models and projected them onto the synthetic images. This approach enables the deployment of high-quality AI models for quality inspection on day 1 of a new production line, delivering a high issue-recognition rate from the outset.

High-fidelity synthetic data for industrial applications is primarily generated by generative deep learning models. The most effective approach is AI-generated (sample-based) synthesis, which requires a real dataset as input to train a generative model, such as a *Variational Autoencoder* or a *Generative Adversarial Network* (GAN) [97]. GANs operate using two competing neural networks: A generator that creates synthetic samples and a discriminator that iteratively assesses their realism. This adversarial training ensures that the final synthetic data captures the nuanced patterns and statistical distributions required for robust model training [98].

This methodology contrasts sharply with *simulation data*, which models specific real-world processes through pre-defined mathematical equations and physics engines (e. g., atmospheric models or vehicle behavior rules). While simulation data is valuable for controlled-scenario testing, it models the underlying physics rather than the observed statistical output of a system, making generative AI essential for systems whose internal physics are unknown or prohibitively complex to model.

Simple mock data, generated by rules or templates, generally lacks the statistical grounding necessary for complex industrial AI applications.

Industrial synthesis faces distinct challenges across data modalities. For physical systems, the synthesis of sensor data (time-series readings for pressure, vibration, or temperature) is critical. The difficulty here lies not only in the scarcity of rare failure events but in accurately replicating the rich, relational structure and multivariate correlations present in highly structured data. If the generative model oversimplifies these precise temporal and correlational shifts – often evaluated using metrics like mutual information or correlation preservation – the resulting AI models will inevitably overfit the synthetic patterns and perform poorly under complex, real-world conditions [99]. Conversely, the challenge in rendering realistic images for computer vision applications (such as defect detection or robotic control) centers on scale and annotation efficiency [100].

3D simulation tools (several from the gaming industry, such as *Unreal Engine* and *Blender*) generate vast, automatically labeled environments, optimized for feature representation learning rather than for capturing precise statistical correlations among low-dimensional variables. Workflows and scripts help with required d*omain randomization*, generating a statistically sufficient number of environment variants, for example, different weather conditions for computer vision of an autonomous truck or different lighting conditions for every hour of a day for an AI model spotting quality defects in production.

Post-processing pipelines to advance image generation from *photo-realistic images* (perceived by humans as realistic) to *sensor-realistic images* (tuned to be best detected by cameras and AI models).

Solution Brief 9-1: Training Data Generation for Safe and Reliable AI (Rabbit AI)

Challenge

- Developing reliable 3D perception, action, and gesture recognition on low-end hardware.
- Overcoming limitations in XR or in-cabin sensing solution development.
- Addressing discovered data gaps quickly with new scenarios.

Solution

- Device-specific ground truth accelerating the algorithms' learning process, allowing them to specialize efficiently on specific hardware.
- Ultrarealistic 3D scanning of humans with dense depth and body poses of 1 mm precision.
- High scenario variance and throughput.
- Capturing complex, dynamic scenarios with innovative recording technology.

Benefits

- Creates more scope for optimization and reduces hardware costs.
- Enables quicker inference times and shorter development cycles.
- Increases overall inference quality and system reliability.
- Accelerates system integration and prototyping to save time.

Customers: Diverse automotive customers

Provider: Rabbit AI, Heidelberg, Germany; *rabbitai.de*

9.4 Reinforcement Learning

Reinforcement Learning (RL) significantly reduces the need for data by using simulation results (e. g., the speed and energy consumption of a machining process) as penalty and reward functions to train an AI model (see related Section 2.7.1.7). In other words, RL skips the intermediate step of synthetic data generation (see Section 9.3) and ties AI model training and simulation together.

Solution Brief 9-2: Reinforcement Learning for Motion Control (Siemens)

Challenge

- Traditional, low-level motion control solutions work with simple logic such as 'electric drive on/off'. From an efficiency perspective (energy consumption and equipment wear & tear), this is sub-optimal.
- Certain motion control challenges are too complex to be solved with traditional PLC programming.

Solution "AI Motion"

- *AI Motion* reinforcement learning and simulation framework tailored explicitly to optimization problems of motion control systems, for example, conveyor belts.
- Resulting models can be compiled to C code and, leveraging Siemens' TIA Portal, be deployed on PLCs to run synchronously within the PLC cycles.

Benefits

- Increased machine throughput while reducing mechanical wear & tear and energy consumption.
- Enables the implementation of motion control solutions for programmatically unvolvable challenges (see [101]).

Customers: Sollas, Valvan

Provider: Siemens, Munich/Berlin, Germany; *siemens.com*

9.5 Physics-Informed Neural Networks

Physics-Informed Neural Networks (PINNs) combine the strengths of ML with the fundamental laws of physics, see Section ABC.

Because PINNs require less training data, they can still work well even with limited information. Imagine an oil pipeline with only a few sensors installed over hundreds of miles; a PINN can combine those sparse measurements with fluid-dynamics equations to estimate conditions everywhere in the system. Similarly, in aerospace design, a PINN can simulate airflow around a new aircraft shape without the heavy computational power required by traditional simulations, which can take days or even weeks.

Another strength is that PINNs can be used to solve "inverse problems" – that is, working backwards from observed outcomes to figure out hidden causes. For example, engineers could use them to estimate a material's strength or the location of a pipe leak based on a small number of measurements.

9.6 Federated Learning

Federated Learning (see Section 2.7.1.8) provides a mechanism for establishing an AI-based self-optimizing system while leaving raw data and related trade secrets in their local environments. While mastering FL is complex, its setup effectively addresses the IP and trade secret concerns described in Section 4.6.1.

Solution Brief 9-3: Federated Learning Platform (katulu)

Challenge

- Sensitive industrial data is siloed due to compliance (e. g., GDPR, export control).
- Centralizing data for AI training is costly, risky, and legally impossible globally.
- Local factory data is insufficient alone to build highly accurate AI models.

Solution

- Federated Learning trains a single AI model across decentralized data sources.
- Raw data remains local while only encrypted model updates are shared.
- Provides Federated Data Pipelines to harmonize data across different sites.
- Their platform is ISO 27001 certified and includes differential privacy mechanisms.

Benefits

- Enables cross-site learning and robust models without compromising privacy.
- Accelerates AI deployment by eliminating costly data transfer and red tape.
- Reduces costs and deployment time compared to centralized cloud solutions.
- Achieves higher model performance and better first-pass yields (e. g., Siemens).

Provider: Katulu, Hamburg, Germany; *katulu.io*

9.7 Data Spaces

To enable collaboration along supply chains, new data ecosystems are being built on the principles of data sovereignty and trust. *Data Space* initiatives such as *Catena-X* (primarily for the automotive industry) and *Factory-X* (for broader manufacturing) are creating decentralized data spaces. Based on European standards such as Gaia-X, they enable a company to make specific data points available to its partners (e. g., a supplier sharing the carbon footprint of a component with a manufacturer) without relinquishing control or ownership of the data. These ecosystems can provide a secure foundation for training AI models on data from multiple companies, thereby optimizing entire value chains (see Table 9.2).

The RO-X initiative (Robotics-and-AI eXchange) is a German/European ecosystem project that aims to unify robotics, AI, and the related data exchange to drive industrial innovation. RO-X seeks to do more than develop individual robotic systems: it is building a decentralized data and services ecosystem that supports the entire life cycle of AI-based robotics, from development and commissioning through operation and maintenance to continuous improvement. Central tenets of RO-X include data sovereignty, sustainability, and energy efficiency.

To a certain extent, these trusted data access platforms are a response to fairly new European legislation: The *EU Data Act* establishes a legal framework that grants customers and third-party service providers the right of access to the vast amounts of data generated by connected industrial machines and IoT devices. By requiring manufacturers to design products for data portability, it fosters a competitive secondary market for data-driven services such as predictive maintenance and advanced operational analytics.

Table 9.2 Examples for industrial data spaces initiatives

Data Space/URL	Goal	Key Participants
Gaia-X *gaia-x.eu*	Digital sovereignty ecosystem, where data is shared and made available in a trustworthy environment	Airbus, Siemens, SAP, Fraunhofer ISST, Orange, OVHcloud, EDF, BMW, Volkswagen, Bosch, Continental, Valeo, etc.
Catena-X *catena-x.net*	Global, trusted, and collaborative data ecosystem for the automotive industry	>100, including BMW, Daimler, Magna, Volkswagen, Volvo, BASF, Siemens, Faurecia, Grammer, Ford, etc.
RO-X *project-rox.ai*	Building a digital ecosystem for scalable, AI-based robotic solutions in industry.	ABB, Siemens AG, Boehringer Ingelheim, Dürr, Rheinmetall, Schunk, Würth, T-Systems, etc.
Semiconductor-X *semiconductor-x.com*	Building resilient semiconductor supply chains	Fraunhofer, Intel, Infineon, Merck, Siemens, Bosch, Merck, etc.

Data Space/URL	Goal	Key Participants
Aerospace-X *aerospace-x.net*	Aims to digitalize supply chains in the aerospace industry	Airbus, Diehl, GKN, MTU, Rolls-Royce, Thyssenkrupp, Liebherr, etc.
Cofinity-X *cofinity-x.com*	Provider of technology for the secure, sovereign exchange of data between industry participants, such as Catena-X.	Joint venture of BASF, BMW, Henkel, Mercedes-Benz, SAP, Schaeffler, Siemens, T-Systems, VW, and ZF, etc.
Factory-X *factory-x.org*	Digital ecosystem for factory outfitters and operators, built on the foundations of Catena-X and the principles of Platform Industrie 4.0	Siemens, SAP, Trumpf, DMG Mori, Festo, Phoenix Contact, Schunk, Lenze, Uhlmann Group, Wittenstein, Sick, etc.

9.8 Public and Commercial Datasets

Leveraging external datasets to enrich internal data can be a valid option, but the industrial world is short of publicly – and even commercially – available datasets. Table 9.3 lists several of them. A further valuable overview of publicly available degradation datasets for condition monitoring of engineered systems is provided in [102].

Table 9.3 Examples for curated public and commercial datasets

Dataset Name/URL	Description
Lens.org *lens.org*	Global, open platform for searching and analyzing patent and scholarly metadata.
CAMPUS® *campusplastics.com*	Material information system for the plastics industry.
Material-Digital *material-digital.de*	German initiative for cross-supply chain material information, primarily metals.
OpenAlex *openalex.org*	Research paper database with 250 million+ scholarly documents across application fields.
DatenservicePlus *datenservice.plus*	Database of 57 million buildings in Germany for insurance, real estate, and banking use cases.
Synthetic Object Recognition Dataset for Industries (SORDI) *sordi.ai*	Set of synthetic images of production equipment from automotive shop floors.

Table 9.3 Examples for curated public and commercial datasets *(continued)*

Dataset Name/URL	Description
Personal Protection Equipment *universe.roboflow.com/perso-nal-protective-equipment*	A community-driven repository of computer vision datasets for PPE detection.
MVTec anomaly detection dataset *mvtec.com/company/research/datasets/mvtec-ad*	5000 annotated high-resolution pictures for anomaly detection.
ABC Dataset *deep-geometry.github.io/abc-dataset*	A 1,000,000 CAD model dataset for geometric deep learning.
Z2Data *z2data.com*	1 billion+ electronic parts: technical information and supply chain-related data points.
A2mac1 *a2mac1.com*	Automotive benchmarking database with BOMs and scores for 1,100+ vehicle models.
CADENAS *cadenas.de*	Commercial provider of parts catalogs for standard mechanical – and, to a limited extent, electrical and electronic – parts with detailed material master data information, including CAD files.
Open Corporates *opencorporates.com*	Curated database with >200,000,000 company records, the macthing master data, and information on how they are related.

10 Access to AI Talent

This data-centric approach must be complemented by a strategic Access to Talent that encompasses not only data scientists and machine learning engineers but also domain experts who can bridge the gap between AI model outputs and real-world industrial applications. Cultivating or acquiring this talent is critical for translating business challenges into solvable AI problems and for interpreting results that drive meaningful operational change.

10.1 Hiring and Retaining AI Talent

The rapid proliferation of AI has created an intensely competitive landscape for specialized talent, presenting organizations with distinct acquisition challenges. The primary impediment lies in the acute scarcity of professionals with the ideal industrial skill mix: experienced MLOps engineers, AI architects, and domain-specific data scientists who can bridge deep theoretical knowledge with the practical realities of industrial deployment.

Solution Brief 10-1: AI Top Talent Tracking (Zeki Data)

Challenge

- Identification of top AI talent with the ability to scale AI solutions effectively.

Solution

- Identification of top talent from 30,000 data sources such as professional networks, patent databases, startup-databases, code repositories, and award listings.
- Tracking of 800,000 AI talents globally (outside of China) across all aspects of AI software, hardware, and compute.
- Analysis of levels of performance and teamwork, career path, influence, reputation, and evolving skills.

Solution Brief 10-1: AI Top Talent Tracking (Zeki Data) ***(continued)***

Benefits

- Companies that select talents with high Zeki scores achieve a 100% increase in innovation compared to their competitors.
- Recruiters use Zeki to source the best top AI talents directly, particularly those who are not actively on the market.
- Investors use Zeki to spot opportunities ahead of the market.

Customers: Leading AI labs, investment funds

Provider: Zeki Data, London, Great Britain; *zekidata.com*

In addition to this, the market commands exceptional compensation packages. Traditional industrial enterprises often find themselves structurally unable to compete with the liquidity and salary bands of hyperscaler technology operations. To overcome these structural disadvantages, employers must articulate a value proposition that extends beyond monetary compensation. They must highlight the tangible impact of the role on core business goals, offering access to unique, proprietary datasets and the opportunity to solve physical-world problems – factors often more intellectually compelling to top-tier talent than salary alone.

Global Mobility as a Differentiator

The internal audit organization of Siemens faced a persistent need to recruit high-caliber data analysts within a corporate salary structure that precluded outbidding Big Tech competitors. To counter this, management leveraged its global footprint to create a unique "Grow & Develop" model. Because the department managed headcount at the global level rather than locally, they could offer international rotation programs to high-performing analysts. The prospect of "experiencing the world" through professional rotation became a powerful non-monetary asset, effectively attracting younger, ambitious talent who prioritized global exposure over immediate salary maximization.

While acquiring AI talent is difficult, retaining highly specialized AI talent is often the more arduous task. The market is liquid, and external offers to poach top performers are constant. However, the primary driver of attrition in the industrial sector is rarely compensation; instead, it is professional stagnation and a lack of purpose.

AI professionals are prone to rapid disengagement if they are relegated to the role of "data janitor" – spending most of their time cleaning unstructured data, fighting brownfield connectivity issues, or maintaining legacy models. Equally damaging is the assignment to science experiments – proof of concepts that never scale to production. Burnout is a significant risk, driven not only by workload but also by the friction of productionizing complex pipelines in rigid OT environments without adequate support.

Procter & Gamble's Scaling Partnership

Procter & Gamble (P&G) partnered with *Siemens* to scale AI across their 100+ factories globally. To maintain morale and focus among their data scientists, P&G had Siemens manage IT/OT integration, freeing their internal AI team to concentrate on model development and innovation.

To mitigate attrition, industrial organizations must cultivate an internal environment that is intellectually stickier than the external market. Best practices center on three pillars:

- *Infrastructure and continuous learning:* Top talent requires top-tier tools. Teams must have dedicated budgets and time allocations for upskilling in novel architectures. They need access to modern infrastructure – including the latest GPU compute resources and enterprise-grade MLOps platforms – to efficiently productize their work. Denying a data scientist appropriate computing power is the industrial equivalent of asking a master carpenter to work with dull tools.
- *Critical mass and community:* Organizations must ensure that individual data scientists are not isolated. A lone data scientist embedded in a traditional engineering unit often suffers from professional isolation. To counter this, companies should create "nuclei" of competence – centralized AI labs or centers of excellence – where practitioners can collaborate with peers. Strategically locating these labs in innovation hubs or university campuses can further bridge the gap between academic theory and industrial application.
- *Impact and domain ownership:* Finally, leadership must shift the focus from task execution to domain ownership. Engineers and scientists should be given end-to-end responsibility for specific business domains and be rewarded based on the value their models deliver. This encourages "intrapreneurship" and loyalty. It is vital to instill the understanding that in the industrial sector, there is no excellence in AI without excellence in the use case. Therefore, a data scientist's professional growth is inextricably linked to their ability to anchor their mathematical skills within the realities of the industrial domain.

10.2 Employee AI Literacy

However, the challenge runs deeper than a simple lack of specialists. To truly succeed, an industrial organization needs more than a small, isolated team of AI experts. It requires a broad upskilling of the existing workforce. Mechanical engineers need to understand how to work with AI-driven design tools. Plant managers need to interpret data from predictive maintenance systems. The entire organization, from the shop floor to the executive suite, must become AI-literate. Notably, some AI regulations, such as the EU AI Act, require workforce AI literacy training.

This is a massive challenge in training and organizational change. Companies must invest in continuous education, build new career paths, and foster a culture that embraces data-driven decision-making. The long-term winners will not be those who hire the most expensive data scientists, but those who successfully elevate the capabilities of their entire workforce.

Solution Brief 10-2: AI Literacy Trainings for Workplaces (MinnaLearn)

Challenge

- Workforce lacks practical AI literacy for safe, effective use.
- Need to scale AI adoption while managing internal risk quickly.
- Compliance with new AI regulations such as the EU AI Act is mandatory.
- Generic online learning fails to drive actionable business results.

Solution

- Offers structured, expert-led training programs, like "Get AI Ready".
- Focuses on hands-on skills such as high-quality AI prompting.
- Content is continuously updated to reflect the latest tools and legislation.
- Courses are LMS-ready, customizable, and embedded with company policies

Benefits

- Ensures organization-wide compliance with external regulatory frameworks.
- Mitigates AI risk by teaching responsible use and hallucination limits.
- Accelerates effective AI tool adoption and inspires immediate action.
- Boosts employee confidence and curiosity toward emerging technologies.

Customers: AI Reactor, Diversidays, groupm, Johnson & Johnson

Provider: MinnaLearn, Helsinki, Finland; *minnalearn.com*

11 Mastering AI Technology

Alongside human capital, enterprises need effective Access to AI Technology, which involves navigating the complex landscape of off the shelf AI solutions, open-source frameworks, and custom-built platforms. This requires a discerning approach to technology selection, prioritizing tools that align with the enterprise's specific operational needs and existing IT infrastructure while remaining flexible enough to adapt to future advancements.

11.1 Make vs. Buy

Implementing AI in an industrial enterprise is not a monolithic IT project – it is a portfolio of strategic decisions. The most critical of these is the *make versus buy* choice. This is not merely a procurement question but a fundamental determination of a company's future competitive posture. The decision rests on a single, binary distinction: Efficiency versus Differentiation.

- *Efficiency:* Are we automating a standard process (e.g., invoice processing, basic demand forecasting) that our competitors also perform? If so, we need *speed and standardization.*
- *Differentiation:* Are we optimizing a unique production process or a proprietary product feature that defines your market edge? If so, we need *control and exclusivity.*

Treating AI as a commodity to be bought off-the-shelf for everything leads to competitive parity – we are only as good as the vendor's roadmap allows. Conversely, trying to build everything in-house leads to technical bankruptcy – drowning in maintenance debt for systems that could have been rented for a fraction of the cost.

11.1.1 Speed and Semantics

When the process is standard, the data is structured, and the goal is operational efficiency, a BUY strategy plays out its strengths. For functions such as Finance, HR, and supply chain planning, established software vendors (SAP, Salesforce, Oracle) offer Semantic Context as a decisive advantage. A generic AI model does not know what an invoice or a maintenance work order is. Vendor-embedded AI comes pre-trained on these definitions. It understands the data structure of our ERP or CRM out of the box, eliminating the expensive, multi-year data engineering projects required to teach an in-house model these basics.

Buying vendor-embedded AI for standard processes accelerates time-to-value from years to weeks. It allows an organization's scarce engineering talent to focus on core production challenges rather than reinventing the wheel for back-office automation.

11.1.2 Access to External Data and Fleet Learning

Access to and integration with external data is a second major reason for the BUY option. Let us consider a platform that supports ideation and research, with analytics on venture capital spending, patent activity, and market-forecast data (see Section 14.1). We can easily agree that this has the potential to become a differentiator. The effort to obtain access to the required data sources and to curate them on an ongoing basis clearly suggests a BUY strategy. Building this internally is rarely justifiable.

A credible approach to fleet learning is a similar pattern. Let's use *predictive maintenance* as an example: An AI model provider (e. g., Siemens, Rockwell, PTC) has set up a system that feeds intelligence from a broad, cross-company fleet of machines. For standard assets such as motors, pumps, and drives, pre-trained models promptly and accurately detect issues, including bearing faults. There is no ROI in training a proprietary model to identify a broken bearing; most likely, we would not be able to obtain suitable data at the required scale.

11.1.3 Differentiation and the Digital Thread

If the process is unique, the data is proprietary, and the goal is a defensible competitive advantage, let's consider a MAKE approach. If a factory employs a unique, patented chemical process or a custom-designed assembly line, a standard vendor model will be ineffective. It cannot optimize what it has not seen. In these scenarios, the unfair advantage is proprietary data – the specific sensor readings, quality logs, and design parameters that only we possess. To leverage this, we must build the models ourselves.

Example: Detecting microscopic defects in a novel composite material requires a model trained specifically for quality inspection on our defect library.

If the secret source of our market success is not a specific product component (think of a recipe) or task (think of a unique way of forging high-precision bearings) but 'process DNA', an AI MAKE approach will group around a *Digital Thread* – a continuous flow of data linking product design to production engineering and execution (see Section 2.6.4). By training custom algorithms on this unified dataset, we create IP that competitors cannot replicate by simply buying a software license.

Controlling the thermal gradients in a proprietary 3D printing process requires an AI agent trained via Reinforcement Learning on our specific machine physics, potentially linking AI model inputs even to the 3D design and additive CAM for feature recognition.

Proprietary AI models turn unique operational complexity into a barrier to entry. If we outsource the core algorithm of a differentiating process, we are essentially outsourcing a competitive advantage.

11.1.4 Hybrid Approaches

For most mature industrial players, the world is not just black and white, and the following hybrid options evolve (see Figure 11.1):

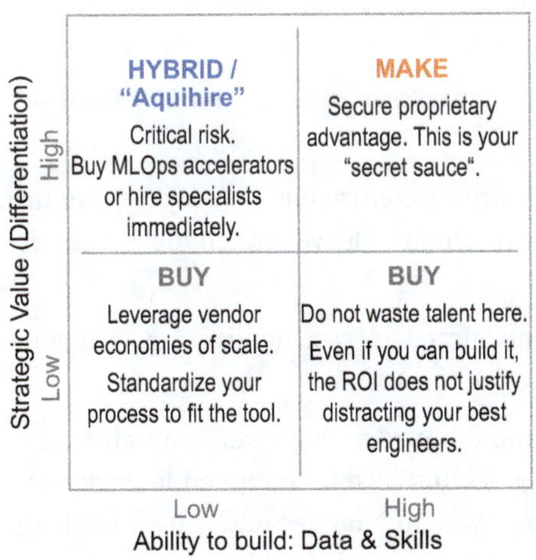

Figure 11.1 Decision matrix Buy vs. Make

Buy the platform, build the brain: This tactical option accelerates AI deployments by a BUY approach to the infrastructure: We do not build our own versioning tools, model registries, or deployment pipelines. Instead, licensing an industrial-grade MLOps platform helps us handle the "plumbing" while we use that rented infrastructure to build and host our proprietary models. This approach mitigates the risk of technical debt while preserving data sovereignty.

Build investment ties with the AI model provider: If we choose a BUY option for fast access to specific external capabilities and the AI deployment area is strategically important, we can consider partnering with a provider that is open to a strategic investment. By doing so, we can tie their capabilities to our strategic goals – at least to a certain extent.

G+D's Investment in Blockbrain

Giesecke+Devrient, a leading provider of security services and applications, invested in *Blockbrain*, a startup specializing in enterprise-grade, LLM-driven knowledge management solutions. Knowledge management is a key discipline in the security application space, as the complexity of threats and attacks against secure systems continues to rise [103].

11.2 Open Source vs. Commercial LLMs

The decision between Open Source and commercial models has evolved into a four-point spectrum of control, balancing *reasoning capability* against *sovereignty*:

- *Public Commercial API:* Maximum speed, minimum privacy (e. g., ChatGPT via web). See Section 11.2.1.
- *Private Commercial Environment:* High reasoning, contractual privacy (e. g., Azure OpenAI), and, to a certain extent, decoupling from model weight changes. See Section 11.2.2.
- *Managed Open Source:* Open weights, outsourced infrastructure (e. g., Hugging Face Endpoints, Databricks Mosaic AI). See Section 11.2.3.
- *Self-Hosted Open Source:* Maximum operational burden, however, maximum sovereignty, both from a data perspective (e. g., Llama 3[1]) on air-gapped factory servers) and from a stability perspective (model weight changes under own control). See Section 11.2.4.

[1] Technically, Llama 3 is not an open-source but an open-access model.

Our enterprise architecture will likely be "polyglot": We will use all four approaches depending on the risk profile of the specific use case (e.g., writing a marketing email vs. analyzing the root cause of a turbine failure). The mature industrial AI strategy is not about choosing a single model; it is about proper routing. An "AI Gateway" should sit between our users and the models, automatically routing a generic coding question to a *public commercial API*, a contract review to a *private commercial instance*, and a shop-floor defect detection task to a *self-hosted edge device*. Whether we build our own models or buy them, one risk remains constant: an unmanaged model is a liability. Once we have acquired the technology, we must control it. This is the domain of *AI governance* (see Section 12).

11.2.1 Public Commercial API

This is the standard consumption model (e.g., calling the OpenAI API directly). It provides the latest "Frontier Model" intelligence but exposes the organization to data-use policies that may permit vendors to train on its data. We use this deployment option for low-risk, high-variability tasks in which data are non-sensitive.

- *Risk:* Data leakage and model drift (vendor updates weights without notice).
- *Best Use:* Creative writing, coding assistance (generic), summarizing public news.

11.2.2 Private Commercial Environment

This approach involves deploying a commercial model (e.g., GPT-4 or Gemini) within a dedicated enterprise cloud perimeter, such as the Microsoft Azure OpenAI Service or AWS Bedrock.

- *Contractual zero-retention:* Unlike public APIs, these services offer enterprise agreements (including HIPAA/GDPR compliance) guaranteeing that our prompts are not used to train the vendor's base model.
- *VPC peering:* The traffic moves through private network backbones, not the open internet, reducing latency and the attack surface.
- *Stability:* We can often pin a model version (e.g., "GPT-4-0613") for a set period, preventing the drift that breaks industrial workflows. However, we still do not own the model weights. If the vendor deprecates the model, we are forced to migrate.
- The clear contractual relationship between an enterprise-grade provider and a customer typically includes the contractual *deflection of the 3rd party copyright litigation risk.*

11.2.3 Managed Open Source

This approach uses managed service providers such as Hugging Face Inference Endpoints, Databricks Mosaic AI, or Anyscale. We select an open-source model (e. g., Llama 3 or Mistral), and the provider manages GPU provisioning, auto-scaling, and driver updates.

- *MLOps abstraction:* We benefit from open-source (weight transparency, no vendor lock-in on the logic) without needing a team of Kubernetes engineers to manage GPU clusters.
- *Portability:* Since we are using standard open weights, we can move the model from one managed provider to another (or to on-premise) if pricing changes.
- *Fine-tuning agility:* These platforms often provide simplified pipelines for fine-tuning open models on proprietary data without managing the underlying training infrastructure.
- Naturally, we would pay a premium on top of the raw compute costs for the management layer.

11.2.4 Self-Hosted Open Source

This involves running open weights on our own metal – either in a private data center or on an edge device.

- *Air-gapped security:* The only option for defense-regulated data, classified IP, or safety-critical loops where internet connectivity is a liability.
- *Total immutability:* We control the exact hash of the model weights forever.
- *AI copyright litigation:* Using open-source models in a self-hosted mode does not provide any opportunity to mitigate the risk of third-party copyright litigation related to data used to train the model or to its potential outputs.

12 AI Governance

Whether at the international, intra-national, industry, or corporate level, *AI governance* can be defined as the system of rules, policies, institutions, and mechanisms used to steer the development, deployment, operation, and use of AI technologies.

The rapid ascent of AI, particularly GenAI, has led to an immediate, widespread, and largely unvetted deployment across different industries. Its momentum has fundamentally outpaced traditional legislative and regulatory cycles, resulting in significant delays in implementing adequate AI Governance. Legislators struggle to define, assess, and create effective, durable policies for complex technologies that evolve monthly. This *oversight gap* means that powerful AI models are deployed without clear, standardized rules governing safety, transparency, bias mitigation, and legal accountability, particularly given the multifaceted issues surrounding intellectual property protection and copyright.

While policy discussions center on rising societal risks such as deepfakes and mass misinformation, an AI system that miscalculates stress tolerance in a bridge construction project or misroutes chemicals in a plant can have catastrophic real-world consequences. This makes robust governance – including human-in-the-loop oversight, detailed audit trails, and formal risk assessments – *a foundational requirement* for industrial AI adoption, not an afterthought.

Relevant (inter)national and industry-level approaches to laws and regulations are outlined in Section 2.4.3. This chapter continues with several ingredients of an enterprise-level AI Governance setup:

- AI governance begins with clearly defined *AI guardrails*: technical and policy-based boundaries that ensure AI systems operate ethically, legally, and within acceptable risk thresholds.
- *AI literacy and risk awareness:* AI literacy training is an instrumental component of any effective AI governance setup, ensuring that employees across all depart-

ments understand the fundamental capabilities, risks, and ethical principles of the technology. These programs empower staff, from data scientists to executive leadership, to identify potential issues, such as algorithmic bias and data privacy violations, inherent in the AI models they deploy or use. By standardizing knowledge, AI literacy training reduces shadow AI adoption and ensures that human judgment remains properly integrated into AI-driven industrial workflows.

- *AI ethics committees and review boards:* An AI ethics committee in an industrial enterprise provides oversight for the responsible development and deployment of AI systems, ensuring they align with human values, regulatory compliance, and organizational safety standards. Potential participants typically include the Chief Data Officer, the Chief Legal Officer, the Head of Engineering or AI Development, representatives from Human Resources, and representatives from the relevant business unit or field experts. Their function is to proactively review AI projects for issues such as algorithmic bias, data security, and systemic risk before they affect critical operations or physical processes.
- *AI component registry:* One vital governance requirement is the AI component registry, a central inventory that catalogs every model, dataset, and pipeline used in production. This registry must document key metadata, including the model's purpose, risk classification, training data lineage, version history, and ownership.
- *AI risk management frameworks:* The AI component registry is the foundational tool that enables *systematic AI risk assessments* that categorize solutions based on potential impact (e. g., high-risk for autonomous control vs. low-risk for back-office forecasting). These assessments drive the level of scrutiny and required governance controls.
- *MLOps procedures and practices:* MLOps practices are instrumental for proper AI governance because they enforce standardized, auditable, and repeatable pipelines for the entire AI lifecycle, from data preparation to model deployment. By ensuring that models are version-controlled, tested for performance and bias, and monitored in production, MLOps provides the transparency and accountability necessary for regulatory compliance and ethical standards.
- The *capability to audit:* Finally, the organization needs robust capabilities to audit AI development and deployment. Auditability ensures that the entire model lifecycle – from data preparation and training to deployment and drift monitoring – is transparent and traceable. This involves capturing comprehensive logs, using *Explainable AI* techniques to interpret high-risk decisions, and establishing defined governance gates (Go/No-Go decisions) before a model is deployed.

IBM's failed attempt to disrupt the healthcare industry with its *Watson* for Oncology offering may illustrate a lack of AI governance, explainability, and rigid data-validation protocols.

Solution Brief 12-1: AI Governance and Testing Platform (Calvin Risk)

Challenge

- AI models are often "black boxes" that lead to unpredictable behavior.
- Companies struggle to meet the requirements of the EU AI Act.
- Traditional risk assessments are slow, inconsistent, and difficult to scale.
- Organizations struggle to quantify the potential financial impact of AI failures.

Solution

- Automated Testing: Standardized quantitative metrics to evaluate model performance, robustness, fairness, and safety.
- A central inventory provides a single source of truth for all AI assets.
- Calculating value at risk translates technical model risks into business metrics.
- Flexible workflows and digitalized questionnaires align AI development with internal policies.

Benefits

- Automated validation reduces testing efforts by 50%, accelerates AI time-to-market.
- Seamlessly ensures compliance with the EU AI Act through automated evidence management.
- Clear dashboards provide executives with transparent, evidence-based insights for confident decision-making.
- Proactive identification of ethical and technical vulnerabilities before they lead to reputational damage.

Customers: Primarily financial services enterprises

Provider: Calvin Risk, Zurich, Switzerland; *calvin-risk.com*

13 ML Operations

Finally, to move beyond pilot projects to enterprise-wide implementation, an organization must master the capability to operate AI (*Machine Learning Operations*, MLOps). This is the operational engine that handles the continuous lifecycle of AI models, from deployment and monitoring to retraining and version control. MLOps ensures that models remain accurate and reliable in dynamic industrial environments, providing the scalability and resilience needed for AI to become a core, value-generating asset rather than a fragmented set of experiments.

To avoid confusion: *AIOps*, as a term, typically refers to AI used to operate large IT environments ("AI for IT Operations"), such as event correlation and automated runbook scripts to manage a server farm. Refer to Section 31.1.2 for more insights into AIOps.

MLOps can be seen as an extension of the DevOps paradigm, developed by leading software companies over the last two decades. *Data operations* (see Section 13.2) is another key component of MLOps.

13.1 DevOps

DevOps is both a movement and a methodology that bridges the traditional divide between software development (Dev) and IT operations (Ops). Through collaboration and shared responsibility, DevOps aims to shorten the systems development life cycle while ensuring high software quality and continuous delivery. At its core, it relies on automation and the *Shift Left* principle, where testing and security checks are performed earlier in the process rather than at the end.

Understanding DevOps in our context is essential for the following reasons:

- It serves as the foundational framework upon which MLOps is built: While DevOps manages deterministic code and binaries, MLOps extends these rigorous principles to manage the unique, probabilistic lifecycle of data and machine learning models.
- The promises of DevOps and its related agility are the promises of *Software-defined Automation* (see Section 2.6.2). Virtualization and subsequent Infrastructure as Code concepts have significantly impacted software development agility and stability, which are the industry's north stars.

Netflix's Radical Approach to Robustness

Netflix faced a critical challenge in 2008 when database corruption halted DVD shipments for days. This failure led them to migrate to AWS and decompose their monolithic application into hundreds of loosely coupled microservices. By adopting microservices, Netflix enabled small, cross-functional teams to work independently. Using tools such as Spinnaker, Netflix engineers deploy code thousands of times per day. There are no release windows or approval committees; if a developer's code passes automated tests, it goes live. This ensures features reach customers instantly. Counterintuitively, Netflix achieved stability by deliberately breaking its own systems. They introduced the Simian Army, a suite of tools designed to test system resilience in production, including Chaos Monkey, which randomly terminates server instances during business hours. This requires engineers to design services that automatically recover from failures without human intervention.

Key technical practices include *Continuous Integration* and *Continuous Deployment* (CI/CD), Infrastructure-as-Code, and real-time monitoring. Unlike the rigid "waterfall" approach of the past, DevOps treats infrastructure and deployments as flexible, code-defined assets.

13.2 Data Operations

Data Operations (DataOps) is a methodology that applies the principles of DevOps (agility, automation, collaboration) to the entire data lifecycle. It is an organizational approach that professionalizes the process of building and managing data pipelines. Using automated testing, continuous integration, and monitoring tools, DataOps aims to reduce the cycle time of data analytics projects and improve the quality, reliability, and security of the data that feeds AI models.

13.2.1 DataOps and Data Governance

While *DataOps* and *Data Governance* are distinct disciplines, they are symbiotic: We cannot scale industrial AI effectively without both.

Data Governance builds the legislative branch. It establishes the policies regarding data access, security, privacy, and quality standards. It answers the question: *"What are we allowed to do with this data, and what standard must it meet?"*

DataOps acts as the executive branch: It builds the infrastructure and processes to adhere to those laws automatically. It focuses on the how: *how* to deliver data rapidly while respecting the constraints set by governance.

In a mature setting, DataOps operationalizes governance. Instead of manual compliance checks, a DataOps pipeline automatically flags noncompliant data (e.g., missing sensor timestamps or export control classifications) before it reaches the AI model.

Why should an industrial company invest in DataOps? The business case rests on three core assumptions regarding ROI:

- *Reduction of "data debt":* Without DataOps, data scientists spend an estimated 60–80% of their time cleaning and wrangling data. DataOps automates this, flipping the ratio so that high-value talent can focus on modeling, not plumbing.
- *Risk mitigation:* In industrial settings, inadequate data leads to catastrophic predictions that can cause physical machine damage or safety incidents. Automated testing (a core DataOps tenet) catches these errors before they cause harm.
- *Agility and time-to-market:* Traditional data projects can take months to deploy. By using CI/CD pipelines for data, organizations can deploy model and pipeline updates in hours or days, enabling faster responses to market or supply chain changes.

13.2.2 Data Pipelines

At its core, a *data pipeline* is a set of processes that move data from various sources to a destination where it can be stored, analyzed, and used to train models.

As outlined in Figure 13.1, a typical industrial data pipeline consists of:

- *Collection:* Extracting raw telemetry from SCADA systems, PLCs, or IoT sensors, PLM, ERP, and CMR Systems
- *Ingestion:* Cleaning and normalizing data. This might involve converting analog signals to digital values, resolving timestamp issues, and addressing other data-quality issues (see Section 4.6.6).

- *Preparation:* This step covers aspects of data correlation, of dealing with a golden record concept, and building data products (see next section) as a means to foster the reuse of data throughout the enterprise and potentially in the ecosystem.
- *Computation:* Computation already does something with the transformed data: Re-organizing data into vector databases and knowledge graphs that are accessible to AI components, training ML models, or populating data warehouses (this typically also includes reorganizating of data for a specific purpose).
- *Presentation:* The presentation layer makes use of the computed artifacts as it provides dashboards or other forms of visualization to humans, offers conversational chatbots to users, or supports workflow automation with "informed" agents.

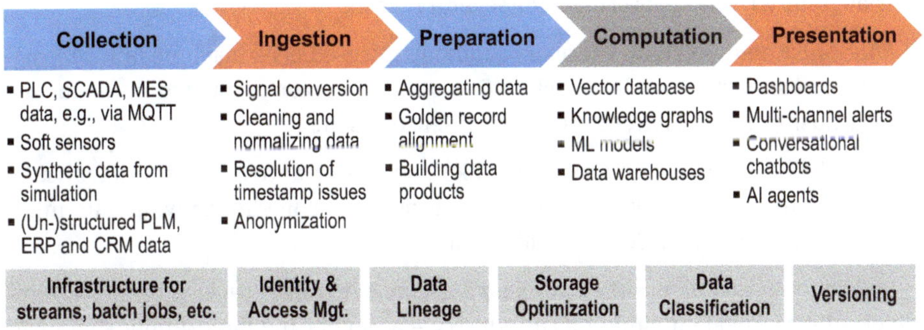

Figure 13.1 Process steps of a data pipeline

DataOps platforms help to build and run data pipelines with a set of standard services and features such as infrastructure to run different flavors of data transfer (streaming, batch jobs, etc.), identify and access management (integration), tools for data lineage (see Section 13.2.4), storage optimization (think of deduplication, compression and tiered support for fast (expensive) and slower (and cheaper) storage types), and naturally data (set) versioning.

13.2.3 Data Products

A *data product* is a curated, high-quality data asset designed to solve a specific business problem or support a particular use case. Unlike raw data, it is a self-contained unit that includes the data itself, essential metadata, and code. By applying "product thinking", organizations ensure these assets are discoverable, trustworthy, and interoperable. To be considered an actual data product, an asset should follow the FAIR principles and standard data mesh criteria [104]:

- *Findable:* Easily found via a data catalog.

- *Addressable:* Having a unique, permanent location for programmatic access.
- *Interoperable:* Using standardized formats to work seamlessly with other products
- *Reusable:* Metadata and data should be well-described so that they can be replicated and/or combined in different settings.

13.2.4 Data Lineage

Data lineage is the life story of a data point. It maps the journey of data from its origin (e. g., a shop-floor sensor) through every transformation, aggregation, and calculation, culminating in its final consumption (the predictive maintenance dashboard). For industrial-grade AI, lineage is critical for several reasons:

- *Root cause analysis:* If an AI model suddenly mispredicts a machine failure, engineers need to trace the data back to find out if the error originated in the model, the transformation logic, or the physical sensor itself.
- *Auditability:* In regulated industries (like pharma or aerospace manufacturing), we must be able to prove exactly how a decision was made and what data influenced it. Lineage provides that audit trail.
- *Deletion requests across the data supply chain:* Whenever several parties are involved – a prevalent situation in industry – a part of the data supply chain can potentially request the deletion of identifiable data by contract or law. To comply with just requests, proper data lineage is vital.

13.2.5 Data Lakes

In technical terms, a *data lake* is a centralized repository that stores structured and unstructured data at any scale. Data is stored “as-is”, without having first to structure the data or define a schema. A *data warehouse*, by contrast, organizes data in a rigidly purified, clean, and sorted manner.

In industrial settings, data is often messy, high-volume, and varied. A data lake is the preferred storage solution for AI for three main reasons:

- *Schema-on-read flexibility:* In a traditional database, we must define the table structure before we can load data (“schema-on-write”). In a data lake, we load the raw data first and determine the structure only when we read it for analysis. This is crucial for IoT sensors, which often change data formats or introduce new fields without prior notice.

- *Diverse data types:* Industrial AI models need more than just rows and columns. They need thermal images for computer vision, acoustic files for sound analysis, and PDF maintenance logs for NLP. A data lake can store all these distinct file types side-by-side.
- *Historical fidelity:* Because data is stored in its raw format, we never lose the original signal. If we discover a better way to remove sensor noise in two years, we can return to the original raw data in the lake and reprocess it. In a data warehouse, the original "noise" might have been permanently cleaned away during entry.

Note: One common pitfall is the *data swamp*". Without the DataOps principles mentioned earlier (governance, cataloging, lineage), a data lake becomes an unmanageable dumping ground where data flows in but is impossible to find or trust.

Solution Brief 13-1: Industrial DataOps Platform (HighByte)

Challenge

- Tag mapping and contextualizing millions of data points is time-consuming and unscalable.
- Raw industrial data is often esoteric and lacks the structure needed for AI.
- Critical operational data is siloed in legacy and local edge systems, preventing real-time AI analysis.

Solution

- AI-Assisted Contextualization: Uses LLMs to identify and map machine instances across large address spaces automatically.
- Industrial MCP Server: Exposes data pipelines as tools that AI agents can use via the Model Context Protocol.
- Standardized Modeling: Creates reusable Digital Twins to provide consistent, high-quality data payloads for AI/ML.

Benefits

- Reduces the time required to build AI-ready data products from months to hours.
- Provides complete, contextualized datasets that reduce AI hallucinations and improve model performance.
- Enables consistent deployment of AI agents and analytics across multiple global factory sites.

Customers: Anglian Water, Gusto, Northrop Grumman, Siemens Gamesa, Toyota

Provider: HighByte, Portland, Maine, USA; *highbyte.com*

13.3 Machine Learning Operations

A successful proof of concept is often the easiest part of the journey. The real challenge is moving that model into a rugged, high-stakes industrial environment and ensuring it remains accurate over time. This is the domain of *Machine Learning Operations* (MLOps). While *DataOps* (see previous chapter) ensures the quality and flow of the "raw material" data, MLOps provides the factory floor, the quality control sensors, and the maintenance crew for the models themselves.

Before describing the most essential aspects of MLOps, let us look at the different stages of AI maturity (see Figure 13.2). While the focus and characteristics of each maturity level (and potentially phase) are apparent, the analogy to the financial management helps understand the enormous lift in maturity that is needed to progress from a bunch of wild data scientists in project mode to a properly managed AI product: It is nothing less cumbersome than lifting a financial reporting function from reporting in Excel to a robust system of auditable financial reporting. Stable interfaces and reproducible results are paramount.

	AI as a Project	AI as a Reusable	AI as a Product
Focus	**Idea to Notebook[1]:** ▪ Discovering useful data correlations ▪ Algorithmic and data feasibility	**Notebook[1] to Data Pipeline:** ▪ Repeatable approach to data transformation ▪ Dataset versioning, dataset cards ▪ Training pipeline	**Data Pipeline to MLOps:** ▪ CI/CD pipeline for all system components ▪ Continuous training, active learning loop ▪ 24x7 Monitoring ▪ AI Bill of Materials
Key Resources	▪ Data scientists ▪ AI / ML tools ▪ Project methodology, e.g., CRISP-DM	▪ Configuration managers ▪ Data engineers	▪ Product managers ▪ SW integration engineers ▪ Product management methodology
Financial Management Analogy	▪ A business analyst with Excel creating top-line reports on request.	▪ A BI platform with managed interfaces to ERP systems	▪ Repeatable and auditable financial reporting. ▪ Continuous controls monitoring

1) The term 'Notebook' here refers to a Data Scientist development environment, e.g., Jupyter

Figure 13.2 AI maturity levels

In a laboratory setting, ML is 90% code and 10% infrastructure. In an industrial setting, the ratio flips. As illustrated in the famous "Hidden Technical Debt" paper by Google researchers (see Figure 13.3), the actual ML code is a small fraction of the overall system [105].

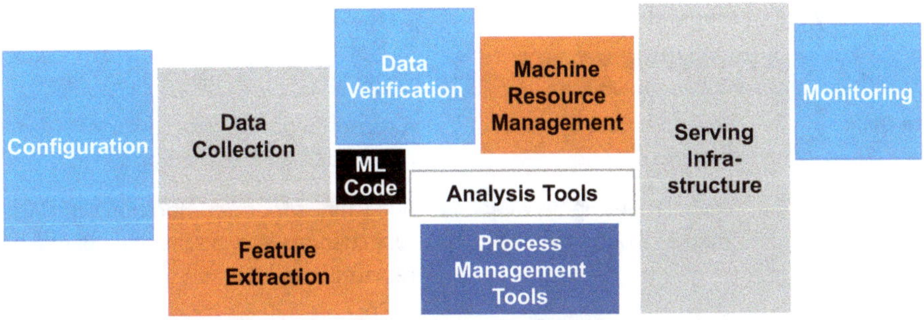

Figure 13.3 Significance of ML code for technical debts (adopted from [105])

For a factory or power plant, MLOps must account for:

- *Safety constraints:* Models cannot be allowed to output hallucinations that might damage hardware.
- *Edge deployment:* Running models on local gateways with limited compute power. Reasons can be performance, often related to limiting latency towards high-speed machines, or confidentiality.
- *Environmental drift:* Changes in ambient temperature or humidity that subtly alter sensor readings.

To manage AI at scale, the MLOps lifecycle offers three distinct, looping phases:

- *Model development (experimentation):* This phase focuses on *reproducibility*. In an industrial context, it isn't enough to find the best algorithm; we must be able to prove why a model made a specific prediction (Explainable AI).
- *Version control:* Using tools like DVC (Data Version Control) to link specific datasets to specific model weights.
- *Experiment tracking:* Logging parameters, hyperparameters, and results to ensure that a winning experiment can be recreated months later.
- *Model deployment* (the CI/CD/CT Pipeline): Unlike traditional software, ML requires a third "C": Continuous Training (CT):
  - *CI (Continuous Integration):* Testing the code, the data schemas, and the model architecture.
  - *CD (Continuous Delivery):* Automating the push of the model to the "edge" (the factory floor) or the cloud.
  - *CT (Continuous Training):* A unique ML trigger that automatically retrains the model when new data suggests the old model is no longer valid.
- *Model monitoring and governance:* In Industrial AI, the "silent killer" is Model Drift. Different types of model drift are listed in Table 13.1.

Table 13.1 Types of model drifts

Type of Drift	Description	Example
Data Drift	The input data distribution changes.	A sensor begins to degrade or is replaced by a different brand.
Concept Drift	The relationship between input and output changes.	A machine's "normal" vibration signature changes after a scheduled part replacement.
Model Decay	General loss of predictive power over time.	Natural wear and tear on assets not captured in the original training set.

Part IV: Enterprise Functions and AI Use Cases

There are as many ways to structure enterprise functions as there are operating models. Is Sales a function that initiates production (as in a system business) or a function that follows production (as in a pure product business environment)? Is Facility Management a sub-function of Asset Management, or does it stand on its own?

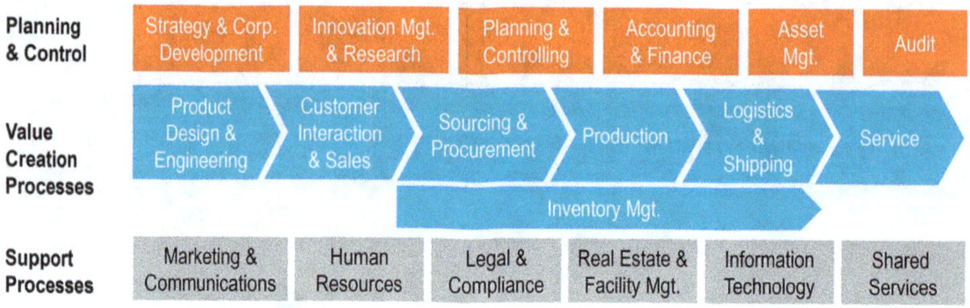

In any case, the structure above serves as the starting point for a comprehensive overview of enterprise functions, subfunctions, and solution briefs, describing commercially available AI offerings that support these subfunctions in their specific forms.

14 Strategy & Corporate Development

14.1 Strategy and Foresight/Market Research

Strategy and Foresight include trend scouting, which can begin with societal, economic, and political trends with connections to markets, eventually leading to demand pull and technology push, thereby increasing competitiveness on either the product or production side.

Strategy and foresight research is fed by different data sources, from *academic research* via *venture capital spend* (or other categories of investment indicating expected commercial momentum) to *market studies* with predicted market volumes, hooks to determine the addressable market volume, as well as lists of vendors for competitor analysis or as an input into partnering and acquisition activities.

GenAI supports the identification and exploration of both structured and unstructured data sources, cohesive integration into internal technology landscapes, and conducting targeted market studies and projections to inform future financial investments and opportunities. Almost all major LLMs now offer *Deep Research* agents, typically as premium offerings of their base LLMs (see Table 14.1).

Deep Research is a new paradigm in which an LLM operates much like a human researcher, actively retrieving and analyzing information in near-real-time. This goes beyond a simple, single-step question-and-answer process. Instead, the model engages in *multi-step problem solving*: first, planning a strategy; then searching for data, reading sources, cross-checking facts, and, if necessary, running computations; and finally *synthesizing a comprehensive, evidence-based answer or report* [106].

Table 14.1 Leading commercial deep research offerings

Offering/URL/Provider	Specifics
You.com *you.com* by You.com	▪ Includes several pre-licensed commercial data sources ▪ Allows hosting of proprietary agents supporting research processes, for example, with internal data sources.
o3-Deep Research Model *openai.com* by OpenAI	▪ Integration with Bing Search via MS Azure offerings
Gemini Pro Deep Think *gemini.google.com* by Google	▪ No specific data sources above "web search" integrated
BloombergGPT by Bloomberg	▪ Trained to deal particularly well with financial data ▪ Includes access to Bloomberg's database
Claude *claude.com* by Anthropic	▪ Tailored offering for financial institutions with several related data sources

14.2 Mergers & Acquisitions

The *Mergers and Acquisitions* (M&A) function is the strategic process of combining companies, divesting business units, or acquiring assets to accelerate growth, gain market share, or realize synergies. It involves identifying targets, conducting due diligence, valuing the deal, negotiating terms, and implementing post-merger integration to realize expected value and strategic objectives. Typical activities within this function are:

- *Strategy and target identification:* This initial phase involves the acquiring company defining its objectives (e.g., market expansion, acquiring technology, achieving cost synergies) and establishing search criteria. This enables the systematic identification, screening, and preliminary evaluation of potential target companies aligned with the core strategy.
- *Valuation and initial offer:* Once a target is selected, the acquiring firm performs a detailed financial valuation using methods like Discounted Cash Flow analysis, comparable company analysis, and precedent transactions to determine a fair purchase price. A non-binding document, often referred to as a Letter of Intent or Heads of Terms, is submitted, outlining the proposed price, structure, and key conditions.
- *Due Diligence (DD):* The buyer gains access to the target's confidential data – usually in a secure Virtual Data Room – to verify its claims and uncover potential risks or liabilities. Due diligence typically includes a financial DD (verifying financial statements, earnings quality, and debt), a legal DD (reviewing contracts, litigation, compliance, and intellectual property), and an operational/commercial DD (assessing the target's market position, technology, and integration complexity).

- *Negotiation and closing:* Assuming the due diligence does not uncover deal-breaking issues, the parties move to final negotiations on the definitive purchase agreement. This legal contract specifies the final price, warranties, indemnities, payment structure, and closing conditions. Once all conditions (including regulatory approvals, such as antitrust filings) are met, the transaction reaches Closing, at which the funds and ownership are formally transferred.
- *Post-merger integration:* The success of an M&A deal is often determined here. Post-merger-integration involves combining the two companies' systems, processes, people, and cultures to realize the expected synergies defined in the initial strategy. This includes harmonizing IT systems, consolidating redundant roles, aligning company cultures, and creating a unified operating model.

AI is used across all phases of M&A, from initial scoping to post-merger integration [107, 108]:

- *Target identification & market scanning:* AI systems ingest and analyze vast amounts of data (financial filings, news articles, patent databases, social media sentiment, etc.) to discover companies with specific characteristics, growth potential, and strategic fit. AI models can estimate the likelihood that a company will go to market within a specified timeframe (e. g., 6–18 months) by identifying historical patterns and signals.

Solution Brief 14-1: AI-assisted M&A Target Scanning (McKinsey)

Challenge
- Information overload makes identifying high-potential targets time-consuming.
- Traditional screening can miss valuable opportunities in adjacent or niche markets.
- Manual diligence is too slow to compete in fast-moving deal environments.
- Subjective biases can lead to overlooking targets with strong strategic or cultural fit.

Solution dealscan.ai
- Proprietary AI algorithms screen a database of over 40 million companies globally.
- GenAI synthesizes vast amounts of (un)structured data for deeper insights.
- Applies prioritization criteria along specific strategic, financial, and cultural metrics.
- Visualizes data to highlight "programmatic" M&A opportunities and synergy potential.

Benefits
- Uncovers viable, non-obvious targets that competitors often miss.
- Significantly accelerates the M&A timeline from sourcing to initial diligence.
- Enables a programmatic M&A strategy, statistically linked to higher shareholder returns.
- Reduces investment risk through objective, data-driven assessment of target fit.

Provider: McKinsey, San Francisco, CA, USA;
mckinsey.com/capabilities/m-and-a/how-we-help-clients
youtube.com/watch?v=g4TILHS49tk

- *Due Diligence* (DD): This is where AI offers the most substantial time and cost savings by dramatically accelerating the review of large document sets. GenAI and NLP can scan thousands of legal documents, contracts, and financial records in hours, a task that traditionally takes human teams weeks. Document scanning entails flagging critical issues, such as change-of-control clauses that could void contracts post-acquisition, hidden liabilities or unusual termination mechanics, and compliance issues or regulatory red flags.
- *Valuation and financial analysis:* AI rapidly aggregates and processes market data, transaction precedents, and comparable company financials, allowing dealmakers to refine their valuation assumptions. Advanced AI can run complex probabilistic modeling to simulate various financial scenarios, predict future performance, and stress-test the target company's business model.

Solution Brief 14-2: Data-driven Talent Due Diligence Service (Zeki Data)

Challenge
- Difficulty identifying hidden risks and "execution capability" before committing to an investment.
- Missing unique intelligence required to make accurate go/no-go investment decisions.
- Massive effort, cost, and time required to research target company talent manually.

Solution
- Applies counter-terrorism-grade analytics to track millions of global scientists and innovators as a foundation to compare a target and their competitors.
- Uses a unique scoring system that extracts data from 30,000 open-access sources.
- Delivers 10-page talent reports and enriched datasets with over 50 variables.

Benefits
- Identifies risks early and reveals hidden technical or go-to-market talent gaps.
- Delivers decision-ready reports and datasets within two business days.
- Empowers advisor and talent teams to build and scale portfolio companies faster post-investment.

Provider: Zeki Data, London, Great Britain; *zekidata.com*

- *Post-merger integration:* AI tools can analyze operational data and IT infrastructure from both companies to identify redundancies, overlaps, and synergies in systems, processes, and assets. Furthermore, AI can analyze employee feedback and HR data to identify potential cultural clashes and key talent-retention risks (talent retention modeling), enabling management to proactively address integration friction points.

15 Innovation Management & Research

Innovation management is the systematic approach to fostering, developing, and implementing new ideas, processes, or products within an organization to create value and achieve competitive advantage. Its most essential subfunctions include

- *Strategy and foresight* to identify future trends, market needs, and technological advancements to guide innovation efforts.
- *Idea generation, collection, and prioritization,* focusing on cultivating a culture where new ideas are encouraged, captured, and evaluated from various sources; promising ideas are selected, prioritized, and allocated resources based on strategic fit and potential return; and
- *Intellectual Property Management,* which involves the administration, protection, and strategic use of a company's intellectual assets, such as patents, trademarks, and copyrights.

According to Doblin's 10 Principles of Innovation, innovation is a discipline that shapes profit models, supply chain networks, brand experience, and service processes, and is thus far broader than the invention-related functions described in this section [109].

Research is the discipline that creates new insights and knowledge. Subfunctions described here are *Material Discovery, Patent Analytics,* and *Laboratory and Experiment Management.*

This function involves the strategic decision-making process for launching new research and development projects. It is the formal trigger for innovation, driven by a deep understanding of market needs, competitive analysis, and an assessment of technological and financial feasibility.

15.1 Idea Management

Idea management is the systematic, structured process of generating, collecting, screening, developing, and implementing ideas from diverse groups (employees, customers, partners) to drive innovation, efficiency, and continuous improvement within an organization. It is a critical component of the broader discipline of innovation management. The process aims to move ideas from initial thought to successful implementation, creating a reliable, repeatable funnel for corporate innovation.

The discipline of idea management follows a structured lifecycle:

- *Idea generation:* Supporting the creative and communicative processes that produce new ideas.
- *Idea capture/submission:* Establishing channels for contributors to submit ideas, along with relevant information, to the innovation team.
- *Collaboration:* Allowing other contributors and subject-matter experts to review, provide feedback, and potentially vote on or rate submitted ideas.
- *Evaluation/screening:* A team of reviewers assesses submissions based on predefined criteria (e. g., feasibility, strategic alignment, potential impact/ROI), see also Section.
- *Development/validation:* The most promising ideas are refined, which often involves creating business cases, concept development, prototyping, and small-scale pilots.
- *Implementation/realization:* The developed concepts are launched as new products, services, or internal process improvements.

Idea management benefits from the powers of AI as it

- *facilitates brainstorming* (e. g., canvas and mind-mapping work) and requirements management processes (e. g., generation of user stories);
- *fuels internal and external platforms for ideation campaigning* with data analytics, smart search, and matchmaking (e. g., assigning team members to hackathon teams according to their interests and skills);
- *provides rapid prototyping platforms* (see Section 31.4.7); and
- accelerates the *creation of pitch materials such as presentations and videos.*

Solution Brief 15-1: Virtual Hackathon Platform (Angelhack)

Challenge

- Need to build and nurture authentic relationships with a global developer community.
- Requirement to market products and drive adoption of new software tools.
- Necessity to crowdsource innovation to stay competitive in the market.
- Difficulty of effectively and verifying top-tier technical talent.

Solution

- End-to-end organization of virtual, in-person, and hybrid hackathons.
- Educational developer quests to encourage learning and technology usage.
- Strategic bounty programs to solve unique challenges and expand ecosystems.
- Incubator programs to guide projects from concept to market launch.

Benefits

- Access to a community of over 300,000 developers.
- Acceleration of product roadmaps through rapid prototyping and innovation.
- Efficient hiring of skills-verified candidates directly from hackathon participants.
- Enhanced brand visibility and product traction within the tech ecosystem.

Customers: AWS, Cisco, Hasbro, IBM, Mastercard, P&G

Provider: Angelhack, San Francisco, CA, USA; *angelhack.com*

15.2 Intellectual Property Management

Intellectual Property (IP) Management involves the administration, protection, and strategic use of a company's intellectual assets, such as patents, trademarks, and copyrights. This includes filing for patents, managing trademark portfolios, and defending against infringement, ensuring that the company's innovations are legally protected from competitors.

AI, and particularly the capability of LLM technology, significantly streamlines corporate IP management by automating time-intensive legal tasks. It accelerates patent drafting and prior art searches by analyzing vast technical and legal databases, suggesting relevant claims, and quickly identifying potential challenges. GenAI also enhances trademark watching and brand protection by continuously monitoring new filings and online content for possible infringements.

Siemens ID Drafter

Siemens developed the AI assistant "ID Drafter" to help researchers and engineers formally capture invention disclosures. Naturally, ID Drafter will not invent itself but will guide its users through a series of structured questions to capture all relevant aspects for the rapid processing of invention disclosures, such as a rating of whether a patent request process makes sense.

15.3 Research

Research is the exploratory discipline that seeks to understand the "what" and "why", generating new insights and knowledge, while (Product) Development (see Chapter 20 "Product Design and Engineering") focuses on its practical application, solving problems.

15.3.1 Materials Discovery

Fundamental challenges facing humanity, such as addressing plastic pollution, removing PFAS, carbon capture, and developing efficient battery technologies, depend primarily on our ability to discover new materials and develop efficient production methods for them. ML models can be trained on the known properties of thousands of materials to predict the properties of novel chemical compounds or alloys, thereby guiding researchers toward the most promising candidates for a given application.

Tesla Reinvented Die Casting

When *Tesla* disrupted car body assembly by their Giga Press approach - a gigantic die casting machine that would produce a car underbody as one piece - they leveraged material discovery to make this innovation happen: Only a new aluminum alloy would combine the desired material attributes for the car design, such as strength, ductability, resistance against road chemicals such as salt and the material properties required for the new approach of die casting in new dimensions, such as solidifying behavior over time (to fill the die cast form consistently in one go) [110].

Solution Brief 15-2: Material Discovery for Metal Alloys (Fehrmann MaterialsX)

Challenge

- The exploration of new aluminum alloys meeting application-specific requirements takes so much time that it is typically on the critical path for a new application's go-to-market timeline.

Solution

- MatGPT LLM as a materials knowledge platform to organize customer materials knowledge (material attributes and production process knowledge).
- MatAIM for AI materials modeling.
- "Rapid lab-validation" ecosystem.
- Technology Partners: Fraunhofer IAPT, Microsoft.

Benefits

- Reduction of material discovery time for new materials from years to weeks.
- Reduction of expensive real-work lab tests to just a few pre-validated alloy variants.

Customers: Aston Martin Yachting, Brain of Materials, leading turbine manufacturer

Provider: Fehrmann MaterialsX, Hamburg, Germany; *fehrmann-materials.com*

15.3.2 Patent Analytics

The retrieval of patent prior art is a foundational step in innovation assessment, intellectual property planning, and technological advancement. Millions of technical disclosures published by patent offices globally constitute a vital source of knowledge for inventors, examiners, and researchers. However, the continuously expanding volume and increasingly interdisciplinary complexity of modern inventions make effective prior art discovery difficult, particularly when the relevant technical information is spread across numerous fields.

NLP and LLMs support humans in intelligently indexing and finding patent information. Countless GenAI application providers have included publicly and commercially available patent databases, such as lens.org, in their "smart search" offerings. A particularly innovative approach combines LLM technology with the *Theory of Inventive Problem Solving* (TRIZ) [111] methodology: The LLM understands TRIZ's 40 principles of invention and identifies solution approaches from one problem domain that are likely to work in another.

Solution Brief 15-3: NLP- and Pattern-based Patent Analysis (INSA Strasbourg)

Challenge

- Manual analysis of patents is very time-consuming.
- The transfer of a solution pattern from one problem domain to a different problem domain is almost impossible without automation.
- The publicly available datasets often lack key attributes, such as "explicit in-domain and out-of-domain labeling, multi-jurisdiction coverage". They are often too large for efficient sub-document-level experimentation on standard computational resources.

Solution

- A specific RAG layer for patent analytics.
- Transformer-based special models BERT and RoBERTa for a question-answering system designed to identify inventive solutions and contradictions in patents.
- Creation of a domain-aware patent retrieval dataset, aggregated at the patent family level.
- TRIZ methodology (translated: "Theory of Inventive Problem Solving") supported by AI discoveries.

Benefits

- Automated cross-domain discovery of related solution approaches and patents.

Customers: Accor Mittal, Arburg

Provider: INSA Strasbourg, Strasbourg, France, Prof. Denis Cavallucci; *insa-strasbourg.fr/en; arxiv.org/pdf/2506.22141*

15.3.3 Laboratory & Experiment Management

This function includes overseeing testing procedures, managing laboratory equipment and resources, and ensuring compliance with safety and quality standards, thereby supporting the R&D process through a controlled environment for experimentation and verification. *Laboratory and Experiment Management* is a lighthouse example for how fundamental the changes in innovation management are:

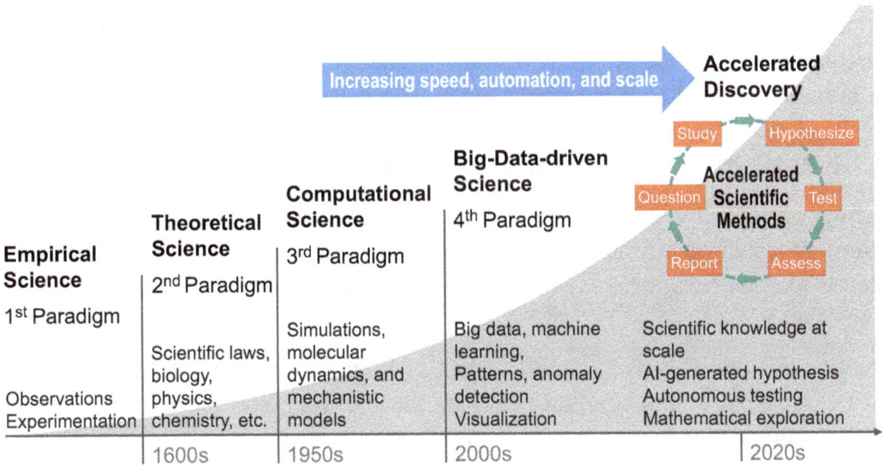

Figure 15.1 Evolution of exploratory concepts in science [112]

AI supports in *Research and Experiment Design, Lab Operations and Resource Management, Real-time Execution and Quality Control,* and *Data Processing and Compliance.*

15.3.3.1 Research and Experiment Design

- *Hypothesis generation:* LLM-based applications, sometimes called AI co-scientists, analyze vast amounts of scientific literature to generate novel hypotheses, propose research directions, and suggest appropriate methodologies.
- *Optimal experimentation:* Predictive analytics can forecast experiment outcomes and identify optimal conditions (e.g., temperature, concentration, timing) before physical trials begin, dramatically reducing time and cost compared with traditional trial-and-error methods.
- *Protocol generation:* GenAI can translate high-level research goals into detailed, step-by-step experimental protocols and even generate the necessary code for data analysis.

15.3.3.2 Lab Operations and Resource Management

- *Smart scheduling and resource allocation:* AI-driven laboratory information management systems and scheduling tools optimize the use of high-demand equipment, minimizing idle time, resolving scheduling conflicts, and accounting for maintenance schedules.
- *Predictive inventory:* ML algorithms analyze historical usage data, seasonal trends, and vendor lead times to accurately forecast stock consumption for reagents and consumables, preventing both costly overstocking and disruptive shortages.

- *Predictive maintenance:* AI monitors real-time operational data from laboratory instruments to predict equipment failures, enabling proactive maintenance and minimizing costly downtime.

15.3.3.3 Real-Time Execution and Quality Control

- *Robotics and automation:* AI powers advanced lab robotics, enabling robots to autonomously execute complex, repetitive tasks such as sample preparation and high-throughput testing, reducing human error and improving throughput and consistency.
- *Data validation:* AI uses computer vision to monitor experiments, detect issues with sample placement or equipment function, and suggest corrections, creating a self-improving loop for experimental consistency.
- *Automated quality control:* AI systems monitor instrument performance, environmental conditions (such as temperature and humidity), and data integrity in real time, immediately flagging any deviations or anomalies that could compromise results.
- *Hygiene management:* AI, particularly machine vision, can monitor the proper use of protective clothing as required [113].

15.3.3.4 Data Processing and Compliance

- *Automated data analysis:* AI can process and integrate massive, multimodal datasets from various instruments and sources in real time, identifying patterns, correlations, and outliers faster than human researchers. Additionally, AI data assistants help democratize complex data analysis for domain experts and reduce their dependence on data analysts and scientists.
- *Data extraction and entry:* NLP tools automate the extraction of key information from unstructured text (like historical lab notes or external publications), streamlining data entry into laboratory information management systems and electronic lab notebooks.
- *Regulatory compliance:* AI enhances compliance by automatically monitoring standard operating procedures, creating detailed audit trails, and generating reports to ensure that labs adhere to industry regulations.

Solution Brief 15-4: Scientific Experiment and Lab Management (Dotmatics)

Challenge

- Long drug development timelines and high costs.
- High rates of clinical trial failures.
- Risk of AI bias due to poorly curated data.
- Lack of transparency in AI predictions is impacting patient safety.

Solution "LUMA"

- Integrating AI directly into scientific R&D workflows.
- Centralizes structured and unstructured data from across lab instruments and scientific disciplines.
- Employs domain-specific, assistive, and generative AI to predict outcomes and automate workflows.
- Creates a continuous Lab-in-the-Loop cycle between physical "wet lab" experiments and digital "dry lab" simulations.

Benefits

- Significant reduction in drug development timelines and costs.

Customers: AntaBio, BASF, Charles River, LeadPharma

Provider: Dotmatics, USA; *dotmatics.com*

16 Planning & Controlling

16.1 Planning

Planning is a responsibility across two dimensions: the first is the set of enterprise functions themselves, as planning must take place in and across all of them. The second dimension is the time horizon as follows:

- *Strategic planning (long-term):* Setting the "north star". This involves defining the mission, vision, and high-level goals for the next 3–5 years. This can be supported by strategy and Foresight activities (see Section 14.1), but remains primarily a very human and cultural activity of aligning the organization towards common goals.
- *Tactical planning (medium-term):* Breaking those big goals into departmental milestones. For example, "To hit our 20% growth target, Marketing needs to generate 5,000 leads". Examples include Production Planning (see Section 24.3) or Supplier Selection and Coordination (see Section 22.1).
- *Operational planning (short-term):* The day-to-day "how-to". Schedules, budgets, and specific tasks for teams. Examples include Production Scheduling (see Section 24.5) and Inventory Planning (see Chapter 23).
- *Contingency planning:* The "What if?" layer. Preparing for market crashes, supply chain issues, or competitive shifts. See Supply Chain Monitoring (Section 22.2) as an example.

16.2 Controlling and Reporting

Let us consider *Reporting* to be the technical side of Controlling, while Controlling adds the human interaction on top of it. Reporting involves integrating information and insights across various departments or business units within an organization. It ensures collaboration, consistency, and goal alignment across functional areas, including finance, marketing, operations, and human resources. *Data analytics* and *dashboarding* have become popular disciplines across all corporate functions. However, the dependency of business functions on data analytics expertise remains a bottleneck. Tools such as Tableau and QlikView still require visualization experts to configure the dashboards. Finally, complex database queries against data source systems are best left to experts due to the performance and data-quality risks they pose.

Database queries are equivalent to software source code. Consequently, GenAI has the potential to translate natural-language requests from business analysts into executable queries and visualizations, thereby increasing self–service and citizen development in the reporting field.

Solution Brief 16-1: AI-based Ad hoc-Generation of Dashboards (App Orchid)

Challenge

- Enterprises accumulate large volumes of structured and unstructured data across many systems (ERP, CRM, document stores, sensor feeds), but data remains siloed and hard to reconcile. Non-technical users struggle to extract insights: natural-language queries are often inaccurate; dashboards and BI reports require analyst or engineering support.
- Key metrics, business context, and semantic meaning are often missing or inconsistent, making interpretation, governance, and trust in analytics difficult.

Solution

- An ontology-driven semantic intelligence fabric connects structured and unstructured data, enriches schema with business meaning, and supports consistent interpretation. Users can ask questions in plain English, and the system interprets with high accuracy, transparent reasoning and lineage.
- Over 50 pre-built insight models (trend, anomaly, correlation, etc.), automatic visualization generation, dashboards, and integration with BI tools.
- Connects >150 enterprise data sources, maintains role-based access, data lineage, compliance, and supports hybrid or existing infrastructure.

Benefits

- Reduced time to insight: Users can ask questions and receive meaningful visual answers without waiting for BI teams; claimed ~85% reduction in time to insight.
- Lower cost and greater self-service: Because non-technical users can explore data, ask questions, and generate dashboards, reducing dependency on specialist resources.
- Increased trust, interpretability, and consistency: Transparent query logic, semantic enrichment, and complete data lineage; results are more accurate and explainable.
- Better leverage of existing infrastructure and investments: Integrations with BI tools (Tableau, Power BI, ...), connectors to many enterprise systems, so less rework.

Customers: American Water, fracsun, Pierer Innovation

Provider: App Orchid, California, USA; *apporchid.com*

17 Finance & Accounting

17.1 Finance

The financial management function is as the enterprise's nervous system, orchestrating the planning of, organizing, directing, and controlling financial activities to ensure stability and profitability. Its core responsibilities encompass managing cash flow, optimizing capital structure, mitigating risk, and delivering strategic insights through financial reporting. Both effective bottom-line and top-line management rely on correlating internal data and external information – think of currency fluctuations and raw material price developments, as well as competitor behavior and customer industry forecasts.

AI enhances decision-making through predictive analytics; machine learning algorithms can forecast market trends, detect real-time fraud anomalies, and simulate complex financial scenarios (e. g., cash flow stress tests) with speed and accuracy that legacy systems cannot match.

AI-driven platforms can improve consistency in *three statement modeling*, a financial modeling technique that integrates the income statement, balance sheet, and cash flow statement into a single cohesive model. This approach enables dynamic connections among the three statements, improving analysis and forecasting of a company's financial performance. Key components include:

- *Income statement:* Shows the company's revenues and expenses over a specific period.
- *Balance sheet:* Provides a snapshot of the company's assets, liabilities, and equity at a specific point in time.
- *Cash flow statement:* Tracks the flow of cash in and out of the business, highlighting operational, investing, and financing activities. This model serves as the founda-

tion for more advanced financial models, such as discounted cash flow and leveraged buyout models, and is essential for informed financial decision-making.

Solution Brief 17-1: AI-supported Financial Planning & Reporting (drivetrain.ai)

Challenge

- Slow, manual data gathering across departments delays critical decision-making and reporting.
- Critical business metrics remain trapped in siloed tools such as ERPs, CRMs, and HR systems.
- Static planning models fail to adapt quickly to dynamic market conditions.

Solution

- Integrates deeply with 200+ business tools to create a unified, automated data layer.
- Offers a flexible modeling engine allowing custom metrics using simple, Excel-like formulas.
- Enables infinite "what-if" scenario planning to test assumptions and forecast outcomes instantly.
- Provides a collaborative interface for department heads to input budgets and track performance.

Benefits

- Reduces manual data consolidation time significantly, freeing up finance teams for strategic analysis.
- Establishes a single source of truth, eliminating debates over data accuracy.
- Accelerates decision-making with real-time insights into actuals versus planned performance.
- Improves forecast accuracy through continuous, data-driven rolling forecasts and variance analysis.

Customers: Primarily SaaS companies such as Observe.ai, javvy, and rightwork.

Provider: Drivetrain.ai, Bengaluru, India; *drivetrain.ai*

17.2 Accounting

Accounting covers a couple of distinct disciplines:

- Cost and Performance Accounting helps managers analyze, track, and report company costs and performance to improve internal decision-making.
- General Ledger Accounting is used for recording and maintaining all the company's financial transactions.
- Subsidiary Ledger Accounting takes care of detailed accounts such as accounts receivable, accounts payable, and fixed asset records to support the general ledger.

Of course, adopting automated ledger posting isn't a new discipline; therefore, ERP systems, by themselves, and *Robotic Process Automation* solutions spanning heterogeneous applications (see Section 31.4.6.1) are freeing up human capacity for oversight and increasing data-entry accuracy at the same time. Faster automated record-keeping enables real-time access to financial data, supporting quicker, better-informed decisions and eliminating the need to wait for monthly reports.

While traditional automation is excellent for basic repetitive jobs, AI goes further by handling complex accounting challenges:

- *Reconciling payments and invoices*, especially where there are discrepancies, becomes much easier with AI, which intelligently matches transactions and significantly lowers manual workload.
- AI also *enhances data quality* by cleaning and standardizing messy information from places like banks, payment processors, and CRM systems.
- Beyond tidying up data, AI offers *ongoing vigilance* – it watches for unusual activity, flags potential fraud, duplicate payments, or unexpected charges, and strengthens our financial security overall (see, for example, Section 22.6).
- Deduction management is a crucial function, particularly in the consumer packaged goods and retail industries. Prescriptive analytics prioritizes deductions based on their likelihood of being invalid or unauthorized [114].

Solution Brief 17-2: AI-supported Revenue Recognition (HubiFi)

Challenge

- High transaction volumes make manual data management and revenue recognition nearly impossible in SaaS-type businesses.
- Legacy ERP systems lack the granularity needed for complex financial analysis.
- Human error in data entry leads to revenue leakage and audit risks.

Solution

- AI-driven engines automate complex "order-to-cash" cycles and multi-system data reconciliations.
- ML identifies patterns in unstructured data to standardize messy financial records.
- Autonomous bots handle "mid-stream" changes, disputes, and backdating without manual intervention.

Benefits

- Reduces monthly accounting close times from several weeks to just a few hours.
- Provides real-time, audit-proof financial insights at the individual subscriber or transaction level.
- Reclaims 80% of finance team time by eliminating repetitive manual tasks.

Customers: Copy.ai, Covertree, Cursor, Helium10, Loop, Perplexity

Provider: HubiFi, Columbus, Ohio, USA; *hubifi.com*

17.3 Regulatory Intelligence & Monitoring

Tax laws and tariff regulations change daily globally (e.g., new e-invoicing mandates in Brazil or Poland). Specialized GenAI tools crawl global legislative databases and websites in real-time. They not only flag changes but "diff" the new law against a multinational corporation's specific structure to generate a tailored impact assessment (e.g., "The new Hungarian corporate tax hike impacts subsidiary X's deferred tax assets by US$ 2 million").

Monitoring the new Tariff Dynamics

Corning, a leading provider of glass applications, built an AI application that screens government agency websites to detect tariff changes. The model performs analysis with regard to geographies, respectively nations, shipping routes, and material declarations ("what is the definition of a finished product?", "what counts as a raw material?"), provides an impact analysis and decision support to mitigate the adverse effects of tariffs by altering the supply chain [115].

17.4 Transfer Pricing

Transfer Pricing (TP) is one of the most high-impact areas for AI within the corporate tax function. Because TP relies heavily on analyzing vast datasets to prove that intercompany transactions adhere to the Arm's Length Principle (pricing transactions as if they were between unrelated parties), it is ideally suited for AI's pattern recognition and data processing capabilities:

- *Intelligent benchmarking (comparability analysis):* The core difficulty in TP is finding comparable independent companies to set a benchmark margin. Traditionally, this involves manual keyword searches in databases such as Orbis or Amadeus. AI models using NLP and LLMs can analyze unstructured text in business descriptions stored in databases. Instead of just matching industry codes, the AI understands a company's function (e.g., distinguishing a "distributor with low risk" from a "distributor with high marketing expenditure") to identify comparables that are far more accurate, reducing the risk of rejection by tax authorities.
- *Operational TP (real-time monitoring):* Most multinational corporations set prices at the start of the year and perform a messy "true-up" adjustment at year-end to ensure subsidiaries earned the correct profit margin. AI agents can monitor ERP data in real-time. They track the profitability of specific product lines or entities throughout the year and predict whether a subsidiary is drifting out of the target

arm's length range. The system can then suggest mid-year price adjustments to restore margins to a safe level, eliminating massive, audit-triggering year-end adjustments.

- *Automated documentation:* Multinational corporations must produce thousands of pages of documentation annually. GenAI can ingest financial data and prior-year reports to draft the narrative sections of these files. It can update functional analyses, describe industry trends based on current news, and ensure consistency across hundreds of jurisdictions, reducing the documentation workload by 60–80%.

It is essential to recognize that tax authorities already use AI to audit taxpayers. They use algorithms to scan thousands of tax returns and flag anomalies (e. g., a distributor with consistently low margins compared to industry peers). Adopting AI enables multinationals to run these same checks preemptively, spotting and fixing audit red flags before regulators see them.

18 Asset Management

18.1 Plant Inspection & Change Management

18.1.1 Red-lining

In process plant management, *red-lining* is a critical, informal procedure used to rapidly flag temporary changes or overrides to standard operating conditions, procedures, or equipment limits [116]. It involves physically marking up a document, such as a *Piping and Instrumentation Diagram* (P&ID) or a procedure sheet, with a red pen to highlight the change. This immediate, highly visible notation alerts all personnel – operators, technicians, and engineers – to a deviation from the norm, signaling an urgent or temporary modification that requires special attention, caution, or a follow-up formal "Management of Change" review.

Solution Brief 18-1: Red-lining and Digital Twin Building (samp.ai)

Challenge

- P&ID revalidation must be performed every two years according to regulatory requirements and is cumbersome when performed on paper ("red-lining").
- Consistency issues between the digital representation of a process plant and reality can have expensive effects on maintenance work orders.

Solution

- Samp's platform uses machine vision, augmented reality, and positioning technology to digitalize the process of red-lining.
- Integration with P&ID tools: Autodesk, Aveva, Hexagon, and Bentley; Integration with GIS platforms such as Esri, QGIS, and MapInfo; Integration with SCADA tools such as OSIsoft, Emerson.

Solution Brief 18-1: Red-lining and Digital Twin Building (samp.ai) *(continued)*

Benefits

- Higher consistency between the digital representation of a plant and its real implementation.
- Less effort for red-lining.

Customers: Engie, Suez, Terega, Trapil

Provider: Samp.ai, Paris, France; *samp.ai*

18.1.2 Plant Inspection

Plant inspection involves systematically examining machinery, structures, and systems to detect defects, wear, corrosion, and other potential issues that could lead to failures or accidents. The main objective of plant inspections is to maintain operational integrity, prevent unplanned shutdowns, and ensure compliance with safety and environmental regulations. Inspectors assess the condition of pressure vessels, pipelines, boilers, and other components to ensure that they meet design and quality standards. Regular inspections also help identify maintenance needs and support preventive maintenance programs, thereby extending equipment lifespan and reducing costs. In addition, plant inspections ensure compliance with national and international standards, contributing to overall workplace safety and sustainability.

AI's helping hands range from feeding data to handheld inspection devices and augmented reality glasses, through supporting data analytics, to controlling autonomous robots and drones to conduct autonomous inspection tours.

Solution Brief 18-2: Autonomous Robotic Inspection (Anybotics)

Challenge

- Industrial and routine inspections are key to improving operational efficiency, reducing downtime, and enhancing worker safety.
- Hazardous and remote areas make manual inspections particularly expensive.

Solution "ANYmal"

- Automated inspection robots, able to navigate and move in process plant environments.
- Thermal anomalies, gas leak and presence detection, partial discharge and other electrical faults, visual inspection of abnormal conditions and indicators on meters, valves, gauges, and levers.
- Certified to work in hazardous, even explosive areas.
- Technology Partners: Accenture, AWS, Cognite, Leica, NVIDIA.

Solution Brief 18-2: Autonomous Robotic Inspection (Anybotics)

Benefits

- Automated inspections, gathering critical data in real-time, and enabling proactive maintenance.
- Improve safety by removing workers from hazardous areas.

Customers: BASF, Grace, Implenia, Petronas

Provider: Anybotics, Zürich, Switzerland; *anybotics.com*

18.2 Machine Maintenance

This is the function of maintaining and repairing a company's equipment and machinery. It involves various strategies, including reactive (fixing after a breakdown), preventive (scheduled maintenance), and predictive (using data to anticipate failures) actions. A well-executed maintenance plan minimizes downtime and extends the lifespan of critical assets.

The adoption of technologies such as IoT sensors and AI is driving the evolution of this function from a reactive to a predictive model. By turning equipment health into a data stream, a company can optimize its entire production schedule and link maintenance directly to PPC functions (see Section).

According to several surveys, predictive maintenance has been the most popular industrial AI use case for some time [117]. This is noteworthy, as the commercial value of predictive maintenance use cases is typically limited: As a rule of thumb, reducing unplanned machine downtime to zero is equivalent to 1‰ of the asset value per month. In other words, a machine worth EUR 1 million translates into EUR 12,000 in annual revenue for a predictive maintenance solution provider, assuming there is *no unplanned downtime*. One explanation is that predictive maintenance solutions do not interfere with the production process and, for that reason, have a low risk profile for organizations entering the industrial AI learning curve.

According to *IoT Analytics'* 2024 market analysis, the popularity of predictive maintenance use cases has declined, with quality prediction and inspection use cases gaining traction [118].

Solution Brief 18-3: Predictive Maintenance for Automotive Clamps (inpro)

Challenge

- Micro-faults cause cycle delays and lower production throughput.
- Wear or misalignments stay hidden until a full system breakdown.
- Static maintenance misses early signs of performance drift.

No real-time insights into asset behavior or root causes

Solution "clamp.io"

- AI monitoring using edge-deployed machine learning models.
- Sensors capture asset status (e. g., clamp positions) continuously.
- Predictive alerts follow industry and OEM-specific parameters.
- Flexible deployment on the Siemens Industrial Edge platform.

Benefits

- Higher equipment uptime through proactive issue detection.
- Maintenance only when needed, reducing service costs overall.
- Integration with existing brownfield equipment is seamless.
- Minimal effort needed to tailor the AI system per customer, scales efficiently.

Customers: Volkswagen

Provider: inpro, Berlin, Germany; *inpro.de*

18.3 Fleet Management

Fleet Management refers to the organized system companies use to manage and track their vehicle assets – including trucks, vans, cars, and other vehicles – to ensure they operate efficiently and safely [119].

Side Note: In an industrial setup, fleet management can also mean coordinating, monitoring, and optimizing the movement of multiple AGVs within a facility. Its primary function is to efficiently assign transport tasks, manage traffic flow to prevent congestion, and dynamically charge or dispatch vehicles to maximize material handling throughput. See related Section 24.7.1.

AI supports Fleet Management tasks as follows [120]:

- *Route optimization:* Real-time data analysis on traffic, road conditions, and delivery schedules to instantly determine and update the most efficient routes; it can automatically reroute vehicles if unexpected events (such as traffic jams) occur. This leads to faster deliveries and lower fuel consumption.
- *Predictive maintenance* through vehicle sensor data and maintenance records to predict precisely when a vehicle will need servicing.

- *Driver safety and monitoring:* Driving pattern analysis detects risky behaviors such as harsh braking, rapid acceleration, or speeding. Fleet managers can use this information to provide targeted training and feedback, thereby reducing the likelihood of accidents and related insurance costs.
- *Resource allocation:* By tracking vehicle usage and demand patterns, AI helps managers efficiently assign the right vehicles and drivers to the right jobs.

Solution Brief 18-4: AI-based Fleet Management (Geotab)

Challenge

- High operational costs from fuel usage, idling, and frequent maintenance.
- Safety risks from driver distractions, collisions, and unsafe behaviors.
- Inefficient operations are causing reduced productivity and unnecessary fleet downtime.
- Difficulty managing regulatory compliance and achieving sustainability targets.

Solution Geotab Platform

- Unified open platform connecting entire fleets for comprehensive management.
- Telematics hardware captures real-time location and engine health data.
- AI-powered dash cams deliver instant in-cab driver coaching.
- An extensive marketplace with integrations to customize and extend functionality.

Benefits

- Reduced costs for fuel, maintenance, and insurance premiums.
- Improved safety with fewer accidents and better driver performance.
- Increased productivity and efficiency through actionable, data-driven insights.
- Streamlined compliance and support for sustainability and electrification goals.

Customers: California Freight, Enterprise (car rental), PepsiCo, State of Utah

Provider: Geotab, Oakville, Ontario, Canada; *geotab.com*

19 Audit

The *audit* function is a critical, independent assurance and consulting activity within an enterprise. Its primary role is to evaluate and improve the effectiveness of governance, risk management, and internal control processes. It provides objective insights for management and the supervisory board, ensuring regulatory compliance, safeguarding assets, and enhancing the organization's overall value.

Data analytics and AI transform the audit profession from a historically interview-driven process to a dynamic, data-centric discipline [121]. The days of auditors primarily relying on anecdotal evidence are fading, replaced by a sophisticated approach that leverages vast datasets, particularly from ERP systems [122]. This shift allows auditors to analyze transactional data, identify anomalies, and uncover potential risks with precision and efficiency.

The integration of AI tools enables auditors to process and scrutinize 100% of a company's data, rather than relying on sampling [123]. AI algorithms can automatically detect unusual payment patterns, duplicate invoices, or unauthorized transactions in ERP data and flag them for human review.

Moreover, this data-driven approach builds a crucial bridge to *continuous controls monitoring*. Instead of periodic point-in-time checks, AI-powered systems can continuously monitor key controls and alert auditors to any deviations in real time. This constant vigilance transforms audit from a reactive exercise into a proactive risk-management function, allowing organizations to address control weaknesses before they escalate into significant problems (see the Three-Way-Match in Section 22.6 as an example).

GenAI further amplifies these capabilities, particularly by unlocking the corporate memory of past audits. For new auditors, navigating a company's historical audit findings, recommended measures, and implemented solutions can be daunting. GenAI can process and synthesize years of unstructured audit reports, internal memos, and corrective action plans. By querying a GenAI model, a new auditor can instantly access insights into recurring issues, effective mitigation strategies, and the overall control environment, effectively democratizing institutional knowledge. This not only accelerates the learning curve for new professionals but also ensures a consistent, informed approach to future audits, leveraging the collective experience to strengthen future assurances [122].

Solution Brief 19-1: Correlating Data in Unstructured Documents (Datasnipper)

Challenge

- Past audit procedures and ongoing audits are primarily based on unstructured documents, including financial statements, PDF exports of transactional data, and documentation of financial procedures, such as handbooks.
- Auditors need to review extensive documentation for their tests.

Solution

- Datasnipper extracts data from unstructured file formats such as PDFs and helps correlate transactional data wherever feasible.
- AI supports this process in an audit-proof way, drawing stringent and transparent conclusions.
- Document processing is supported in many languages. An Excel plug-in aligns with how auditors work in daily life.

Benefits

- Increased efficiency in document reviews (reportedly >60% efficiency gains).
- Increased quality in auditing as "spaghetti documents" can be flattened for better review.

Customers: Deloitte, EY, Grant Thornton, KPMG, Siemens Healthineers

Provider: Datasnipper, Amsterdam, Netherlands; *datasnipper.com*

20 Product Design & Engineering

Product Design & Engineering is the starting point of a product's lifecycle. It sets the foundational blueprint for all subsequent manufacturing and business processes.

This chapter follows through from Computer-Aided Design, where 2D and 3D models of a product build the conceptual design, Computer-Aided Engineering with its simulation-heavy work on achieving engineering maturity, Computer-Aided Process Planning, which generates manufacturing routines and instructions, to Computer-Aided Manufacturing, where machine-level instructions are derived, for example, for machining or additive processes.

20.1 Computer-Aided Design

Computer-Aided Design (CAD) software is used to create 2D and 3D models of a product. It focuses on the conceptual and visual aspects of design, allowing engineers and designers to explore ideas and create virtual models before any physical work begins.

These AI assistants can automate repetitive design tasks, suggest component placements based on best practices learned from past projects, and provide real-time feedback on the manufacturability and cost implications of design choices. *Similarity search* in designs is becoming increasingly mature and relevant, helping to avoid duplication of design work and contributing to sourcing consolidation.

Several market players are working to extend the modalities of large models to 2D and 3D CAD. In addition to enabling a new level of similarity search, this would allow natural language to be used to create and modify CAD models and to query them.

20.1.1 Mechanical CAD

Mechanical Computer-Aided Design (MCAD) helps engineers to create, analyze, and optimize 3D models and 2D technical drawings of mechanical parts, assemblies, and systems. It facilitates precise design and bridges to CAE (e. g., simulation of real-world performance, such as stress and motion) and to PDM/PMI (see Section 20.2.3), including manufacturing data such as bills of materials.

AI can support:

- the *creation of CAD models from scratch*: Several R&D initiatives and first offerings provide "CAD as a Modality" of LLMs. In a nutshell: As programmatic commands can describe CAD models in a specific 3D language, LLMs are useful for transforming requirements expressed by natural language prompts into CAD models, in the same way that LLMs do this for software code.

Solution Brief 20-1: CAD as an AI Model Modality (Autodesk)

Challenge
- Design tools struggle with interpreting geometry and systems beyond textual prompts.
- Traditional CAD workflows are slow and constrained by legacy parametric engines.
- Engineers need to move quickly from concept to detailed layout without re-work.
- Integrating design, make, and build phases remains fragmented across tools.

Solution "Neural CAD"
- Neural CAD model trained to reason about geometry and building systems.
- Text prompts, sketches, or spatial constraints help generate editable CAD geometry.
- AI integration from early concept to detailed design and manufacturing pipelines.
- Trained on professional design data for industry-relevant outputs.

Benefits
- Accelerated design generation and iteration, driving faster concept-to-CAD output.
- Better collaboration between design and manufacturing, reducing hand-offs.

Customers: Isar Aerospace, RFA Rocket Factory, Siemens

Provider: Autodesk, San Francisco, California, USA; *autodesk.com/solutions/autodesk-ai/neural-technology*

- *3D Scan to CAD model conversion:* This is a non-trivial task, as 3D scanning provides point clouds as an output. Transforming point clouds into 3D models with minimal human rework is an art form. Still, it clearly helps engineers substantially, for example, by enabling the reproduction of spare parts for which 3D CAD models are unavailable.

Particularly in industries where field services are provided by companies other than the original producer of a system, spare part reengineering is almost a core process – think of maintenance services for small- and medium-sized gas turbines.

Solution Brief 20-2: 3D Part Scans to CAD Conversion (backflip.ai)

Challenge
- Traditional 3D design software is complex and requires specialized skills.
- Broken manufacturing parts cause costly production downtime.
- Manual measurement and recreation of replacement parts is slow.
- 3D scanning often produces unusable, complex surface textures.

Solution
- Proprietary AI foundation model trained on over 100 million 3D geometries.
- Converts text, images, or sketches into 3D printable models.
- Automated "Scan-to-CAD" converts 3D scans into parametric CAD files.
- Novel neural representation teaches AI to "think" in 3D.

Benefits
- Reduces design time from days to minutes.
- Makes 3D creation accessible to users without CAD expertise.
- Minimizes manufacturing downtime by quickly producing replacement parts.
- Delivers clean, manufacturable geometries compatible with existing software.

Customers: Gillette, Honda, KUKA, Lockheed Martin, SpaceX

Provider: Backflip AI, Miami, Florida, USA; *backflip.ai*

- *AI-assisted CAD Quality Assurance*: AI in different flavors plays an essential role in MCAD (and ECAD) quality assurance. This can include engineering design rule checks, drawing consistency checks (remember that drawings of large systems can span several sheets of paper), and testing for compliance with specific modeling standards.

Solution Brief 20-3: AI-based Reviews of Engineering Drawings (CoLab Software)

Challenge
- Engineering teams waste 23% of their time on repetitive, non-value-added administrative design checks.
- Critical tribal knowledge is buried in siloed spreadsheets or lost.
- Manual reviews often miss subtle geometric flaws, cross-sheet inconsistencies, or complex Design for Manufacturability issues.

Solution Brief 20-3: AI-based Reviews of Engineering Drawings (CoLab Software)

Solution "Auto Review"
- AI Peer Checker automatically annotates 3D models and 2D drawings against technical standards.
- Similarity Engine identifies related past designs to surface relevant historical lessons learned proactively.
- Automated Issue Tracking transforms AI-generated markups into structured, actionable tasks within the digital thread.

Benefits
- Reclaims nearly a quarter of engineering capacity by automating routine documentation and validation.
- Collapses design cycles from months to hours through rapid, parallelized AI-powered feedback loops.
- Drastically reduces the cost of poor quality by catching errors before production release.

Customers: Bissell Homecare, Hoshiza, Molex, Schaeffler

Provider: CoLab Software, St. John's, Canada; *colabsoftware.com/product/autoreview*

20.1.2 Electrical CAD

Electrical CAD (ECAD) supports the design and development of a wide range of electrical and electronic components, including *Printed Circuit Boards* (PCBs), integrated circuits, cable harnesses, and electrical cabinets. ECAD, as a discipline, encompasses many aspects of MCAD; consider the 3D geometry of a large cable harness or the challenge of stacking automation control equipment into an electrical cabinet with a minimized form factor. Structurally, electrical design can be supported through MCAD AI, including design generation and the quality assurance of schematics and designs. As in the semiconductor industry, place-and-route algorithms significantly contribute to product quality, as form factor, electrical performance, and side effects on other system components (e. g., robustness against radio interference) are related to optimal place-and-route choices.

Solution Brief 20-4: AI-powered Electrical Engineering (non-PCB) (WSCAD)

Challenge
- Routine electrical CAD tasks consume excessive time and clicks.
- Design errors remain undetected until late in the process, increasing rework and costs.
- Shortage of skilled electrical CAD engineers limits project capacity.
- Complex tool menus challenge occasional users and slow onboarding.

Solution Brief 20-4: AI-powered Electrical Engineering (non-PCB) (WSCAD) ***(continued)***

Solution "ElectriX for Building Automation", "Cabinet Engineering"

- AI Copilot interprets natural-language commands to execute CAD tasks instantly.
- Automated error-checking and diagnostics surface issues in seconds.
- Unified platform supports multiple disciplines: electrical, cabinet, fluid, and automation.

Benefits

- Design tasks completed in seconds instead of minutes/hours.
- Significant reduction in errors and rework, improving quality.
- Less-experienced users can perform advanced tasks, reducing dependence on experts.

Customers: Isar Aerospace, RFA Rocket Factory, Siemens

Provider: WSCAD, Bergkirchen, Germany; *wscad.com*; *wscaduniverse.com*

Solution Brief 20-5: AI-powered Electrical Engineering (PCB) (Celus)

Challenge

- Electronics design projects take weeks or months due to manual workflows.
- Engineers struggle to select components amid supply-chain risks and many variants.
- Fragmented data and component libraries slow down BOM generation.

Solution

- Automatically converts technical requirements into schematics and BOMs.
- CUBO™ component database recommends parts and designs.
- Integrations with primary EDA tools (e. g., native exports, ecosystem connectors).
- Component manufacturers & distributors enrich data, expedite sourcing and design.

Benefits

- Up to ~90% reduction in design time by automating key engineering tasks.
- Improved component choice and supply-chain visibility, reducing risk and re-work.
- Engineers at various skill levels can produce viable hardware designs.
- Ecosystem collaboration (design, manufacturing, sourcing) with high innovation throughput.

Customers: AGS Devices, Renesas Electronics

Provider: **Celus.io**, München, Germany; *celus.io*

20.2 Computer-Aided Engineering

Computer-Aided Engineering (CAE) software then uses these models to simulate real-world conditions by applying engineering principles. It analyzes the design for properties such as structural integrity, fluid dynamics, and thermal performance, enabling engineers to optimize the product virtually.

20.2.1 Simulation

Simulation as an art form is very dependent on computing resources, and it is no surprise that the largest *High-Performance Computing* (HPC) clusters, the 'supercomputers of this world', are all used to run military and non-military simulations. Large corporations with simulation-intensive CAE processes and IP protection needs have built their own HPC clusters (e. g., semiconductor, automotive, aerospace).

As *Design Space Exploration* (see Section 20.2.2) for product attributes and even for manufacturability requires even more product "dimensions" to be simulated, AI can shortcut computationally expensive calculation runs by AI model-based estimations.

Within the discipline of simulation, simulation accuracy is a constant concern: The more accurate a simulation is, the more physical and costly prototyping can be avoided. On the other hand, simulation accuracy typically comes at the cost of additional computational time and costs. AI can accelerate simulation performance and, as AI estimations replace calculations, adds to the "uncertainty" in simulation results. It is a common approach to work along the lines of a simulation and prototyping funnel:

- 1,000 s of AI-accelerated simulation runs identify the top 10 design variants.
- 10 design variants are simulated with less uncertainty, accepting longer simulation runs and higher compute costs.
- Just the best 2–3 design variants are then physically built to enter field testing.

In addition to the funnel concept, AI-supported high-speed simulation supports a *Shift-left*. Historically, design engineers had to wait days or even weeks for simulation feedback on proposed design changes (e. g., the impact of a change to an exterior car rear mirror on wind resistance and fuel consumption). Using accelerated simulation methods, such as surrogate models, provides engineers with instant feedback, ultimately shortening go-to-market times while avoiding idle time waiting for simulation results.

The following techniques replace or augment computationally intensive traditional solvers:

- *Surrogate models:* These are computationally cheap, data-driven approximations of expensive simulations or experiments. They work as black-box models, mapping inputs to outputs learned from a limited dataset. For example, a neural network is trained on results from a few hundred expensive CFD runs (see Section 20.2.1.2) to predict aerodynamic drag for new designs in real time.
- *Reduced Order Models* (ROMs): ROMs are mathematical simplifications of complex, high-fidelity, physics-based systems (e. g., a Finite Element Model; see related Section 20.2.1.1). They reduce the degrees of freedom by projecting the original equations onto a small set of basic functions.
- *Physics-Informed Neural Networks* (PINNs): PINNs are a hybrid approach that integrates the governing physical laws (*Partial Differential Equations*, or PDEs) directly into the neural network's loss function during training. This forces the model to adhere to known physics, enabling accurate predictions with less training data and better generalization than purely data-driven surrogates. They are used to solve PDEs or to infer unknown parameters, such as material elasticity, from minimal sensor data.
- *Geometrical deep learning* extends deep learning to handle non-Euclidean data like 3D meshes, graphs, and the point clouds common in engineering. It uses models such as *graph neural networks*, which analyze relationships between interconnected nodes (e. g., atoms in a molecule or nodes in a simulation mesh). It facilitates the creation of robust surrogates that can predict complete 3D fields (e. g., stress or airflow) for designs with highly variable, non-parametric geometries.

20.2.1.1 Finite Element Analysis

Finite Element Analysis (FEA) predicts how structures and materials will respond to external forces, heat, vibrations, and other physical effects. By dividing complex geometries into simpler elements, FEA enables precise analysis of stress, strain, and deformation. It is widely applied in mechanical, civil, and aerospace engineering to optimize designs, reduce material costs, and ensure safety and performance before physical prototypes are built.

AI accelerates FEA by acting as a powerful, rapid *surrogate model*: ML algorithms are trained on datasets of traditional FEA results to learn the complex, non-linear relationships between a component's design and its physical performance (e. g., stress, heat flow). This enables the algorithms to predict outcomes in milliseconds, drastically cutting the computational time required by classical solvers. For example, an AI model can instantly predict stress hotspots on hundreds of car frame designs, allowing engineers to iterate and optimize a structure for safety and weight far faster than traditional, hour-long FEA runs.

20.2.1.2 Computational Fluid Dynamics

Computational Fluid Dynamics (CFD) is constrained by significant computational time. ML models are trained on vast datasets of full CFD simulation results (solving the Navier-Stokes equations). Once trained, these models can predict complex fluid behavior, such as pressure and velocity fields, in seconds rather than hours.

Solution Brief 20-6: AI-accelerated Physics Simulation (Luminary Cloud)

Challenge

- Traditional simulations take days, creating bottlenecks in rapid design cycles.
- On-premise hardware limits massive parallel simulations or complex physics.
- High barriers to entry due to specialized expertise required for meshing and setup.

Solution

- Physics AI (SHIFT Models): Pre-trained industry models providing near-instant performance predictions without meshing.
- Cloud-Native GPU Acceleration: Massively parallel NVIDIA GPU clusters deliver speeds up to 100x faster.
- Lumi AI Copilot: AI assistant that automates simulation setup, orchestration, and complex engineering workflows.

Benefits

- Reduces early-stage development costs by up to 80% through virtual wind tunnels.
- Accelerates time-to-market by evaluating thousands of design iterations in seconds, not weeks.
- Democratizes high-fidelity engineering insights for designers earlier in the product development process.

Customers: Flighthouse Engineering, Joby, Nautilus, Northrop Grumman

Provider: Luminary Cloud, Redwood City, California, USA; *luminarycloud.com*

Supporting CFD with AI-driven predictions has become a significant area of startup momentum, with notable players including PhysicsX.ai, Emmi AI, SimmulAItion, and BeyondMath [124].

20.2.1.3 Test Plan Management

Effective test plan creation and management are the cornerstones of high-quality engineering, ensuring systems meet rigorous performance and safety standards. This discipline involves defining a strategic scope, identifying critical risks, and allocating resources to validate complex architectures. By systematically organizing test cases and tracking execution metrics, engineers proactively mitigate defects. Given the complexity of an engineered system, test data poses a 'big data' challenge that requires structure and rigor, as well as pattern detection, to uncover quality issues in the sheer volume of data.

Solution Brief 20-7: ML-enhanced Test Plan Management (Monolith AI)

Challenge

- Test plans are inefficient with 50–5000 channels, causing delays and high costs.
- Test data often contains undetected errors, leading to costly retesting.
- Failures in late-stage validation risk brand reputation and budgets.
- Physical testing is time-consuming and expensive, especially for complex systems.

Solution

- AI-driven platform automates test plan optimization and data validation.
- Self-learning models detect anomalies and predict system behavior.
- Integrates with existing test infrastructure and engineering workflows.
- Provides a user-friendly interface tailored for engineering teams.

Benefits

- Reduces test plans by up to 70%, saving time and resources.
- Detecting over 90% of errors faster, improving data reliability.
- Accelerates time-to-market without compromising product safety.
- Enhances engineering precision, reducing the risk of costly failures.

Customers: BMW, Honeywell, Siemens

Provider: Monolith AI, Cambridge, UK; *monolithai.com*

20.2.2 Design Space Exploration

Design Space Exploration (DSE) is a systematic process of evaluating a large number of potential design alternatives to identify an optimal or near-optimal solution that meets a client's specific requirements. Unlike a simple trial-and-error approach, DSE evaluates trade-offs among design parameters, including performance, cost, energy consumption, and reliability. By exploring the full spectrum of possibilities, DSE helps to uncover innovative and efficient solutions that might otherwise be missed

- in the *development phase of new products* with improved product feature performance (e.g., the size of a consumer electronics product needs to be minimized while keeping the thermal behavior of the PCB in line with parameters for the targeted product lifetime); and
- in the *context of system and project sales*, where a standard solution is insufficient (e.g., the hull form of a naval vessel is optimized against target performance parameters and harbor layout conditions).

AI benefits DSE in two ways: it reduces the time required for an individual simulation run. Furthermore, AI can be trained to assess interim results of several simulation runs: If the AI-based assessment of the simulation result already concludes that a specific design variant will never make it into the top 10 design variants, the rest of the simulation is skipped, and the next design variant enters the simulation phase. This reduces simulation time across multiple design variants by up to 60% [125].

Regaining Competitive Edge with Accelerated Design Space Exploration

Siemens Energy's competitiveness struggled in the market for large gas turbines as a competitor was beating their turbine efficiency by a percentage point – a significant business case disadvantage in energy generation. The engineering team faced intense pressure to improve the gas turbine design in a short period. Because many tuning parameters for turbine blade design contradict each other, they relied heavily on DSE. To accelerate simulation, their team implemented *reduced order modeling* in combination with an AI prediction, skipping further computation for a simulation run on a design unlikely to outperform previous runs. This saved over 15,000 h of compute time (and costs), sped up the Go-to-Market, and even increased the lifespan of turbine blades by 20% [125].

Solution Brief 20-8: Generative Design for Maritime Assets (Compute Maritime)

Challenge

- Ships and other maritime vessels are not fully leveraging the best designs for fuel efficiency and reduced environmental impact.
- Manually iterating through design options is too cumbersome.

Solution "NeuralShipper"

- AI-driven design exploration specifically to the naval architecture and maritime industry, optimizing ship hull designs for factors like fuel efficiency and stability.
- Generates high-fidelity NURBS geometries for direct CAD workflows, delivering industry-ready, mathematically precise, CAD-native outputs.

Benefits

- Generated designs improve ship fuel efficiency and overall performance.
- Superior hydrodynamics at lower OpEx and reduced environmental impact.

Customers: BAR Technologies, BYD Naval Architects, Fram Marine

Provider: Compute Maritime (UK); *computemaritime.com*

20.2.3 Product Data Management

Product Data Management (PDM) centralizes the storage and organization of all product-related technical data, acting as a single source of truth for engineering and manufacturing teams. Its core function is to securely manage intellectual assets, such as

CAD files, drawings, specifications, and *Bills of Materials* (BOMs). PDM provides key features, including version control to track every change and workflow automation to streamline approvals and revisions. By ensuring that all stakeholders, from design through production, access only current, accurate information, PDM significantly improves collaboration, reduces costly errors, and accelerates the product's time-to-market. Ever-increasing compliance reporting requirements, such as product CO_2 footprint reporting, export control classifications, and supply chain partner compliance, have heightened the significance of PDM over the last decade. PDM is a foundational layer within the broader *Product Lifecycle Management* (PLM) concept.

20.2.3.1 Part Classification

Part classification organizes a company's products, parts, and documents based on shared attributes like design characteristics (e. g., geometry, size, material) and manufacturing attributes (e. g., required process steps) or sourcing attributes. This organization typically employs a structured coding system, such as eCl@ss or ETIM, to create part families [126].

Text-based similarity searching has long supported part classification tasks. First AI (and non-AI) solutions have been launched that handle geometric similarity searches across CAD files, further maturing automated part classification. Design characteristics can be extracted from mechanical or electrical CAD files and used as input for part family selection and attribute specification.

Solution Brief 20-9: Automated Part Classification (Siemens)

Challenge
- Time-intensive effort to manually classify and rationalize high volumes of parts.
- Time-intensive effort to identify brownfield parts without an identifier.

Solution Teamcenter X
- AI engine learns from classified objects in Teamcenter.
- Supports human-in-the-loop or complete automation of classification tasks.
- Visual search finds parts by matching photos with CAD geometry.
- Natural language interface for users.

Benefits
- Lower cost of classifying product data while reducing errors.
- Faster identification of legacy parts.

Customers: Apple, Bosch, CycloTech, Ford, GM

Provider: Siemens, Munich/Berlin, Germany; *siemens.com, blogs.sw.siemens.com/teamcenter/plm-genai-teamcenter*

20.2.3.2 Bill of Material Management

Large enterprises often have thousands of products with sprawling *Bills of Materials* (BOMs). A BOM is a comprehensive, structured list of all the items, assemblies, components, parts, and quantities required to manufacture, build, or service a product, but its content and structure vary significantly based on the intended use within the enterprise. Examples include [127]:

- The *Design BOM* (DBOM) is the initial, product-centric list created by R&D or CAD software, focusing on the functional and geometric relationships of parts as drawn.
- The *Engineering BOM* (EBOM), created by the engineering team, refines the DBOM by incorporating non-geometric components such as standard fasteners, bulk materials, and packaging specifications, making the product ready for industrialization.
- The *Manufacturing BOM* (MBOM 1) is process-centric; it restructures the EBOM to reflect how the product is built, listing items in the sequence of assembly operations, often grouping parts into kits or defining labor and machinery requirements for a specific manufacturing plant.
- The *Sales BOM* (SBOM) is customer-facing, detailing the product and its configuration options as sold, often defining the final deliverable items for a sales order.[1)]
- The *Maintenance BOM* (MBOM 2) – also known as the Service BOM – lists parts needed to maintain or repair the product after sale, focusing on service kits and easily replaceable modules.
- Finally, the *Recycling or Disassembly BOM* is structured to define the materials and sequence needed to efficiently take the product apart at its end-of-life for recycling or component recovery.

AI supports bill of materials management as follows:

- *AI-assisted BOM creation:* AI algorithms can crawl through CAD files and derive a draft for a design or engineering BOM.
- *BOM synchronization:* Keeping the different BOM types synchronized is a painstaking task, specifically as data links between, say, an EBOM and an MBOM 1 are challenging to maintain. Example: When a production site updates MBOM 1 due to a change in part geometry from a part supplier, the EBOM update is missed.
- *BOM consolidation:* NLP, clustering algorithms, and similarity search in related CAD files can identify redundant or functionally equivalent parts across different product lines. This enables engineers to consolidate the parts catalog, leading to

1 The abbreviation SBOM is also used for Software Bill-of-Materials in a software engineering context.

significant savings through volume purchasing, reduced inventory, and simplified logistics.

- *Bill of Process creation:* AI can crawl through the EBOM and generate drafts for a bill of process (see Section 20.4.1).
- *Obsolescence forecasting:* AI models systematically monitor and evaluate extensive streams of external data, including supplier announcements, market trends, component lifecycles from platforms such as SiliconExpert BOM Manager [128], and historical part failure rates. These capabilities enable AI to forecast which components are at risk of becoming obsolete, along with the anticipated timing and underlying causes, often well in advance of formal end-of-life notifications. This approach facilitates proactive management of BOM obsolescence [129].

Solution Brief 20-10: CAD Drawings to Bill of Materials (Markovate)

Challenge

- Converting complex CAD drawings into accurate bills of materials is slow and labor-intensive.
- Manual blueprint interpretation often results in costly errors, inconsistencies, and production rework.
- Traditional rule-based automation fails to adapt to diverse drawing styles or unstructured data.

Solution "AI Blueprint Classifier"

- DL-based image processing to identify, segment, and color-code critical regions on blueprints.
- Intelligent AI models extract dimensions, GD&T symbols, and materials to generate production-ready BOMs.
- AI interprets relationships between components, assembly sequences, and manufacturing specifications.

Benefits

- Accelerates project completion and plan review times by up to 30%.
- 90% reduction in manual marking errors and associated operational risks.
- Decreases labor costs by 15%.

Customers: ProForge Industries, Titan Manufacturing

Provider: Markovate, San Francisco, CA, USA; *markovate.com*

20.2.4 Model-Based Systems Engineering

Model-Based Systems Engineering (MBSE) means the conception, design, and maintenance of complex industrial systems – from smart factories to autonomous vehicles. It moves away from document-centric engineering, where requirements, designs, and analysis artifacts are scattered across disparate Word documents, spreadsheets, and drawings. Instead, MBSE formalizes the entire engineering process by creating a single, integrated, and authoritative digital model of the system. This digital artifact serves as the single source of truth, capturing requirements, functional definitions, architectural structure, and verification methods using standardized graphical modeling languages, most notably the *Systems Modeling Language* (SysML) [130].

By centralizing all system knowledge, MBSE significantly enhances communication and clarity across large, multidisciplinary teams, drastically reducing the ambiguity and misinterpretation inherent in text-based specifications. The core value of MBSE lies in its ability to manage the overwhelming complexity inherent in modern cyber-physical systems that merge mechanical, electronic, and software components. The modeling environment enforces rigor and strict traceability, ensuring that every functional requirement is directly linked to an architectural element and a corresponding validation test – a necessity for regulatory compliance and safety-critical applications. This digital continuity enables engineers to perform sophisticated trade-off analysis and simulations – evaluating factors such as performance, reliability, safety, and cost – far earlier in the design cycle, a practice known as “shifting left”. By integrating analysis tools directly into the master design model, design flaws are identified and corrected before they become costly downstream manufacturing issues.

Furthermore, because the MBSE model can serve as a detailed, structured, and machine-readable representation of the intended system (especially with SysML v2), it serves as the essential blueprint for commissioning and maintaining a high-fidelity Digital Twin throughout the system’s operational lifecycle.

AI, particularly LLMs and NLP, plays an instrumental role at the interface between requirements engineering and the construction of a consistent model representation of a complex system.

Requirements Engineering in the Power Plant Industry

Assystem, a French-based global provider of power plant engineering services, fine-tuned an LLM to understand codes, regulations, and engineering rules for nuclear power plants. Their CurieLM is used to crawl large-scale tender documentation, extract system-component relationships, and draft visual models of a function diagram and a project breakdown structure. Requirements from the tender documentation are linked to respective model artifacts. This saves engineers significant manual modeling work.

Solution Brief 20-11: Dynamical System Modeling (Collimator)

Challenge

- Legacy engineering tools are desktop-bound, siloed, and lack native support for AI/ML workflows.
- Modeling complex, nonlinear dynamical systems using only physics-based equations is slow and imprecise.
- Local hardware constraints limit the ability to run massive parallel simulations or optimizations.

Solution

- Python-native platform integrates deep learning libraries such as PyTorch and TensorFlow for hybrid modeling.
- AI-driven "System Identification" (SINDy) automatically creates mathematical plant models from experimental data.
- JAX-powered backend enables automatic differentiation and high-performance cloud computing for rapid optimization.

Benefits

- Accelerates design cycles by shifting simulation run times from hours to minutes via high-performance computing.
- Reduces verification and validation time by up to 75% through automated AI-powered testing.
- Enables Digital Twins that combine real-world data with physics, for example, for superior predictive maintenance.

Customers: Grace, Nesa Innovation Labs, Redback Technologies

Provider: Collimator, Denver, CO, USA

20.3 Product Design Quality Assurance

This is the critical process of validating and verifying the quality and functionality of a product design before it moves to manufacturing. This goes beyond a simple check; it is a formal, systematic activity that ensures the design meets all performance, reliability, and safety standards. It is where the theoretical design is tested against practical requirements, a process greatly enhanced by CAE simulations.

20.3.1 Design Rule Checking

Design Rule Checking (DRC) is a quality-assurance step across numerous engineering disciplines, including mechanical component development and microchip design. DRC is the automated verification of a design against predefined geometrical, electrical, or manufacturing constraints to ensure correctness, manufacturability, and adherence to industry standards.

While traditional DRC systems are highly effective at flagging explicit violations, integrating industrial AI elevates the process to new levels of sophistication. AI-powered DRC can go beyond static rule sets by learning complex patterns from large datasets of successful and failed designs. This enables it to identify subtle, emergent issues that conventional rules might miss, predict potential performance problems, and even proactively suggest design improvements.

20.3.2 Design For Manufacturability

Design for Manufacturability (DFM) is the practice of designing a product or assembly with manufacturing in mind, aiming to create a design that meets all functional and quality requirements while being produced in the simplest, least expensive way possible. DFM emphasizes involving all stakeholders – including design, manufacturing, quality, and purchasing – early in the process to adhere to the "Rule of 10", which states that the cost of a change increases tenfold at each successive stage of development (see Figure 20.1).

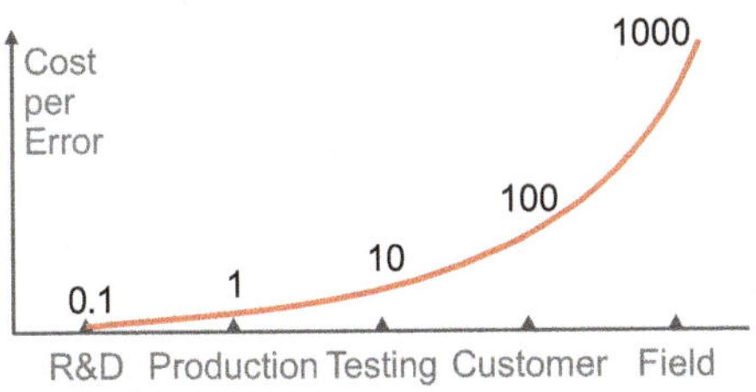

Figure 20.1
Rule of 10: Costs of errors multiply 10x in later stages

DFM focuses on the following key areas [131]:

- *Designing components for ease of fabrication:* Using off-the-shelf or common parts and optimal materials;
- *Designing for ease of assembly:* Reducing part count and using *Geometric Dimensioning and Tolerancing* (GD&T) to enlarge acceptable tolerance zones;
- *Designing for inspection:* Inspection methods and measurement instruments used to certify manufacturing conformity should be considered early in the design of products.
- DFM has recently gained momentum from increased focus on sustainability and Zero-Waste-Zero-Defect concepts, respectively, including Zero-Defect Manufacturing.

20.3.3 Supply Chain Analytics for Parts

Before a product can be built, its components must be sourced. AI models can analyze vast datasets on supplier performance, material costs, and geopolitical risks to create a more resilient, cost-effective supply chain. These systems can predict supplier delays, identify opportunities to reduce costs by using alternative parts, and flag potential supply chain risks long before they become critical.

Solution Brief 20-12: Supply Chain Transparency for Electronic Parts (SupplyFrame)

Challenge

- Limited visibility into market data.
- Reactive decisions cause costly delays.
- Inefficient sourcing, missed savings opportunities.

Solution "NPI", "DirectSource", "DesignSense", "Commodity IQ"

- Aggregates billions of supply chain data points of parts searched, parts used, and parts offered.
- AI-powered predictive market intelligence (e. g., on pricing and availability).
- Centralized platform for actionable insights in a multi-sided market model.

Benefits

- Proactive risk mitigation, enhanced resilience.
- Significant cost savings, optimized sourcing.
- Faster time-to-market, competitive advantage.

Customers: Baker Hughes, Dell, GE, Panasonic, Toshiba

Provider: SupplyFrame, Texas, USA; *supplyframe.com*

20.4 Computer-Aided Process Planning

Computer-Aided Process Planning (CAPP) translates the product design into a detailed manufacturing plan. It comprises a systematic approach using computer technology to determine the most efficient and cost-effective manufacturing routines, steps, and schedules. It acts as the critical bridge between product design (CAD) and manufacturing execution (CAM).

20.4.1 Discrete Manufacturing: From BOM to BOP

Deriving a *Bill of Process* (BOP) from a *Bill of Materials* (BOM) is a critical step that translates what is needed (the parts) into how it will be built (the steps). The process begins with the *Engineering BOM* (EBOM) or *Manufacturing BOM* (MBOM), which provides the component list.

Manufacturing engineers then define the specific sequence of work centers, operations, and tooling required to assemble those components. This involves grouping parts into kits, assigning them to discrete assembly steps, defining the time standards for each task, and specifying quality checks.

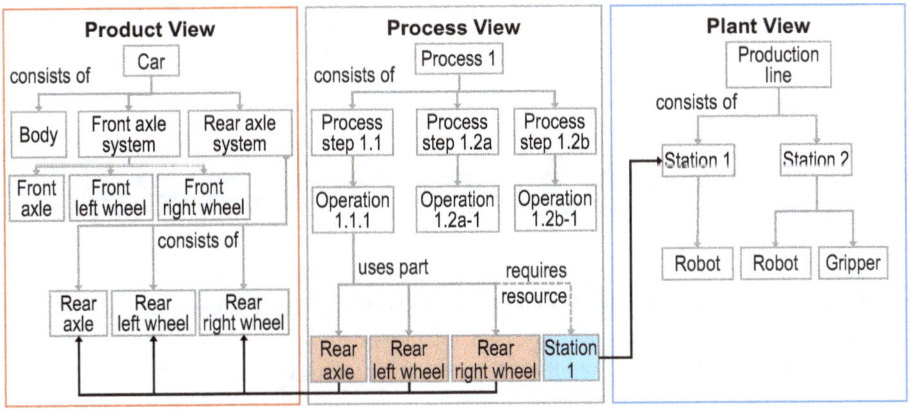

Figure 20.2 Production process definition using product data and plant setup

A modern BOP management solution simplifies complex process updates by integrating engineering changes with production planning. Examples are:

- *Centralized BOP definition:* Links process plans with MBOM for accurate manufacturing sequences.
- *Change management:* Synchronizes MBOM updates, enabling quick impact analysis and process adaptation.
- *Digital work instructions:* Delivers real-time, visual assembly guidance to the shop floor.
- *Automated change propagation:* Ensures process consistency across multiple production sites.
- *Process validation & optimization:* Supports virtual simulations, quality checks, and compliance verification.

> Believe it or not, BOM to BOP conversion, almost a holy grail for the industry, is in its infancy concerning AI support. Anyone tackling this challenge: *Please contact the author*!

20.4.2 Computer-Assisted Synthesis Planning

Computer-Assisted Synthesis Planning (CASP) defines the process by which new chemical compounds are designed and manufactured. At its core, CASP leverages sophisticated algorithms and vast chemical databases to help chemists and engineers devise optimal synthetic routes for target molecules. This is not just about finding a way to make something; it is about discovering the most efficient, safest, and most cost-effective pathways, often uncovering novel approaches that human intuition alone might miss.

Solution Brief 20-13: AI-assisted Protein Engineering (Cradle)

Challenge

- Traditional protein engineering is slow, costly, and sequential.
- Difficulty optimizing a protein for multiple desired properties in a single step.
- Need to explore a vast sequence space beyond human intuition quickly.
- High risk and expense from numerous experimental rounds (wet lab cycle).

Solution

- Generative AI models propose novel, optimized protein sequence candidates.
- AI fine-tunes models by iteratively learning from the customer's wet lab data.
- Enables co-optimization of complex properties like stability and affinity.
- Secure, user-friendly platform integrates AI directly into R&D workflows.

Benefits

- Achieves 1.5x to 12x faster development timelines.
- Significantly reduces experimental cycles, cutting R&D cost and time.
- Democratizes access to complex protein design for all scientists.
- Increases the probability of success by designing non-intuitive variants.

Customers: Corteva, IFF, Novonesis

Provider: Cradle, Amsterdam, Netherlands; *cradle.bio/solutions/industrial*

By integrating AI and machine learning, CASP systems can predict reaction outcomes, assess feasibility, and even suggest precursors, thereby significantly accelerating research and development cycles across industries such as pharmaceuticals, agrochemicals, and advanced materials. This intelligent automation not only boosts productivity and reduces waste but also enables the creation of entirely new substances with tailored properties, making it an indispensable tool for innovation in modern industrial chemistry.

20.5 Computer-Aided Manufacturing

The term *Computer-Aided Manufacturing* (CAM) is conceptually flexible, with its specific implementation dictated by the nature of the physical process it controls. While CAD defines the what – the geometry and specifications of a part – CAM defines the how – the step-by-step instructions for a machine to create that part. The diversity of CAM systems across industries is a direct consequence of the manufacturing processes themselves. The "how" in machining is a tool path; in additive manufacturing, a slicing recipe; in electronics, a data-rich stack of layers; and in process industries, a real-time control signal. Despite these functional and conceptual distinctions, all forms of CAM share a common purpose: to enable precision, consistency, and efficiency that far exceed those of manual methods.

This underlying conceptual framework clarifies the significant operational differences, as summarized in Table 20.1.

Table 20.1 High-level differences of CAM concepts by production type

CAM for	Primary Task	Conceptual Model	Typical Output
... Machining	Generate tool paths to remove material.	Subtractive geometry, tool-material interaction	NC code (G-code) for CNC machines.
... Additive Manufacturing	Generate build recipes to add material.	Layer-by-layer material deposition	Sliced data (G-code, SLC, CLI) for 3D printers.
... Electronics Manufacturing	Verify and prepare layered fabrication data.	Data management, verification, and alignment.	Fabrication files (Gerber, Excellon) for diverse machines.
... Process Industries	Monitor and control continuous material flow.	Supervisory and distributed control of variables.	Control signals, alarms, and HMI visualizations

The evolution of these systems points to a fundamental shift in automation's role. Historically, CAM systems automated the physical acts of machining or fabricating. Today, the focus is increasingly on automating human tasks such as programming and optimization. Features such as *automatic feature recognition* automate the labor-intensive process of toolpath creation, while generative design can autonomously generate thousands of optimized part designs based on constraints.

In process control, AI predicts upcoming issues using real-time data, enabling proactive intervention and reducing the need for manual operator oversight. This progression signifies a move from simple automation to the intelligent augmentation of human decision-making and expertise.

The ultimate direction of modern CAM is the convergence of these disparate systems. The existence of hybrid additive and subtractive machines, or modular, prefabricated factories, demonstrates that the rigid boundaries between discrete and process manufacturing are blurring. This synthesis requires a new generation of software and AI that can manage a unified digital thread, seamlessly translating design data into instructions for a multi-disciplinary workflow, encompassing everything from design optimization to a combined set of additive and subtractive manufacturing commands.

20.5.1 CAM for Machining

In machining and other subtractive processes, CAM's function is to translate a three-dimensional digital model into a set of actionable instructions that guide a CNC machine tool. This is accomplished by generating a tool path, a precise, mathematically calculated trajectory that a cutting tool follows to remove material from a workpiece. These toolpaths are converted into machine-readable numerical control code, most commonly *G-code*, which controls every aspect of the machining process, including axis movement, spindle speeds, and feed rates.

Solution Brief 20-14: AI-based CNC Machine Programming (Lambda Function AI)

Challenge

- CNC programming is slow, manual, and reliant on individual expertise.
- If done wrong, there is a risk of adverse events such as tool breakage and scrap.
- Lack of consistency and knowledge retention across different shifts/programmers.
- Need to significantly reduce cycle time and recurring operational costs.

Solution AMAS

- AI software integrated directly into CAM tools (NX, Mastercam, Fusion).
- AI recommends optimal machining strategies, tools, and cutting parameters.
- Real-time monitoring of tool load and process variables on the shop floor.
- Closed-loop learning uses shop-floor data to improve future programs.
- Technology Partners: Siemens, Mastercam, Autodesk.

Solution Brief 20-14: AI-based CNC Machine Programming (Lambda Function AI)

Benefits

- 10x+ faster programming time, saving hours of manual work.
- 30%+ lower recurring costs by optimizing tool use and efficiency.
- Enhanced precision and improved first-pass yield on complex parts.
- Better knowledge retention and continuous process improvement.

Customers: Leesta Industries, Kaneri Group, several aerospace and defense OEMs

Provider: Lambda Function AI, USA; *lambdafunction.ai*

A CAM workflow for machining is typically broken down into distinct operational phases. The initial phase, known as roughing, focuses on rapidly removing most of the material, leaving a small amount for later removal. The next phase, finishing, involves a series of fine, light passes to achieve the final, precise dimensions and the desired surface finish. Modern CAM software has advanced significantly to support complex operations such as 5-axis machining, enabling intricate geometries and providing access to parts from multiple angles in a single setup, thereby reducing the need for time-consuming manual retooling.

By simulating the operation in advance, engineers can identify potential issues such as tool collisions or un-machined areas, preventing costly mistakes and material waste before production even begins.

20.5.2 CAM for Additive Manufacturing

Instead of removing material, *CAM for Additive Manufacturing* (3D printing), or Additive CAM, creates instructions for a machine to precisely add material, layer by layer, until a physical part is constructed. The central operation in Additive CAM is slicing, in which the digital 3D model is decomposed into a series of horizontal 2D layers. The CAM software then generates the toolpath for each layer, guiding the machine's deposition head or laser to build the part from the ground up. Several critical preparatory steps accompany this process. For complex geometries and overhanging features, the software automatically generates and places support structures to prevent the part from collapsing during the build. It also performs nesting, which involves optimizing the orientation and placement of multiple parts on the build plate to maximize material utilization and minimize post-processing requirements.

20.5.3 CAM for Electronics Manufacturing

CAM for Electronics, specifically for *Printed Circuit Boards* (PCBs), operates on a different conceptual model. Unlike shaping a three-dimensional part, manufacturing a PCB involves creating and aligning a series of two-dimensional, data-rich layers. The core software in this domain is a *CAM processor*, which serves as a sophisticated data management and verification hub. Its primary task is to receive design files from the engineer, typically in formats like Gerber and Excellon, and prepare them for fabrication.

The CAM processor's functions are centered on ensuring manufacturability and data integrity. Its primary responsibilities include *Design Rule Checking* (DRC) (see Section 20.3.1), which continuously checks the design for compliance with rules for the final application, such as correct clearances and via density. A second critical function is *Design for Manufacturability* (DFM) (see Section 20.3.2), which evaluates the design against the specific physical requirements and limitations of the manufacturer's equipment to minimize production risks. This can involve automatically accounting for anticipated distortions during PCB layer lamination.

The output of this CAM process is not a single file for a single machine, but a suite of digital data modules for a variety of specialized tools, including photoplotters, CNC drills, and *Automated Optical Inspection* (AOI) machines, each with its own set of instructions. This multi-file, multi-machine output is a key differentiator for PCB CAM, distinguishing it from the single-machine focus of traditional machining.

20.5.4 On-Demand Manufacturing Marketplaces

On-demand manufacturing platforms like *Xometry* and *Protolabs* serve as a bridge between businesses that need custom parts and a vast, distributed network of manufacturers specializing in CNC machining, additive manufacturing, and other processes such as polishing.

At the heart of their business model stands an instant quoting engine that automates a process that once took days or even weeks: When an engineer uploads a 3D CAD file, the platform's algorithms analyze the part's geometry (*automatic feature recognition*), material, and required tolerances. The engine then instantly calculates production costs and lead times by referencing a massive dataset of past jobs and current market conditions. In addition to rapid feedback, the job is matched to the most suitable supplier within the network, optimizing for cost, location, and capability.

As machining job shops and end customers also benefit from costing automation as well, several SaaS providers are tackling this challenge with their own solutions, including Up2parts, MTK, Limitless NC, Paperless Parts, and LaserHub.

Solution Brief 20-15: AI-based PMI Extraction from Technical Drawings (werk24)

Challenge

- Many companies have a vast archive of valuable product designs stored as old 2D drawings in formats such as PDF or TIFF. Manually digitalizing these is a slow, error-prone process.
- Geometric tolerances and other quality properties embedded into legacy drawings are vital for machining job shops selecting suitable machines.

Solution

- werk24.io's AI models can read these technical drawings much like a human engineer, whether the drawings follow european or american CAD standards.
- Computer vision models extract all critical information – including dimensions, geometric tolerances, features, materials, and notes – and convert it into a machine-readable format, making legacy designs accessible for modern digital workflows.

Benefits

- Automated costing workflows of machining marketplaces benefit greatly from being able to deal with legacy drawings.
- End users can accelerate their engineering digitalization journey and feed their PDM systems quickly with quality data extracted from drawings.

Customers: DiManEx, Laserhub, Saphirion

Provider: Werk24, Munich, Germany; *werk24.io*

20.5.5 CAM for Process Industries

The term "CAM" as used in discrete manufacturing is not typically applied to process industries such as chemicals, pharmaceuticals, and food and beverage production. This is because these industries do not produce individual parts by shaping or adding material; instead, they manage the continuous or batch-based flow and transformation of substances. However, the core function of converting a design or recipe into actionable machine instructions remains, and distinct but analogous control systems fulfil it.

For large-scale, geographically dispersed operations, the functional equivalent of CAM is a *Supervisory Control and Data Acquisition* (SCADA) system. SCADA is a centralized system that gathers real-time operational data from remote locations and provides operators with a comprehensive view of the entire process via a Human-Machine Interface (HMI). Its primary focus is on data acquisition and high-level supervisory control, allowing human operators to monitor and make decisions to ensure efficiency and safety. For more complex and localized operations, a *Distributed Control System* (DCS) is the preferred solution. DCS uses a decentralized architecture with dedicated controllers near the process units, enabling more precise, real-time control of critical parameters such as temperature and pressure. This distributed, rapid-response control makes DCS the closest functional parallel to the direct machine control seen in traditional machining CAM. The increasing adoption of modular, prefabricated factories in process industries, such as the *factory-in-a-box* solution for pharmaceutical plants, further demonstrates how principles of discrete manufacturing and CAM are beginning to intersect with the process world.

Advanced Process Control (APC) is a layer of process control built on top of basic industrial control systems to optimize complex manufacturing processes. Unlike traditional controls that react to deviations in a single variable, APC uses advanced algorithms and mathematical models to manage multiple, interdependent variables simultaneously. This enables the system to predict future process behavior, proactively adjust, and operate closer to safety and quality limits without risking instability. By continuously monitoring and fine-tuning operations in real-time, APC systems significantly improve efficiency, increase product yield and consistency, and reduce energy consumption and waste.

21 Customer Interaction & Sales

Customer Interaction and Sales are fundamental, interdependent functions driving revenue. Unlike consumer sales, B2B transactions often involve *complex sales cycles*, multiple decision-makers, and higher contract values. *Customer interaction* goes beyond simple support: It encompasses building deep relationships based on trust, industry expertise, and understanding the client's strategic needs. This interaction is key to identifying pain points and opportunities. The *sales function* then leverages these insights to offer tailored solutions, not just products, ensuring that the proposal aligns with the client's business objectives. A strong, consultative approach to interaction and sales is critical for securing deals, fostering customer loyalty, and generating repeat business and valuable referrals within the B2B market.

While AI in the sales domain deserves a book in its own right, this chapter covers the following sub-functions: *Prospect and customer profiling*, *customer interaction support*, and *order intake*. It also distinguishes between *product sales*, *system sales*, and *project sales*.

21.1 Prospect and Customer Profiling

The primary motivation for customer and prospect profiling in B2B is to move beyond generic outreach by gaining deep insights into the complex needs, organizational structures, and pain points of target businesses. This intelligence allows organizations to focus resources on high-value accounts through tailored marketing and sales strategies, ultimately improving conversion rates and accelerating long sales cycles.

Solution Brief 21-1: Targeted Market Intelligence (Coral Innovation)

Challenge

- Insights are scattered across fragmented sources, many of them behind paywalls.
- Market intelligence "managed by Excel" kills agility and efficient collaboration.

Solution "Nuntium.ai"

- Leverages fragmented sources such as patent filings, press releases, research project announcements, niche publications, and startup ecosystem news.
- Monitors news on target accounts, provides personalized updates for sales teams.
- Tracks competitor activities without the costs of traditional intelligence platforms.
- Collaboration platform to assess and comment on news and signals across silos.

Benefits

- Market intelligence becomes a living, interactive resource.
- Hidden signals are revealed through data correlation.

Customers: Leading machine tool builder, producer of labeling machines

Provider: Coral Innovation, Stuttgart, Germany; *coral-innovation.de/product/sales*

The *Share of Wallet* (SoW) is an important KPI in B2B commerce; its analysis provides insight into the proportion of a customer's total potential expenditure in a specific category that the company captures. In essence, the SoW reflects the customer's financial commitment and loyalty to a specific supplier relative to competitors. In complex B2B environments, contracts are often deliberately structured as *share-of-wallet contracts*, designed to induce and reward customer loyalty by offering discounts contingent on the customer committing to buy a threshold share from the supplier [132].

Historically, quantifying SoW has been an inaccurate science, often relying on high-level surveys or market aggregates [133]. However, for SoW to drive significant growth, it must be quantified for every single customer or prospect. The move toward AI, leveraging relevant data sources, can transform SoW from an abstract, high-level metric into a set of next-best actions.

One core challenge in B2B SoW analysis is calculating the customer's total potential spend (the total wallet), as data on expenditures with competitors (the unserved wallet) is typically unavailable. This contrasts sharply with sectors like the credit card industry, where card issuers can leverage centralized credit records from bureaus to calculate total wallet size and subsequent share. Traditional B2B approaches relied on top-down methodologies, starting with public aggregate industry estimates, which inherently lack the customer-level granularity required for effective sales action [132].

Buyer intent data is catalytic to operationalizing SoW analysis: It provides information about the target audience's online behavior – the "behavioral breadcrumbs" left behind as they navigate the digital realm seeking solutions – and predicts whether a prospect is ready to buy a solution in the relevant category [134].

Solution Brief 21-2: Buyer Intent Analytics for B2B Markets (Bombora)

Challenge
- Struggling to identify active, high-potential B2B buyer accounts.
- Ineffective engagement with anonymous website visitors and first-party data.
- Need to proactively identify and mitigate customer churn risk.
- Lack of clear visibility into B2B market trends and competitive performance.

Solution "Company Surge"
- Collects exclusive intent data through the trusted B2B data co-op.
- Uses Company Surge to signal high-potential, in-market accounts.
- Resolves identity and enriches anonymous first-party customer data.
- Provides premium B2B digital audiences for targeted omnichannel deployment.
- Integration Partners: Salesforce, HubSpot, LinkedIn, Apollo, The Trade Desk, Yahoo DSP, DV360, Outreach, Similarweb, Outbrain.

Benefits
- Accelerates revenue by focusing on accounts with active buying intent.
- Delivers highly personalized messaging and relevant content to visitors.
- Enhances marketing automation with superior audience segmentation.
- Gaining a holistic view and sophisticated measurement of campaign performance.

Customers: Cloudera, Siemens, Splunk, Tanium

Provider: Bombora, New York City, USA; *bombora.com*

To maximize the efficiency of sales resources, AI assigns a Propensity Score to each account. This score reflects the mathematical likelihood (often a range, e. g., 0 to 100) that the account is currently in-market and will convert on a specific expansion offer. The score is synthesized from multiple inputs, including the predictive SoW calculation, first-party data (such as pricing or demo page visits), and third-party intent data from providers such as Bombora. Accounts registering high scores indicate strong, immediate buying intent and are prioritized for outreach [135].

21.2 Customer Interaction Support

21.2.1 Follow-Up Automation

This function is a multi-phase process that encompasses the entire customer interaction lifecycle, from planning and preparation through execution to follow-up. Effective support is increasingly personalized, proactive, and multi-channel, leveraging CRM software to provide a unified, empathetic experience that builds trust and loyalty.

Solution Brief 21-3: Follow-up Automation (Outreach.io)

Challenge

- Sellers waste critical hours on administrative tasks such as CRM updates and email drafting.
- Managers struggle to identify at-risk deals or predict revenue with high accuracy.
- Sales teams often fail to follow best practices, leading to missed revenue targets.

Solution

- Smart Email Assist drafts personalized, context-aware messages to accelerate buyer engagement.
- Analyzes activity signals to score deals and recommend the next best actions.
- Automatically transcribes calls, identifies sentiment, and extracts action items for coaching.

Benefits

- Automates repetitive "grunt work", allowing reps to focus on human-to-human relationship building.
- Provides revenue leaders with data-driven predictions to call their numbers with confidence.
- Empowers teams to spot risks early and replicate top-performing sales motions across the organization.

Customers: Adobe, Tableau, Okta, Splunk, DocuSign, SAP, Siemens

Provider: Outreach, Seattle, USA; *outreach.io*

21.2.2 Account and Sales Manager Support

B2B sales are heavy on relationship management, and in many cases, key account managers (KAMs) are assigned to navigate the complex decision-making structures within large customer organisations. AI can support KAMs by freeing them from keeping record of their interactions as writing minutes, deriving next best actions, and maintaining respective data in a typical CRM system, which can be largely automated as outlined in Section 31.5.1. Establishing AI support for KAMs kills several birds with one stone:

- Employee satisfaction increases as KAMs are freed up from a heavy portion of administrative work.
- CRM data quality improves, particularly Next Best Actions, ultimately leading to better sales.
- By CRM data quality improvements, an organization's dependency on individual KAMs diminishes; this can be instrumental in tackling the consequences of attrition and retirements in our sales community.

Solution Brief 21-4: Voice-based Meeting Documentation (Blockbrain)

Challenge

- Sales representatives spend on average 6h per week on backend admin work.
- CRM data quality suffers from a certain degree of admin aversion.
- Poor record keeping increases an organization's dependency on individuals.

Solution "Blockbrain Mobile App"

- Meeting documentation templates specify a conversation structure between AI and a sales representative. Templates can contain "must-have" data points.
- Blockbrain Mobile App calls sales reps after their customer meeting, or can be called when they are driving back.
- Sales reps provide voice input, which is structured to update the CRM system. If sales reps do not provide "must-have" data points, the mobile app prompts proactively.

Benefits

- Meeting documentation time shrinks by 5–15 minutes per report.
- Sales reps love to be able to talk to the AI to document their customer meetings.
- Increased CRM data quality increases sales opportunities and decreases dependency on certain individuals.

Customers: Fischer Group, Harting, Schunk

Provider: Blockbrain, Stuttgart, Germany; *theblockbrain.ai/en/sales-use-case/*

21.3 Product Sales

For companies specializing in product sales, the process is streamlined and highly transactional. This model is typical for selling high-volume, standardized goods or raw materials. The focus is on efficiency and speed. The sales process is often self-service or triggered by simple quotation requests. Once a purchase order is received, it is quickly validated against inventory, and a sales order is created. An ERP system plays a significant role here, automating tasks such as credit checks, inventory allocation, and confirmation generation.

The order fulfillment process is a predictable sequence of picking, packing, shipping, and invoicing. The key to success is a seamless, automated workflow that minimizes manual intervention and ensures a rapid, accurate delivery, thereby reducing costs and improving customer satisfaction for repeat orders.

AI can support product selection and configuration in several ways:

- *Simple Product Configurators* help reduce order-entry inconsistencies and leverage the potential of cross- and up-selling.

- *Recommendation Engines:* Using data analytics on transaction histories, customer similarity search, and product configuration data, AI can recommend additional products.
- *AI chatbots* can provide a personalized, lightweight sales consulting experience.

Custom Connector Design Automated with AI

Harting is transforming industrial connectivity design through its "Connectivity AI" initiative, a collaboration with Siemens and Microsoft. Harting enables engineers to describe connector requirements in simple, natural language. A specific LLM version can instantly translate these prompts into technical specifications, identify suitable existing products, or autonomously generate new 3D CAD models and simulations for custom solutions. This innovation drastically reduces design cycles [136].

21.4 System Sales

System sales represent a significant step up in complexity. This model involves selling a combination of products, software, and services to create a complete solution, such as a factory automation line or a complex HVAC system. The sales process is consultative and solution-oriented, with a longer sales cycle. It begins with a detailed needs analysis, followed by designing a customized solution and a comprehensive proposal. The order management phase is far more intricate. It involves coordinating the delivery of multiple components, scheduling specialized services such as installation and configuration, and managing separate billing schedules for hardware and software. This process requires close collaboration between sales, engineering, manufacturing, and service teams to ensure that all parts of the solution are correctly delivered and integrated.

Configure, Price, Quote (CPQ) activities are crucial for streamlining the complex sales process in B2B companies, especially for those that deal with highly customizable products or services. The primary role is to ensure speed, accuracy, and profitability when generating sales quotes.

- *Configure* ensures sales representatives or customers can select options without creating impossible or non-manufacturable combinations.
- *Price* ensures that the resulting configuration adheres to all relevant pricing rules, discounts, and contract terms, maximizing margins.
- *Quote* automates the generation of polished, professional, and accurate proposals and contracts. In essence, CPQ transforms complex system sales into rapid, error-free, and optimized transactions.

Product configurators play a major role in reducing a system's complexity to a level that transactional sales become possible. While product configurators themselves contain configuration logic that is typically rule-based, AI can support product configuration in several ways:

- *Rule and configuration harvesting:* Using the power of LLMs to analyze legacy documentation such as product manuals, data sheets, and internal documentation to extract configuration rules and populate configurators.
- *Proposal of suitable configurations:* Translating customer requirements, articulated in natural language, into a suitable product or system configuration.
- *Capturing customer environment parameters:* Machine vision applications – often deployable on smartphones – can help to capture important parameters of a customer's environment, such as part numbers of replacement parts or measures sufficiently captured for a fast or even automated quoting process.
- *Variant Management Pruning Recommendations:* Data analytics can recommend which low-value, high-cost variants to rationalize or eliminate in order to simplify the internal product structure (components, manufacturing) without significant impact on external sales.

Solution Brief 21-5: Configure Price Quote (Tacton)

Challenge

- Managing billions of valid configurations manually leads to engineering bottlenecks and order errors.
- Highly customized technical quotes often take weeks, causing manufacturers to lose competitive deals.
- Inconsistent pricing and excessive discounting across global sales teams significantly reduce overall profitability.

Solution

- Combines deterministic logic with generative models for error-free product and pricing recommendations.
- Uses AI to analyze historical win-loss data and optimize real-time deal structures.
- AI-driven prompts help non-technical users navigate complex requirements to find optimal solutions.

Benefits

- Reduces the time to generate complex technical quotes from weeks to minutes.
- Ensures 100% accurate, manufacturable orders through advanced AI-based constraint checking and validation.
- Protects deal profitability by providing data-driven pricing guardrails and automated discount controls.

Customers: Atlas Copco, Siemens Energy, Valmet, Vantage, Yaskawa

Provider: Tacton, Stockholm, Sweden; *tacton.com*

21.5 Project Sales

Project sales are at the apex of complexity. This model involves large-scale, one-of-a-kind undertakings such as building a new manufacturing plant or a power generation facility. The process is relationship-driven and often spans years. The sales cycle is extensive, starting with a deep-dive discovery phase to define precise project scope, budget, and timeline. The order itself is often not a single transaction but a complex contract with phased deliveries and payments tied to project milestones. Order management is replaced by rigorous project management, with a dedicated team overseeing the entire lifecycle, from engineering and procurement through installation, testing, and final commissioning. This process demands a high degree of flexibility, risk management, and continuous communication with the client to manage scope changes and ensure the project is successful, on time, and on budget.

Requirements analysis for *Requests for Quotations* (RfQs) or tenders is a critical function to ensures that all technical, financial, and compliance specifications are clearly understood and accurately addressed before submitting a proposal. It involves interpreting client needs, identifying mandatory requirements, and aligning them with an organization's capabilities and resources.

AI enhances this process by automating document review and data extraction from complex tender documents, helping teams quickly identify key criteria, deadlines, and eligibility conditions. NLP tools can summarize lengthy specifications and flag ambiguous or conflicting requirements for clarification. AI-driven analytics can also assess historical bid data to predict success probabilities and recommend optimal pricing or strategy adjustments.

Solution Brief 21-6: Analysis of Tender Documents and Technical Standards (Drimco)

Challenge
- Manual analysis of large quantities of sequential text, including dependencies, is painstaking.

Solution DRIMCO RfQ/Tender Management
- Tender Compare, Risk Management, Auto Commenting, Topic Recognition, Department Assignment, Auto Document Segmentation.
- Integration with leading ALM and Requirement Management Systems.

Benefits
- Increased traceability of requirements.
- Integration between Sales and Project Execution.
- Faster proposals, for example, due to faster risk management and faster identification of reusable solutions.

Customers: Innomotics, KSB, Siemens Energy

Provider: Drimco, Munich, Germany; *drimco.ai*

The extraction of requirements from tender documents and references to regulatory and industry requirements informs Risk Management (risk quantification, derivation of mitigation measures, input to calculations, review by risk review boards) and *Project Management* (pre-structuring project plans, identification of similar (sub-)projects, etc.).

22 Sourcing & Procurement

Sourcing & Procurement are responsible for acquiring the materials, components, and services necessary for production, acting as a crucial link in the supply chain. While Sourcing focuses on establishing an effective and efficient supplier network, Procurement handles demand fulfillment.

22.1 Supplier Selection and Coordination

This function involves the systematic evaluation and selection of suppliers, followed by the ongoing coordination of business relationships. This is no longer a simple transaction; it is a collaborative effort to ensure reliability, quality, and ethical compliance (see Section 22.2).

AI can support this process by various means:

- GenAI-based research platforms can help identify requirements in a structured format and *compact vendor long-lists to vendor short-lists* as a starting point for negotiations.
- GenAI and NLP technology can help prepare the *Request for Quotation (RfQ)* documents and evaluate the related responses. The same applies to shaping contracts (see Section 21.5).
- Much like AI support for documenting customer interactions as described in Section 21.2.2, AI can *document supplier meetings* in the selection phase or later.

Solution Brief 22-1: Vendor Evaluation and Preselection (Spend Matters)

Challenge

- Manual software sourcing is time-consuming, fragmented, and prone to expensive human error.
- Organizations struggle to filter vast vendor landscapes for specific, high-priority business requirements.
- Lack of objective, data-driven market intelligence leads to high-risk software selection decisions.

Solution "Tech Match", "Solution Map"

- Uses AI-driven matching algorithms to pair organizational needs with vetted technology vendors.
- Leverages a proprietary database to deliver research-backed recommendations.
- Automates the creation of tailored RFQs using AI to align with category-specific parameters.

Benefits

- Accelerates the selection timeline through rapid AI-powered shortlisting.
- Reduces procurement risks by replacing subjective web searches with objective, AI-filtered insights.
- Minimizes sourcing costs by automating intensive research and stakeholder collaboration tasks.

Customers: OpenAI, P&G, Nestlé, Samsung, Duracell

Provider: Spend Matters, Chicago, USA; *spendmatters.com*

22.2 Supply Chain Monitoring

Supply Chain Monitoring has evolved from simply tracking shipments to a complex, strategic function that ensures transparency and manages risk across the entire supply chain. It involves collecting data across the entire supply chain to identify and mitigate risks, such as labor abuse, environmental violations, and supplier disruptions.

The increasing regulatory pressure, exemplified by the German Supply Chain Act (LkSG), and consumer demand for ethical products necessitate greater transparency. This forces companies to implement new data-collection and reporting systems, which, in turn, improve their risk-management capabilities. This transformation illustrates how a seemingly operational function is becoming a high-stakes issue in corporate governance. The ability to monitor a supply chain is no longer just about operational efficiency; it is a critical component of brand reputation, legal compliance, and long-term business resilience.

Solution Brief 22-2: Supply Chain Risk Management (Prewave)

Challenge

- Lack of transparency into their complex, multi-tier supply chains.
- Difficult to detect and prevent disruptions and emerging risks at an early stage.
- Need to comply with strict regulations such as CSDDD and LkSG.
- Manual risk monitoring is time-consuming and error-prone.

Solution

- AI monitors 400+ languages and media for real-time risk alerts.
- Uses proprietary Tier-N technology to map the full supply chain.
- Generates a 360° risk score for every supplier profile.
- Provides an action platform for due diligence and mitigation.

Benefits

- Prevents disruptions and reputational damage by acting fast.
- Ensures full compliance with global supply chain regulations.
- Reduces manual overhead by automating due diligence and reporting.
- Increases supply chain resilience and business continuity.

Customers: Audi, Eberspächer, Kärcher, Porsche, Volkswagen

Provider: Prewave, Vienna, Austria; *prewave.com*

22.3 Materials Requirements Planning

Materials requirements planning is the strategic process of planning and controlling material ordering. It is a core part of operational procurement, ensuring that the right materials are available in the right quantity at the right time. This function involves forecasting demand, determining reorder points, and calculating optimal order quantities.

This strategic approach is critical for avoiding two costly risks: overstocking, which ties up capital and increases storage costs, and understocking, which leads to production bottlenecks and lost sales. Therefore, precise planning and management directly improve cost optimization and process reliability, demonstrating a direct, tangible impact on a company's financial health.

22.4 Costing

AI systems analyze vast, complex datasets – including historical spend, market trends, supplier performance metrics, and geopolitical factors – to create highly accurate cost forecasts and identify potential savings at the part level. This informs RfQs and negotiation strategies and helps proactively manage risks such as price volatility and supply chain disruptions.

An automotive manufacturer uses AI to analyze a component's 3D geometry in real time, cross-reference it against global commodity prices (e.g., steel or aluminum), and benchmark it against thousands of historical supplier quotes. This rapid analysis provides a precise should-cost model for the part, giving the manufacturer a powerful position to negotiate the best possible price with a supplier, rather than relying solely on the quoted price.

Solution Brief 22-3: AI-based Part Sourcing Intelligence (Easy2Parts)

Challenge

- ERP systems struggle to manage parts based on design files and therefore fail to provide intelligent search and part comparison features.
- This intransparency leads to unaddressed savings potential.

Solution "Abella AI"

- Similarity search of parts according to parts master data and geometry.
- Analysis of earlier procurement transactions and related suppliers.
- Price comparisons.

Benefits

- Better sourcing decisions resulting in significant savings across a corporation's BOMs.

Customers: BHS, Grenzebach, Horsch, Krones, Siemens

Provider: Easy2Parts, Deggendorf, Germany; *easy2parts.com*

22.5 Incoming Goods Inspection

This is the process of inspecting incoming deliveries to ensure that the goods' quantity, quality, and specifications of the goods match the purchase order. This quality control gate is the last step in the procurement process before materials are officially accepted into inventory.

AI can support several receiving stages:

- *Arrival & identification:* Scanning barcodes and other ID information on labels of incoming goods and correlating them to purchase orders.
- *Unloading & counting:* Inspection gates or forklifts with machine vision equipment can count boxes on pallets.
- *Defect detection:* Automated Quality Inspection solutions can detect quality issues, potentially on 100% of incoming goods, as opposed to just sampling.
- *Sorting decision:* Goods sorting by types and quality, feeding into intralogistics.

Solution Brief 22-4: High Speed Incoming Goods Inspection (overview.ai)

Challenge
- Manual inspection processes are slow, inconsistent, and prone to human error.
- Traditional machine vision is rigid, expensive, and requires specialized experts.
- Statistical sampling methods allow critical defects to slip through to customers.
- Existing systems struggle to adapt quickly to frequent product or design changes.

Solution
- User-friendly, browser-based AI vision platform deployable in a matter of just hours.
- Deep learning models capable of training on as few as five images.
- Edge-based architecture processes data locally without complex external infrastructure, allowing high-speed processing.
- No coding or specialized technical knowledge required to set up and operate.
- Vision Transformer, few-shot learning.

Benefits
- Significantly reduces manufacturing waste, scrap, and costly customer returns.
- Lowers total cost of ownership compared to traditional vision systems.
- Empowers existing staff to manage quality control without external help.
- Delivers higher inspection accuracy and consistency at full production speeds.

Customers: Honda, Mitsubishi, Schaeffler, Toyota, Tyson Foods

Provider: Overview.ai, San Francisco, California, USA; *overview.ai*

22.6 Three-Way-Match (Continuous Controls Monitoring)

Continuous Controls Monitoring (CCM) significantly enhances the *three-way-match* in procurement by moving beyond periodic, manual checks. CCM uses automated technology to monitor 100% of purchase transactions in real time. It instantly verifies that the purchase Order, goods receipt note, and vendor invoice data align within set tolerance limits. Any discrepancies – such as a price deviation or a quantity mismatch – are immediately flagged as exceptions and sent to a workflow for review. This shift from detective (auditing later) to preventive/predictive (constant monitoring) drastically reduces the risk of fraud and payment errors, ensuring ongoing financial compliance [137].

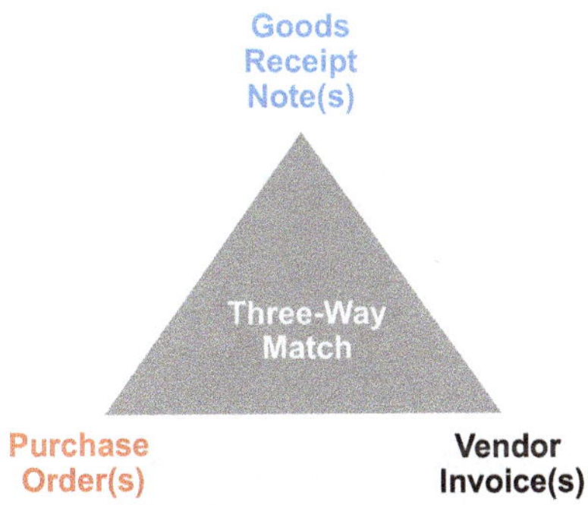

Figure 22.1 Three-Way-Match Principle

Solution Brief 22-5: Process Mining for Purchase-to-Pay (Celonis)

Challenge

- Hidden inefficiencies and out-of-ERP communication cause high cycle times.
- Frequent non-compliance: Maverick buying and "Invoice before PO".
- Delayed goods receipts and invoice matching create payment holds, regularly missing possible cash discounts for early payments.

Solution (Process Mining Platform)

- Extracts real-time event log data across all Purchase-to-Pay systems (e. g., ERP).
- Creates a living digital process twin of the actual Purchase-to-Pay process flow.
- AI/ML identifies root causes of friction, bottlenecks, and deviations.

Benefits

- Reduces cycle time and manual touches in requisition-to-payment.
- Increases touchless invoice rate and on-time payment compliance.
- Optimizes working capital by maximizing cash discounts.

Customers: Mann+Hummel, Siemens, Vodaphone, Wien Energy

Provider: Celonis, Munich, Germany; *celonis.com*

23 Inventory Management

This function manages the physical flow and storage of goods, bridging the gap between procurement, production, and shipping. The goal is to ensure that the right products are available to meet demand while avoiding the costs of overstocking and the risks of stockouts.

Demand forecasting plays a significant role in many industries, both on the production and retail sides. Time-series prediction models handle demand forecasting particularly well when demand follows patterns (e.g., ice cream sales primarily depend on weather conditions). AI can help uncover related demand patterns and calibrate statistical models with optimal parameter sets. A first generation of "universal" time-series models has been pre-trained on a large set of patterns, such as AWS Chronos and NXAI TiRex.

Solution Brief 23-1: Universal Time- Series Prediction (NXAI)

Challenge

- Key processes in demand planning and logistics depend on forecasting.
- Traditional forecasting models require complex feature engineering.

Solution "TiRex"

- xLSTM algorithm class delivers transformer-like performance while consuming far fewer resources.
- Uses a zero-shot inference capability; no prior training needed.
- Maintains a state, that is to remember AI conclusions from recent forecasts for improved accuracy and performance.

Benefits

- State-of-the-art accuracy, outperforming many traditional methods.
- Generates forecasts a number of orders of magnitude faster (high speed).
- Significantly reduces model development and deployment time and effort.

Solution Brief 23-1: Universal Time- Series Prediction (NXAI)
Customers: Festo, n8n, Witron
Provider: NXAI, Linz, Austria; *nx-ai.com*

- *Inventory auditing* is the process of physically counting and verifying inventory to reconcile records with actual stock. This is a critical activity for ensuring data accuracy and compliance with financial reporting requirements, and for identifying discrepancies or errors in the system. Several AI-based solutions, mainly leveraging computer vision on mobile devices or, increasingly, autonomous drones, reduce the manual labor required for physical inventory audits.

Solution Brief 23-2: Autonomous Inventory Scanning (Gather.ai)
Challenge ▪ Human inventory checks are error-prone, expensive, and, specifically in cold-chain environments, very inconvenient.
Solution "3D Case Counting" ▪ AI-powered drones. ▪ Algorithms for 3D case counting, bar code/QR code, and label reading. ▪ Specific support for cold chain logistics
Benefits ▪ Drones scan inventory 15x faster than manual methods. ▪ No constructional changes needed, high brownfield fit. ▪ Up to 99.95% inventory precision.
Customers: Barret, Geodis, Langham Logistics, NFI, Taylor
Provider: Gather.ai, Pittsburgh, PA, USA; *gather.ai*

- *Inventory valuation:* This is the accounting process of assigning a monetary value to the materials held in inventory. Different valuation methods, such as FIFO (First-In, First-Out), are used to determine the cost of goods sold and the value of remaining inventory. This directly impacts the company's financial statements, linking physical inventory to the accounting and finance sectors. The choice of valuation methods directly affects profitability metrics and tax obligations. The reduction of *slow-moving or obsolete inventory* (SLOB) is a discipline that, when properly mastered, reduces storage costs, bound capital costs, and tax burdens [138]. Both demand forecasting and inventory auditing play an instrumental role in SLOB reduction.

24 Production

Production is the complex orchestration of technical precision and strategic management. This chapter explores the manufacturing lifecycle, beginning with *plant design and engineering* and *production engineering*. We discuss how *production planning and control* align with *scheduling* and capacity planning to optimize throughput. On the shop floor, we detail *manufacturing execution* and *quality control*, and the physical coordination of *material handling*, *assembly*, and *machine tending*. Finally, we address the critical tactical elements of *machine operation*, including setup, tool management, and process parameter calibration to ensure operational excellence, before going on to explore connected worker concepts.

24.1 Plant Design and Engineering

Plant design and engineering is the foundational process that encompasses conceptual modeling, detailed spatial engineering, asset layout definition, and meticulous generation of all engineering artifacts, including the 3D models, piping schematics, and electrical drawings, required before physical construction can begin. This function establishes the structure of the plant, which dictates operational efficiency for decades [139].

Industrial AI introduces a proactive, optimization-driven design paradigm: Generative design analyzes complex design inputs, constraints, and projected operational requirements to generate a wide range of optimized design configurations that manual human effort cannot achieve. AI-driven systems are also pivotal in proactively minimizing errors. Solutions such as iSolve Easy Hanger automate routine design tasks and are engineered to produce error-free documentation and clash-free 3D models in real time [140]. This upstream design accuracy eliminates costly downstream rework and material waste during construction.

Solution Brief 24-1: AI-supported Plant Design (iSolve Technologies)

Challenge

- Engineers struggle with time-consuming, manual workflows for designing complex pipe supports.
- Manual calculations and drafting often lead to design errors and costly re-work.
- Estimating material costs and preparing technical bids takes too long for manufacturers.

Solution "Easy Hanger"

- Provides a comprehensive digital library for automated 3D assembly of hanger parts.
- Uses intelligent design rules to ensure technical integrity and regulatory compliance.
- Instantly generates BOMs, 2D manufacturing drawings, and real-time cost quotations.

Benefits

- Automates engineering parts design to maximize workflow speed and output quality.
- Accelerates the transition from initial bid preparation to final manufacturing orders.
- Prevents clashes and design mistakes through real-time validation and centralized data.

Provider: iSolve Technologies, Charlotte, North Carolina, USA; *isolveglobal.com*

Furthermore, AI simulation tools facilitate virtual prototyping and Digital Twins. These virtual models accurately replicate the behavior of physical prototypes, enabling predictive analysis of wear and tear, ergonomics, and structural risks without the time and expense of multiple physical tests, thereby drastically accelerating the design-to-market cycle. Naturally, all value propositions of the Industrial Metaverse apply (see Section 2.6.3).

Process Mining (see Section 2.7.1.10), when paired with motion sensors and computer vision, can provide compelling insights and improvement recommendations for shop-floor layouts, as demonstrated by MotionMiners.

Solution Brief 24-2: Motion-Mining for Layout Optimization (MotionMiners)

Challenge

- Manual process analysis (stopwatch/clipboard) is slow and inaccurate.
- Lack of transparency into the efficiency and ergonomics of manual tasks.
- Difficulty gaining acceptance from works councils for monitoring.
- Inefficient utilization of internal fleet vehicles and personnel resources.

Solution

- Employees and vehicles wear/carry anonymized sensors (wearables/beacons).
- AI analyzes motion data to identify 50+ activities and KPIs automatically.
- Visualizes workflows, heatmaps, and activity diagrams.
- Integrates with ERP/warehouse management system data for in-depth, holistic process matching.
- Sophisticated anonymization to find acceptance by worker representation bodies.

Solution Brief 24-2: Motion-Mining for Layout Optimization (MotionMiners) *(continued)*

Benefits

- Finds potential savings and efficiency gains between 15% and 40%.
- Reduces manual analysis effort by approximately 80% (vs. traditional methods).
- Improves working conditions by identifying ergonomically critical movements.

Customers: Dachser, DB Schenker, DHL, Miele, REWE, ZF

Provider: Motion Miners, Dortmund, Germany; *motionminers.com*

24.2 Production Engineering

Production engineering then bridges the gap between a validated product design and its mass manufacturing. This field focuses on optimizing the processes and systems required to produce the product efficiently and cost-effectively. Production engineers design and implement production lines, select and configure machinery, develop assembly procedures, and establish quality control measures. Their focus is on streamlining workflows, reducing waste, improving efficiency, and ensuring consistent product quality at scale. They troubleshoot manufacturing issues, continuously seek process improvements, and work to make the transition from engineering design to high-volume production as smooth and economical as possible.

24.2.1 Production Engineering in Process Industries [139]

Piping and Instrumentation Diagrams (P&IDs) are detailed schematic representations used in the process industries to illustrate the functional relationships among piping, instrumentation, and system equipment components. They are fundamental engineering documents that show the interconnection of process equipment and the instrumentation used to control the process. P&IDs use standardized graphical symbols for components such as valves, pumps, vessels, heat exchangers, and control instruments, providing a comprehensive visual language for engineers, operators, and maintenance personnel. They are crucial for process design, construction, operation, and troubleshooting, offering a complete overview of the process flow and control strategy.

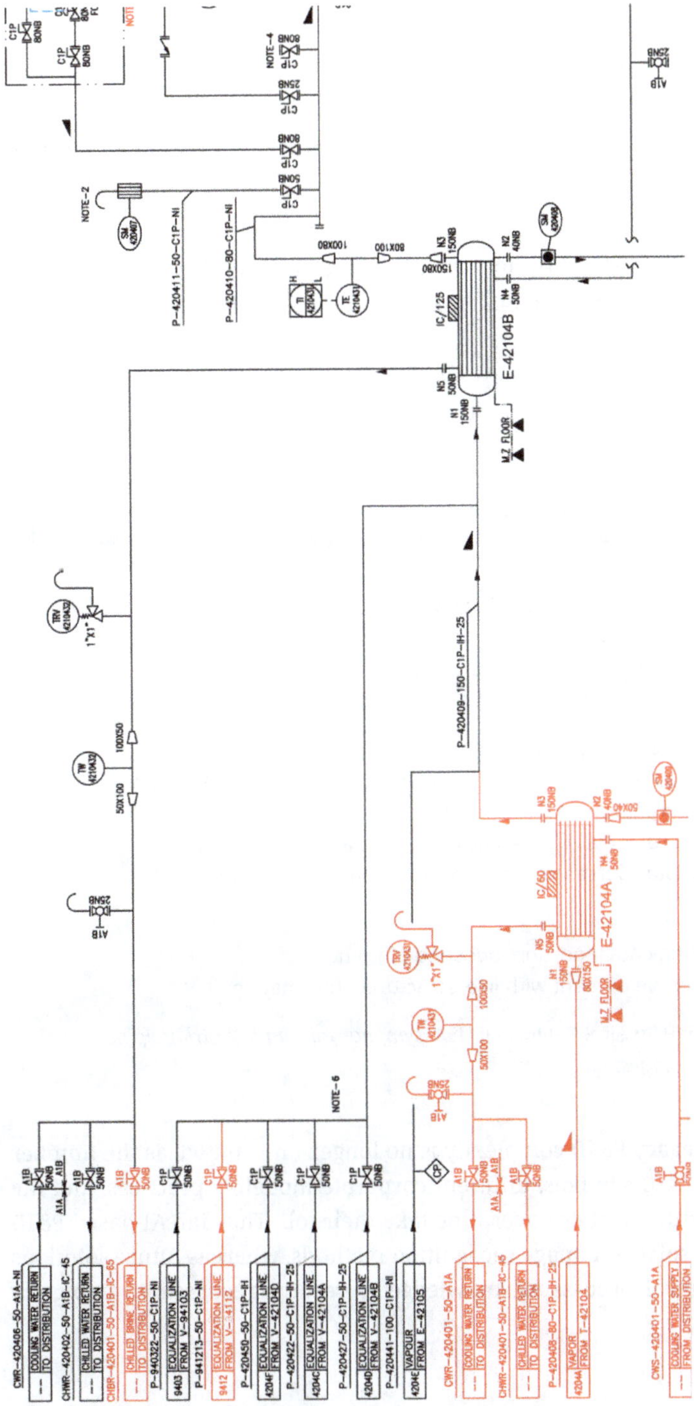

Figure 24.1 Example of a piping & instrumentation diagram (P&ID)

AI support covers the use cases:

- *P&ID generation:* AI analyses textual descriptions of process industry plants or subsystems and drafts a P&I diagram.
- *Interpretation of legacy P&IDs:* AI interprets P&I diagrams, stitches them together if they span multiple pages, and converts them into, say, DEXPI for downstream systems.
- *Enrichment of legacy P&IDs:* AI interprets P&I diagrams, specifically component names/labels and links system and component-level documentation for fast retrieval by experts.
- *Consistency checking:* AI interprets P&I diagrams and performs a set of rule checks, for example, when sending subsystem supplier documentation into a regulatory approval process.

Solution Brief 24-3: Digitalizing Piping & Instrumentation Diagrams (Symphony.ai)

Challenge
- Valuable engineering data is trapped in flat P&ID documents.
- Traditional ingestion processes are slow and inefficient.
- Difficulty updating and synchronizing P&ID changes organization-wide.
- High risk of asset failures without predictive operational insights.

Solution: "Symphony.ai P&ID Ingestion"
- Uses Vision AI, optical character recognition, and ML to interpret P&ID drawings.
- Automatically extracts components, connections, labels, and metadata.
- Creates a digital model and asset hierarchy from the diagrams.
- Intelligently models data sources within a data orchestration pipeline.

Benefits
- Automates engineering data ingestion, boosting efficiency.
- Supports digital twin development with live, structured information.

Provider: Symphony.ai, Palo Alto, California, USA; *symphonyai.com/industrial/piping-instrumentation-diagrams-ingestion*

AI's ability to master legacy P&ID complexity is no longer undisputed, as the number and heterogeneity of P&ID symbols, different corporate modeling practices, and the evolution of symbol and font styles over time take their toll. Thus far, AI-based P&ID recognition has relied solely on image recognition methods, whereas future solutions will incorporate chemical processing knowledge to resolve recognition ambiguity [141].

24.2.2 Production Engineering for Discrete Manufacturing

In discrete manufacturing, *production engineering* involves designing and implementing the automation layer, including developing operational logic for PLCs, designing HMIs, and programming industrial robot controls.

GenAI can help by:

- *Generating automation code* for PLCs, HMIs, and robot control systems, accelerating system deployment and reducing common manual programming errors.
- Visualizing and *documenting legacy PLC code*, which is instrumental to performing updates when the originator of a PLC-driven solution cannot be involved.
- *Mapping PLC code parameters to OPC UA data points*, supporting the upgrade of brownfield environments to become I4.0 ready.
- Managing *compliance with corporate or industry automation standards*: Large users of automation technology define their own automation architecture standards, such as VASS[1]. Adherence to these standards can be fostered by respective copilot technology.

Furthermore, every automation solution is a complex system comprising software (PLC and HMI code), network configurations (e.g., sensors, subsystems, and gateways), electrical dimensioning and wiring plans, documentation, and a bill of materials. Keeping these different aspects of a production system in sync, particularly when changes are made in a live environment (e.g., an end-of-life device that needs replacement), is cumbersome and error-prone. First copilots for engineering implementations indicate that agentic AI in particular can have a positive impact.

Solution Brief 24-4: GenAI for Production Line Automation (Siemens)

Challenge

- Increasing complexity and time pressure in industrial automation.
- Repetitive, standard coding tasks consume significant amounts of engineering time.
- Difficulty finding information quickly in extensive technical documentation

Solution "Industrial Copilot for Engineering"

- Hosting in a security-managed and controlled Microsoft Azure Environment with extensive legal clearance of different security and IP concerns.
- Industrial Copilot seamlessly integrated with the Siemens TIA Portal.
- Supports generation of WinCC Unified visualization panels from natural language.
- Agentic architecture to integrate future AI features from Siemens and 3rd parties.

[1] VASS stands for Volkswagen, Audi, Seat and Skoda.

Solution Brief 24-4: GenAI for Production Line Automation (Siemens) *(continued)*
Benefits ▪ Significantly reduces engineering workload and repetitive tasks. ▪ High-quality code generation; 60% better than the leading LLMs ▪ Helps address the shortage of skilled workers by augmenting capabilities.
Customers: Schaeffler Special Machinery, Thyssen Krupp Automation
Provider: Siemens, Munich/Berlin, Germany; *siemens.com/industrial-copilot*

24.3 Production Planning and Control

Production Planning and Control (PPC) is the central nervous system of the production process, a strategic function that coordinates material flow, capacity, and scheduling to ensure production runs smoothly and efficiently. It guarantees that the right products are made at the right time and at the right cost to meet demand.

24.4 Material Requirements Planning

Material Requirements Planning (MRP I) is a standard system used by manufacturers to manage inventory and schedule production. It determines the precise quantities of materials and components needed and when they are required by analyzing sales orders, demand forecasts, and bills of materials. MRP is a critical subset of the broader PPC system.

MRP creates a direct causal link between sales forecasts and purchasing decisions. By breaking down a finished product's requirements into parts and applying lead times, the system can generate a precise schedule for procurement and production. This ensures that materials arrive just in time to meet production needs, minimizing inventory costs and production delays.

The function formalizes and automates procurement planning (see Section 22.3) and inventory management (see Chapter 23), turning these manual activities into a single, integrated, and highly efficient process.

24.5 Production Scheduling

Production scheduling is the process of sequencing and scheduling manufacturing orders to optimize resource utilization and meet delivery dates. It involves detailed planning of setup and production times, considering available capacities and machine assignments to create an efficient production schedule. Scheduling all the jobs, machines, materials, and personnel in a factory is a massive combinatorial optimization problem that humans cannot solve optimally.

Solution Brief 24-5: Production Scheduling with Genetic Algorithms (Pailot)

Challenge

- Great complexity of manufacturing makes simple rule-based scheduling suboptimal.
- Production schedules are constantly disrupted by unexpected events, making manual planning slow and inefficient.

Solution "Pailot Engine", "Pailot Bridge", "Pailot Cockpit"

- Cloud-based SaaS platform, Rest-API integration with established MES systems.
- Under the hood, Pailot relies on genetic algorithms and simulation-based digital twins to generate feasible, optimized schedules. Each scheduling request is handled as a fresh problem via the API, ensuring flexibility and speed.

Benefits

- Up to 20% production scheduling efficiency gains.

Customers: EDAG, Fritsch Elektronic, Sick, Star Team

Provider: Pailot, Karlsruhe, Germany; *pailot.com*

AI-powered schedulers can analyze all these variables in real time and generate a production schedule that maximizes throughput, minimizes bottlenecks, and dynamically adapts to unexpected events such as machine failure or an urgent new order.

24.6 Manufacturing Execution

Manufacturing execution refers to the real-time management of activities on the production floor. The *Manufacturing Execution System* (MES) ensures that work orders are executed according to the production schedule, resources are allocated, and data is collected to monitor progress and performance. It is the tactical execution of the strategic PPC plan.

AI transforms MES from passive data logging into a proactive digital co-pilot: By integrating ML with real-time shop-floor data, AI-enhanced MES can dynamically reschedule production orders in response to unplanned downtime or supply shifts, optimizing throughput without human intervention. Anomaly detection identifies quality drift across machines during production, rather than after completion, minimizing scrap. In closed-loop approaches, the system continuously learns from each production cycle to fine-tune process parameters across machines to maximize efficiency.

24.7 Material Handling

24.7.1 AGVs, AMRs, and Fleet Management

This function covers the automated internal transport of materials. *Automated Guided Vehicles* (AGVs) follow fixed paths, while *Autonomous Mobile Robots* (AMRs) use algorithms and sensors for dynamic navigation and obstacle avoidance.

The operation interfaces with the host *Warehouse Management System* (WMS), which defines pick-and-drop locations and communicates when a load is ready. It relies on *Real-Time Location Systems* (RTLS) and sensor networks to support environmental mapping and localization. Coordination requires communication with robotic cell communication systems to ensure safe load transfers.

AI enables AMRs to be autonomous. AI algorithms enable autonomous navigation by allowing AMRs to scan and map structures, plan multiple optimal routes freely, and detect barriers to reroute dynamically without stopping. Sophisticated *fleet management* optimization involves the AI fleet controller choosing the most efficient route for the entire fleet based on current facility conditions, maximizing overall throughput. This capability relies on multi-agent coordination principles to manage dependencies and allocate complex tasks across multiple robots, enabling clustered intelligence and efficient operation in human-filled, complex environments.

Solution Brief 24-6: Intelligent Fleet Management (Node Robotics)

Challenge

- Struggling to coordinate individual robots to create a cohesive, collaborative team (fleet fragmentation).
- Difficulty in efficiently assigning transport jobs across dynamic, multi-robot environments (complex task dispatching).
- Frequent deadlocks and traffic congestion are slowing down automated material flow (navigation bottlenecks).

Solution Brief 24-6: Intelligent Fleet Management (Node Robotics)

Solution

- Synchronizes live data from all robots to create a real-time global environment (AI map fusion).
- Uses adaptive lane-based movement and path planning to prevent robot collisions (intelligent traffic management).
- Dynamically dispatches jobs to the best-suited robot via smart ERP/WMS integration (automated task optimization).

Benefits

- Maximizes fleet throughput by identifying bottlenecks through AI-driven performance analytics.
- Minimizes commissioning and maintenance expenses through streamlined, modular software integration.
- Easily adapts to complex environments using a low-code editor for custom behaviors.

Customers: Bär, Bleichert, BMW, Idealworks

Provider: Node Robotics, Stuttgart, Germany; *node-robotics.com*

24.7.2 Depalletizing, Palletizing, and Singulation

These specialized functions involve high-precision robotic manipulation to handle unstructured or mixed items, separating goods (singulation) or unloading items from a pallet (depalletizing).

These tasks require 3D machine vision cameras for depth perception and object localization, precise motion control via robot controllers, and adaptive force regulation.

Solution Brief 24-7: Turnkey smart feeder for small metal parts (EPF)

Challenge

- A combination of a rattle plate and a robot gripper is used to singulate and sort small metal parts (e. g., hooks). If the robot arm cannot grip the next metal part, the rattle plate vibrates to dislodge the part and move it into position.
- Whenever the system needs to adjust to metal parts of a different geometry, an expensive AI retraining project has to be run.

Solution "Supata Assembly"

- EPF and Siemens implemented a CAD to AI gripping workflow to generate synthetic images of new parts solely based on their CAD models and have the AI understand possible gripping points for a robot gripper.

Solution Brief 24-7: Turnkey smart feeder for small metal parts (EPF) ***(continued)***

Benefits

- Customers can adjust the singulation solution to accommodate new parts without project work. The adjustment step simply becomes a workflow with CAD files as the only input.

Customers: Bulgari Gioielli, Springfix

Provider: EPF, Carrù, Italy; *epf.it/supata*

24.7.3 Machine Tending

Machine tending uses robots or automated systems to load raw materials into processing machinery, such as CNC machines or presses, and unload finished parts from it. AI optimizes sequence planning for the tending operation, calculating the most efficient motion sequence to minimize overall cycle time. It utilizes vision feedback to ensure fault tolerance, verifying the status of critical machine components before initiating a load sequence.

Machine tending is probably one of the subfunctions of production where hopes for robotic autonomy and universality have most frequently crystallized. Shop floor owners seek to avoid equipping each and every machine with a static robot arm for loading and unloading, as those would remain underutilized most of the time. A mobile robot operating across multiple machine types would require substantial dexterity and the ability to understand different machine types to be useful.

Machine Tending – a Use Case for Humanoids?

In 2025, *Figure AI* concluded a successful 11-month deployment of its second-generation humanoid robot, Figure 02, at the BMW plant in Spartanburg. Operating on an active assembly line, the robots handled sheet-metal loading – a pick-and-place task requiring 5 mm tolerances. This real-world pilot provided critical data on hardware reliability and cycle times, which directly informed the design of the newly released Figure 03 [142].

24.8 Press Shop

The *press shop* handles high-speed, high-force metal-forming processes, with a notable risk of tool damage from foreign objects or positioning errors. A press control system monitors force, stroke, and component position in real-time. Digital twins support simulation and predictive failure analysis [143].

AI supports press shops as follows:

- *AI-supported materials discovery* is a catalytic discipline for efficiency gains in the press shop. For instance, new steel and aluminum alloys expand the capabilities of presses (e. g., workpiece sizes) and the product's properties (e. g., chemical resistance in an automotive part). See Section 15.3.1.
- *Predictive defect and damage prevention*, moving beyond end-of-line detection to monitor subtle process anomalies indicative of potential future defects.
- *Tool protection systems*, using cameras, continuously check component positioning and detect foreign objects, such as residual scrap metal from a previous pass, during the high-speed press cycle.
- *Real-time process optimization* by comparing live performance against the digital twin to maintain optimal throughput.

24.9 Machining

Machining encompasses high-precision subtractive processes such as CNC drilling, milling, turning, and polishing. Success requires managing complex kinematics and analyzing large volumes of sensor data, including acoustics, vibration, and thermal profiles.

- At the programming level, AI systems help to *generate G-code* (see Section 20.5.1).
- AI algorithms analyze real-time sensor data from the machines to *optimize tool usage* (see Section 24.10) and predict tool wear, ensuring that tool replacements are scheduled precisely when needed, minimizing both costly breakage and unnecessarily early changes.
- These self-learning capabilities also drive the *continuous optimization of tool paths*, dynamically adjusting parameters, such as feed rates and cutting speeds, to maximize material removal rates and improve surface finish quality in real-time. This use case typically requires a local edge environment with ultra-low latency, as described in Section 2.3.2.4, "Edge Applications".

- *Machine tending* (see Section 24.7.3) helps automate loading and unloading machines, in many cases extending the machine utilization into off-shift times where no or little human labor capacity is available.
- Computer vision *detects metal parts and tools where they do not belong*: Systems monitor the work area to instantly spot anomalies, debris, or unauthorized human entry, triggering immediate shutdowns or alerts to prevent injuring the operator, or damaging the machine or workpiece.
- Finally, *predictive maintenance* functions monitor vibration, temperature, and spindle load data to forecast component failures weeks in advance, shifting maintenance from reactive repairs to proactive, scheduled interventions that maximize machine uptime and sustain operational efficiency.

24.10 Tool Management

Tool management involves monitoring, inventorying, and replacing all cutting, shaping, and forming tools. Tool condition is a direct driver of both final product quality and machine stability [144]. Furthermore, tools are a substantial cost factor that requires tool management and the use of sophisticated optimization routines, much like *Material Requirement Planning* [145].

AI supports highly accurate predictive tool wear monitoring: ML models analyze sensory data, including cutting-sound signatures, spindle torque, and current, to estimate tool flank wear in real time. Based on these predictions, AI enables optimal tool replacement scheduling, preventing the use of worn tools (which compromise quality) and avoiding the costs associated with premature replacement.

Tool management is another example where industrial shopfloor realities ground optimization ambitions: One primary challenge in establishing AI-supported tool management is identifying and tracking the tools themselves, especially where tool picking automation from automated tool magazines is not used.

24.11 Additive Manufacturing

Additive Manufacturing (AM, also known as 3D Printing) involves layering material and requires precise, dynamic control of hundreds of variables (e.g., laser power, temperature gradients).

AI is crucial for mastering the complexity of AM, enabling end-to-end automation and intelligent control. AI enhances design accuracy, predicts failure points, and automates process adjustments to minimize waste and accelerate production timelines.

Last but not least: Machine tending, as laid out in Section 24.7.3, is a very complementary function for AM [146].

The most advanced application is closed-loop process optimization. AI-enabled Digital Twins leverage real-time sensor data and ML to simulate and autonomously control the printing process.

This capability allows the system to dynamically adjust parameters during printing to maintain optimal conditions and part quality, enabling fully self-monitoring and self-optimizing workflows. If it becomes clear that the 3D printing process is deviating too far from the targeted work item parameters, AI provides timely notifications allowing the printing process to be stopped at the earliest possible time and freeing up the expensive 3D printing resource for the next production job (or a restart).

24.12 Welding

Welding processes (arc, laser, resistance spot) are critical to structural integrity. Quality control must be rigorous due to the significant impact of defects such as porosity or incomplete fusion.

AI supports real-time defect detection and classification. AI-based visual inspection and acoustic systems can identify welding inconsistencies, pinpoint missed welds, and detect critical defects, including porosity and gas pockets. What can be challenging is that this requires high-speed inline inspection, operating at frame rates (30 frames per second or more) that keep pace with high-speed robotic cells [147, 148].

AI also enables predictive quality modeling, where models can correlate inputs with outputs to predict final weld quality and failure load, enabling quality assurance before physical testing.

Finally, the quality documentation of welding seams and spots, for example, as needed in automotive and aerospace applications, can be supported by both AI-based robotics and pattern recognition, such as non-destructive ultrasound inspection methods [149].

Solution Brief 24-8: AI Control for Welding Robots (Path Robotics)

Challenge

- Critical shortage of skilled welders limits manufacturing capacity and growth.
- Traditional automation fails when handling imperfect parts or fit-up variations.
- High capital expenditure requirements create barriers to adopting robotic solutions.
- Rising demand in defense and infrastructure sectors is outpacing manual labor availability.

Solution Brief 24-8: AI Control for Welding Robots (Path Robotics) ***(continued)***

Solution
- Intelligent welding cells powered by proprietary Obsidian-1™ AI for autonomy.
- Vision systems allow robots to see and adapt to imperfect parts in real-time.
- Continuous AI learning improves capabilities across all deployed cells.

Benefits
- Achieves up to 4x productivity compared to traditional welding methods.
- Reduces welding costs by approximately 30%.
- Delivers consistent quality with over 97% first-pass yield.

Customers: LAD Services, Millerbernd, Tycrop

Provider: Path Robotics, Columbus, Ohio, USA; *path-robotics.com; youtu.be/GcNogDy32uE*

24.13 Assembly

Assembly combines components into the final product, ranging from high-speed automated lines (*final assembly*) to complex human-driven tasks (*guided worker assembly*).

24.13.1 Guided Worker Assembly

In high-variance manufacturing, workers often face cognitive overload when managing thousands of different parts or configurations.

AI supports workers along the following lines:

- *Creating and updating of Standard Operating Procedures* as a part of computer aided process planning (see Section 20.4). This does not need to remain at the documentation level; it can extend to the generation of training content, helping workers quickly familiarize themselves with production process updates or new product variants.

Solution Brief 24-9: AI-assisted Creation of Assembly Instructions (Assemblio)

Challenge
- Creating assembly instructions manually often takes weeks instead of minutes.
- Relying on individual expertise makes assembly processes vulnerable to staff turnover.
- Disconnects between CAD engineering data and the actual production shop floor (information silos).

Solution Brief 24-9: AI-assisted Creation of Assembly Instructions (Assemblio)

Solution

- Automatically generates standardized digital assembly guides directly from 3D CAD data.
- Uses AI to convert engineering data into assembly-ready bills of materials.
- Automatically updates instructions and tracks variations when design modifications occur.

Benefits

- Reduces assembly planning effort from weeks down to just a few minutes.
- Accelerates worker onboarding through interactive, language-independent 3D visual instructions.
- Minimizes assembly errors by validating and simulating process steps before production.

Customers: Daimler Truck, Rauch, Schaeffler, Siemens, Voith

Provider: Assemblio, Stuttgart, Germany; *assemblio.com*

- *Augmented reality* applications can overlay digital instructions directly onto the physical workspace. These systems act as a real-time quality gate. By monitoring the assembly process with overhead cameras, the AI can validate *kitting* (completeness checks for a complex kit) and/or ensure precise adherence to standard operating procedures (SOPs), dramatically reducing human error and enhancing process consistency [150].
- Unlike static manuals, these AI guides are *dynamic* – they adapt to the worker's pace and provide corrective haptic or visual feedback before a mistake moves down the line. This significantly reduces quality costs by preventing rework at the source.
- Furthermore, data captured during assembly enables manufacturers to identify ergonomic bottlenecks, ultimately creating a safer, more efficient environment for the human workforce [150].

Solution Brief 24-10: Visual Shop Floor Analytics (Leela.ai)

Challenge

- Time and motion studies can be costly, subject to bias, and provide limited data restricted to a specific point in time.
- IIoT sensors miss out on the human actions between the machines.
- MES prompts frontline workers to enter codes or push buttons, but these steps are frequently missed or handled incorrectly.

Solution "Leela Creator", "Leela Viewer", "Tactsync"

- Visual Intelligence Platform leverages large activity models (LAMs). The AI engine combines symbolic reasoning with neural networks and vision AI to deliver cause-and-effect insights, a hybrid approach that trains on 100x less data.
- Scales easily by adding more cameras to compare workstations, shifts, and facilities.
- Ensures privacy with face/body blurring and optional disabling of video review.

Solution Brief 24-10: Visual Shop Floor Analytics (Leela.ai) *(continued)*

Benefits

- LAMs deliver deeper contextual insight, clearer explainability, superior accuracy, and far leaner training and inference.
- Immediate video understanding that captures not just what happened but why - then takes informed, autonomous action.

Customers: Amsted Rail, Baltimore Aircoil

Provider: Leela.ai, Somerville, MA, USA; *leela.ai*;

24.13.2 Robotic Assembly

Unlike the early stages of production – such as welding or stamping, where robots handle heavy, raw materials – final assembly requires a sophisticated blend of high-payload strength and delicate dexterity. Robots in this phase handle high-precision tasks such as windshield and seat installation, as well as the intricate routing of wiring harnesses. By utilizing advanced end-effectors, such as soft grippers and vacuum suctions, they can manipulate fragile materials without causing surface damage.

Furthermore, the rise of *collaborative robots* (cobots) has transformed the workspace into a hybrid environment. While heavy industrial arms handle physically demanding or hazardous lifting, cobots work alongside human operators to perform ergonomically intensive tasks, such as underbody bolting.

Computer vision and force-torque sensors enable robots to "feel" and "see" their environment. This is critical for tasks such as screwdriving or part joining, where the robot must adapt to micro-tolerances and real-time vibrations.

Apropos force-torque sensors: While robots excel at rigid parts, they still struggle with deformable objects (cables, fabrics, gaskets). Human hands remain superior for feeling a snug fit or threading a flexible wire; having said this, progress in extending industrial robot capabilities to handle deformable objects has been incremental yet steady.

Solution Brief 24-11: Robotic Wiring of Electric Cabinets (Wirebot)

Challenge

- Heavy reliance on time-intensive, manual wiring processes in manufacturing.
- A growing shortage of skilled labor hinders production capacity.
- High physical strain on employees from repetitive, non-ergonomic tasks.

Solution Brief 24-11: Robotic Wiring of Electric Cabinets (Wirebot)

Solution "Wire Bot"

- Modular robotic system with automated conductor preparation and wiring capabilities.
- Automates cutting, stripping, crimping, and printing for up to 16 conductors.
- Performs rigorous quality checks, including pull-out tests and optical monitoring.
- Integrates easily without 3D-CAE, using simple cable lists and data.
- Channel and solution partner: WAGO (*wago.com*)

Benefits

- Reduces manual wiring labor by up to 60%, relieving skilled workers from monotonous, physically demanding tasks.
- Ensures consistently high-quality results with automated error detection.

Provider: WireBot, Zur Yigal, Israel; *wirebot.tech*

24.13.3 Electronics Assembly

While surface-mount technology has been driving pick-and-place automation in electronic assembly at astonishing speeds, large capacitors, coils, connectors, or switches in *Through-Hole Technology* (THT) are often mounted manually.

Progress in force-controlled robotics solves remaining THT mount challenges step by step, enabling fully automated electronic assembly in the foreseeable future.

Reflow oven control by AI process parameter calibration is also making progress; heat zone settings and conveyor belt speed no longer depend solely on human experience [151]. This helps both by reducing energy consumption and increasing product quality.

Automated Optical Inspection (AOI) is a vital process in electronics production. *Pre-reflow-oven AOI* checks parts for completeness and correct orientation. *Post-reflow-oven AOI* checks PCBs for scratches, hair cracks, cold solder joints, and solder bridges.

However, the rate of false positives is traditionally high in electronics AOI. False positives in this case mean a PCB is flagged as faulty and diverted for further, sometimes manual, quality inspection. Quality prediction models can assess the likelihood that a faulty PCB will be falsely flagged and override the divert to secondary inspection decision to improve throughput (false call reduction).

Pseudo Error Reduction in Electronics

In their Amberg and Chengdu electronics factories, *Siemens* trained an AI model to reduce frequent pseudo defects from optical quality inspection, flagging perfect solder joints as defects. This has reduced false alarms by 75%, significantly decreasing the need for X-ray inspections. The X-ray inspection station is a costly bottleneck in electronics assembly.

24.14 Paint Shop

The *paint shop* is characterized by automated coating applications, where quality depends on material usage and environmental control. Significant cost drivers are water consumption and, particularly, energy consumption for drying, which account for 45%–70% of the energy required for the entire production process of a car [152].

AI can help by facilitating

- *material discovery* to find new coating recipes, optimized along the dimensions of protection performance, visual appearance, and production efficiency;
- *immersion tank design* by computational fluid dynamics simulation;
- *water treatment* for deionizing, dosing chemicals for optimal bath balance, filtering, and recycling;
- *robot path planning*, either for spray robots or for quality inspection robots;
- *integrated quality control* through scanning systems that operate on a moving line without interrupting production cycle times (e. g., a paint quality tunnel), thereby maintaining high efficiency.
- *first time quality:* ML models select and investigate the main characteristics within the data that critically affect the painting outcome, allowing engineers to isolate causal factors for defects; and
- *energy savings in the drying process:* Minimizing heat dissemination when car bodies leave the drying tunnel, allowing the systems to calibrate efficiently when rebooting after a shutdown in off-shift times, optimizing fan control.

24.15 Quality Control

Computer-Aided Quality Control (CAQ) involves systematically monitoring the production process to reduce manufacturing inefficiencies, maintain high customer satisfaction, and ensure regulatory compliance across demanding sectors such as healthcare and aerospace. Quality control, supported by AI, can be structured into three components: quality prediction, quality inspection, and root cause analysis, as outlined below.

24.15.1 Quality Prediction

Batch control manages discrete production runs across industries such as chemicals, requiring rigorous control of recipes and process variables. The process interfaces with DCS/SCADA for data logging and control, and leverages process digital twins. AI supports real-time batch prediction, tracking batch evolution, and forecasting final quality metrics [153]:

It enables closed-loop optimization and supervisory control by autonomously managing parameters to enhance yield.

Digital twins allow for simulation to test the impact of process changes on recipe compliance before they are implemented physically, mitigating risk in high-value operations.

AI also provides virtual sensors (see Section 9.1) to estimate product properties before laboratory results are available, enabling immediate preventative intervention.

Beyond its role in reducing AOI false calls, as described in Section 24.13.3, quality prediction is beneficial whenever a production process consumes an expensive resource for an extended period. The earlier a quality prediction indicates that the required output quality will be missed, the sooner the process can be stopped and restarted with a new batch. This applies to many processes in the process industries (e. g., brewing beer), where it is critical to detect fermentation failure as early as possible so that the brew kettle can be emptied, cleaned, and the process restarted. The same applies, for instance, to 3D printing.

24.15.2 Quality Inspection

24.15.2.1 Machine Vision

Machine Vision (MV) is a vital tool in modern CAQ. Related systems offer a substantial advantage over manual inspection, delivering consistent accuracy and high-speed operation. By automatically inspecting every product on the line, machine vision achieves quality assurance, detecting minute flaws – such as micro-cracks or dimensional deviations – that human inspectors are likely to miss, due to, say, fatigue or speed limitations. AI supports MV along the following lines:

- *Setup and calibration support:* AI-supported wizards can help non-experts to quickly set up an MV solution, including required tuning of the optical system and the lighting setup.

  Example: Siemens Inspekto leverages specialized AI to help shop-floor workers set up the system in under 45 minutes.
- *Image acquisition support:* AI identifies work items, their rotation, and the region of interest for a quality check. This improves production flexibility as items do not need to be precisely positioned.

- *Anomaly detection:* DL models identify anomalies, following training with a limited number of good parts (few-shot learning). This approach keeps the project overhead required to introduce a quick quality inspection low; however, the inspection algorithm only provides a binary OK/Not-OK decision, and in most cases, everything flagged as Not-OK ends up in a separate, typically manual inspection task.
- *Quality issue classification:* DL models even classify different fault types, which is a precondition to automating the process of fixing or scraping parts.

  Example: A paintshop quality inspection separates scratches from blisters and paint drops; several fault types can be corrected through robotic polishing. In contrast, others require human intervention, including repainting the car body or a component.
- *Synthetic data generation* (see Section 9.3) is becoming increasingly instrumental in the training of AI models for MV applications.

Solution Brief 24-12: Supply Chain Integrity with Visual Inspection (Cybord)

Challenge

- High risk of counterfeit, defective, or manipulated electronic components.
- Lack of real-time, comprehensive quality inspection during assembly.
- Traditional traceability systems lack visual, component-level verification.
- Costly product recalls and rework due to undetected component flaws.

Solution

- Visual-AI software integrates seamlessly with existing SMT machines.
- Inspects 100% of components (top and bottom) in real-time before placement.
- Real-time interception instantly identifies and rejects faulty components.
- Collects and analyzes visual data for a forensic, micro-traceability record.

Benefits

- Ensures 100% authenticity and quality of all assembled components.
- Significantly reduces manufacturing rework, scrap, and recall costs.
- Instantly enforces approved vendor list compliance on the line.
- Provides unmatched visibility and control over the entire supply chain.

Customers: Fuji, Siemens, several customers in automotive and defense.

Provider: Cybord.ai, Tel Aviv (Israel)/New York City (USA); *cybord.ai*

24.15.2.2 Acoustic Quality Inspection

Acoustic quality inspection is a non-destructive tool for ensuring product integrity. By analyzing the unique sonic fingerprint of a component, sensors can detect internal flaws – such as microscopic cracks, loose fittings, or casting voids – that are often invisible to the naked eye, or computer vision applications.

This process uses advanced microphones and piezoelectric transducers to capture sound waves or vibrations emitted during operation or from intentional impact. ML algorithms then compare these real-time signals against a baseline of "healthy" acoustic patterns.

Critical Welding Spot Inspection

Vogt Ultrasonics partnered with the reinforcement learning specialist *Evoptima* to reinvent the approach to processing and leveraging massive datasets from ultrasonic phased-array spot weld inspections in automotive manufacturing. By integrating AI time-series models (based on xLSTM) to analyze raw acoustic signals directly, accuracy in predicting weld nugget size improved by 30%, enabling more robust, automated quality gates for safety-critical welding spot inspection in automotive [149].

Solution Brief 24-13: Acoustic Testing of Structural Integrity (Resoniks)

Challenge

- Traditional methods such as X-ray or manual checks are too slow for 100% inspection.
- Undetected internal defects lead to costly scrap, warranty disputes, and risk-fraught product recalls.
- Legacy testing requires expensive, specialized labor and hazardous chemicals or radiation.

Solution

- AI-powered acoustic analysis detects structural flaws by identifying a part's unique sonic fingerprint.
- Plug-and-play units provide fully automated, inline testing for metal and composite parts.
- ML models are trained on reference parts to provide instant pass/fail results.

Benefits

- Enables 100% real-time inspection, ensuring zero-defect quality.
- Significantly lower CapEx and OpEx compared to CT scans or ultrasonic testing.

Customers: Audi, Brose, Magna, Oras, Rational, Schaeffler, Temco

Provider: Resoniks, The Hague, Netherlands; *resoniks.com*

24.15.3 Root Cause Analysis

Quickly identifying the root cause of a quality issue improves production efficiency. The parameters can vary tremendously, be it a counterfeit electronic part on a PCB, a change of a supplier with minimal differences in part tolerances, or an ever-varying quality of raw materials (natural ones such as leather, cotton, or synthetic ones such as plastic granulate for injection molding with differences in the recycled plastics portion). It can be tool wear, changes in environmental conditions (e. g., humidity), or even differences in expert knowledge, depending on the shift staffing plan.

AI can correlate almost any data source and help identify potential root causes quickly.

Solution Brief 24-14: Root Cause Analysis for Manufacturing (Xplain Data)

Challenge

- Traditional AI often lacks the "why" behind results, leading to ineffective interventions.
- Businesses possess massive datasets but struggle to distinguish actual causation from simple correlation.
- High-dimensional data in manufacturing and healthcare is difficult to interpret for actionable insights. Conventional SQL databases are too rigid for analyzing complex, interconnected business objects.

Solution

- Causal AI algorithms are designed to uncover direct cause-and-effect relationships in real-world data.
- The XD ObjectAnalytics database analyses entire objects rather than tables.
- Automated causal discovery tools identify drivers of outcomes without manual feature selection.
- Industry-specific applications tailored for electronics manufacturing, discrete manufacturing, and healthcare sectors.

Benefits

- Deeper insights into production yield and quality by identifying root causes.
- Intelligent business interventions based on proven causal links, not just trends.
- Reduced manual data preparation efforts through an object-oriented architecture.

Customers: Siemens, SW Machines, Trumpf

Provider: Xplain Data, Munich, Germany; *xplain-data.de*

24.16 Robotics

The central tension in industrial robotics lies between universality and task-specific performance. Historically, robots were task-specific, excelling at high-speed, high-precision repetitive actions such as welding or palletizing, but requiring months of either rigid programming or AI training projects in a customer-specific environment.

The current trend is shifting toward general-purpose physical AI and robotic foundation models (see Section 2.7.4.4, "World Models"), which enable robots to perform millions of diverse tasks with zero-shot generalization. While universal models – often embodied in humanoid forms – promise unmatched flexibility and natural language control, they struggle to match the micron-level precision and cycle-time efficiency of specialized hardware designed for single, high-output industrial operations.

In any case, AI is already catalytic for the flexibility, autonomy, and coordination of industrial robots today in the following areas:

- *Perception:* ML-based pose estimation, object detection (including gripping points), etc.
- *Sequence planning:* AI uses optimization and RL to calculate the most efficient order and timing for a robot to execute a series of tasks, minimizing cycle time.
- *Path planning:* AI solves complex kinematics to generate collision-free paths. It excels at multi-arm coordination, managing dynamic dependencies and communication between multiple robots (including cobots) operating in a shared workspace, a cornerstone of collective robotic intelligence.
- *Actuator control:* DL and computer vision enable adaptive actuator control, allowing robots to adjust gripping force or orientation based on real-time perception of irregular or fragile objects.

Solution Brief 24-15: AI-powered Robot Programming (intrinsic)

Challenge
- Traditional robot programming requires hundreds of hours of manual, rigid hard-coding by experts.
- Robots struggle in dynamic environments due to a lack of adaptive perception and sensing.
- High costs and specialized expertise keep automation out of reach for most smaller businesses.

Solution "Flowstate"
- Intrinsic's Flowstate provides an AI-integrated environment for rapid simulation-to-real-world deployment.
- Intrinsic's Vision Model uses foundation models for automated, one-shot object detection and pose estimation.
- Reinforcement learning and graph neural networks automate complex multi-robot motion planning and collision avoidance.

Benefits
- Reduces development time from months to weeks through automated, AI-generated robot trajectories.
- Enables high-mix production by allowing robots to adapt instantly to new parts and environments.

Customers: Comau, Foxconn, Martin Automation, Trumpf

Provider: Intrinsic, Mountainview, California, USA; *intrinsic.ai*

24.17 Machine Setup and Parameter Calibration

Process parameter calibration prepares a machine for a new product run (setup) and fine-tunes operational variables, tasks historically reliant on expert knowledge and manual iteration.

Besides reducing dependence on human expertise, this reduces changeover time and minimizes the scrap generated during fine tuning (e. g., by using parameter settings to compensate for factors such as tool wear or variations in raw materials, ensuring consistent, high-quality output).

Solution Brief 24-16: Metal Sheet Cutting Parameter Calibration (Trumpf)

Challenge

- Laser metal cutting machines provide numerous settings to adjust laser beam energy, cutting speed, nozzle type, and nozzle/sheet distance to material properties such as metal type and thickness
- Tuning machine parameters for new materials is an iterative process, requiring skilled personnel
- Skilled personnel are becoming increasingly scarce.

Solution "Cutting Assistant"

- Several settings models were trained to optimize settings for different metal types.
- An initial selector model uses machine vision input from a test laser cut of the new material, selects 2–3 suitable settings models, and relies on transfer learning to determine the best parameter set.
- The models are computationally optimized to run locally on machines.
- Technology Partner: Fraunhofer IPA

Benefits

- Optimal machine parameters for both maximized speed and accuracy.
- Shorter calibration times than for human-performed calibration.

Provider: Trumpf, Ditzingen, Germany; *youtube.com/watch?v=o1MlP6calrk* | *arxiv.org/html/2503.15928v2*

24.18 Machine Operations

Industrial machine operators perform critical tasks to maintain efficient, safe production flows in manufacturing environments. Their core responsibilities include machine setup, process parameter calibration and monitoring, quality control, maintenance, and troubleshooting.

AI for machine operations can support these activities, for instance, by acting as a copilot with access to domain expertise, machine data, system logs, and standard operating procedures. Its primary functions for machine operations include:

- *Real-time diagnostics and troubleshooting:* It connects to live machine data (IoT sensors, MES, ERP) and allows operators to query the machine's status or alarms using natural language (voice or text). It instantly provides step-by-step resolution guidance or recommends next steps.
- *Predictive maintenance:* By continuously analyzing data, it identifies trends and anomalies, proactively suggesting maintenance actions to prevent unexpected downtime before machine failure occurs.
- *Knowledge democratization:* It provides immediate access to scattered corporate knowledge (manuals, documents, historical repair logs) in a simple, conversational format, allowing new or less-skilled workers to troubleshoot like seasoned experts.

Solution Brief 24-17: Copilots for Machine Operations (40 Factory)

Challenge

- Servitization and Revenue: OEMs struggle to transition to new servitization business models and monetize machine data to generate new revenue streams.
- End-users face poor operational equipment effectiveness (OEE) and costly unexpected downtime due to traditional maintenance strategies.
- After-sales support and in-house technicians struggle with slow, knowledge-based troubleshooting across a heterogeneous fleet of machines and complex manuals.

Solution "40 Factory's Machine Copilots"

- MAT (Machine Analytics Tool): An Industrial IoT white-label platform for end-to-end data acquisition, real-time monitoring, and advanced analysis, enabling predictive maintenance.
- Wilson.ai: A generative AI virtual assistant trained on proprietary company knowledge (manuals, reports) to provide instant, expert answers for maintenance and training.

Benefits

- New Income: Enables OEMs to launch digital services, creating new income flows and strengthening their competitive position.
- Cost & Efficiency: Significantly reduces maintenance costs and unplanned downtime by shifting to a predictive strategy, thereby boosting OEE.
- Rapid Support: Streamlines after-sales service and internal processes, allowing for faster problem resolution and turning machine data into actionable insights.

Customers: Arol, Macotec, MEP Group, Persico

Provider: 40 Factory, Piacenza, Italy; *40-factory.com*

24.19 Occupational Health and Safety

Not only does poor health and safety cost companies money (see Figure 24.2), but good Occupational Health and Safety (OSH) pays dividends. Studies estimate that for every euro invested in OSH, there is a return of EUR 2.2 and that the cost-benefit ratio of improving safety and health is favorable [154].

The economic advantages of strong OSH for businesses are significant: it improves worker productivity, reduces absenteeism, lowers compensation costs, and meets the sourcing requirements of public- and private-sector contractors.

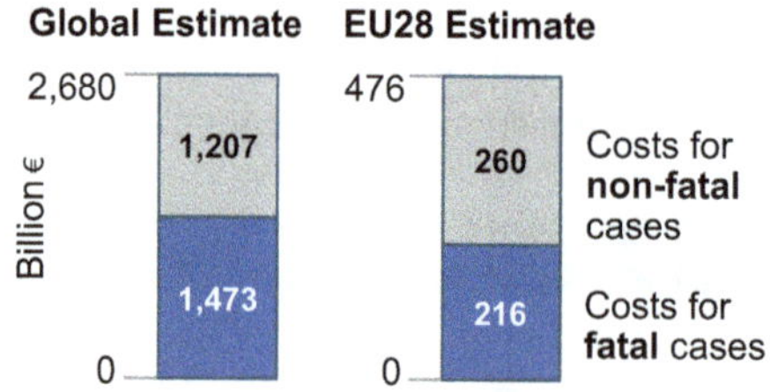

Figure 24.2 Costs of work-related accidents and illnesses, globally and in EU28

Examples of AI supporting continuous, automated, preventative risk mitigation:

- NLP or LLMs can help *analyze safety incident reports of the past.*
- AI-powered computer vision automates *Personal Protective Equipment* (PPE) compliance monitoring, continuously detecting whether necessary PPE is being used in designated areas and issuing immediate alerts upon non-compliance.
- It also enables the *detection of personnel in safety areas*, providing real-time analysis to identify unauthorized personnel in restricted zones, preventing exposure and potentially triggering system slowdowns or shutdowns [155].
- AI-powered computer vision can capture *ergonomics metrics* such as the number of bending movements, steps taken, or time spent in a bent-over posture or overhead activities. This facilitates design changes to improve ergonomics, thereby reducing long-term health impacts.
- Recent research suggests feasibility even for the machine-vision-based *detection of unsafe behavior when workers climb ladders* [156].

Solution Brief 24-18: AI-Detection of Humans for Industrial Safety (Neura Robotics)

Challenge

- Traditional safety systems struggle to distinguish humans from objects, causing false alarms.
- Complex safety setups and physical barriers restrict workspace layout.
- Unnecessary machine stops interrupt workflows, leading to production downtime.
- Standard sensors perform poorly in harsh conditions like dust or low lighting.

Solution "Omnisensor"

- Uses multi-modal sensor fusion to detect humans accurately in real-time.
- Modular design supports creation of custom safety zones for complex facility layouts.
- Differentiates between static objects and humans to prevent false triggering.
- Integrates flexible mounting options, including ceiling and mobile platform configurations.

Benefits

- Enables removal of physical fences, optimizing valuable factory floor space.
- Reduces unplanned downtime through automatic machine restarts without human intervention.
- Lowers installation and maintenance costs compared to traditional safety systems.
- Enhances productivity by allowing safe, uninterrupted human-robot collaboration.

Provider: Neura Robotics, Metzingen, Germany; *neura-robotics.com/omnisensor*

24.20 Connected Worker

The *connected worker* is a culmination of concepts already laid out. At its core, this solution empowers frontline staff with mobile devices, wearables, and AR headsets to bridge the gap between physical tasks and digital insights:

- AI further enhances this role through *augmented work instructions*, where computer vision recognizes components and overlays step-by-step digital guides to ensure precision.
- NLP allows *hands-free interaction* with technical manuals via voice-activated AI copilots, enabling workers to troubleshoot complex systems without leaving their stations.
- By analyzing movement and environmental data, AI also monitors safety, identifying ergonomic or hazardous risks such as gas levels in process industries, non-compliance with PPE rules, humans in no-go-safety zones, etc.

Solution Brief 24-19: Worker Guidance and Task Verification (Augmented Industries)

Challenge

- Training new technicians for complex machinery and processes is slow.
- Valuable expertise remains trapped in experts' heads or outdated paper documents.
- High machine downtime and quality issues due to slow/inaccurate troubleshooting.

Solution "Flow Tool"

- Instantly transforms documents, including videos, into digital work instructions.
- Provides technicians with AI-powered step-by-step instructions and troubleshooting via chat just in time.
- Manages audit-proof training paths and skill metrics, ensuring compliant operations.

Benefits

- Lowers onboarding and training expenses by up to 60% using AI automation.
- Minimizes downtime through faster, accurate problem-solving at the point of work.
- Boosts instruction effectiveness and reduces scrap rates through consistent task verification.

Customers: BMW Group, Mehnert, Siemens, Vestas,

Provider: Augmented Industries, Heroldsberg, Germany; *flow-tool.com*

25 Distribution Logistics

Distribution logistics is the process of moving finished products from the company to the customer. Intralogistics topics are addressed in Section 24.7 “Material Handling”.

25.1 Demand Forecasting & Inventory Balancing

In the product business, demand forecasting is a vital function for planning and steering production capacity and, naturally, for managing inventory levels.

ML models examine past sales data along with external influences – such as economic trends, seasonal patterns, and competitor offers – to accurately forecast the required inventory for each warehouse (Inventory Balancing). This reduces working capital because less safety stock remains unused, and it also helps prevent stock-outs [157].

Amazon and Unilever use large-scale forecasting models *to pre-position* inventory near customers *before* customers place an order. See also Solution Brief Throughput AI in Section 25.2.1.

25.2 Order Allocation, Picking & Packaging

25.2.1 Order Allocation

Order allocation is the system-driven process of reserving specific inventory for confirmed customer orders before any physical movement, effectively blocking stock to prevent it from being sold to others. It applies business logic (e. g., First-In-First-Out, customer priority, or inventory availability) to determine which units to use to fulfill a request.

AI upgrades this process from static rules to dynamic optimization. Instead of simply asking "Is stock available?", an AI model asks "Which specific unit of stock should I allocate to this order to maximize profit and minimize delivery time?"

Solution Brief 25-1: De-bottlenecking of Industrial Supply Chains (Throughput AI)

Challenge

- Critical business data is trapped in disconnected IT silos (ERP, WMS, Excel).
- Traditional forecasting is static and fails to account for real-time market volatility.
- Suboptimal inventory management. leads to millions in tied-up working capital and lost sales.

Solution

- Patented AI Algorithms sit on top of existing data to put material flow on autopilot.
- AI Demand Sensing leverages real-time signals to generate granular, SKU-level forecasts every week.
- Automated Rebalancing uses AI to move stock between locations based on actual consumption data.

Benefits

- Unlocks up to 60% of working capital by identifying and reducing excess, slow-moving stock.
- Delivers measurable operational impact within three weeks without requiring massive IT support.
- Maximizes profitability by aligning supply with the highest-margin customers and priority demand.

Customers: Indorama, MTA, Transnational Foods

Provider: Throughput AI, Palo Alto, California, USA; *throughput.world*

25.2.2 Picking & Kitting

Picking is the physical execution phase in which warehouse personnel or automated systems travel to designated storage locations to retrieve the items previously allocated to an order. It involves extracting the correct quantities of goods from shelves or bins and consolidating them for subsequent packing and shipment.

While picking is an umbrella term, it focuses primarily on selecting items (from partially chaotic bin content), kitting groups several items to form a kit (often with a dedicated stock keeping unit) so that customers receive an organized set of items that meets their specific expectations.

25.2.3 Packaging

In distribution logistics, *packaging* is a coordinated system for preparing goods for safe, efficient, and cost-effective transport, storage, and delivery to the final consumer.

While marketing focuses on how packaging looks on a shelf, logistics packaging focuses on how the item moves through the supply chain. It acts as the silent guardian of the product, ensuring it survives the rigors of shipping while maximizing space in trucks and warehouses.

25.2.4 Palletizing

Palletizing is the process of stacking and organizing goods (such as boxes, bags, or crates) onto/on a pallet to create a single, stable load unit for shipment.

Integrating AI with robotics has transformed palletizing from a rigid, labor-intensive chore into a dynamic, high-speed operation. Modern systems leverage computer vision and ML to identify diverse stock keeping units (SKUs), optimize stacking patterns (boxes, totes, bags), and adapt to changing box dimensions in real time. This ensures maximum load stability while reducing product damage and labor costs.

Solution Brief 25-2: Automated Palletizing (Bastian Solutions)

Challenge

- Manual palletizing is labor-intensive, leads to physical strain, and causes operational bottlenecks.
- High SKU variety and mixed-load pallets are difficult for traditional, rigid robotic systems.
- Constant product changes require expensive, time-consuming manual reprogramming of robotic workcells.

Solution

- AI-powered vision identifies and locates products in 3D space without prior training.
- StackOrder™ Software allows real-time visualization and implementation of complex, dynamic pallet patterns.
- ML builds a shared object library, allowing fleet-wide improvement and zero-programming updates.

Benefits

- Reduces labor dependency and turnover issues by automating repetitive, ergonomically taxing tasks.
- Enhances flexibility by enabling autonomous handling of millions of SKUs and mixed-case loads.
- Accelerates ROI through high-uptime performance and rapid deployment without custom software coding.

Customers: Boeing, Puma, SMC, Trace Die Cast

Provider: Bastian Solutions, Indianapolis, Indiana, USA; *bastiansolutions.com*

25.3 Shipping & Transportation Logistics

This is the function of planning, implementing, and controlling the movement and storage of goods from their point of origin to the customer. It involves selecting carriers, managing freight, and ensuring timely and cost-effective delivery.

25.3.1 Freight Carrier Selection

Transportation typically accounts for the lion's share of the logistics spend, making even incremental efficiencies highly impactful for a company's bottom line. AI transforms this from a reactive struggle into a proactive strategy: predictive analytics anticipate market rate shifts and port congestion weeks in advance, allowing shippers to lock in favorable rates or reroute shipments before delays occur.

Solution Brief 25-3: Real-time Freight Carrier Selection (Project44)

Challenge

- Fragmented data across thousands of carriers leads to visibility gaps and manual follow-ups.
- Reactive firefighting during global disruptions results in high expedited shipping and inventory costs.
- Siloed, poor-quality data makes it impossible to achieve autonomous supply chain execution.

Solution "Movement"

- Multi-agent orchestration deploys specialized AI agents to fix data and resolve exceptions autonomously.
- The "AI Disruption Navigator" maps global events directly to impacted inventory for predictive impact analysis.
- The "MO AI Assistant" provides a natural language interface for instant, conversational supply chain insights.

Benefits

- Reduces data gaps by 50% through autonomous, 24/7 AI-driven carrier and driver engagement.
- Lowers disruption-related costs by up to 40% via earlier detection and automated rerouting.
- Accelerates decision-making speed by 90% by replacing manual analysis with AI-powered answers.

Customers: Absolute, Continental, Georgia Pacific, HCS Group, T-Group

Provider: Project44, Chicago, Illinois, USA; *project44.com*

25.3.2 Customs & Import/Export Clearance

Customs and import/export clearance involves preparing and submitting the necessary documents to customs authorities and handling duties and taxes, ensuring that goods can legally and smoothly cross international borders [158]:

- NLP can extract data from unstructured documents – such as invoices and certificates – with high accuracy, eliminating manual data entry and cross-referencing errors.
- This automation is applied to the harmonized system code classification, where AI instantly suggests the correct codes.
- Furthermore, AI-supported systems can constantly monitor global sanctioned party lists and export regulations in real-time, drastically cutting down the time compliance teams spend on screening and ensuring due diligence, allowing them to focus on strategic risk mitigation.

25.3.3 Freight Cost Control

GenAI can support complex tasks, such as auditing thousands of freight invoices to identify billing errors. Typical errors are:

- *Duplicate invoicing:* The most frequent error, where a carrier accidentally bills for the same shipment multiple times, often under different reference numbers.
- *Incorrect accessorial charges:* Carriers may apply extra fees for services not performed, such as lift-gate delivery, residential surcharges, or inside delivery, even if the dock was accessible.
- *Classification errors:* In less-than-truckload shipping, items are billed on the basis of their freight class. A slight error in density or commodity description can result in significantly higher rates.
- *Weight discrepancies:* This occurs when the carrier's re-weigh differs from the shipper's stated weight, often due to uncalibrated scales or including the weight of the pallet twice.
- *Fuel surcharge inaccuracies:* Fuel surcharges fluctuate weekly. Errors occur when carriers apply the wrong week's index or use an incorrect percentage based on the contract.
- *Distance/mileage miscalculations:* Billing for practical miles or hub miles when the contract specifies short-route miles.
- *Discount omissions:* Failing to apply the negotiated contract discounts or base rate incentives specifically agreed upon during the procurement phase.

Solution Brief 25-4: Freight Cost Auditing (Blue Cargo)

Challenge

- Lack of real-time visibility into container status causes expensive, preventable port terminal fees.
- Manual auditing of complex freight invoices is slow and prone to human error.
- Fragmented data across carriers and terminals makes disputing unfair detention charges nearly impossible.

Solution

- AI-First audit platform automatically flags billing errors, duplicate charges, and regulatory non-compliance.
- Predictive analytics monitor port congestion and container dwell times to forecast potential fees.
- AI agents and automated workflows centralize documentation for rapid, evidence-based dispute resolution.

Benefits

- Significantly reduces drayage and detention costs by identifying millions in incorrect freight charges.
- Cuts invoice review time by up to 70% through data extraction and analysis.
- Increases working capital by recovering overpayments and preventing unfair accessorial fees at scale.

Customers: Cargomatic, GE Appliances, Next Trucking, Samsung

Provider: Blue Cargo, San Francisco, California, USA; *bluecargo.io*

26 Customer Service

26.1 Service Desk Agent Training

Service desk agent training moves beyond static manuals and role-play scripts: AI simulates *role-play scenarios* based on anonymized, real customer interactions, allowing new hires to practice handling diverse, emotionally charged issues without risk. This accelerates speed-to-proficiency, which is particularly useful in an environment traditionally plagued by high staff attrition. In addition, this training can be conducted without an on-site trainer.

Furthermore, AI acts as a *real-time coach* during customer interactions, assisting agents by generating suggested responses, summarizing complex ticket histories, and providing instant feedback on communication skills and tone.

By analyzing the performance of top agents, *AI tailors learning paths* and focuses training on specific skill gaps, ensuring continuous improvement and higher quality, consistent service across the entire support team.

Solution Brief 26-1: AI-led Service Agent Trainings (Spitch AI)

Challenge

- High agent turnover and lengthy, costly onboarding processes.
- Traditional training lacks realism for complex or emotional calls.
- Difficulty ensuring consistent quality and compliance across all agents.
- Excessive workload and time burden on trainers and coaches.

Solution

- AI-powered simulator creates realistic, dynamic customer call scenarios.
- Customizable training scenarios that vary customer emotion and tone.
- The feedback system provides agents with concrete improvement suggestions.
- Provides 24/7 on-demand access to practice in a safe, secure environment.

Solution Brief 26-1: AI-led Service Agent Trainings (Spitch AI) *(continued)*

Benefits

- Up to 50% reduction in agent onboarding and training time.
- Up to 40% lower training costs and less effort for coaches.
- Agents gain confidence and higher competency before handling live calls.
- Increased agent job satisfaction, leading to lower employee attrition.

Customers: Etihad, Swiss Banks, and Insurance Companies.

Provider: Spitch AI, Zurich, Switzerland; *spitch.ai*

26.2 Complaint and Issue Management

This function does not just involve handling customer complaints but also means analyzing them to identify root causes, implement corrective actions, and improve product quality and customer satisfaction. It is a feedback loop from the market to the production floor.

AI supports complaint and issue management as follows:

- NLP and LLMs *extract entities* (e.g., a customer identity or a referenced purchase order) from unstructured communication (e.g., an email), improving routing and reducing agents' lookup times.
- It *pre-generates* and, to a certain extent, *personalizes outgoing customer communication.*
- It supports the *extraction of knowledge base entries* from repeating tickets and proven solution approaches
- Whenever knowledge base entries feed customer-facing chatbots, *issues and related tickets can be deflected* as users are enabled to solve their problem by self-help mechanisms.

26.3 Technician Field Force Management

Service field force management is the process of organizing and optimizing the activities of off-site personnel, such as technicians, engineers, and inspectors. Core responsibilities include complex scheduling and dispatching to match the right skills with the right job, real-time tracking of staff and equipment, managing work orders from creation to completion, and ensuring field inventory availability [159].

AI enhances these operations as follows [160]:

- AI-powered algorithms analyze historical data, traffic patterns, and technician expertise to create highly efficient, dynamic schedules and routes, drastically reducing travel time.
- Furthermore, AI assists in predictive maintenance by analyzing data from IoT devices to forecast equipment failures, allowing for proactive repairs.
- LLMs, respectively, NLP helps to interpret legacy field force repair and maintenance reports, unlocking a potentially precious set of historical data points. Of course, both tools can now support the rapid generation of field-force repair and maintenance reports, potentially even via voice input.
- Furthermore, most of the AI benefits for fleet management (see Section 21.3) apply.

26.4 Disposal & Recycling

This function refers to support for the compliant disposal or recycling of a product at the end of its life, a key component of end-of-life management in PLM and a growing sustainability concern.

Solution Brief 26-2: Dangerous and Valuable Waste Identification (WeSort)

Challenge
- Large fires caused by exploding lithium batteries often result in a total loss of a waste sorting system.
- Related insurance policies are costly.
- Waste sorting returns are directly related to the purity of sorting.

Solution "Battery.Sort", "Vision.Family"
- X-ray scanner and AI models identify batteries and devices with batteries.
- Different AI vision models improve the purity of different waste types.
- Very powerful air pressure nozzles shoot the identified waste part into separate, secured containers.

Benefits
- Decreased risk of battery-induced fires. Consequently, reduced insurance fees.
- Improved purity of waste leading to higher earnings.

Customers: Korn, pre-zero, Recycling Park Harz, Siemens

Provider: WeSort.ai, Würzburg, Germany; *wesort.ai*

27 Marketing & Communication

In the context of an industrial enterprise – characterized by complex supply chains, high-value capital goods, and technical buyer journeys – the *Marketing and Communication* (MarCom) function is the strategic bridge between engineering excellence and market demand.

Unlike consumer-facing sectors, industrial MarCom focuses on building long-term credibility, articulating technical value propositions, and managing stakeholder relationships across long sales cycles. It is responsible for brand positioning, lead generation through trade shows and digital channels, and internal communications that align a global workforce. However, the sheer volume of technical content and the need for personalized, multi-channel engagement often strain traditional MarCom resources.

Naturally, AI helps to generate content for engineering reports, localized press releases, white papers, and social media updates. This ensures that global offices maintain a consistent brand voice while catering to local languages and regional nuances. And for a simple starting point: The power of AI-driven translation services (see Section 32.4) is a classic example of how easy and agile translation work has become.

The interface between content creation and publishing, on the one hand, for lead generation, and sales follow-up, on the other, has high potential for efficiency gains through a data analytics-driven approach to content evaluation.

Rockwell faced a challenge common to automation technology providers: they had hundreds of technical assets (white papers, datasheets, guides) but struggled to attribute value to them or to follow up effectively globally. They used intelligent progressive profiling and automated content gating (in partnership with *Formulayt*). Instead of asking for 10 fields of data upfront (which scares away engineers), the system remembered users. If an engineer downloaded a general guide, the system would wait. If they returned a week later to view a specific PLC spec sheet, the system recognized the intent increase and triggered a specific, lower-friction form. This automated relevance led to a 700% increase in contact conversions, effectively automating the qualification step before a human representative ever had to intervene [161].

28 Human Resources

The comprehensive process of acquiring, onboarding, and managing an employee's lifecycle.

28.1 Recruitment & Hiring

AI-powered *recruitment analytics* tools bring together data from job postings, applicant tracking systems, interviews, and assessments to uncover patterns and inefficiencies that humans might overlook. Hiring platforms exemplify this transformation by capturing and standardizing interview conversations – both in-person and video – then turning notes and recordings into actionable insights that help evaluate interviewer effectiveness, identify candidate drop-offs, and guide hiring improvements. In addition, AI can automatically *analyze video interviews*, assessing both verbal and nonverbal communication to provide structured, bias-free feedback to hiring teams.

However, integrating AI into recruitment also presents significant ethical and technical challenges, particularly regarding *algorithmic bias*. Historical data used to train AI systems often reflects past human biases, leading to unfair outcomes in application screening.

Amazon discontinued its AI-driven CV analysis tool after discovering that it unintentionally favored male candidates because of biased training data [162]. Another example is a collective-action lawsuit against *Workday*, alleging that the company's AI used to screen job applicants discriminated against candidates 40 years of age and older [163].

Such cases highlight the importance of continuous monitoring, transparency, and human oversight in AI-assisted hiring.

Solution Brief 28-1: Preventing Bias in Hiring Decisions (Knockri)

Challenge

- Manual screening causes long time-to-hire and high cost-to-fill.
- Human interviewer bias results in poor diversity and unfair hiring.
- Difficulty assessing soft skills and job competencies objectively at scale.
- Traditional recruitment methods offer a suboptimal candidate experience.

Solution

- AI analyzes transcripts of structured video and audio assessments.
- Algorithms assess content based solely on scientific skill frameworks.
- Bias is mitigated by ignoring demographics, appearance, and accent.
- Provides a branded, seamless candidate experience on any device.

Benefits

- Achieves up to 90% reduction in time-to-hire and screening costs.
- Organically increases racial and gender diversity in candidate pools.
- Improved quality of hire and up to 80% better employee retention.
- Delivers fast, objective, and fair candidate evaluation at enterprise scale.

Customers: Deloitte, IBM, Shopify

Provider: Knockri, Toronto, Canada; *knockri.com*

Hiring temporary staff via temporary employment agencies is a variant of the hiring process that benefits particularly well from AI acceleration:

- *Receiving customer requests* ("We need three additional welders in the morning shifts on Tuesdays and Wednesdays for the upcoming 12 weeks") can already be taken and converted into a structured selection and scheduling workflow.
- *Screening CVs* on both sides, the agency hiring candidates and the customer temporarily hiring supporting temporary workers, benefits from CV-specific text analysis and AI-supported match-making.
- LLMs can further *support communication between all parties*, including the creation of documentation required to meet regulatory rules.

Solution Brief 28-2: AI-supported Temporary Hiring Workflows (PD Connect)

Challenge
- Dealing with unstructured customer requests, specifically at business peak times
- Risk of fines due to non-compliance with regulatory requirements
- Manual effort of screening skill profiles and matching them to customer demand

Solution "PDConnect24"
- AI chatbots to receive temporary hiring requests from customers
- AI-based CV analysis and match-making
- AI-supported communication

Benefits
- Reduction of time-to-hire KPI by 38%
- Improved quality in compliance-related documentation, reduced risk of fines.

Customers: emsland.work, DEKRA, Wackler Personalservice

Provider: PD Connect, Lingen, Germany; *pdconnect.de*

28.2 Timesheeting

Timesheeting describes the process of tracking and managing employees' (and contractors') working hours. This serves several purposes:

- Checking whether work contracts are being fulfilled (e. g., tracking whether an employee has worked the agreed 40 h per week).
- Determining which internal projects consumed what resources. Aggregated project hours can be fed into project management tools to provide insights into hours worked versus project milestones achieved.
- Feeding into charging and billing wherever work performed is charged to customers (e. g., service orders or software projects with a time and material charging model).

AI-supported timesheeting systems (e. g., *laurel.ai*) automate timesheet creation by tracking user activity across applications and URLs, generating descriptive entries, and instantly capturing billable minutes that would otherwise be lost. Similarly, ML can provide smart suggestions, automatically populating timesheets based on previous entries and data pulled from other systems like calendar events (leveraging, for example, Microsoft Outlook) and tasks (e. g., Journyx). Furthermore, users can interact with their timesheets in natural language, as demonstrated by Cognitus [195] with its agentic timesheeting integration into Microsoft Teams. Integration with ERP systems accelerates related approvals and subsequent reporting and billing workflows.

Solution Brief 28-3: AI-supported Time Sheeting (Journyx)

Challenge

- Filling in timesheets is a non-productive task and typically unpopular among employees.
- A resulting lack of timesheeting discipline creates lags in transparency and steering a business

Solution "Smart Timesheets"

- Integration with MS Office Outlook calendars to extract calendar entries and tasks to pre-populate timesheets
- A feedback mechanism lets the AI learn and improve over time.

Benefits

- Faster availability of employee timesheets
- Less effort to create them

Customers: Iridium Communications, Caspian One; Johnson Controls, Boehringer Ingelheim

Provider: Journyx, Austin, Texas, USA; *journyx.com*

28.3 Payroll Processing

Payroll processing covers the administrative function of calculating and processing employee salaries, wages, and pension contributions. AI can become an instrumental tool to manage the multifaceted multi-party interactions required to process large salary volumes smoothly and compliantly:

- *Process documents* (e. g., healthcare insurance payment confirmation)
- *Increase pay transparency and understanding:* Offering employees the opportunity to interact with an AI assistant to understand payment calculation rules and their results, and to address issues.
- *Detect fraud:* By analyzing patterns, verifying data, and identifying irregularities in real-time, AI strengthens payroll security and ensures compliance.
- *Support shadow payroll processing:* Shadow payrolls are a mechanism used by companies to stay tax-compliant when they send employees to work in a different country (temporarily or long-term), but still pay them through their home country payroll. The additional shadow payroll is used solely for reporting and remitting local taxes (such as income tax and social insurance) to the host country's authorities.

Solution Brief 28-4: AI Tools for Payroll Processing (Payslip)

Challenge

- Manual processing of repetitive tasks causes inefficiencies and errors.
- Fragmented data across countries and vendors makes global oversight difficult.
- Legacy systems often lack the specialized AI needed for complex global compliance.

Solution "Alpha Assist", "Alpha Agent", and "Alpha Intelligence"

- Alpha Assist: Task-focused AI tools for repetitive work like pay element mapping.
- Alpha Agent: Intelligent automation that handles time-consuming reporting and reconciliation workflows.
- Alpha Intelligence: Real-time anomaly detection to highlight potential errors before payroll closes.

Benefits

- Provides centralized, harmonized data across all countries, vendors, and systems.
- Enterprise-grade accuracy and security through payroll-first-built AI models.
- Empowers teams to shift from manual tasks to high-value strategic decision-making.

Customers: Booking.com, Cloudera, EQT

Provider: Payslip.com, Mayo, Ireland; *payslip.com/product/payslip-alpha*

28.4 Training

The *training* function designs and delivers *internal programs* for personnel development, enhancing employee competencies, career progression, and overall productivity through workshops, e-learning, and certifications. Its function can also include *training sales partners and customers* to ensure that they deeply understand products, services, and best practices.

Instead of one-size-fits-all materials, GenAI tools analyze learner data to craft adaptive modules, quizzes, and simulations that match individual skill levels and goals. This personalization enhances engagement and retention while reducing instructional designers' development time.

Solution Brief 28-5: AI-based Learning Management System (Docebo)

Challenge

- Creating training content is painstaking.
- Trainings carry static content, so parts of the student community are not challenged enough.

Solution Brief 28-5: AI-based Learning Management System (Docebo)

Solution

- GenAI supported training content creation.
- AI-supported training recommendations (e. g., role-based).
- Integrations with leading directory services, HR systems, digital credential backbones, etc.
- Manages automated recertifications required for several regulatory standards.

Benefits

- Higher employee engagement and retention, with lower costs for training content creation and distribution.

Customers: Ducati, Dyson, Knauf, SONOS

Provider: Docebo, Ontario, Canada; *docebo.com*

One more thought on the role of GenAI in generating content and, to a certain extent, replacing painstaking audio and video production processes: Organisational agility – a quality we certainly all strive for – requires that our teams can adjust their way of working quickly in response to business needs and process changes. The ability to train staff on changes in a flexible, smooth, and efficient way is directly linked to how dynamically a training organization can respond to business needs by providing updates on how a given process should be executed.

Solution Brief 28-6: AI-generated Avatar Videos and Voice Overs (Synthesia)

Challenge

- Production of videos, for example, for service, sales, or training, typically requires external media experts, which is costly but also requires planning and booking, which slows down agility in video production.
- Once produced, it is cumbersome to implement changes and updates.

Solution

- Support for 140+ languages, 230 different avatars, 250+ video templates

Benefits

- Saves up to 90% of time and costs of traditional video production
- Increases agility, particularly when implementing minor updates

Customers: Bosch, Heineken, Reuters, Merck, Mondelez, Moody's, SAP

Provider: Synthesia, London, United Kingdom; *synthesia.io*

29 Legal & Compliance

29.1 Legal & Contract Management

A corporate legal department serves as the essential guardian of an organization's legal health, tasked with navigating complex regulatory environments and mitigating business risks. Its typical responsibilities are extensive, primarily revolving around the entire lifecycle of contract management – drafting, reviewing, and negotiating agreements – as well as ensuring strict compliance with evolving global laws. Furthermore, the department manages litigation, protect intellectual property assets, and provides vital strategic counsel to executive leadership.

AI-driven tools now automate routine, high-volume tasks, such as expediting due diligence during mergers or rapidly reviewing non-disclosure agreements. ML algorithms can also analyze vast contract repositories to identify anomalous clauses or compliance gaps far faster than human review [164].

Solution Brief 29-1: AI-supported In-house-Legal Management (Streamline)

Challenge
- Legal in-house departments can become a bottleneck when scaling a business.
- High OpEx spend for legal work, both for internal resources and external law firms, while standard requests characterize many work items.

Solution
- Predefined workflow solutions to handle sales, partner, contractor agreements, as well as compliance reviews, privacy-related requests, invention disclosures, and employment law issues.
- Integrations with email, Slack, Ironclad, and Salesforce.

Benefits
- Significant response time reductions.
- Cityblock Health reports a legal OpEx spend reduction by 40%.

Solution Brief 29-1: AI-supported In-house-Legal Management (Streamline)

Customers: Cityblock Health, hims, lighthouse, logitech

Provider: Streamline, San Francisco, California, USA; *https://www.streamline.ai*

29.2 Compliance Management

Compliance management builds the framework and ensures that the business operates within the rules (doing the right thing). At the same time, the audit function tests the effectiveness of that framework and verifies that the business is following its own rules (ensuring it did things right).

Both disciplines cover a range of subjects, including operational efficiency, the reliability of financial reporting, and compliance with laws, regulations (e. g., environmental regulations), and industry standards (e. g., ISO 27001 for cybersecurity).

Solution Brief 29-2: Automated Compliance Management (Vanta)

Challenge

- Compliance is a manual, time-consuming, and resource-heavy process.
- Startups need to become compliant with industry standards, for example, HIPAA, ISO 27001, quickly to unblock and close larger sales deals.
- Vendor risk management and security reviews are complex and slow.
- Difficult to maintain continuous compliance after the initial audit.

Solution

- Software agents automate evidence collection and continuous compliance monitoring.
- Single AI-powered platform for GRC, risk, and vendor management.
- Streamlines audits for 35+ frameworks like SOC 2 and ISO 27001.
- Creates a public Trust Center to demonstrate security posture proactively.

Benefits

- Achieves compliance quickly and automatically to unblock revenue growth.
- Saves hundreds of hours of manual work for security teams.
- Provides continuous security assurance, moving beyond point-in-time checks.

Customers: Duolingo, GitHub, Icelandair, Leela.ai, Snowflake

Provider: Vanta, San Francisco, California, USA; *vanta.com*

Environment, Health, and Safety (EHS) compliance spans many different topics. PPE compliance is described in Section 24.19 "Occupational Health and Safety".

30 Real Estate & Facility Management

30.1 Building Security Management

Building security management refers to the coordinated processes, technologies, and strategies used to protect a building's occupants, assets, and infrastructure against security threats, accidents, and unauthorized access. It ensures the safety and integrity of physical spaces by integrating surveillance, access control, emergency response, and cybersecurity systems.

The key functions of building security management include:

- *Access control:* Regulating who can enter specific areas through digital credentials or biometrics.
- *Surveillance and monitoring:* Using cameras and sensors to observe activities in and around the facility.
- *Intrusion detection:* Identifying unauthorized entry or suspicious behavior through alarms and motion detectors.
- *Hazard detection:* Detecting hazards as early as possible while avoiding expensive false alerts (think of a hospital or conference center evacuated because of a false alarm).
- *Emergency management:* Coordinating responses to fire, medical, or security incidents.
- *Incident reporting and compliance:* Documenting events and ensuring adherence to safety regulations and data protection laws.

Solution Brief 30-1: Vision-based Fire Detection (Visionify AI)

Challenge

- Traditional alarms are too slow; smoke must physically reach sensors.
- Fires in large industrial spaces escalate quickly due to detection delays.
- Needs continuous 24/7 monitoring across vast facilities without fatigue.
- High cost and disruption of false alarms from dust or steam.

Solution

- AI vision system analyzes video feed from existing cameras.
- Detects the visual signature of smoke or fire within 30 seconds.
- Edge processing ensures real-time analysis and low-latency alerts.
- Sends immediate, multi-channel notifications (SMS, email, speakers).

Benefits

- Provides critical early warning, minutes faster than conventional systems.
- Dramatically reduces potential property damage and business interruption.
- Lowers insurance premiums through enhanced, documented safety measures.
- Reduces false alarms using intelligent visual discrimination algorithms.

Customers: Adani Power, DB, Henkel, Sefaira

Provider: Visionify AI, Westminster, Colorado, USA; *visionify.ai/articles/vision-ai-next-gen-fire-detection*

30.2 Visitor Management

Visitor management refers to the process of tracking, monitoring, and managing individuals who enter and exit an organization's premises. Its key functions include visitor registration, identity verification, access control, monitoring visitor flow, and maintaining records for security and compliance purposes. Effective visitor management ensures safety, professionalism, and operational efficiency in workplaces, schools, hospitals, and government facilities.

AI-powered tools such as facial recognition and optical character recognition enable quick, reliable identity verification, reducing manual errors and wait times. ML algorithms analyze visitor data to predict traffic patterns, optimize scheduling, and enhance security by identifying unusual behavior or potential threats. NLP allows AI chatbots to manage pre-registrations, answer visitor inquiries, and provide real-time assistance.

Furthermore, AI integrates with smart building systems devices to enable seamless access control and personalized experiences. By automating routine tasks and providing real-time insights, AI-supported visitor management systems enhance security and the visitor experience, helping organizations create safer, smarter, and more efficient environments.

A Finnish high-tech company replaced human-staffed reception desks in remote business buildings with self-service check-in kiosks. Facial recognition features match a camera picture of the visitor, a passport document, and a picture from an earlier registration to allow entry.

Solution Brief 30-2: Visitor Management System (Verkada)

Challenge
- Paper-based tracking is insecure, lacks privacy, and creates unreliable audit trails.
- Staff cannot quickly identify high-risk individuals or verify credentials in real-time.
- Disconnected visitor logs, video, and access control prevent cohesive incident investigations.

Solution
- Uses facial recognition to expedite check-in for returning, opt-in visitors instantly.
- Links visitor profiles with AI-enabled cameras for person-of-interest and trajectory tracking.
- AI-driven tools scan government databases to block unwanted individuals.

Benefits
- Enhanced Security Response: Real-time AI alerts for blocked individuals prevent unauthorized entry before it happens.
- Streamlined Operations: Reduces front-desk manual labor by up to 98% via automated, touchless workflows.
- Accelerated Investigations: AI-powered search allows security teams to find visitor footage in seconds, not hours.

Customers: General Motors, Nestlé, Northrop Grumman, Signify

Provider: Verkada, San Mateo, California, USA; *verkada.com/workplace/guest-visitor-management-system*

30.3 Building Energy Management

Building energy management systems play a crucial role in optimizing energy consumption, reducing costs, and improving sustainability in residential, commercial, and industrial buildings. These systems monitor, control, and analyze energy use across HVAC, lighting, and electrical systems.

AI algorithms process large volumes of sensor data to identify patterns, forecast energy demand, and detect inefficiencies or equipment faults before they occur. ML models can automatically adjust system settings – such as temperature, lighting, and ventilation – based on occupancy patterns and environmental conditions, ensuring comfort while minimizing waste. Additionally, AI supports integration with renewable energy sources and smart grids, enabling buildings to respond dynamically to fluctuating energy prices and grid demands.

31 Information Technology

IT infrastructures have evolved from monolithic, on-premises data centers to distributed, hybrid ecosystems spanning multi-cloud environments, edge computing nodes, and ephemeral microservices. IT sourcing strategies have evolved from a single-outsourcing-provider model towards selective sourcing of best-in-class IT services, which leaves IT management with the self-inflicted noble duty of stitching everything together to deliver a cohesive user experience while managing oversight and technical debts. Modern IT environments are characterized by dynamic complexity: virtualized assets are spun up and down in milliseconds; containerized applications depend on microservices that can be dynamically reconfigured; and the workforce is increasingly distributed, accessing corporate resources from unmanaged networks.

AI provides powerful tools that enable IT management and service delivery to tackle these challenges. The sections *IT Service Management*, *Enterprise Architecture Management*, *Cybersecurity*, and *Software Development* provide many related examples.

31.1 IT Service Management

IT Service Management (ITSM) is the discipline of designing, delivering, managing, and improving the use of IT within an organization. It is the front line of IT, dealing directly with users and operational incidents.

The infusion of AI into ITSM creates what is often termed *Service Management 4.0*, or *cognitive service management*, for example, transforming the service desk user experience, automating incident operations via AIOps, and enhancing change & asset management, as well as configuration compliance management (see Table 31.1).

Table 31.1 From traditional ITSM to AI-enhanced ITSM

	Traditional ITSM	AI-enhanced ITSM	Benefit
Incident Detection	User reports/static thresholds	Anomaly detection/ predictive baselines	Proactive prevention of outages.
Triage	Manual classification & routing	Automated intent recognition & routing	Faster mean time to repair; reduced staff workload.
Resolution	Human agent investigation	Virtual agent/ Self-healing scripts	Scalable 24/7 support; lower cost per ticket.
Change Management	Change Advisory Board meetings for all changes	Risk-based auto-approval	Increased release velocity (DevOps alignment).
Knowledge Management	Manual article creation	GenAI drafting & synthesis	Up-to-date info; reduced training time.

31.1.1 Service Desk

The traditional service desk model is labor-intensive and often frustrating for end-users. It relies on tiered support structures (Level 1, 2, 3) in which tickets are manually transferred between queues, frequently resulting in long wait times and inconsistent resolution quality. AI is dismantling this tiered structure in favor of swarming and immediate, automated resolution.

- *Intent recognition:* The primary interface of a smart service desk is an AI-powered virtual agent. Unlike early chatbots that relied on rigid decision trees and keyword matching – often leading to "I don't understand" loops – modern virtual agents utilize NLP and LLMs.
- *Semantic understanding:* NLP allows the system to digest unstructured text and understand intent, context, and nuance. A user might type "My laptop is crawling", "PC is slow", or "Everything is lagging". A keyword-based system might miss the connection, but an NLP model trained on IT corpus data recognizes the semantic intent: *Performance Issue > Endpoint > High Latency/CPU.*
- *Entity extraction:* Beyond intent, the AI extracts critical entities (variables) from the conversation. If a user says, "I can't access the HR portal from my iPad", the system identifies the service (HR Portal) and the device (iPad), allowing it to immediately check specific knowledge bases or known issues related to mobile access for that service.

- *Sentiment analysis:* AI models continuously analyze the sentiment of user inputs. By detecting frustration, sarcasm, or urgency in the user's language, the system can dynamically prioritize the interaction. A user expressing high anger might be routed immediately to a human agent, bypassing standard automated triage steps, thereby protecting the employee experience score [165].
- *Knowledge management* is historically the "Achilles heel" of ITSM. *Knowledge bases* are frequently outdated, fragmented, or written in dense technical jargon that end-users cannot parse. GenAI is fundamentally solving this problem by automating the lifecycle of knowledge:
- *Dynamic content creation:* When a human agent resolves a complex, novel incident, GenAI can ingest the ticket history – including the chat logs, technical notes, and resolution steps – and automatically draft a structured knowledge base article. This ensures that tribal knowledge is captured and codified instantly across the entire organization.
- *Contextual synthesis:* For the end-user, GenAI replaces the traditional search and link experience. Instead of returning a list of ten blue links to PDF manuals, the AI acts as an intelligent synthesizer. It reads the relevant manuals, extracts the steps for the user's error code, and generates a concise, step-by-step response directly in the chat window [166].
- *Gap analysis:* AI agents continuously monitor search queries that return no results or result in a ticket creation. These failed searches are flagged as knowledge gaps, prompting subject-matter experts to create the missing documentation. This creates a self-improving knowledge ecosystem [167].
- *Standard request automation:* The "Shift-Left" strategy aims to move resolution closer to the user (or to automation). AI enables this by handling high-volume, low-complexity requests via integration with backend systems.
- *Transactional workflows:* Virtual agents are integrated into enterprise platforms such as Microsoft Teams or Slack. Through APIs, they can execute workflows such as password resets, software provisioning, or guest Wi-Fi access [166].
- *Contextual approvals:* For requests requiring approval (e. g., a new laptop), the AI can analyze the user's role and the cost of the asset. If the request falls within pre-approved policy limits (e. g., "Sales Directors can auto-approve mobile devices costing less than US$ 1,000"), the AI grants immediate approval, speeding up fulfillment.

31.1.2 Autonomous Operations

While the service desk handles user interactions, the backend infrastructure is managed by *Artificial Intelligence for IT Operations* (AIOps). AIOps is the application of ML to the massive datasets generated by IT infrastructure (logs, metrics, traces, events) to automate operations [168].

31.1.2.1 Event Correlation

The primary challenge in modern operations is alert fatigue. A single router failure can trigger thousands of downstream alerts (event storm) from every server and application dependent on that network segment. Human operators cannot process this flood of red lights.

- Topology-Based Correlation: AIOps platforms ingest topology data (dependency maps) to understand relationships. When an alert storm occurs, the AI uses this graph to correlate thousands of symptoms with a single root cause ("the router") [168].
- Temporal Correlation: The AI also looks at time-series data. It recognizes that the database latency spike happened exactly 200 milliseconds after the storage array reported a disk failure.
- Outcome: The system suppresses the symptom alerts and presents the operator with a single root cause, reducing noise by up to 99% and allowing the team to focus on the fix rather than the diagnosis [169].

Solution Brief 31-1: AI-supported Observability Platform (Dynatrace)

Challenge

- Managing billions of dependencies across dynamic, multi-cloud environments is humanly impossible.
- IT teams are overwhelmed by alert storms and manual, time-consuming troubleshooting tasks.
- Organizations struggle with skilled labor shortages and losing expertise during staff transitions.

Solution

- Hypermodal Davis AI combines causal, predictive, and generative AI to provide precise, context-aware answers.
- Automated Root-Cause Analysis instantly pinpoints the exact source of problems using deterministic, dependency-based logic.
- Davis CoPilot allows users to query complex data using simple conversational prompts.

Solution Brief 31-1: AI-supported Observability Platform (Dynatrace) ***(continued)***

Benefits

- Reduces mean time to repair by providing automated, actionable remediation steps.
- Forecasts future performance issues to stop incidents before they impact customers.
- Democratizes data access and automates routine tasks to free up innovation time.

Customers: AirFrance/KLM, Deutsche Telekom, SAP, Siemens Healthineers

Provider: Dynatrace, Waltham, Massachusetts, USA; *dynatrace.com*

31.1.2.2 Predictive Analytics and Proactive Remediation

Traditional ITSM is reactive: wait for a break, then fix it. AIOps enables predictive service management as follows:

- *Anomaly Detection:* Using unsupervised learning, AIOps tools establish dynamic baselines for normal behavior for every metric (CPU, memory, transaction rate). These baselines adjust for seasonality (e. g., higher traffic on Black Friday). When a metric deviates from this baseline – even if it hasn't crossed a static failure threshold – the AI flags it as an anomaly [170].
- *Outage Prediction:* By recognizing fingerprints of past failures (e. g., a specific pattern of memory creep combined with increasing thread count), the AI can predict an outage hours or days in advance. It creates a proactive incident ticket, alerting engineers to intervene before the service crashes [169].
- *Sustainable Operations:* This predictive capability extends to energy efficiency. AI can analyze server utilization patterns and dynamically consolidate workloads or power down idle infrastructure during low-demand periods, thereby significantly reducing the IT estate's carbon footprint [166].

31.1.2.3 Automated Root Cause Analysis and Run Book Automation

The ultimate goal of AIOps is the self-healing data center:

- *Automated root cause analysis*: When an incident occurs, AI agents automatically gather diagnostic context – grabbing logs, comparing configuration snapshots, and checking recent change records. They can, for example, identify that a specific code deployment 15 minutes ago is likely the root cause of the current performance degradation [166].
- *Auto-remediation:* For known issues, the AI can trigger runbooks. If the print spooler service hangs, the AI detects the issue and restarts the service. If a disk fills up, the AI clears temporary files. This creates a resilient infrastructure where Level 1 and Level 2 technical issues are resolved by machines, freeing humans for complex engineering tasks.

31.1.3 Change and Asset Management

Beyond immediate operations, AI enhances the governance processes of ITSM:

- *Predictive change management:* Change is the leading cause of incidents. Rigid change-control processes (such as Change Advisory Board (CAB) meetings) slow innovation. AI enables adaptive governance:
- *Risk scoring:* AI models analyze the history of thousands of past changes. They evaluate attributes such as the team's implementation, the service involved, the time of day, and the code's complexity. Based on this, the AI assigns a numeric risk score to a new change request [166].
- *Auto-approval:* High-scoring (low-risk) changes are automatically approved and routed for deployment. Only outlying, high-risk changes are flagged for human CAB review. This intelligent triage significantly accelerates release velocity without compromising stability.
- *Intelligent asset management:* Managing the lifecycle and cost of IT assets is critical for financial efficiency:
- *Utilization analysis:* AI monitors software usage patterns to identify zombie assets – licenses that have been paid for but are never used. It can recommend license reclamation, saving millions in enterprise software spend [166].
- *Predictive hardware lifecycle:* Instead of replacing laptops on a fixed 3-year cycle, AI analyzes device performance data (battery health, crash frequency). It identifies devices that are degrading early for replacement and extends the life of devices that are still performing well, optimizing capital expenditure [166].

31.2 Enterprise Architecture Management

Historically, *Enterprise Architecture Management* (EAM) has suffered from the ivory tower problem: Architects create beautiful diagrams that are disconnected from the messy reality of IT operations. By the time an as-is architecture document is published, it is already obsolete. AI transforms EAM from a static documentation discipline into a dynamic, data-driven practice of continuous architecture. The foundation of any EAM practice is the repository – the database of applications, servers, business capabilities, and their relationships. AI automates the population and maintenance of this repository, creating a living architecture graph through AI-based discovery and dependency mapping [171].

31.2.1 AI-based Discovery

Modern discovery is not just about finding IP addresses; it is about understanding the application-level purpose of components and the network traffic between them.

- *Discovery agents:* Specialized software agents use deep internal metrics from software installed on hosts to monitor the digital signals of the enterprise continuously. These agents are typically local software components that monitor hardware, the operating system, or specific software (observability platforms), or software agents that feed software license management backbones and components within CI/CD pipelines, e. g., leveraging cloud APIs. They extract metadata from these operational sources to update the architecture model in real-time.
- *Agent-less network scanning:* AI algorithms analyze the behavior of discovered assets to classify them. A device listening on port 80 and sending traffic to a database on port 1433 is automatically classified as a web server, even if it lacks descriptive metadata tags. This semantic discovery ensures that the repository reflects functional reality, not just administrative records. Application-aware firewalls are particularly well-suited to support this task.
- *Hybrid discovery methods:* AI combines agent-based data with agentless scanning (network packet analysis) to build a complete picture [172].

31.2.2 Dependency Mapping

The most critical and challenging aspect of EAM is mapping dependencies. Understanding what breaks if a specific server is decommissioned is the holy grail of both preventive impact analysis (e. g., as input to Change Advisory Board decisions, root cause analysis, and the derivation of automated or manual corrective actions).

- *Deep dependency analysis:* AI utilizes *Graph Neural Networks* (GNNs) to analyze traffic flows and code references. It maps the *lineage of data* as it moves from a customer-facing mobile app via an API gateway to a microservice and, finally, to a legacy mainframe database [173].
- *Inferred dependencies:* Unlike simple topology tools, AI can infer logical dependencies. By analyzing ticket data and user behavior, it might become apparent that two seemingly unconnected systems are functionally dependent because users consistently access them in sequence. This reveals hidden architectural coupling that static analysis misses [171].
- *Visualizing complexity:* These tools render complex, multi-layered graphs that allow architects to zoom in from a high-level business capability (e. g., order processing) down to the specific Kubernetes pods running the service, providing full vertical traceability [174].

Solution Brief 31-2: Discovery-based Data Modeling (Ellie.ai)

Challenge

- Business experts struggle to communicate complex data requirements to technical teams.
- Manually describing 1,000 s of database tables and columns is slow and error-prone.
- Analytics engineers lose roughly 60% of their time on non-development tasks and assumptions.

Solution

- GenAI agents generate initial entity-relationship diagrams from text descriptions, drawings, or interactive chats.
- AI agents automatically generate business-friendly descriptions for existing data warehouse tables and columns.
- Domain experts use a chatbot to design data products without needing technical modeling skills.

Benefits

- Teams can meet analytics KPIs up to 60% faster using automated workflows.
- Non-technical stakeholders can participate in creating accurate, business-driven data models.
- AI-generated documentation provides instant clarity on raw data.

Customers: DNA, ecore, Siemens, Vopa, YIT

Provider: Ellie.ai, Helsinki, Finland; *ellie.ai*

31.3 Cybersecurity

As industrial systems become more connected, they become more vulnerable to cyberthreats. AI supports *cybersecurity* and related regulatory compliance in manufacturing, moving the industry from a reactive approach to a proactive, automated one. Systems continuously monitor network traffic and machine behavior, establishing a baseline to instantly detect anomalies that signal potential cyberattacks, enabling faster responses than human teams. After collecting, classifying, and managing data, AI systems can generate comprehensive audit reports that meet regulatory requirements, including IEC 62443 and FDA regulations. The role of explainable AI is vital here, as it provides a clear, auditable trail of decision-making, allowing manufacturers to prove to regulators why an AI system flagged a defect or executed a response [175].

Solution Brief 31-3: AI-based Intrusion Detection (Palo Alto Networks)

Challenge

- AI-accelerated attackers generate threats faster than human teams can manage.
- Security is complex, needing simpler, more intuitive, automated platforms.
- Organizations must secure their GenAI usage and AI-powered applications.
- Adversarial AI creates polymorphic threats that are difficult to detect.

Solution "Precision AI"

- High-fidelity automation and security copilots to simplify tasks and deliver instant solutions.
- Precision AI covers defense against adversarial AI.
- Module Prisma AIRS secures the entire AI ecosystem: apps, models, and data.

Benefits

- Detect and prevent AI-generated, polymorphic threats in real time.
- Predict and block escalating AI attacks before they can cause damage.
- Scale and automate cyber defense by leveraging a rich security dataset.
- Increase security team efficiency with enterprise-ready AI capabilities.

Customers: Campbell's, Dell, Hill & Smith, NetApp, Salesforce

Provider: Palo Alto Networks, Palo Alto, California, USA; *paloaltonetworks.com/precision-ai-security*

31.4 Software Development

According to a recent IDC report [176], developers responded to the question "How many hours do you spend per week for each of the following activity/task?" as shown in Figure 31.1.

What quickly becomes obvious is that, with all the excitement about *software coding* support through GenAI, the spectrum of software development activities is far broader than that. Certainly good news: Many of the mentioned tasks can be supported by tailored AI solutions!

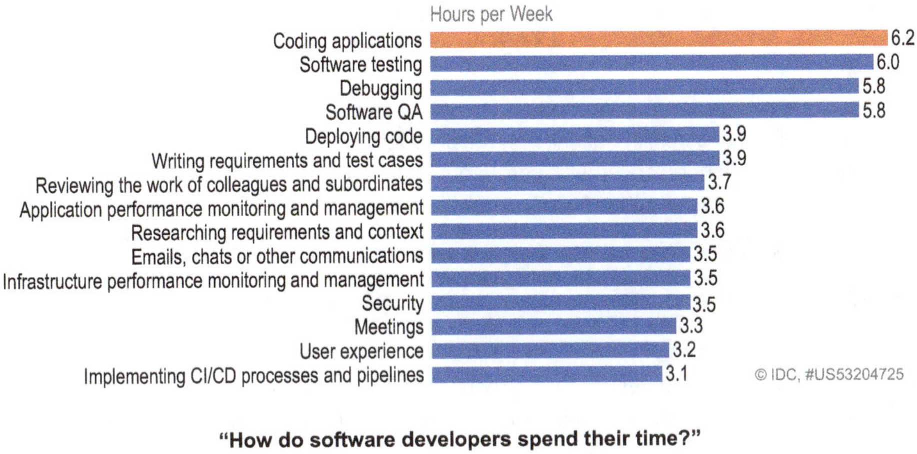

Figure 31.1 Task distribution of software developers [176]

31.4.1 Requirements Engineering

The initial phase of any industrial software project – *requirements engineering* (see also Section 21.5) – is traditionally prone to human error, ambiguity, and communication gaps between business stakeholders and technical teams. By processing large volumes of unstructured input, such as meeting transcripts, functional specifications, or legacy documents, LLMs can automatically identify inconsistencies, highlight potential ambiguities, and enforce logical structures.

Furthermore, GenAI excels at translating high-level business needs into actionable developer tasks. It can generate detailed user stories, complete with acceptance criteria, following standard formats such as *Gherkin syntax* [177]. This rapid translation allows product owners to move from conceptual feature ideas to ready-to-code tickets in a fraction of the time, establishing a clear, standardized, and traceable link between user intent and implementation.

Solution Brief 31-4: User Story Creation & Mapping with AI (StoriesOnBoard)

Challenge

- Development backlogs lack visual clarity for non-technical users.
- Teams struggle to align priorities and manage collected feedback.
- Writing detailed user stories and acceptance criteria is time-consuming.
- Need to integrate planning with development tools (e. g., Jira)

Solution

- Visual user story mapping software plots the user journey and goals.
- AI features generate stories, goals, and acceptance criteria instantly.
- Provides robust tools for feature prioritization and release planning.
- Offers two-way synchronization with Jira, Azure DevOps, and Trello.

Solution Brief 31-4: User Story Creation & Mapping with AI (StoriesOnBoard) *(continued)*

Benefits

- Accelerates product discovery and backlog refinement efficiency.
- Ensures all stakeholders are aligned on the product vision and goals.
- Reduces time spent on documentation with AI-assisted specification.
- Optimizes resource allocation by prioritizing features based on value.

Customers: Deloitte, Lufthansa, SAP, Walgreens

Provider: StoriesOnBoard, Pecs, Hungary; *storiesonboard.com*

Here, requirements engineering for software can transition to a model-based software engineering approach, particularly when formal methods, such as UML, are used to consistently integrate different areas of software development and their respective artifacts.

An application extension requires that its data model, workflow model, and UI model be updated consistently, along with developer and user documentation. A model-based approach ties this together. GenAI helps to feed formal UML models from requirement documentation.

31.4.2 Code Generation

In the actual coding phase, GenAI acts as a powerful *pair programmer*. Modern AI coding assistants offer intelligent coding support by generating boilerplate code, suggesting function completions, and even writing entire methods based on natural language prompts or surrounding code context. This capability significantly reduces the developers' cognitive load, allowing them to focus on the unique, complex business logic rather than repetitive syntax or setup routines.

The quality of code generation varies significantly across programming languages, simply because the most widely used platforms for training coding AI have a bias toward modern languages such as JavaScript and Python. In contrast, legacy languages such as COBOL, low-level C (for hardware controllers), and PLC-related languages are underrepresented in modern DevOps code repositories.

At the intersection of software development and PLC programming, GenAI delivers solutions that enable automation engineers to rapidly generate, optimize, and debug complex automation code (such as PLC code in Structured Control Language, or SCL), significantly shortening engineering development time from weeks to minutes [178].

Solution Brief 31-5: Software Code Generation (Mistral)

Challenge
- Developers spend excessive time on repetitive boilerplate and manual unit test creation.
- Teams struggle to maintain high productivity across dozens of different programming languages.
- Standard AI models often generate code too slowly for real-time IDE completion.

Solution "Codestral"
- Optimized for code completion, fill-in-the-middle tasks, and instruction-based programming.
- Expertly trained on over 80 programming languages, including Python, Java, and C++.
- Offers seamless plugins for VS Code, JetBrains, and advanced agentic workflows.

Benefits
- Automation of routine coding tasks and function generation cuts time by 50%.
- Lightning-fast, low-latency completions maintain the developer's "flow state".
- Provides open-weight models for private, secure deployment on-premises or in Virtual Private Cloud environments.

Customers: ABANCA, Cap Gemini, SNCF

Provider: Mistral, Paris, France; *mistral.ai*

Copyright violations can pose a significant risk to code generation, whether they lead to 3rd-party claims and litigation or to difficulties protecting one's own–generated code. Consequently, *plagiarism scanning* becomes an essential capability in code generation.

Solution Brief 31-6: Software Code Plagiarism Scanning (CopyLeaks)

Challenge
- Developers risk hidden vulnerabilities and unlicensed code reuse.
- Need governance and compliance for AI-assisted code generation.
- Must prevent unauthorized use of proprietary source code.

Solution
- Offers code plagiarism detection and source code verification.
- Tools check code against 20+ public/private repositories.

Benefits
- Avoids legal issues by identifying unlicensed code reuse quickly.
- Streamlines code integrity and governance with API integration.

Customers: Health Union, NSS, Oakland University

Provider: CopyLeaks, Stamford, CT, USA; *copyleaks.com*

31.4.3 Quality Assurance and Documentation

GenAI's impact is equally transformative in *quality assurance*. The models can analyze user stories and acceptance criteria to generate comprehensive test cases and synthetic test data at scale. This goes beyond simple unit tests, extending to integration and end-to-end scenarios, including edge cases that human testers might overlook. By automating the creation of test suites, GenAI enables teams to "shift left", integrating rigorous testing earlier in the development process and dramatically reducing defect introduction.

Finally, documentation, often viewed as a necessary evil, is streamlined: LLMs can analyze source code, APIs, and configuration files to automatically generate and maintain documentation, including in-line comments, API reference material, and comprehensive user guides.

31.4.4 Run-time Debugging

Generative AI dramatically accelerates debugging in run-time environments by efficiently correlating application error logs with the codebase. LLMs, trained on vast code repositories, perform real-time log analysis to detect anomalies and patterns in log streams, such as sudden spikes in HTTP 500 errors or specific 'NullPointerExceptions'. It then analyzes the associated log data, including stack traces and contextual timestamps, and maps the cryptic runtime error directly to the specific line of code and the functional root cause.

Essentially, the AI doesn't just identify the error; it uses its generative capability to immediately propose a code fix that resolves the issue, often reducing the time spent on bug isolation and correction from hours to seconds [179].

31.4.5 Refactoring

While GenAI is robust for generating new code and localized fixes, its use for large-scale, complex software refactoring remains immature. *Refactoring* involves restructuring existing code without altering its external behavior – a task that demands a deep, semantic understanding of system architecture, inter-module dependencies, and historical context.

Current LLMs supporting software refactoring often struggle with complex control flows, ensuring behavior preservation across large codebases, and avoiding the subtle introduction of functional errors. A further refactoring quality challenge is that legacy languages (e.g., FORTRAN, COBOL, or even low-level C), which are due for replacement to modernize applications, are significantly underrepresented in code repositories (e.g., GitHub) used to train these LLMs' coding capabilities.

The consensus among industry practitioners is that LLMs are best suited as a recommendation engine for refactoring opportunities, but human expertise remains mandatory for safe execution and validation.

31.4.6 Application Integration

31.4.6.1 Robotic Process Automation

Robotic Process Automation (RPA) is a technology that uses software bots to automate repetitive, rule-based tasks across digital systems, mimicking human interactions with applications. These bots can perform actions such as logging into systems, copying and pasting data, filling out forms, or generating reports with speed and accuracy. For example, in accounting, RPA bots can reconcile financial statements. In healthcare, they can manage patient records and billing, while in human resources, they handle employee onboarding or payroll updates. A logistics company might use RPA to track shipments and update inventory systems in real-time.

A key success factor for RPA has been the availability of a continuum of application integration options: some RPA platforms use deep API integration with business applications, while others use lightweight screen recorders to integrate with legacy or custom applications by filling in and capturing UI form data.

AI primarily supports RPA through image analytics (e. g., scanned documents or user interface screenshots) and semantic text interpretation (e. g., understanding the content of an incoming email and routing it to the most appropriate workflow).

Solution Brief 31-7: AI Agents for Paperwork (Rossum.ai)

Challenge
- Handling rising document volumes and strict compliance rules.
- Errors and a lack of control in traditional document processing.
- High manual overhead for data capture and validation.
- Slow exception handling and document turnaround time.

Solution "Rossum AI Agents for Paperwork"
- Uses AI Agents to read, capture, validate, and transform data.
- Leverages a proprietary transactional LLM supporting 276 languages.
- Automates approval workflows and vendor communication rules.
- Cross-validates document data with master data and ERPs.

Benefits
- High data accuracy with zero hallucinations and continuous AI learning.
- Significant time savings and reduction in manual effort.
- Ensures full compliance and provides a complete audit trail.
- Faster decision-making with real-time strategic insights.

Customers: Bosch, Flexport, Panasonic, Siemens

Provider: Rossum.ai, London, United Kingdom; *rossum.ai*

31.4.6.2 Agents-based Integration

Application integration will shift from rigid, pre-defined workflows to autonomous, goal-driven orchestration. Instead of human developers coding fixed API calls (the "how"), AI agents will be given high-level business objectives (the "what"). These agents will dynamically plan, execute, and self-correct multi-step integrations across disparate systems (CRMs, ERPs, databases) using available APIs. This transition can enable a proactive, event-driven architecture, making applications more resilient and adaptable, and capable of completing autonomous business processes with minimal human oversight.

Solution Brief 31-8: AI Agents Platform for Engineering (Synera)

Challenge

- Manual, repetitive tasks significantly slow down engineering cycles.
- Delays between experts cause long wait times for quotes and designs.
- Fragmented tool landscape hinders efficient collaboration and data flow.
- Manual process bottlenecks limit engineering capacity.

Solution

- AI Agents platform automates engineering tasks with a digital workforce.
- Visual, low-code platform integrates with 60+ existing engineering tools.
- AI agents automatically collaborate on CAD, FE analysis, and costing.
- Deployable on AWS and Azure for enterprise-level scaling and security.

Benefits

- Reduces development cycles from weeks to hours.
- Increases RFQ win rates with faster response times.
- Minimizes errors and drives down part costs with accurate predictions.
- Transforms operations into a scalable, 24/7 engineering organization.

Customers: Airbus, BMW, Hyundai, NASA, Volkswagen

Provider: Synera, Bremen, Germany; *synera.io*

31.4.7 Vibe Coding

Coined recently, *vibe coding* describes a paradigm in which a citizen developer guides an LLM to produce an application mockup. The citizen developer gives high-level instructions – the vibe – for the desired outcome, and AI generates the code. Natural language is also used to refine the application's behavior.

Vibe coding is enjoying significant momentum for the following reasons:

- Business unit representatives can start and evolve projects for critical business applications (or updates) without the need to have scarce IT specialist resources assigned. This is particularly helpful in the early phases of experimentation, when it is still unclear whether to invest in a new IT endeavor.

- Secondly, "appetite comes with eating": the definition of what a new application should do and what it should look like is an iterative process of specifying, reviewing, and refining. Enabling this realization process on the business-unit side without tying up expensive IT expert resources can improve application development efficiency.

Nevertheless, one should be aware of the shortcomings of vibe coding:

- Debugging vibe code can become a nightmare as GenAI does not necessarily create stringent code for application mock-ups.
- Many hygiene factors of application development, such as meeting secure coding practices, are ignored in the vibe coding environments.
- Embedding applications into an application management environment, that is, the process of productizing them from a support process perspective, is not covered, and can add serious overhead.

The role of vibe coding is to support hackathon-type exercises. It does not replace application coding practices, but is an instrument for driving agility.

Solution Brief 31-9: Rapid Software Prototyping (Lovable)

Challenge

- Creating a prototype to demonstrate a new application's impact on business requires IT specialists, who are in limited supply.
- This slows down the desired pace of innovation, whether in product management for digital offerings or in applications for internal processes.

Solution

- Users can specify web apps in natural language and generate clickable mockups using templates and generative AI within a controlled environment.
- GitHub integration and clear context/requirements documentation foster a smooth handover to developers if the mock-up is elevated to a full implementation.
- Lovable offers an interface to wireframe modeling environments such as Figma.

Benefits

- Business units can quickly create and improve application mock-ups using NLP.
- Scarce IT resources can start with the actual implementation once business representatives have matured what they really want.

Customers: Bain & Company, Google, LinkedIn, Shopify

Provider: Lovable.dev, Stockholm, Sweden; *lovable.dev*

31.5 Workplace Services

31.5.1 Note Taking

AI-supported *note-taking* transforms spoken conversation into structured, actionable data. Tools automatically transcribe audio from meetings with high accuracy, identify speakers, and generate concise summaries using NLP. These summaries capture critical details such as decisions, next steps, and assigned action items, saving users hours of manual transcription and cleanup.

It is noteworthy ;-) that the more sophisticated solutions generate domain-specific summaries (e. g., a sales meeting summary differs structurally from an applicant interview summary) and provide backend system integration (e. g., with a CRM or HR system).

Solution Brief 31-10: Automated Note Taking (fireflies.ai)

Challenge

- Manually taking notes during meetings is distracting and time-consuming.
- It is difficult to capture all key details, action items, and decisions accurately.
- New hires or absent members lack complete visibility and meeting context.
- Time is wasted reviewing long transcripts or replaying complete recordings.

Solution

- AI bot joins calls to automatically record, transcribe, and take notes (summaries, action items, and meeting outlines).
- Offers smart search filters and topic trackers across all conversations.
- Integrates seamlessly with leading video conferencing platforms and integrates with several CRM platforms for sales-related use cases, as well as HR platforms for applicant management.

Benefits

- Saves time by eliminating the need for manual note-taking efforts and allows participants to engage and focus on the discussion entirely.
- Provides in-depth conversation analytics, actionable insights, and automated interfaces to downstream systems for record keeping.

Customers: Delta, Expedia, Nike

Provider: Fireflies.ai, San Francisco, California, USA; *fireflies.ai*

31.5.2 Real-Time Voice Translation

Platforms like Zoom and Teams, and dedicated services like Wordly or Talo, employ advanced neural machine translation and speech-to-text algorithms to *transcribe speech in real time* and deliver *translated audio* or captions. This process facilitates seamless, two-way communication across dozens of languages without the delays or high costs of human interpreters. The user experience is typically enhanced by lip-syncing video processing. Real-time voice translation holds the promise that several parties can communicate in their mother tongues without sacrificing semantic richness for the sake of being understood in a language that serves only the "common denominator" among all participants.

Solution Brief 31-11: Real-Time Audio/Voice Translations (Google)

Challenge

- A common language spoken between several non-native speakers hinders communicative nuances.
- Human interpreters are expensive
- Human translation creates unwanted latency in real-time communication.

Solution "Google Meet"

- Google's AI can translate English, Spanish, Italian, German, and Portuguese in real-time and 69 languages by captions
- Google's AI can adjust the speaker's video for lip syncing.

Benefits

- Low-cost translation of verbal communication, capturing nuances without latency.

Provider: Google, Mountain View, California, USA; *google.com/meet*

32 Shared Services

32.1 Business Partner Master Data Management

Business partner master data management encompasses the creation and maintenance of a single, unified, high-quality record for all external entities with which an organization interacts, primarily customers, suppliers, and vendors. It consolidates fragmented data – such as contact details, financial terms, and relationship hierarchies – into a single source of truth.

Business partner master data changes frequently, partly because business transactions such as takeovers and insolvencies occur, and partly because changing names, legal forms, and directors are camouflage patterns in the context of money laundering and other compliance violations. Hence, maintaining smooth business partner master data is a prerequisite for addressing several compliance risks.

Solution Brief 32-1: Supplier Data Management (CDQ)

Challenge

- High admin costs and errors from manually searching and entering supplier data.
- Approx. 20% of master data becomes outdated annually, creating operational risks.
- Inconsistencies across ERP systems cause duplicates and poor spend transparency.

Solution

- AI-Driven Data Cleansing: Uses machine learning for automated deduplication, pattern recognition, and anomaly detection.
- Collaborative Data Sharing: Leverages a community pool of 200 million+ peer-validated records and 70+ global sources.
- Proactive Data Monitoring: AI-powered alerts monitor compliance, risk signals, and address changes in real time.

Solution Brief 32-1: Supplier Data Management (CDQ)

Benefits

- Reduces data maintenance costs by up to 40% through intelligent updates.
- 100% accurate vendor onboarding by pre-filled fields using AI and external reference data.
- Minimizes fraud and compliance penalties via automated bank account and sanction checks.

Customers: Fresenius, Schaeffler, SAP, Siemens, Unilever, Vaillant

Provider: CDQ, St. Gallen, Switzerland; *cdq.com/products/cdq-suite*

32.2 Invoicing & Credit Note Issuance

Invoicing is the process of generating and sending invoices to customers for goods or services delivered. This is more than just a bill; it is a financial instrument and a key trigger for financial services like factoring, which companies use to convert receivables into immediate cash. *Credit note issuance* is the process of issuing a credit note to a customer, typically to correct an invoicing error, grant a price adjustment, or provide a refund for returned or faulty goods.

The process of invoicing triggers the financial service of *factoring*: a company facing an immediate cash-flow need can sell its accounts receivable (invoices) to a third party at a discount, receiving immediate capital in return. The factor then assumes the responsibility for collecting the full payment from the customer. This demonstrates a direct link between the shipping/logistics function and the financial sector, illustrating how a seemingly routine administrative process can be a powerful strategic tool for managing liquidity, especially for businesses with high operational costs and slow-paying customers.

32.3 Business Travel Management

Business travel management involves coordinating all aspects of corporate travel to ensure efficiency, cost-effectiveness, and compliance with company policies. Core functions include

- *Trip planning*, where itineraries are optimized for time and budget;
- *Trip booking*, which secures flights, hotels, and transportation; Visa and Tax Management, ensuring travelers meet legal requirements and benefit from applicable tax recoveries;
- *Expense claims management*, streamlining reimbursements and auditing costs; and
- *Policy enforcement*, maintaining compliance with organizational travel rules.

AI enhances these functions significantly – for example, AI-powered systems can analyze past travel data to recommend the most cost-effective routes during trip planning, automate flight and hotel bookings based on traveler preferences, and flag potential visa or tax issues before departure.

AI tools, such as chatbots, support real-time itinerary changes. At the same time, expense management platforms automatically scan receipts and verify claims against corporate travel policies, reducing manual effort and improving accuracy in corporate travel management.

Solution Brief 32-2: AI-assisted Business Travel Management (Navan)

Challenge
- Tedious expense reporting and manual data entry waste employee time.
- Controlling struggles with fragmented data and delayed insights into company spend.
- Difficulty enforcing travel guidelines leads to overspending.

Solution
- Consolidates travel booking, corporate cards, and expense management. into one super app.
- Ava AI helps with automated rebooking, personalized searches, and instant expense categorization.
- Syncs real-time payment and travel data directly with major ERP systems.

Benefits
- Workflows reduce booking time and eliminate traditional expense reports.
- Dynamic policy enforcement and "set it&forget it" guardrails prevent overspending.
- Access to corporate rates and auto-reconciliation reduces operational overhead.

Customers: Glassdoor, MongoDB, Primark, Thomson Reuters, Zoom

Provider: Navan, Palo Alto, California, US; *navan.com*

32.4 Document Translation

Document translation is critical for global enterprises, ensuring product documentation, legal agreements, and training materials are accurate across markets. It enables regulatory compliance and supports local customers and partners. High-quality translation builds trust, facilitates faster market entry, and ensures consistent global brand messaging.

Solution Brief 32-3: Automated document translation (DeepL) [180]

Challenge

- Enterprises and research institutes must provide documentation and customer communication in several languages.
- Human translation services are costly.

Solution "DeepL Translation", "DeepL Clarify"

- Founded in 2009 as Linguee, a dictionary website with a lively community of freelancers. Started AI training with vast sets of publicly accessible EU documents (e. g., bills, meeting minutes, studies, etc.), as their translation had to be exact.
- Data center in Iceland (see Section 2.3.3), where the naturally cool climate and abundant energy meant low-cost power. Their supercomputer is the world's 23rd largest, capable of translating a million words in under a second.
- "Clarify" on-demand assistant asks questions back to the user in case nuanced transactions require user tuning.

Benefits

- The most exact automated translation engine for documents and websites.

Customers: Deutsche Bahn, Elsevier, Siemens

Provider: DeepL, Cologne, Germany; *deepl.com*

Part V: Conclusion and Annexes

33 Conclusion

The promises of AI must be reconciled with the industry's uncompromising realities, navigating the fine line between seductive tech hype and the constraints of physical laws. Every industrial leader is also a private person, constantly confronted with polished, hyper-optimistic social media messages and AI's momentum in the purely digital space. Specifically, middle management suffers from high expectations from top management regarding AI productivity and the fragility introduced into daily operations when immature solutions are deployed.

As *Rainer Brehm* from Siemens Digital Industries famously observed, "Production does not have an UNDO button". Therefore, AI for industry must become truly *industrial-grade* – robust, secure, and governed by the same engineering rigor that defines modern manufacturing. While the path from a lab-based pilot to a profitable, enterprise-wide implementation is often a cumbersome and frustrating journey through "pilot purgatory", this book offers more than 80 solution briefs and many best practises showing that there are many ways to take that critical first step. Climbing the mountain of industrial intelligence is a step-by-step exercise; it requires patience, a tiered focus on foundational capabilities, and the willingness to learn through experimentation.

Our AI journey is energized by a global ecosystem of notable industrial AI startups working with immense passion and speed to solve specific, high-value use cases – from automated 3D modeling to root-cause analysis. However, these innovators face a complex reality: balancing solving a customer's unique, specialized problem with building scalable platforms that venture capital demands as its highest priority.

Ultimately, the world's increasing fragility – political, economic, and environmental – leaves no room for hesitation. Whether addressing fragile supply chains or striving for grandchild-compatible entrepreneurship through zero-waste strategies, the mandate is clear: We must start our AI journey now, with passion, ensuring that industrial AI becomes the engine of the next great revolution in human productivity and global sustainability.

34 Annexes

34.1 References

[1] P. Mertens, Integrierte Informationsverarbeitung 1: Operative Systeme in der Industrie., 18. Auflage ed., Springer Fachmedien, 2013.

[2] M. Minsky and S. Papert, Perceptrons: An Introduction to Computational Geometry, Cambridge, MA: The MIT Press, 1969.

[3] H. Dolfing, "Case Study 20: The $4 Billion AI Failure of IBM Watson for Oncology," 7.12.2024. [Online]. Available: *https://www.henricodolfing.ch/case-study-20-the-4-billion-ai-failure-of-ibm-watson-for-oncology/*. [Accessed 24.9.2025].

[4] K. Foote, "A Brief History of the Internet of Things," Dataversity, 22.1.2022. [Online]. Available: *https://www.sustainablemanufacturingexpo.com/en/articles/overcoming-iot-challenges.html*. [Accessed 24.9.2025].

[5] Visible Flow Consulting, "How GE burned $7B on their platform," Platform Engineering, [Online]. Available: *https://platformengineering.org/blog/how-general-electric-burned-7-billion-on-their-plat form*. [Accessed 24.9.2025].

[6] J. Lee, Definition and Meaning of Industrial AI, Singapore: Springer, 2020.

[7] J. Coleman, "Nvidia's Jensen Huang on why DeepSeek's new model will need '100 times more computing'," CNBC, 12.3.2025. [Online]. Available: *https://www.cnbc.com/2025/03/19/nvidia-ceo-jensen-huang-why-deepseek-model-needs-100-times-more-computing.html*. [Accessed 20.12.2025].

[8] World Economic Forum, "How AI-powered innovation can democratize breakthrough science," 25.6.2025. [Online]. Available: *https://www.weforum.org/stories/2025/06/ai-innovation-democratizes-breakthrough-science/*. [Accessed 20.12.2025].

[9] M. K. Pasupuleti, "AI-Driven Fusion: Unlocking Net-Positive Energy for a Sustainable Future," in AI-Enhanced Fusion Energy: Achieving the First Net-Positive Reactor, National Education Services, 2025, pp. 37–49.

[10] C. Paoli, "Analysts Warn of AI Cooling with Microsoft Cancellation of AI Datacenter Leases," Redmond Magazine, 24.2.2025. [Online]. Available: *https://redmondmag.com/articles/2025/02/24/analysts-warn-of-ai-cooling.aspx;*. [Accessed 20.12.2025].

[11] "AI Reasoning: Gold-Medal Performance at the 2025 IMO," Intuition Labs, 23.12.2025. [Online]. Available: *https://intuitionlabs.ai/articles/ai-reasoning-math-olympiad-imo*. [Accessed 23.12.2025].

[12] N. Benaich, "State of AI Report," Air Street Capital, USA, 2025.

[13] McKinsey, "Humanoid robots: Crossing the chasm from concept to commercial reality," 15.10.2025. [Online]. Available: *https://www.mckinsey.com/industries/industrials-and-electronics/our-insights/humanoid-robots-crossing-the-chasm-from-concept-to-commercial-reality*. [Accessed 20.12.2025].

[14] D. Romero, "Machine Economy 2030: Why Autonomous Customers Are the Next Big Trend.," Technologic Innovation, 6.9.2025. [Online]. Available: *https://technologicinnovation.com/2025/09/06/machine-economy-2030-the-rise-of-autonomous-customers*. [Accessed 17.12.2025].

[15] M. Doyle, "Four Steps in the Evolution of the Machine Economy," IOT for All, 2.12.2024. [Online]. Available: *https://www.iotforall.com/four-steps-in-the-evolution-of-the-machine-economy*. [Accessed 17.12.2025].

[16] K. Wynroe, D. Atkinson and J. Sevilla, "Literature review of transformative artificial intelligence timelines," Epoch.ai, 23.1.2023. [Online]. Available: *https://epoch.ai/blog/literature-review-of-transformative-artificial-intelligence-timelines*. [Accessed 17.12.2025].

[17] IoT Analytics, "Data Center Equipment & Infrastructure Market Report 2025–2030," Hamburg, 2025.

[18] M. Frąckiewicz, "Global Semiconductor Industry Trends and 2025 Outlook: AI Boom, Advanced Nodes, and Geopolitics," TechStock², 27.6.2025. [Online]. Available: *https://ts2.tech/en/global-semiconductor-industry-trends-and-2025-outlook-ai-boom-advanced-nodes-and-geopolitics-report-june-27th-2025*. [Accessed 17.12.2025].

[19] "Is Moore's Law Still Applicable?," McKinsey Electronics, 4.6.2025. [Online]. Available: *https://www.mckinsey-electronics.com/post/is-moores-law-still-applicable*. [Accessed 17.12.2025].

[20] R. Dean, "Compute Forecast," 2025.

[21] D. Owen, "What will AI look like in 2030?," Epoch.ai, USA, 2025.

[22] TierPoint, "The Future of Cloud Computing in Edge AI," 11.12.2025. [Online]. Available: *https://www.tierpoint.com/blog/cloud-computing-edge-ai/*. [Accessed 17.12.2025].

[23] Nlyte, "Mastering Mission-Critical Thermal Management," 4.11.2025. [Online]. Available: *https://www.nlyte.com/blog/mastering-mission-critical-thermal-management/*. [Accessed 17.12.2025].

[24] V. Lee, P. Seshadri, C. O'Niell, A. Choudhary, B. Holstege and S. A. Deutscher, "Breaking Barriers to Data Center Growth," Boston Consulting Group, 10.1.2025. [Online]. Available: *https://www.bcg.com/publications/2025/breaking-barriers-data-center-growth*. [Accessed 13.11.2025].

[25] "China bans tech companies from buying Nvidia's AI chips," The Financial Times, 17.9.2025. [Online]. Available: *https://www.ft.com/content/12adf92d-3e34-428a-8d61-c9169511915c*. [Accessed 17.12.2025].

[26] "AI firm DeepSeek writes less-secure code for groups China disfavors," The Washington Post, 16.9.2025. [Online]. Available: *https://www.washingtonpost.com/technology/2025/09/16/deepseek-ai-security/*. [Accessed 17.12.2025].

[27] W. Chang, "China's "AI+" drive aims for integration across sectors: a wake-up call for Europe," Merics, 2.10.2025. [Online]. Available: *https://merics.org/en/comment/chinas-ai-drive-aims-integration-across-sectors-wake-call-europe*. [Accessed 26.12.2025].

[28] J. Finkle, "2015 Ukraine power grid hack," Reuters, 2.7.2017. [Online]. Available: *https://www.reuters.com/article/us-ukraine-cybersecurity-sandworm-idUSKBN0UM00N20160108/*. [Accessed 23.9.2025].

[29] M. Agostini, "Digital Sovereignty: The Hidden Architecture of Trust in the Age of AI," 29.5.2025. [Online]. Available: *https://medium.com/@tarifabeach/digital-sovereignty-the-hidden-architecture-of-trust-in-the-age-of-ai-75370532f2df*. [Accessed 17.12.2025].

[30] J. A. McGuire, Power, Data Protection, Pragmatism and Digital Sovereignty, Vienna: Drupal Association, 2025.

[31] M. Kodama, "California Senate Bill 53," 2025. [Online]. Available: *https://sb53.info/*. [Accessed 17.12.2025].

[32] R. W. Green, "AI Regulation in the Middle East: Balancing Innovation and Data Privacy," CustomAI Studio, 2.10.2025. [Online]. Available: *https://medium.com/@custom_aistudio/ai-regulation-in-the-middle-east-balancing-innovation-and-data-privacy-cbdb73989506*. [Accessed 16.12.2025].

[33] "Press Release: Joint initiative for trustworthy AI," ETH Zurich, 4.12.2023. [Online]. Available: *https://ethz.ch/en/news-and-events/eth-news/news/2023/12/press-release-joint-initiative-for-trustworthy-ai.html*. [Accessed 17.12.2025].

[34] "Your Practical Guide to the EU AI Act and GPAI Guidelines," applied AI, 2.8.2025. [Online]. Available: *https://www.appliedai.de/en/trustworthy-ai-the-ai-act/eu-ai-act-rules-2025*. [Accessed 17.12.2025].

[35] ZEKI Data, "State of AII Talent 2025," Zeki Data, London, 2025.

[36] H. Schmidt, "ChatGPT und KI: Weniger Stellenanzeigen in Deutschland," Frankfurter Allgemeine Zeitung PRO Digitalwirtschaft, 21.1.2026.

[37] E. Brynjolfsson, R. Chen and B. Chandar, "Canaries in the Coal Mine? Six Facts about the Recent Employment Effects of Artificial Intelligence," Digital Economy Lab, Stanford University, 11 2025. [Online]. Available: *https://digitaleconomy.stanford.edu/wp-content/uploads/2025/11/CanariesintheCoalMine_Nov25.pdf*. [Accessed 17.12.2025].

[38] "Krakow layoffs reflect broader shift to AI, automation in CEE," Central European Times, 8.4.2025. [Online]. Available: *https://centraleuropeantimes.com/krakow-layoffs-reflect-broader-shift-to-ai-automation-in-cee/*. [Accessed 23.11.2025].

[39] Digital Twin Interoperability Taskforce, "Digital Twins for Industrial Applications," Industrial Internet Consortium, USA, 2020.

[40] R. Argolini, F. Bonalumi, J. Deichmann and S. Pellegrinelli, "Digital twins: The key to smart product development," McKinsey, USA, 2023.

[41] "IDTA Homepage," Industrial Digital Twin Association, [Online]. Available: *https://industrialdigitaltwin.org/en/*. [Accessed 20.12.2025].

[42] NIST, "Digital Thread for Smart Manufacturing," 2018. [Online]. Available: *https://www.nist.gov/programs-projects/digital-thread-smart-manufacturing*. [Accessed 17.12.2025].

[43] Durolabs, "What is a Digital Thread? Why it Matters for Modern Manufacturing," 2.4.2025. [Online]. Available: *https://durolabs.co/blog/digital-thread/*. [Accessed 17.12.2025].

[44] MIT Sloan Management Review & Deloitte, "Following the Digital Thread: Revolutionizing Supply Chains," (youtube.com), 28.2.2018. [Online]. Available: *https://www.youtube.com/watch?v=ULFKLHzsA4E*. [Accessed 17.12.2025].

[45] Northrop Grumman, "Digital Pathfinder," USA, 2024.

[46] Sollas, "33% Higher Packaging Machine Throughput – With Siemens' AI Motion (Presentation)," in AI with Purpose Summit, Munich, 2024.

[47] D. S. A. B. Humam Kourani and W. M. P. v. d. Aalst, "Process Modeling With Large Language Models," Aachen, 2024.

[48] S. Z. M. V. W. ... v. d. A. C. M. Anne Rozinat, "Analyzing Multi-agent Activity Logs Using Process Mining Techniques," in Distributed Autonomous Robotic Systems, Berlin/Heidelberg, Springer, 2009, pp. 251–260.

[49] Sima.ai, "Cerence AI and SiMa.ai Partner to Power Next-Gen Conversational AI at the Edge," 4.9.2025. [Online]. Available: *https://sima.ai/blog/press-release/cerence-ai-and-sima-ai-partner-to-power-next-gen-conversational-ai-at-the-edge/*. [Accessed 17.12.2025].

[50] M. Holland, "Generative AI models like DSLMs outperform LLMs in value," Tech Target Network, 11.3.2025. [Online]. Available: *https://www.techtarget.com/searchenterpriseai/news/366620407/Generative-AI-models-like-DSLMs-outperform-LLMs-in-value*. [Accessed 3.10.2025].

[51] A. Cosmas, J. Seeley, K. Ungerman, R. Mann and a. V. Krishnan, "Remapping travel with agentic AI," Skift Research & McKinsey, 16.9.2025. [Online]. Available: *https://www.mckinsey.com/industries/travel/our-insights/remapping-travel-with-agentic-ai*. [Accessed 17.12.2025].

[52] Microsoft Research, "The Agentic Economy," 29.3.2025. [Online]. Available: *https://arxiv.org/html/2505.15799v2*. [Accessed 26.9.2025].

[53] M. Schnitger, "Autodesk wants you to pay for outcomes, not just access," Schnitger Corp., 8.10.2025. [Online]. Available: *https://schnitgercorp.com/2025/10/08/autodesk-wants-you-to-pay-for-outcomes-not-just-access/*. [Accessed 27.12.2025].

[54] K. Wiggers, "What are AI 'world models,' and why do they matter?," Tech Crunch, 14.12.2024. [Online]. Available: *https://techcrunch.com/2024/12/14/what-are-ai-world-models-and-why-do-they-matter/*. [Accessed 17.12.2025].

[55] J. D. Ser, J. L. Lobo, H. Müller and A. Holzinger, "World Models in Artificial Intelligence: Sensing, Learning, and Reasoning Like a Child," 19.3.2025. [Online]. Available: *https://arxiv.org/abs/2503.15168*. [Accessed 17.12.2025].

[56] "The GenAI Divide: State of AI in Business 2025," MIT, Boston, MA, USA, 2025.

[57] McKinsey, "How digital manufacturing can escape 'pilot purgatory'," McKinsey, USA, 2018.

[58] Rockwell Automation, "State of Smart Manufacturing Report 2024," Rockwell Automation, USA, 2024.

[59] M. Chui, R. Roberts, L. Yee, E. Hazan, A. Singla, K. Smaje, A. Sukharevsky and R. Zemmel, "The economic potential of generative AI," McKinsey, USA, 2023.

[60] M. Anderson, "Andrew Ng criticizes the Culture of Overfitting in Machine Learning," Unite AI, 5.5.2021. [Online]. Available: *https://www.unite.ai/andrew-ng-criticizes-the-culture-of-overfitting-in-machine-learning/*. [Accessed 6.12.2025].

[61] C. Gorges, "IT-Praxis: Hauck Aufhäuser Lampe und Halley zeigen Hyperscalern, wie das mit Enterprise-KI läuft," IT Finanzmagazin, 28.10.2025. [Online]. Available: *https://www.it-finanzmagazin.de/it-praxis-hauck-aufhaeuser-lampe-und-halley-zeigen-hyperscalern-wie-das-mit-enterprise-ki-laeuft-234853/*. [Accessed 26.12.2025].

[62] B. Scharinger, A. Vogelsang, T. Olsson and M. Borg, "Can RE Help Better Prepare Industrial AI for Commercial Scale?," IEEE Software, vol. 39, no. 6, 2022.

[63] N. Hassan, "How and why to create an AI bill of materials," 8.8.2024. [Online]. Available: *https://www.techtarget.com/searchenterpriseai/tip/How-and-why-to-create-an-AI-bill-of-materials*. [Accessed 27.12.2025].

[64] A. S. O. M. D. B. Sascha Kaltenpoth, "A Step Towards Cognitive Automation: Integrating LLM Agents with Process Rules," in Business Process Management. BPM 2025. Lecture Notes in Computer Science., Cham, Springer, 2025.

[65] M. V. N. K. Johannes Jakubik, J. Walk and G. Satzger, "Data-Centric Artificial Intelligence," Business & Information Systems Engineering, vol. 66, no. 4, p. 507–515, 2024.

[66] S. Steve Cullimore, S. J. C. Rod Koborsi, P. D. Anil Somani, P. S. Sean Turner and J. Wood, "Differences between transfer pricing and financial reporting valuations," The Tax Advisor, 1.5.2022. [Online]. Available: *https://www.thetaxadviser.com/issues/2022/may/differences-transfer-pricing-financial-reporting-valuations/*. [Accessed 19.11.2025].

[67] V. Romanov, "The Truth About PLC Scan Cycles and Polling: Why Your SCADA System Misses Critical Data," Joltek, 22.8.2025. [Online]. Available: *https://www.joltek.com/blog/plc-scan-cycles-polling-scada-systems-data*. [Accessed 24.12.2025].

[68] R. Tiwari, "The Impact of AI and Machine Learning on Job Displacement and Employment Opportunities," International Journal of Scientific Research in Engineering and Management, 2023.

[69] J. L. Joe Seydl, "How AI can boost productivity and jump start growth," JP Morgan, 24.7.2024. [Online]. Available: *https://privatebank.jpmorgan.com/nam/en/insights/markets-and-investing/ideas-and-insights/how-ai-can-boost-productivity-and-jump-start-growth*. [Accessed 19.12.2025].

[70] M. Cazzaniga, F. Jaumotte, L. Li, G. Melina, A. J. Panton, C. Pizzinelli, E. J. Rockall and M. M. Tavares, "Gen-AI: Artificial Intelligence and the Future of Work," Staff Discussion Notes, vol. 001, 2024.

[71] The Economic Times, "JPMorgan warns AI boom needs $650 billion a year, just for 10% return – bubble brewing?," 14.11.2025. [Online]. Available: *https://economictimes.indiatimes.com/news/international/us/jpmorgan-warns-ai-boom-needs-650-billion-a-year-just-for-10-return-bubble-brewing/articleshow/125280375.cms*. [Accessed 19.12.2025].

[72] "Unlocking the potential of GenAI in industrial manufacturing," Germany, 2025.

[73] R. Horton, J. Michalski, S. Winters, D. Gunn and J. Holland, "AI ROI: The paradox of rising investment and elusive returns," Deloitte, 22.10.2025. [Online]. Available: *https://www.deloitte.com/uk/en/issues/generative-ai/ai-roi-the-paradox-of-rising-investment-and-elusive-returns.html*. [Accessed 19.11.2025].

[74] Immuta, “Quantifying the ROI of Data Governance: How to Get Buy-In,” 21.8.2025. [Online]. Available: *https://www.immuta.com/blog/data-governance-roi/*. [Accessed 19.12.2025].

[75] Compunnel, “The ROI of Data Governance: Beyond Compliance to Competitive Advantage,” 8.7.2024. [Online]. Available: *https://www.compunnel.com/blogs/the-roi-of-data-governance-beyond-compliance-to-competitive-advantage/*. [Accessed 19.11.2025].

[76] Alation, “What's Your Data Governance ROI? Here's What to Track,” 7.7.2025. [Online]. Available: *https://www.alation.com/blog/data-governance-roi/*. [Accessed 19.11.2025].

[77] Worklytics, “Calculating the ROI of Employee AI Adoption,” [Online]. Available: *https://www.worklytics.co/resources/calculating-roi-employee-ai-adoption-power-bi-template*. [Accessed 19.11.2025].

[78] inpro, Siemens, “Checklist for initiating scalable industrial AI solutions,” 4 2023. [Online]. Available: *https://www.inpro.de/en/ai-checklist/*. [Accessed 19.12.2025].

[79] Siemens, “Siemens Mobility wins German Mobility Award 2020 (Press Release),” 20.10.2020. [Online]. Available: *https://press.siemens.com/global/en/pressrelease/siemens-mobility-wins-german-mobility-award-2020*. [Accessed 26.12.2025].

[80] F. Dyson, Disturbing the Universe, New York: Sloan Foundation, 1981.

[81] P. Jia Gai, J. Hou and Y. Tu, Competence Penalty Is a Barrier to the Adoption of New Technology, Peing, Hongkong, May 2025.

[82] P. Kabel, Interviewee, KI-Grafiken OHNE nervige Einschränkungen. [Interview]. 23.10.2025.

[83] SentinelOne, “AI Model Security: A CISO's Complete Guide,” [Online]. Available: *https://www.sentinelone.com/cybersecurity-101/data-and-ai/ai-model-security/*. [Accessed 1.12.2025].

[84] Microsoft, “Confidential AI,” [Online]. Available: *https://learn.microsoft.com/en-us/azure/confidential-computing/confidential-ai*. [Accessed 1.12.2025].

[85] JDSupra, “The Pros And Cons Of Protecting AI As Trade Secrets,” 5.3.2024. [Online]. Available: *https://www.jdsupra.com/legalnews/the-pros-and-cons-of-protecting-ai-as-3161472/*. [Accessed 19.12.2025].

[86] Harris Beach Murtha, “Strategies for Patenting AI-Related Inventions,” 31.10.2024. [Online]. Available: *https://www.harrisbeachmurtha.com/insights/strategies-for-patenting-ai-related-inventions/*. [Accessed 19.12.2025].

[87] Wikipedia, “Defensive publication,” [Online]. Available: *https://en.wikipedia.org/wiki/Defensive_publication*. [Accessed 1.12.2025].

[88] Wigwe & Partners, “Copyright Infringement And Generative Artificial Intelligence: Emerging Legal Challenges,” 26.12.2024. [Online]. Available: *https://wigweandpartners.com/copyright-infringement-and-generative-artificial-intelligence-emerging-legal-challenges*. [Accessed 27.12.2025].

[89] D-Carbonize, “Comparison of carbon footprints by sector,” 21.10.2024. [Online]. Available: *https://d-carbonize.eu/comparison-carbon-footprints-sector*. [Accessed 19.12.2025].

[90] Microsoft and PwC, “How AI can enable a Sustainable Future,” 6.6.2019. [Online]. Available: *https://www.pwc.co.uk/sustainability-climate-change/assets/pdf/how-ai-can-enable-a-sustainable-future.pdf*. [Accessed 19.12.2025].

[91] M. Suer, “MIT's 4 Stages of Enterprise AI Maturity,” 19.12.2024. [Online]. Available: *https://www.vktr.com/ai-technology/mits-4-stages-of-enterprise-ai-maturity/*. [Accessed 19.12.2025].

[92] McKinsey Global Institute, “Notes from the AI Frontier – Modeling the Impact of AI on the World Economy,” McKinsey Global Institute, 9 2018. [Online]. Available: *https://www.mckinsey.com/featured-insights/artificial-intelligence/notes-from-the-ai-frontier-modeling-the-impact-of-ai-on-the-world-economy*. [Accessed 26.12.2025].

[93] OPC UA Foundation, “Unified Architecture – Landingpage,” [Online]. Available: *https://opcfoundation.org/about/opc-technologies/opc-ua/*. [Accessed 19.12.2025].

[94] EUROMAP, “Overview OPC UA Specifications,” [Online]. Available: *https://euromap.org/i40/OPCUA*. [Accessed 19.12.2025].

[95] Paragon ID, “The Digital Product Passport: what you need to know about data carriers and product identifiers,” 24.5.2024. [Online]. Available: *https://www.paragon-id.com/en/inspiration/the-digital-product-passport-what-you-need-to-know-about-data-carriers-and-product*. [Accessed 19.12.2025].

[96] J. S. Leinar Ramos, "Maverick Research: Forget About Your Real Data – Synthetic Data Is the Future of AI.," Gartner, 24.6.2021. [Online]. Available: *https://www.gartner.com/en/documents/4002912*.

[97] "Synthetic Data Basics," 6.8.2025. [Online]. Available: *https://mostly.ai/synthetic-data-basics*. [Accessed 19.12.2025].

[98] IBM, "8 best practices for synthetic data generation," 6.12.2024. [Online]. Available: *https://www.ibm.com/think/insights/synthetic-data-generation*. [Accessed 19.12.2025].

[99] C. Dilmegani, "Synthetic Data vs Real Data: Benefits, Challenges," AI Multiple, 10.11.2025. [Online]. Available: *https://research.aimultiple.com/synthetic-data-vs-real-data/*. [Accessed 19.12.2025].

[100] J. C. Keith Man, "A Review of Synthetic Image Data and Its Use in Computer Vision," Journal of Imaging, vol. 8, no. 11, p. 310, 2022.

[101] Siemens, "AI and the Chocolate Factory," 2 2023. [Online]. Available: *https://www.siemens.com/global/en/company/stories/research-technologies/artificial-intelligence/ai-and-the-chocolate-factory.html*. [Accessed 30.12.2025].

[102] F. Mauthe, C. Braun, J. Raible, P. Zeiler and M. F. Huber, "Overview of Publicly Available Degradation Data Sets for Tasks within Prognostics and Health Management," 28.1.2025.

[103] Giesecke+Devrient, "G+D Ventures becomes lead investor in AI knowledge management start-up Blockbrain (Press release)," 17.9.2025. [Online]. Available: *https://www.gi-de.com/en/group/press/press-releases/g-d-ventures-becomes-lead-investor-in-ai-knowledge-management-start-up-blockbrain*. [Accessed 28.12.2025].

[104] "The FAIR Principles," 2020. [Online]. Available: *https://www.go-fair.org/fair-principles/*. [Accessed 10.1.2026].

[105] D. Sculley, G. Holt, D. Golovin, E. Davydov, T. Phillips, D. Ebner, V. Chaudhary, M. Young, J.-F. Crespo and D. Dennison, "Hidden Technical Debt in Machine Learning Systems," in NeurIPS Proceedings, 2015.

[106] V. Q. Ha, "Modern LLM Frameworks for Deep Research: Open-Source vs Proprietary Solutions," 24.7.2025. [Online]. Available: https://medium.com/@vi.ha.engr/modern-llm-frameworks-for-deep-research-open-source-vs-proprietary-solutions-642136c20078. [Accessed 19.12.2025].

[107] "AI for M&A: Applications, benefits, implementations, technologies, and solutions," Leeway Hertz, 13.5.2025. [Online]. Available: *https://www.leewayhertz.com/ai-for-mergers-and-acquisitions/*. [Accessed 19.12.2025].

[108] McKinsey, "Gen AI: Opportunities in M&A," 21.5.2025. [Online]. Available: *https://www.mckinsey.com/capabilities/m-and-a/our-insights/gen-ai-opportunities-in-m-and-a*. [Accessed 19.12.2025].

[109] Deloitte Digital, "Ten Types of Innovation – The discipline of building breakthroughs," 6.10.2024. [Online]. Available: *https://www.deloittedigital.com/us/en/accelerators/ten-types.html*. [Accessed 19.12.2025].

[110] "Tesla's Gigacasting Alloy – Patent Application & Science," The Limiting Factor, 1.12.2021. [Online]. Available: *https://www.youtube.com/watch?v=xtBIb0UyikQ*. [Accessed 7.10.2025].

[111] "TRIZ," Wikipedia, [Online]. Available: *https://en.wikipedia.org/wiki/TRIZ*. [Accessed 19.12.2025].

[112] E. O. Pyzer-Knapp, J. W. Pitera, P. W. J. Staar, S. Takeda, T. Laino, D. P. Sanders, J. Sexton, J. R. Smith and A. Curioni, "Accelerating materials discovery using artificial intelligence, high performance computing and robotics.," Computational Materials, vol. 8, no. 24, 2022.

[113] C.-H. H. J.-Y. W. Y.-Y. T. W. J. C. M.-S. L. F.-R. H. L.-D. L. Yi-Ling Fan, "Enhancing safety with an AI-empowered assessment and monitoring system for BSL-3 facilities," Heliyon, vol. 11, no. 1, 2025.

[114] M. Liu, "Top AI Use Cases For Accounts Receivable Automation In 2025," Forrester, 20.3.2025. [Online]. Available: *https://www.forrester.com/blogs/top-ai-use-cases-for-accounts-receivable-automation-in-2025/*. [Accessed 1.1.2026].

[115] C. C. Prasad Kulkarni, Interviewee, GenAI Solutions at Corning. [Interview]. 4.12.2025.

[116] Moyo, "From Hidden Hazards to Optimised Operations: The Role of Redlining in Engineering Change Management," 22.7.2024. [Online]. Available: *https://moyo.co/from-hidden-hazards-to-optimised-operations-the-role-of-redlining-in-engineering-change-management/*. [Accessed 19.12.2025].

[117] IoT Analytics, "Industrial AI Market Report 2021," IoT Analytics, Hamburg, 2021.

[118] IoT Analytics, "Industrial AI Market Report 2025," IoT Analytics, Hamburg, 2025.

[119] IBM, "What is Fleet Management?," [Online]. Available: *https://www.ibm.com/think/topics/fleet-management*. [Accessed 11.11.2025].

[120] Talking Tech Trends, "How Does AI Improve Fleet Management?," USA, 2025.

[121] M. Friedlich, "Audit's digital revolution: how technology is reshaping the industry," Wolters Kluwer, 12.3.2024. [Online]. Available: *https://www.wolterskluwer.com/en/expert-insights/audits-digital-revolution-how-technology-is-reshaping-the-industry*. [Accessed 19.12.2025].

[122] Thomson Reuters Institute, "How GenAI can transform compliance and risk management," 15.8.2024. [Online]. Available: *https://www.thomsonreuters.com/en-us/posts/corporates/genai-compliance-risk-management/*. [Accessed 26.9.2025].

[123] Wolters Kluwer, "Artificial intelligence in auditing: Enhancing the audit lifecycle," 17.4.2024. [Online]. Available: *https://www.wolterskluwer.com/en/expert-insights/artificial-intelligence-auditing-enhancing-audit-lifecycle*. [Accessed 19.12.2025].

[124] Next47, "The Future of Physics AI," Next47, 15.9.2025. [Online]. Available: *https://www.n47.com/insights/future-of-physics-ai*. [Accessed 16.12.2025].

[125] Siemens, "Siemens revolutionizes engineering simulation with HEEDS AI Simulation Predictor and Simcenter Reduced Order Modeling (Press Release)," 28.11.2023. [Online]. Available: *https://news.siemens.com/en-us/heeds-ai-simulation-predictor-simcenter-rom/*. [Accessed 19.11.2025].

[126] M. P. Groover, "Parts Classification and Coding," in Automation Production System and Computer Integrated Manufacturing, Hoboken, New Jersey, Prentice Hall, 2008.

[127] OptiPro ERP, "The 10 Types of Bill of Materials (BOMs) Explained," [Online]. Available: *https://www.optiproerp.com/blog/10-types-boms-explained/*. [Accessed 11.11.2025].

[128] Siliconexpert, "Resilience Built Into Every BOM," [Online]. Available: *https://www.siliconexpert.com/products/bom-manager/*. [Accessed 16.12.2025].

[129] CQLsys Technologies, "The AI Revolution in BOM Management: Driving Smarter Manufacturing and Product Development," 25.10.2025. [Online]. Available: *https://cqlsystechnologiesblog.wordpress.com/2025/10/15/the-ai-revolution-in-bom-management-driving-smarter-manufacturing-and-product-development/*. [Accessed 19.12.2025].

[130] Siemens, "Manage the Complexity of Modern Vehicle Development with Product Definition and MBSE," [Online]. Available: *https://webinars.sw.siemens.com/en-US/product-definition-in-the-automotive-product-development-process/*. [Accessed 16.12.2025].

[131] GD&T Basics, "Design for Manufacturability," 5.8.2020. [Online]. Available: *https://www.gdandtbasics.com/design-for-manufacturability/*.

[132] "Share of Wallet," Wikipedia, [Online]. Available: *https://en.wikipedia.org/wiki/Share_of_wallet*. [Accessed 16.12.2025].

[133] Pecan, "Increase Share Of Wallet With Predictive Analytics," 23.4.2023. [Online]. Available: *https://www.pecan.ai/blog/increase-share-of-wallet-with-predictive-analytics*. [Accessed 16.12.2025].

[134] Cognism, "Intent Data: What It Is, How It's Collected, and 7 Ways to Use It," 8.9.2025. [Online]. Available: *https://www.cognism.com/blog/intent-data*. [Accessed 16.12.2025].

[135] Propensity, "Predictive Analytics for Sales Engagement," 10.9.2025. [Online]. Available: *https://support.propensity.com/hc/en-us/articles/38526965350427-Predictive-Analytics-for-Sales-Engagement*. [Accessed 16.12.2025].

[136] Microsoft, "HARTING reduces design time from weeks to minutes with Siemens and Azure A," 7.3.2025. [Online]. Available: *https://www.microsoft.com/en/customers/story/22743-harting-cloud-for-manufacturing*. [Accessed 16.12.2025].

[137] Oracle NetSuite, "What Is Three-Way Matching & Why Is It Important?," 6.5.2022. [Online]. Available: *https://www.netsuite.com/portal/resource/articles/accounting/three-way-matching.shtml*. [Accessed 26.10.2025].

[138] SDI, "Ridding Your Warehouse of SLOB Inventory: How to Eliminate Waste & Unlock Value," 22.9.2025. [Online]. Available: *https://www.sdi.com/resources/blog/ridding-your-warehouse-slob-inventory/*. [Accessed 10.1.2026].

[139] isolve, "How AI is Transforming 3D Plant Engineering for the Oil & Gas Sector," 31.10.2025. [Online]. Available: *https://isolveglobal.com/3d-plant-engineering/how-ai-is-transforming-3d-plant-engineering-for-the-oil-gas-sector/*. [Accessed 16.12.2025].

[140] iSolve, "How AI Can Eliminate 40% of Design Rework in Large Construction Projects," 17.11.2025. [Online]. Available: *https://isolveglobal.com/bim-modeling/how-ai-can-eliminate-40-of-design-rework-in-construction-projects*. [Accessed 23.12.2025].

[141] K. Patry, "Why Industrial AI Requires Hybrid Intelligence: Lessons from P&ID Analysis," 9.9.2025. [Online]. Available: *https://medium.com/@kapilpatry/why-industrial-ai-requires-hybrid-intelligence-lessons-from-p-id-analysis-457eea9fd382*. [Accessed 23.12.2025].

[142] Figure AI, "F.02 Contributed to the Production of 30,000 Cars at BMW," 19.11.2025. [Online]. Available: *https://www.figure.ai/news/production-at-bmw*. [Accessed 24.1.2026].

[143] Digiforming.io, "The Transformative Power of Artificial Intelligence in Modern Press Shops," 5.4.2025. [Online]. Available: *https://www.digiforming.io/article/the-transformative-power-of-ai-in-modern-press-shops*. [Accessed 16.12.2025].

[144] V. V. Q., B. Tien-Ninh and T. Minh-Quang, "AI-based tool wear prediction with feature selection from sound signal analysis," Frontiers in Mechanical Engineering, vol. 2025, no. Volume 11, pp. 2297–3079, 2025.

[145] T. Geib, Geschäftsprozeßorientiertes Werkzeugmanagement, Wiesbaden 1997: Springer Verlag, 1997, pp. 78–91.

[146] F. Altun, A. Bayar, A. K. Hamzat, R. Asmatulu, Z. Ali and E. Asmatulu, "AI-Driven Innovations in 3D Printing: Optimization, Automation, and Intelligent Control," Journal of Manufacturing and Materials Processing, vol. 9, no. 10, p. 329, 2025.

[147] Overview.ai, "AI-Powered Weld Defect Detection: Porosity, Cracks & Incomplete Fusion," 6.10.2025. [Online]. Available: *https://www.overview.ai/blog/weld-defect-detection-ai-vision/*. [Accessed 16.12.2025].

[148] Overview.ai, "AI-Powered Weld Defect Detection: Porosity, Cracks & Incomplete Fusion," 6.10.2025. [Online]. Available: *https://www.overview.ai/blog/weld-defect-detection-ai-vision/*. [Accessed 23.12.2025].

[149] R. Weber and C. Wagner, AI and spot welding inspection: Reinventing Quality Control (Vogt Ultrasonics), Industrial AI Podcast, 2025.

[150] A. Weber, "Using AI to Improve Productivity and Quality," Assembly Mag, 5.2.2025. [Online]. Available: *https://www.assemblymag.com/articles/99042-using-ai-to-improve-productivity-and-quality*. [Accessed 16.12.2025].

[151] P. Yin, J. Yang, J. Ha, K. A. Deo and S. Park, "Reflow Oven Zone Temperature Advisor using the AI-Driven Smart Recipe Generator," in 73rd Electronic Components and Technology Conference, 2023.

[152] N. Holt, "Smart savings in paintshop energy," Automotive Manufacturing Solutions, 2012. [Online]. Available: *https://www.automotivemanufacturingsolutions.com/press-and-body/smart-savings-in-paintshop-energy/540440*. [Accessed 24.12.2025].

[153] Quartic, "AI-Powered Batch Process Manufacturing for Chemical and Advanced Material Industries," [Online]. Available: *https://www.quartic.ai/chemicals/*. [Accessed 19.12.2025].

[154] European Agency for Safety and Health at Work, "Business benefits of health and safety," 8.3.2015. [Online]. Available: *https://osha.europa.eu/en/additional-resources/youtube/business-benefits-health-and-safety*. [Accessed 20.11.2025].

[155] Be Global Safety, "PPE detection with AI: Everything you need to know," 2.3.2022. [Online]. Available: *https://beglobalsafety.com/ppe-detection-with-ai-everything-you-need-to-know/*. [Accessed 16.12.2025].

[156] M. Park, D.Q. Tran, J. Bak, A.S. Kulinan and S. Park, "Real-time Monitoring unsafe behavior of portable multi-position ladder worker using deep learning based on vision data," Journal of Safety Research, vol. 87, pp. 465–480, 2023.

[157] Amazon, "Amazon Science Blog: The evolution of Amazon's inventory planning system," 1.10.2021. [Online]. Available: *https://www.amazon.science/latest-news/the-evolution-of-amazons-inventory-planning-system*. [Accessed 17.12.2025].

[158] Credlix, "AI and Automation in Export Compliance: The Next Big Shift," 7.8.2025. [Online]. Available: *https://www.credlix.com/blogs/ai-and-automation-in-export-compliance-the-next-big-shift*. [Accessed 5.1.2026].

[159] Salesforce, "Field Service Management: What It Is, Benefits, & More," 27.8.2025. [Online]. Available: *https://www.salesforce.com/service/field-service-management/what-is-fsm/*. [Accessed 20.11.2025].

[160] Salesforce, "Field Service AI: The Complete Guide," 27.9.2025. [Online]. Available: *https://www.salesforce.com/service/field-service-management/ai-field-service-management-guide/*. [Accessed 20.11.2025].

[161] Formulayt, "Rockwell Automation Drive 700% Increase in Conversions," 29.10.2025. [Online]. Available: *https://formulayt.com/customers/case-studies/rockwell-case-study*. [Accessed 16.12.2025].

[162] D. Meyer, "Amazon Reportedly Killed an AI Recruitment System Because It Couldn't Stop the Tool from Discriminating Against Women," Fortune, 10.10.2018. [Online]. Available: *https://fortune.com/2018/10/10/amazon-ai-recruitment-bias-women-sexist/*. [Accessed 13.10.2025].

[163] J.G. Asare, "What The Workday Lawsuit Reveals About AI Bias—And How To Prevent It," Forbes, 23.6.2025. [Online]. Available: *https://www.forbes.com/sites/janicegassam/2025/06/23/what-the-workday-lawsuit-reveals-about-ai-bias-and-how-to-prevent-it*. [Accessed 13.10.2025].

[164] Thomson Reuters, "See how CoCounsel Legal elevates your team's capabilities," 10.10.2025. [Online]. Available: *https://legal.thomsonreuters.com/blog/working-faster-and-better-as-an-in-house-team-with-ai-assistance/*. [Accessed 19.12.2025].

[165] AWS, "What is Natural Language Processing (NLP)?," [Online]. Available: *https://aws.amazon.com/what-is/nlp/*. [Accessed 19.12.2025].

[166] U. Chu, "AI in ITSM: Top Use Cases You Need To Know," SmartDev, 18.8.2025. [Online]. Available: *https://smartdev.com/ai-use-cases-in-itsm*. [Accessed 20.11.2025].

[167] G. Espinosa, "Optimizing Efficiency: The Synergy of ITSM and AI," Apex Systems, [Online]. Available: *https://www.apexsystems.com/insights/article/optimizing-efficiency-synergy-itsm-and-ai*. [Accessed 19.12.2025].

[168] Palo Alto Networks, "AIOps Use Cases: How AIOps Helps IT Teams?," [Online]. Available: *https://www.paloaltonetworks.com/cyberpedia/aiops-use-cases*. [Accessed 20.11.2025].

[169] "Edwin AI: The AIOps Agent for Fast Incident Resolution," LogicMonitor, [Online]. Available: *https://www.logicmonitor.com/edwin-ai*. [Accessed 20.11.2025].

[170] ServiceNow, "What is AIOps?," [Online]. Available: *https://www.servicenow.com/products/it-operations-management/what-is-aiops.html*. [Accessed 20.11.2025].

[171] S.V. Charles Betz, "Real-Time Enterprise Architecture In The Age Of AI," Forrester, 2.4.2025. [Online]. Available: *https://www.forrester.com/blogs/the-augmented-architect-real-time-enterprise-architecture-in-the-age-of-ai*. [Accessed 20.11.2025].

[172] Faddom, "Application Dependency Mapping: The Complete Guide," 3.10.2022. [Online]. Available: *https://faddom.com/application-dependency-mapping/*. [Accessed 27.12.2025].

[173] Devox Software, "Using AI for Dependency Mapping in Large Codebases: A Practical Approach," 4.10.2025. [Online]. Available: *https://devoxsoftware.com/blog/using-ai-for-dependency-mapping-in-large-codebases-a-practical-approach/*. [Accessed 25.11.2025].

[174] Dynatrace, "What is dependency mapping?," 2.10.2024. [Online]. Available: *https://www.dynatrace.com/knowledge-base/dependency-mapping/*. [Accessed 20.11.2025].

[175] S. Guha, "AI is Transforming Manufacturing Cybersecurity from Threat Detection to Compliance Automation," Automation World, 24.9.2025. [Online]. Available: *https://www.automationworld.com/cybersecurity/article/55315914/ai-driven-strategies-for-secure-and-compliant-manufacturing-environments*. [Accessed 16.12.2025].

[176] A. Resnick, "How Do Software Developers Spend Their Time?," IDC, USA, 2025.

[177] N. I. Banu, "What is Gherkin: Syntax, Its Uses With Cucumber," 30.10.2025. [Online]. Available: *https://intellipaat.com/blog/gherkin/*. [Accessed 16.12.2025].

[178] Siemens, "Scaling Industrial AI to Help Alleviate the Skilled Labor Shortage," 3.7.2025. [Online]. Available: *https://www.siemens.com/global/en/company/insights/scaling-industrial-ai-to-help-alleviate-the-skilled-labor-shortage.html*. [Accessed 3.10.2025].

[179] J. Henson, "AI-Assisted Debugging: How Generative AI Can Improve Coding Efficiency," Medium, 20.9.2024. [Online]. Available: https://medium.com/@jesse.henson/ai-assisted-debugging-how-generative-ai-can-improve-coding-efficiency-771f5ea85f6e. [Accessed 4.10.2025].

[180] A. Wyndham, "Inside DeepL: The World's Fastest-Growing, Most Secretive Machine Translation Company," Slator Industry News, 15.9.2021. [Online]. Available: *https://slator.com/inside-deepl-the-worlds-fastest-growing-most-secretive-machine-translation-company/*. [Accessed 1.10.2025].

[181] Merill Talks, "NVIDIA vs. Hyperscaler: Who controls the Future of GPUs?," 24.10.2025. [Online]. Available: *https://www.youtube.com/watch?v=6WYE644GpRg*. [Accessed 16.11.2025].

[182] S. Rosset, C. Perlich, B. Zadrozny, S. Merugu, S. Weiss and R. Lawrence, "Wallet estimation models," 7.10.2005. [Online]. Available: *https://www.tau.ac.il/~saharon/papers/wallet-final.pdf*. [Accessed 16.12.2025].

[183] F. Bassetti, "The AI revolution in weather forecasting: Reactions and comments from the mediasphere," Climate Foresight, 24.3.2024. [Online]. Available: *https://www.climateforesight.eu/articles/reacting-to-the-ai-revolution-in-weather-forecasting*. [Accessed 11.11.2025].

[184] P. Seeberg and R. Weber, "Industrial AI Podcast," Pixel Komma Ton, 2022–2025. [Online]. Available: *https://www.aipod.de*.

[185] Transport Adcancements, "DHL Express Deploys AI-powered Sorting Robot," 8.9.2021. [Online]. Available: *https://www.transportadvancement.com/road-traffic/dhl-express-deploys-ai-powered-sorting-robot/*. [Accessed 17.12.2025].

[186] IDS, "Beyond the frame rate," 4.3.2025. [Online]. Available: *https://en.ids-imaging.com/technical-articles-details/items/beyond-frame-rate.html*. [Accessed 17.12.2025].

[187] J. Lario, J. Mateos, F. Psarommatis and Á. Ortiz, "A cost model for the investment feasibility of quality inspection technologies inthe Zero Defect Manufacturing era," International Journal of Production Research, pp. 1–16, 2024.

[188] D. Powell, M. C. Magnanini, M. Colledani and O. Myklebust, "Advancing zero defect manufacturing: A state-of-the-art perspective and future research directions," Computers in Industry, vol. 136, 2022.

[189] Rudderstack, "Unified data platforms: Architecture, benefits, and ROI," 22.10.2025. [Online]. Available: *https://www.rudderstack.com/blog/unified-data-platform/*. [Accessed 19.12.2025].

[190] Thomson Reuters Tax & Accounting, "Auditing in the digital age: Assessing risk with AI precision," 25.4.2025. [Online]. Available: *https://tax.thomsonreuters.com/blog/auditing-in-the-digital-age-assessing-risk-with-ai-precision/*. [Accessed 19.12.2025].

[191] Cognitus, "Homepage," [Online]. Available: *https://cognitus.com/products/generative-ai/*. [Accessed 19.12.2025].

[192] M. R. K. R. C. S. Bryan Petzold, "Designing data governance that delivers value – McKinsey, Zugriff am November 19, 2025," McKinsey, 26.6.2020. [Online]. Available: *https://www.mckinsey.com/capabilities/tech-and-ai/our-insights/designing-data-governance-that-delivers-value*. [Accessed 19.11.2025].

[193] J. K. R. W. Christian Wagner, "AI and spot welding inspection: Reinventing Quality Control," Industrial AI Podcast, 16.10.2025. [Online]. Available: *https://aipod.de/ai-and-spot-welding-inspection-reinventing-quality-control/*. [Accessed 28.12.2025].

[194] X. Lin, Y. Ning, J. Zhang, Y. Dong, Y. Liu, Y. Wu, X. Qi, N. Sun, Y. Shang, P. Cao, L. Zou, X. Chen, C. Zhou, J. Wu, S. Pan, B. Wang, Y. Cao, K. Chen, S. Hu and L. Guo, "LLM-based Agents Suffer from Hallucinations: A Survey of Taxonomy, Methods, and Directions," ACM, 2025.

34.2 Company Direcotry

Company/URL/ Headquarter	Profile	Founding Year	Mentions
40Factory *40-factory.com* Piacenza, IT	Industrial copilot technology for machines and shop floors.	2020	▪ SB 24-17 in Section 24.18
Accenture *accenture.com* Dublin, IE	Global professional services company delivering strategy, consulting, digital, technology and operations services.	1989	▪ Section 4.10.2
AngelHack *angelhack.com* San Francisco, CA, US	As a leading hackathon agency, AngelHack ensures your hackathon's success – from planning to management and beyond.	2011	▪ SB 15-1 in Section 15.1
Anybotics *anybotics.com* Zurich, CH	Automated inspection robots, able to navigate in process plant environments and monitor them (e. g., detecting gas leakages).	2016	▪ SB 18-2 in Section 18.1.2
App Orchid *apporchid.com* San Francisco, CA, US	Deep learning NLP with industry-specific content delivered through knowledge graphs, to create predictive apps.	2013	▪ SB 16-1 in Section 16.2
Assemblio *Assemblio.com* Stuttgart, DE	AI-powered platform that automatically transforms CAD models into digital assembly instructions and production plans.	2022	▪ SB 24-9 in Section 24.13.1
Augmented Industries *flow-tool.com* Heroldsberg, DE	Empowers technicians with digital work instructions and knowledge capture.	2021	▪ SB 24-19 in Section 24.20
Autodesk *autodesk.com* San Francisco, CA, US	Software for 3D design, engineering, and entertainment, empowering professionals to design and make buildings, products, and media.	1982	▪ SB 20-1 in Section 20.1.1
Backflip AI *backflip.ai* Miami, FL, US	GenAI models to instantly transform photos or 3D scans into manufacturable CAD parts.	2020	▪ SB 20-2 in Section 20.1.1

Company/URL/ Headquarter	Profile	Founding Year	Mentions
Bastian Solutions *bastiansolutions.com* Indianapolis, Indiana, US	Automated material handling systems, equipment, and consulting.	1952	▪ SB 25-2 in Section 25.2.4
Blockbrain *theblockbrain.ai* Stuttgart, DE	AI-supported knowledge management and process automation.	2022	▪ Section 11.1 ▪ SB 21-4 in Section 21.2.2
Blue Cargo *bluecargo.io* San Francisco, CA, US	AI-powered freight audit and spend management for international supply chains.	2018	▪ SB 25-4 in Section 25.3.3
Bombora *bombora.com* New York City, NY, US	B2B intent data platform to identify, prioritize, and engage accounts actively researching specific products.	2020	▪ SB 21-2 in Section 21.1
Calvin Risk *calvin-risk.com* Zurich, CH	Automated platform for AI governance, testing, and quantitative risk management to ensure compliance.	2022	▪ SB 12-1 in Chapter 12
CDQ *cdq.com* St. Gallen, CH	Consulting, cloud platform and collaborative community for automating and improving business partner master data.	2006	▪ SB 32-1 in Section 32-1
Celonis *celonis.com* Munich, DE	Process intelligence platform using process mining to visualize, optimize, and automate business operations.	2011	▪ SB 22-5 in Section 22.6
Celus *celus.io* Munich, DE	Streamlines electronics engineering by transforming technical requirements into schematic prototypes and bills of materials.	2018	▪ SB 20-5 in Section 20.1.2
CoLab Software *colabsoftware.com* St. John's, CA	Human and AI design review platform for hardware.	2017	▪ SB 20-3 in Section 20.1.1
Collimator Denver, CO, US	Model, simulate, and optimize complex dynamical systems with a combination of physics and machine learning.	2020	▪ SB 20-11 in Section 20.2.4

Company/URL/ Headquarter	Profile	Founding Year	Mentions
Compute Maritime *computemaritime.com* London, UK	AI tools for design & optimization of maritime assets (e. g., hulls, propellers, hydrofoils).	2024	▪ SB 20-8 in Section 20.2.2
CopyLeaks *copyleaks.com* New York, US	Content analysis platform protecting intellectual property, governing AI use, and setting a standard for responsible AI adoption.	2015	▪ SB 31-6 in Section 31.4.2
Coral Innovation *coral-innovation.de* Stuttgart, DE	Coral Innovation offers AI tools to track market trends, competitors, and tech updates, supporting sales and product teams.	2018	▪ SB 21-1 in Section 21.1
Cradle *cradle.bio* Amsterdam, NL	Helps to leverage AI to generate protein candidates and improve their properties.	2017	▪ SB 20-13 in Section 20.4.2
Cybord *cybord.ai* Tel Aviv, IS	Solutions to eliminate the use of nonconforming electronic components during product assembly.	2018	▪ SB 24-12 in Section 24.15.2.1
Datasnipper *datasnipper.com* Amsterdam, NL	Helping audit and finance teams extract, cross-reference, and verify data in Excel and text files.	2017	▪ SB 19-1 in Chapter 19
DeepL *deepl.com* Cologne, DE	High-accuracy AI language platform for professional-grade machine translation and multilingual writing assistance.	2017	▪ Section 2.3.3 ▪ SB 32-3 in Section 32.4
Dessia Technologies *dessia.io* Antony, FR	AI-powered platform for engineering automation to accelerate product design and decision-making processes.	2017	▪ SB 4-3 in Section 4.10.1
Docebo *docebo.com* Ontario, CA	AI-powered learning management system to automate and personalize enterprise training and development.	2005	▪ SB 28-5 in Section 28.4
Dotmatics *dotmatics.com* Boston, MA, US	Cloud-based R&D scientific software enabling life sciences researchers to manage data, automation, analysis, and collaboration.	2019	▪ SB 15-4 in Section 15.3.3.4

Company/URL/ Headquarter	Profile	Founding Year	Mentions
DRIMCO *drimco.net* Munich, DE	AI NLP and computer vision for the industrial use cases to analyze requirements from RFQs, tenders, or regulations.	2020	▪ SB 21-6 in Section 21.5
Drivetrain.ai *drivetrain.ai* Sunnyvale, CA, US	Business planning platform for SaaS enterprises.	2021	▪ SB 17-1 in Section 17.1
Dynatrace *dynatrace.com* Waltham, MA, US	AI-powered observability platform that automates cloud monitoring and security for enterprises.	2005	▪ SB 31-1 in Section 31.1.2.1
Easy2Parts *easy2parts.com* Deggendorf, DE	AI-platform supporting sourcing processes of mechanical parts, leveraging both, material master and design data for similarity searches.	2019	▪ SB 22-3 in Section 22.4
Ellie.ai *ellie.ai* Helsinki, FI	Full-stack enterprise data modeling platform powered by AI.	2018	▪ SB 31-2 in Section 31.2.2
embraceable.ai *embraceable.ai* Karlsruhe, DE	AI company focused on human-centric explainable agent-based AI systems.	2020	▪ Section 4.5
EPF *epf.it/en* Carrù, IT	Industrial automation, renewable energy and plastic injection molding	1961	▪ SB 24-7 in Section 24.7.2
Fehrmann MaterialsX *fehrmann-materials.com* Hamburg, DE	AI-powered software and simulations to accelerate industrial material development and alloy optimization.	2024	▪ SB 15-2 in Section 15.3
Fireflies.ai *fireflies.ai* San Francisco, CA, US	AI notetaker that records, transcribes, summarizes, and analyzes meetings to automate workflows.	2014	▪ SB 31-10 in Section 31.5.1
Gather AI *gather.ai* Pittsburgh, PA, US	AI to improve order fulfillment in the widest range of logistics environments – from ambient to cold chain storage.	2017	▪ SB 23-2 in Chapter 23

Company/URL/ Headquarter	Profile	Founding Year	Mentions
Geotab *geotab.com* Oakville, On, CA	Global telematics platform using AI-driven data to optimize fleet safety, efficiency, and sustainability.	2000	▪ SB 18-4 in Section 18.3
Google *about.google* Mountain View, CA, US	Cloud computing, productivity tools, and search and advertising solutions to help businesses scale and grow.	1998	▪ SB 31-11 in Section 31.5.2
HighByte *highbyte.com* Portland, ME, US	Industrial DataOps platform to model, contextualize, and orchestrate data for AI.	2018	▪ SB 13-1 in Section 13.2
Hubfi *hubifi.com* Columbus, Ohio, US	Automated revenue recognition platform that streamlines accounting, ensures ASC 606 compliance, and delivers real-time financial reporting.	2023	▪ SB 17-2 in Section 17.2
Inpro *inpro.de* Berlin, DE	Innovation and production systems company in automotive and mechatronics.	1982	▪ SB 18.3 in Section 18.2 ▪ Section 5.6
INSA Strasbourg *insa-strasbourg.fr/en* Strasbourg, FR	National Institute of Applied Sciences of Strasbourg is a prestigious French public Grande École for engineers and architects.	1875	▪ SB 15-3 in Section 15.3.2
Intrinsic *intrinsic.ai* Mountainview, CA, US	AI-powered platform to democratize industrial robotics via intuitive programming.	2021	▪ SB 24-15 in Section 24.16
iSolve Technologies *isolveglobal.com* Charlotte, NC, US	Transforms AEC & EPC projects with next-generation building information management and 3D plant engineering.	1986	▪ SB 24-1 in Section 24.1
Journyx *journyx.com* Austin, TX, US	Cloud-based software to track employee time and expenses for project accounting.	1996	▪ SB 28-3 in Section 28.2
Katulu *katulu.io* Hamburg, DE	Federated AI platform for privacy-preserving training & deployment.	2022	▪ SB 9-3 in Section 9.6

Company/URL/ Headquarter	Profile	Founding Year	Mentions
Knockri *knockri.com* Toronto, CA	AI video assessments to scientifically assess skills, create hiring efficiencies, and deliver an experience candidates actually enjoy.	2017	▪ SB 28-1 in Section 28.1
Lambda Function AI *lambdafunction.ai* San Francisco, CA, US	AI-assisted CNC/CAM software to automate machining programming.	2020	▪ SB 20-14 in Section 20.5.1
Leela AI *leela.ai* Newton, MA, US	Visual intelligence platform to improve performance, quality, and safety on shop floors.	2017	▪ SB 24-10 in Section 24.13.1
Leo AI *getleo.ai* Cambridge, MA, US	Generative AI copilot for mechanical engineers to automate CAD design, calculations, and documentation.	2023	▪ SB 2-4 in Section 2.7.2.3
Lovable *lovable.dev* Stockholm, SE	AI app builder that turns text prompts into full-stack web apps.	2023	▪ SB 31-9 in Section 31.4.7
Luminary Cloud *luminarycloud.com* Redwood City, CA, US	GPU-native simulation platform using physics-based AI to accelerate engineering design cycles.	2019	▪ SB 20-6 in Section 20.2.1.2
Markovate *markovate.com* San Francisco, CA, US	Development house and integrator for AI solutions to master complexity enterprise-grade.	2015	▪ SB 20-10 in Section 20.2.3.2
McKinsey *mckinsey.com* Chicago, IL, US	Multinational strategy and management consulting firm.	1926	▪ SB 14-1 in Section 14.2
MinnaLearn *minnalearn.com* Helsinki, FI	Online platform offering accessible AI literacy and digital skills training for workplaces.	2022	▪ SB 10-2 in Section 10.2
Mistral *mistral.ai* Paris, FR	European large language model provider for various use cases.	2023	▪ SB 31-5 in Section 31.4.2

Company/URL/ Headquarter	Profile	Founding Year	Mentions
Monolith AI *monolithai.com* London, UK	Engineering AI to reduce physical testing and accelerate validation.	2016	▪ SB 20-7 in Section 20.2.1.3
Motion Miners *motionminers.com* Dortmund, DE	AI-driven platform using sensors and wearables to automatically analyze and optimize manual processes.	2017	▪ SB 24-2 in Section 24.1
Munich Re *munichre.com* Munich, DE	Reinsurance, primary insurance, and insurance-related risk solutions worldwide.	1880	▪ SB 4-1 in Section 4.1
Navan *Navan.com* Palo Alto, CA, US	AI-powered platform for integrated corporate travel, expense management, and cards.	2015	▪ SB 32-2 in Section 32.3
Neura Robotics *neura-robotics.com* Metzingen, DE	Cognitive robots using integrated AI and sensors to perceive, learn, and collaborate safely with humans.	2019	▪ SB 24-18 in Section 24.19
Node Robotics *node-robotics.com* Stuttgart, DE	Robust software solutions designed specifically for mobile robot OEMs.	2019	▪ SB 24-6 in Section 24.7.1
NXAI *nx-ai.com* Linz, AT	Industrial AI company commercializing the xLSTM architecture, for example for efficient timeseries predictions.	2024	▪ SB 23-1 in Chapter 23
Outreach *outreach.io* Seattle, WA, US	AI-powered sales execution platform to automate workflows, manage pipelines, and increase revenue.	2014	▪ SB 21-3 in Section 21.2.1
Overview.ai *overview.ai* San Francisco, US	System integrator and solution provider for industrial machine vision.	2018	▪ SB 22-4 in Section 22.5
Pailot *pailot.com* Karlsruhe, DE	Cloud-based production scheduling platform for production planning optimization.	2020	▪ SB 24-5 in Section 24.5
Palo Alto Networks *paloaltonetworks.com* Palo Alto, CA, US	Advanced firewalls and cloud-based cybersecurity offerings.	2005	▪ SB 31-3 in Section 31.3

Company/URL/ Headquarter	Profile	Founding Year	Mentions
Payslip *payslip.com* Mayo, IE	Intelligent payrole processing on international levels.	2016	▪ SB 28-4 in Section 28.3
Path Robotics *path-robotics.com* Columbus, OH, US	AI-based control for welding robots and processes.	2014	▪ SB 24-8 in Section 24.12
PD Connect *pdconnect.de* Lingen, DE	AI-driven recruitment and sales software for personnel service providers and temporary employment agencies.	2023	▪ SB 28-2 in Section 28.1
Prewave *prewave.com* Vienna, AT	Data-driven supply chain risk and compliance management platform.	2017	▪ SB 22-2 in Section 22.2
Project 44 *project44.com* Chicago, IL, US	The decision intelligence platform for the modern supply chain.	2014	▪ SB 25-3 in Section 25.3.1
Rabbit AI *rabbitai.de* Heidelberg, DE	Highly-accurate real-world ground truth capturing solution for reliable & safe AI.	2020	▪ SB 9-1 in Section 9.3
Resoniks *resoniks.com* The Hague, NL	Innovative solutions for quality control processes using AI-powered acoustic analysis.	2022	▪ SB 24-13 in Section 24.15.2.2
Responsible Annotation ervices *annotation.at* Vienna, AT	Inclusive, high-precision annotation and labeling services.	2023	▪ SB 2-2 in Section 2.7.1.2
RIIICO *riiico.com* Düsseldorf, DE	AI platform for the extraction of CAD models from 3D scans (point clouds), such as in the context of populating the industrial metaverse.	2021	▪ SB 2.1 in Section 2.6.3.3
Rossum.ai *rossum.ai* London, UK	Specialist AI agents that automate transactional paperwork by extracting and validating document data for robotic process automation.	2017	▪ SB 31-7 in Section 31.4.6.1

Company/URL/ Headquarter	Profile	Founding Year	Mentions
Samp.ai *samp.ai* Paris, FR	Machine vision, augmented reality and positioning technology for Digital Twins.	2019	▪ SB 18-1 in Section 18.1.1
Siemens *siemens.com* Munich/Berlin, DE	Industrial technology provider of mobility, electrification & automation solutions.	1847	▪ SB 20-9 in Section 20.2.3.1 ▪ SB 4-2 in Section 4.2 ▪ Section 5.7 ▪ SB 9-2 in Section 9.4 ▪ SB 24-4 in Section 24.2.2
Spend Matters *spendmatters.com* Chicago, IL, US	Data-driven, technology-centric content and research platform for vendor selection.	2004	▪ SB 22-1 in Section 22.1
Spitch AI *spitch.ai* Zurich, CH	Conversational agentic AI solutions for customer service center automation.	2014	▪ SB 26-1 in Section 26.1
StoriesOnBoard *storiesonboard.com* Pecs, HU	StoriesOnBoard is an online agile collaboration solution for release planning and project scope management.	2014	▪ SB 31-4 in Section 31.4.1
Streamline AI *streamline.ai* Burlingame, CA, US	Mission control for in-house legal teams with seamless intake, automated review workflows, and real-time reporting.	2020	▪ SB 29-1 in Section 29.1
SupplyFrame *supplyframe.com* Pasadena, TX, US	Design-to-Source intelligence platform for electronics supply chains.	2003	▪ SB 20-12 in Section 20.3.3
Symphony AI *symphonyai.com* Palo Alto, CA, US	Enterprise-grade generative AI solutions to transform workflows across retail, finance, and industrial sectors.	2017	▪ SB 24-3 in Section 24.2.1
Synera *synera.io* Bremen, DE	Low-code AI agent platform to automate complex engineering workflows.	2018	▪ SB 31-8 in Section 31.4.6.2

Company/URL/ Headquarter	Profile	Founding Year	Mentions
Synthesia *synthesia.io* London, UK	Platform for creating studio-quality videos with AI avatars and voice-overs in 140+ languages.	2017	▪ SB 28-6 in Section 28.4
Tacton *tacton.com* Stockholm, SE	AI supported configure-price-quote solutions.	1998	▪ SB 21-5 in Section 21.4
Throughput AI *throughput.world* Palo Alto, CA, US	AI-powered supply chain platform that eliminates bottlenecks to optimize inventory, capacity, and distribution.	2017	▪ SB 25-1 in Section 25.2.1
Trumpf *trumpf.com* Ditzingen, DE	Industrial machine tools, lasers, and electronics for sheet metal processing, automation, and smart factory solutions.	1923	▪ Section 5.7.8 ▪ SB 24-16 in Section 24.17
Vanta *vanta.com* San Francisco, CA, US	Data and AI driven regulatory and cybersecurity compliance management and certifications.	2018	▪ SB 29-2 in Section 29.2
Verkada *verkada.com* San Mateo, CA, US	AI-powered cloud platform that unifies physical security and smart building management.	2016	▪ SB 30-2 in Section 30.2
Visionify *visionify.ai* Westminster, CO, US	AI-powered workplace safety solutions that use existing cameras to detect hazards and PPE violations.	2021	▪ SB 30-1 in Section 30.1
Weidmüller *weidmuller.com* Detmold, DE	Industrial connectivity and automation solutions for power, signals, and data in industrial environments.	1850	▪ SB 2-3 in Section 2.7.1.5
Werk24.io *werk24.io* Munich, DE	AI-based product(ion) management information extraction from technical drawings.	2020	▪ SB 20-15 in Section 20.5.4
WeSort.ai *wesort.ai* Würzburg, DE	AI sorting for harmful and valuable objects in waste management and recycling.	2021	▪ SB 26-2 in Section 26.4

Company/URL/ Headquarter	Profile	Founding Year	Mentions
WireBot *wirebot.tech* Zur Yigal, IL	AI-driven robotic systems that automate electrical cabinet wiring.	2020	▪ SB 24-11 in Section 24.13.2
WSCAD *wscad.com* Bergkirchen, DE	AI-powered electrical CAD for engineers, designers and maintenance personnel.	1990	▪ SB 20-4 in Section 20.1.2
Xplain Data *xplain-data.de* Zorneding, DE	Development of innovative technologies in the field of causal AI for industry.	2015	▪ SB 24-14 in Section 24.15.3
ZEKI Data *zekidata.com* London, UK	Talent intelligence platform with more than 300,000 different data sources.	2022	▪ Section 2.5 ▪ SB 14-2 in Section 14.2 ▪ SB 10-1 in Section 10.1

34.3 Table Index

34.4 Figure Index

34.5 Abbreviations

A2A	Agent to Agent
AAS	Asset Administration Shell
AGI	Artificial General Intelligence
AGV	Automated Guided Vehicle
AIOps	AI for IT Operations
AMR	Autonomous Mobile Robot
ANN	Artificial Neural Network
AOI	Automated Optical Inspection
APC	Advanced Process Control
API	Application Programming Interface
ASIC	Application-Specific Integrated Circuit
B2B	Business to Business
B2C	Business to Consumer
BOP	Bill of Process
CAGR	Compound Annual Growth Rate
CAM	Computer-Aided Manufacturing
CapEx	Capital Expenditure
CAQ	Computer-Aided Quality Control
CD	Continuous Deployment
CFD	Computational Fluid Dynamics
CI	Continuous Integration
CPG	Consumer-Packaged Goods
CRM	Customer Relationship Mgt.

CT	Continuous Training
CUDA	Compute Unified Device Architecture
DCS	Distributed Control System
DD	Due Diligence
DL	Deep Learning
DPP	Digital Product Passport
DRC	Design Rule Checking
DSE	Design Space Exploration
EAM	Enterprise Architecture Mgt.
EHS	Environment, Health and Safety
ERP	Enterprise Resource Mgt.
FDA	Food & Drug Administration
FEA	Finite Element Analysis
FL	Federated Learning
FPGA	Field-Programmable Gate Array
GAN	Generative Adversarial Network
GD&T	Geometric Dimensioning and Tolerancing
GDP	Gross Domestic Product
GDPR	General Data Protection Regulation
GenAI	Generative AI
GNN	Graph Neural Network
GPU	Graphic Processing Unit
HVAC	Heating, Ventilation and Air Conditioning
I4.0	Industry 4.0
IIoT	Industrial Internet of Things
IP	Intellectual Property
ITSM	IT Service Mgt.
KG	Knowledge Graph
KPI	Key Performance Indicator

LLM	Large Language Model
M&A	Mergers & Acquisitions
MCP	Model Context Protocol
MES	Manufacturing Execution System(s)
ML	Machine Learning
MLOps	Machine Learning Operations
NLP	Natural Language Processing
NOA	NAMUR Open Architecture
OECD	Organisation for Economic Cooperation and Development
OEM	Original Equipment Manufacturer
OpEx	Operational Expenditure
OSH	Occupational Safety and Health
PCB	Printed Circuit Board
PDM	Product Data Management
PFAS	Perfluoroalkyl and Polyfluoroalkyl Substances
PINN	Physics-Informed Neural Network
PLC	Programmable Logic Controller
PLM	Product Lifecycle Management
PM	Process Mining
PoC	Proof of Concept
PUE	Power Usage Effectiveness
QC	Quantum Computing
R&D	Research & Development
RAG	Retrieval-Augmented Generation
RBR	Rule-Based Reasoning
RE	Requirements Engineering
RfQ	Request for Quotation
RL	Reinforcement Learning
ROI	Return on Investment

RPA	Robotic Process Automation
RTLS	Real-Time Location System
SDA	Software-Defined Automation
SKU	Stock Keeping Unit
SLMs	Small Language Model
SMT	Surface Mount Technology
SoW	Share of Wallet
SysML	Systems Modeling Language
TP	Transfer Pricing
TPU	Tensor Processing Unit
UAE	United Arab Emirates
USD	Universal Scene Description
VLAM	Vision Language Action Model
VM	Virtual Machine
VPC	Virtual Private Network
WMS	Warehouse Management System

Index

Symbole

A

B

C

D

E

F

G

H

I

J

K

L

M

N

O

P

T

U

V

W

X

Z

www.ingramcontent.com/pod-product-compliance
Lightning Source LLC
LaVergne TN
LVHW060314240926
848814LV00005B/30
9781569906101